# Fodor's

# LOS ANGELES

HOLLYWOOD

# WELCOME TO LOS ANGELES

Los Angeles is a polarizing place, but there's truly a corner of the city for everyone. Drive for miles between towering palm trees, bodega-lined streets, and Downtown's skyscrapers, and you'll still never discover all of L.A.'s hidden gems. Scratch the surface to find people-watching on Rodeo Drive, historic bars on the Sunset Strip, and the glitz and grime of Hollywood Boulevard. From the humble and trendy East Side to the tony beach-adjacent cities of Venice and Santa Monica to the west, experience everything in the city's year-round idyllic weather.

## TOP REASONS TO GO

★ **Star Gazing:** Both through the telescope atop Griffith Park and among the residents of Beverly Hills.

★ **Eating:** From food trucks to fine dining, an unparalleled meal awaits your palate.

★ **Beaches and Boardwalks:** The dream of '80s Venice is alive in California.

★ **Shopping:** Peruse eclectic boutiques or window-shop on Rodeo Drive.

★ **Architecture:** Art deco wonders to Frank Gehry masterpieces abound.

★ **Scenic Drives:** You haven't seen the sunset until you've seen it from a winding L.A. road.

# Fodor's LOS ANGELES

**Editorial:** Douglas Stallings, *Editorial Director*; Salwa Jabado and Margaret Kelly, *Senior Editors*; Alexis Kelly, Jacinta O'Halloran, and Amanda Sadlowski, *Editors*; Teddy Minford, *Associate Editor*; Rachael Roth, *Content Manager*

**Design:** Tina Malaney, *Associate Art Director*

**Photography:** Jennifer Arnow, *Senior Photo Editor*

**Maps:** Rebecca Baer, *Senior Map Editor*; David Lindroth, Mark Stroud (Moon Street Cartography), *Cartographers*

**Production:** Jennifer DePrima, *Editorial Production Manager*; Carrie Parker, *Senior Production Editor*; Elyse Rozelle, *Production Editor*

**Business & Operations:** Chuck Hoover, *Chief Marketing Officer*; Joy Lai, *Vice President and General Manager*; Stephen Horowitz, *Head of Business Development and Partnerships*

**Public Relations:** Joe Ewaskiw, *Manager*

**Writers:** Michele Bigley, Meg Butler, Alene Dawson, Audrey Farnsworth, Paul Feinstein, Rachael Levitt, Kathy A. McDonald, Rachael Roth, Jesse Tabit, Jeremy Tarr, Ashley Tibbits, Clarissa Wei

**Editors:** Rachael Roth (lead editor), Salwa Jabado

**Production Editor:** Elyse Rozelle

**Production Design:** Liliana Guia

27th Edition

ISBN 978-0-14-754684-5

ISSN 1095-3914

PRINTED IN THE UNITED STATES OF AMERICA

10 9 8 7 6 5 4 3 2 1

# CONTENTS

## Fodor's Features

# CONTENTS

## MAPS

# ABOUT THIS GUIDE

### Fodor's Recommendations

Everything in this guide is worth doing—we don't cover what isn't—but exceptional sights, hotels, and restaurants are recognized with additional accolades. Fodor's Choice★ indicates our top recommendations. Care to nominate a new place? Visit Fodors.com/contact-us.

### Trip Costs

We list prices wherever possible to help you budget well. Hotel and restaurant price categories from **$** to **$$$$** are noted alongside each recommendation. For hotels, we include the lowest cost of a standard double room in high season. For restaurants, we cite the average price of a main course at dinner or, if dinner isn't served, at lunch. For attractions, we always list adult admission fees; discounts are usually available for children, students, and senior citizens.

### Hotels

Our local writers vet every hotel to recommend the best overnights in each price category, from budget to expensive. Unless otherwise specified, you can expect private bath, phone, and TV in your room. For full information, visit Fodors.com.

**Top Picks**

- ★ Fodor's Choice

**Listings**

- ✉ Address
- ✉ Branch address
- ☎ Telephone
- 📠 Fax
- 🌐 Website
- 📧 E-mail
- 🎫 Admission fee
- 🕒 Open/closed times
- [M] Subway
- ✣ Directions or Map coordinates

**Hotels & Restaurants**

- 🏨 Hotel
- 🛏 Number of rooms
- 🍴 Meal plans
- W Restaurant
- ✍ Reservations
- 👔 Dress code
- ▭ No credit cards
- [$] Price

**Other**

- ⇨ See also
- ☞ Take note
- ⛳ Golf facilities

### Restaurants

Unless we state otherwise, restaurants are open for lunch and dinner daily. We mention dress code only when there's a specific requirement and reservations only when they're essential or not accepted. For full information, visit Fodors.com.

### Credit Cards

The hotels and restaurants in this guide typically accept credit cards. If not, we'll say so.

## EUGENE FODOR

Hungarian-born Eugene Fodor (1905–91) began his travel career as an interpreter on a French cruise ship. The experience inspired him to write *On the Continent* (1936), the first guidebook to receive annual updates and discuss a country's way of life as well as its sights. Fodor later joined the U.S. Army and worked for the OSS in World War II. After the war, he kept up his intelligence work while expanding his guidebook series. During the Cold War, many guides were written by fellow agents who understood the value of insider information. Today's guides continue Fodor's legacy by providing travelers with timely coverage, insider tips, and cultural context.

# EXPERIENCE
# LOS ANGELES

# LOS ANGELES TODAY

Starstruck. Excessive. Smoggy. Superficial.... There's a modicum of truth to each of the adjectives regularly applied to L.A., but the locals dismiss their prevalence as envy from those who aren't as blessed with year-round sunshine. Pop culture does permeate life here, its massive economy employing millions of Southern Californians, but the city where dreams are made accommodates those from all avenues of life.

## Downtown's Upswing

Los Angeles has been archly described as "72 suburbs in search of a city." Hence the renaissance its once-desolate Downtown is experiencing may come as something of a surprise. Long-neglected neighborhoods here have been spruced up, and streets even the police deemed irredeemable have been revitalized.

The Broad Foundation's 120,000-square-foot, three-story contemporary art museum, simply called "the Broad," has been a highly popular destination since opening its doors in 2015. Across the street from Walt Disney Concert Hall and the Los Angeles Museum of Contemporary Art, the honeycomb-shaped structure holds more than 2,000 art objects and includes pieces by heavy hitters in the art world, like Cindy Sherman and Andy Warhol.

Even with an ailing economy, in the last decade Downtown saw a remarkable development boom—most notably L.A. LIVE, a 27-acre, $2.5-billion entertainment complex, which includes the Nokia Theatre and the innovative Grammy Museum. Restaurants, boutiques, and art studios continue to pop up, more people are moving in, and public spaces are being revitalized.

And that's not all: the $20 million makeover of the galleries at the Huntington Library, Art Collections, and Botanical Gardens have made it a must-see for lovers of European art.

## Access Hollywood

Hollywood may disappoint tourists looking to overdose on glitz; after all, most of its moviemakers departed for the San Fernando Valley decades ago, leaving the area to languish. Even after the much-hyped debut of the Hollywood & Highland Center, the area remains more gritty than glamorous, yet that's part of its charm.

Yet new life continues to be pumped in. In the last few years, vintage venues

## WHAT'S NEW

Downtown Los Angeles is undergoing a major makeover. Longtime residents who once would never have considered venturing into the center of the city are finding lots of reasons to linger. Multimillion-dollar condos and lofts are perpetually in construction

and a new park was recently unveiled in the Arts District. Also in the works is a $20 million bikeway that will run from Downtown Los Angeles to South Los Angeles.

Downtown's Grand Central Market underwent a major makeover in 2013 and

continues to welcome new culinary talent today. From Texas barbecue to Thai sticky rice to a full-blown raw oyster bar, there's something for everyone. Don't worry, it's still a great place to pick up freshly ground spices and other kitchen staples.

such as the Hollywood Palladium have been refurbished; the popular Madame Tussauds constructed a movie-themed museum adjacent to the TCL Chinese Theatre; and Cirque du Soleil began a show with a decade-long run at the Kodak Theatre.

## New Lights on the Coast
Outdoor entertainment can be found at more than just L.A.'s beaches; there are also a number of amusement parks close to the city.

One of the first sites you see driving into Santa Monica is a tremendous Ferris wheel at Pacific Park out on the Santa Monica Pier—and now it stands out even more. The wheel was recently replaced, and the new one is covered with about 160,000 dazzling LED lights that shine much brighter than the 5,000 or so red, white, and blue bulbs on the previous one.

## Food for Thought
Star chefs continue to flock from across the country to make their mark on Los Angeles. Recent big openings have included Maude, Curtis Stone's exquisite tasting menu gem in Beverly Hills, and Cassia, a powerhouse restaurant in Santa Monica known for its infusion of Singaporean and Vietnamese flavors with classic French techniques. For a solid brunch, don't miss Jessica Koslow's Sqirl Kitchen on Virgil Avenue in Silver Lake, known for its seasonal rice bowls and house-made jams.

Eats in L.A. remain relatively egalitarian. Even posh places seldom require jackets, so the dress code is casual. Ditto for the menu. (In the city that invented fast food, it's no coincidence that Govind Armstrong flips gourmet burgers or that Wolfgang Puck built his reputation on pizza.) If you want to go budget, you can easily justify chowing down at McDonald's, Carl's Jr., and In-N-Out Burger; all qualify as "indigenous cuisine" having originated in the Five-County Area.

The next addition to Hollywood will be the Academy Museum of Motion Pictures, which will highlight how film and the moviemaking business has woven its way into pop culture over the course of time since its creation. The 290,000-square-foot museum, estimated to cost around $400 million, is due to open in 2018.

Getting to L.A. is easier than ever. The Los Angeles International Airport recently underwent a $78.3 million makeover of Terminal 2, with chic terrazzo floors and more food options. Next up is a remodel of Terminal 1, scheduled for 2018.

# WHAT'S WHERE

*Numbers refer to chapters.*

**2 Downtown Los Angeles.** Downtown L.A. shows off spectacular modern architecture with the swooping Walt Disney Concert Hall and the stark Cathedral of Our Lady of the Angels. The Music Center and the Museum of Contemporary Art anchor a world-class art scene, while El Pueblo de Los Angeles, Chinatown, and Little Tokyo reflect the city's history and diversity.

**3 Hollywood and the Studios.** Glitzy and tarnished, good and bad—Hollywood is just like the entertainment business itself. The Walk of Fame, TCL Chinese Theatre, Paramount Pictures studio, and the Hollywood Bowl keep the neighborhood's romantic past alive. Universal Studios Hollywood and Warner Bros. are in the Valley.

**4 Beverly Hills, West Hollywood, and the Westside.** Go for the glamour, the restaurants, and the scene. Rodeo Drive is particularly good for a look at wretched or ravishing excess. But don't forget the Westside's cultural attractions—especially the dazzling Getty Center. West Hollywood is an area for urban indulgences—shopping, restaurants, nightlife—rather than sightseeing. Its main

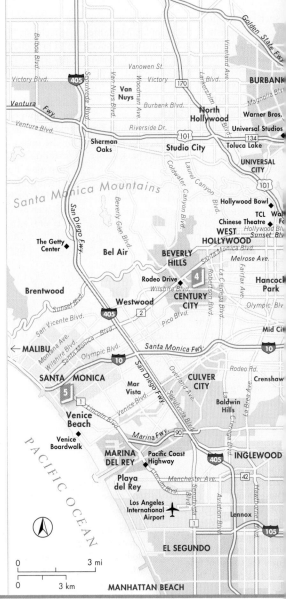

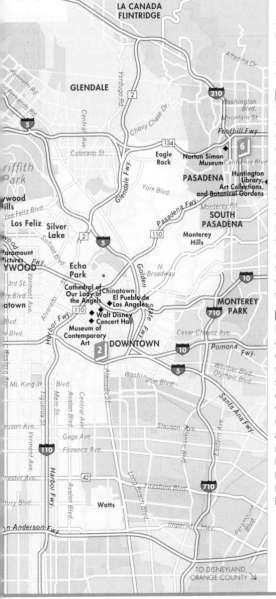

arteries are the Sunset Strip (Sunset Boulevard), and Melrose Avenue, lined with shops ranging from thrifty to couture.

**5 Santa Monica and the Beaches.** In Santa Monica, a lively beach scene plays out daily. Venice, just south of Santa Monica, is a more raffish mix of artists, beach punks, and yuppies, most of whom you can see on the Venice Boardwalk. Drive up the Pacific Coast Highway to Malibu, where the rich and famous reside. An extravagant residence of a different kind, the Getty Villa Malibu is filled with everything from medieval to contemporary art.

**6 Pasadena.** Like Santa Monica, Pasadena may appear to be an extension of L.A., but it's actually a separate city with a strong sense of community. It's a quiet, genteel area to visit, with outstanding Arts and Crafts homes, good dining, and a pair of exceptional museums: the Norton Simon Museum, and the Huntington Library, Art Collections, and Botanical Gardens in adjoining San Marino.

# LOS ANGELES PLANNER

## When to Go

Any time of the year is the right time to visit Los Angeles. From November to May, you can find crisp, sunny, unusually smog-free days. December to April is the rainy season, but storms are usually brief, followed by brilliant skies. Dining alfresco, sailing, and catching a concert under the stars—these are reserved for L.A. summers, which are virtually rainless (with an occasional air-quality alert).

Prices skyrocket and reservations are essential when tourism peaks July through September.

Southern California is a temperate area, moderated by the Pacific Ocean. In addition, mountains along the north and east sides of the Los Angeles coastal basin act as buffers against the extreme summer heat and winter cold of the surrounding desert and plateau regions.

Pasadena and the San Fernando Valley are significantly hotter than Beverly Hills or Hollywood, while coastal areas can be dramatically cooler. Late spring brings "June gloom," when skies tend to be overcast until afternoon.

## Getting Around

In L.A., where the automobile is worshipped—and will be, no matter how high gas prices go—the freeways are the best way to get around town.

**Renting a Car.** Definitely plan to do it at the airport. And if you want to cruise around in a convertible—a quintessential L.A. experience that allows you to catch some sun while sitting in traffic—reserve well in advance.

**Parking.** With the exception of Downtown high-rises, where parking costs can be exorbitant, parking in L.A. is not inexpensive nor plentiful. Avoid

rush hour (before 10 am and between 5 and 7 pm) if at all possible, and remember that even-numbered freeways run east–west, and odd-numbered ones run north–south.

**Taking Taxis.** There are, however, ways to get around Los Angeles without a car. Taxis are not as plentiful as in New York or San Francisco, but you can always find them at major hotels. From LAX to Downtown, a cab ride runs about $42, and shuttle vans cost about $16 per person. Ride-sharing services like Uber and Lyft are other more affordable options.

## Dining and Lodging

Chefs in L.A. are frontrunners in the farm-to-fork mentality, and scour the city's many farmers' markets for the freshest of locally grown ingredients. For lodging, there's everything from ultraluxe hotels in Beverly Hills to quiet beachfront resorts along the coast in Santa Monica, with a range of prices in every area.

## Tips for the Freeway

**Pick a Lane.** The carpool lane, the "fast lane," the truck lane, the merge lane—this isn't your typical freeway. First of all, keep out of the two far right lanes, which buses and trucks are restricted to. To drive the speed limit, pick the middle lane; the fourth lane moves about 5 miles over the speed limit. Newbies should stay out of the far left lane. Speeds here range from 75 to 90 mph and you've got to deal with carpool lane mergers.

**Signaling Is a Must.** You might be able to get away with a quick lane change in other cities, but don't try it in L.A. Drivers may try to merge into the same spot as you from three lanes away. You'll quickly learn that locals are notorious for not using their signal, but it's always a smart idea.

**Get a Freeway Map.** The small, laminated maps that just cover the jumble of freeways are indispensable if you merge onto the wrong freeway, get lost, or get stuck in traffic and want to find an alternative route. Nearly every gas station sells them; you can get a decent one for a few bucks. ■TIP➔ You can also find one on the inside back cover of this guide.

### L.A. DRIVING TIMES

| | |
|---|---|
| From LAX to Downtown L.A. | 30–75 mins/19 miles |
| From LAX to Beverly Hills | 30–75 mins/15 miles |
| From LAX to Santa Monica | 20–60 mins/18 miles |
| From Downtown L.A. to Beverly Hills | 20–45 mins/11 miles |
| From Downtown L.A. to Pasadena | 15–25 mins/11 miles |
| From Downtown L.A. to Burbank | 18–30 mins/12 miles |
| From Downtown L.A. to Universal City | 15–40 mins/10 miles |
| From Santa Monica to Redondo Beach | 25–55 mins/15 miles |
| From Santa Monica to West Hollywood | 25–50 mins/10 miles |
| From Santa Monica to Malibu | 32–75 mins/25 miles |

**Don't Pull Over.** Short of a real emergency, never, ever, pull over and stop on a freeway. So you took the wrong ramp and need to reroute? Take the next exit and find a safe, well-lit public space to stop your car and get your bearings.

### For a Guided Tour

The **Los Angeles Conservancy** (☎ *213/623–2489* ⊕ *www.laconservancy.org*) regularly conducts Saturday morning walking tours of Downtown architectural landmarks and districts.

Tours begin at 10 am, last about 2½ hours, and are offered rain or shine. Call for schedule and fees.

**Starline Tours** (☎ *323/463-3333* ⊕ *www. starlinetours.com/los-angeles-tours.asp*) offers a wide range of sightseeing tours around town. It's an ideal way to get a taste of Los Angeles without the hassle of figuring out transportation.

# LOS ANGELES TOP ATTRACTIONS

## Disneyland

**(A)** "The Happiest Place on Earth" continues to delight children and all but the most cynical adults. A visit here can be enchanting, exciting, romantic, or nostalgic, depending on your age. Disneyland, the original vision of Walt Disney, is now paired with Disney's California Adventure, showcasing more recent Disney characters and Hollywood-oriented attractions.

## Walt Disney Concert Hall

**(B)** Designed by Frank Gehry, the dramatic curves of this stainless steel–clad masterpiece located in Downtown is a signature of the modern metropolis. One of several venues of the Music Center, the 2,265-seat Disney Hall is home to the Los Angeles Philharmonic. It features unrivaled acoustics and a stunning pipe organ.

## TCL Chinese Theatre and the Hollywood Walk of Fame

**(C)** An iconic metaphor for Hollywood, the elaborate Chinese Theatre opened in 1927 with the premiere of Cecil B. DeMille's *King of Kings*. That's when the tradition of stars imprinting their hands or feet into the cement began with an "accidental" footprint by Norma Talmadge. More than 160 stars have contributed, and among the more unique prints are the nose of Jimmy Durante and hoofs of Trigger. The theater is adjacent to the Hollywood & Highland Center. The Walk of Fame runs along 15 blocks of Hollywood Boulevard (and 3 blocks of Vine Street), with more than 2,600 stars bearing the names of celebrities.

## Getty Center

**(D)** On a hillside above Brentwood, the Getty Center is a sign that L.A. has established its place in the art world. The complex has a skin of travertine marble. Natural light floods galleries filled with impressionist canvases, Greek antiquities, and exhibits of furniture and decorative arts from the French monarchy. Pedestrian plazas and gardens abound, and a sunset dinner at the restaurant can be highly romantic.

## Rodeo Drive

**(E)** Dominated by the exclusive names of Gucci, Versace, and Cartier, Rodeo Drive is a shoppers' paradise. Along the cobblestoned Via Rodeo, you can drop $1,000 on python pumps or nosh on a $500 sushi dinner. Fortunately, Rodeo Drive doesn't cater exclusively to the rich and famous, and more moderate shops and restaurants are interspersed with the iconic boutiques.

## Santa Monica Pier

**(F)** Spend a sunny day beside the Pacific Ocean riding the Ferris wheel and playing games at this popular family destination. Cotton candy and other hard-to-resist treats are within easy reach. Drop by in the late afternoon and witness the sunset, or the rumored green light created by the sun hovering over the ocean, seconds before it disappears into the horizon.

## Venice Beach Boardwalk

**(G)** The bohemian lifestyle of this famous boardwalk is constantly threatened by the rapid gentrification of Venice. Still, the magicians, fortune-tellers, and Muscle Beach weight lifters live on. Struggling artists sell their paintings, infiltrated by tackier purveyors of cheap watches and sunglasses. Rent a bicycle or in-line skates, grab a hot dog, and enjoy the sights and the sunset.

# TOP LOS ANGELES EXPERIENCES

Hordes of tourists descend on Los Angeles each year with visions of seeing stars—of the Hollywood Boulevard and celebrity variety, that is—but before you purchase that star map, consider these other options for soaking in true local culture.

### Bike the Strand

Despite urban myths that claim otherwise, Angelenos do abandon their cars every now and then—especially if it's to rent an old-school beach cruiser and bike down the 22-mile-long Strand, which stretches from Will Rogers State Beach in Santa Monica to Torrance County Beach in Redondo.

The Strand runs parallel to the Pacific Ocean through Santa Monica and Venice. Don't miss one-of-a-kind sights, including the oversized Ferris wheel on the Santa Monica Pier, the greased-up bodybuilders of Muscle Beach, and the roller dancers (think disco on roller skates) of Venice Beach. If biking isn't your thing, there are plenty of rollerbladers and walkers as well.

### Drive Through In-N-Out Burger

Whether you recently moved here or are just passing through, going to the In-N-Out drive-through is a rite of passage in L.A. Pro tip: order from the secret menu (available online), and enjoy your burger or fries "Animal Style" from the comfort of your car. The chain's popularity ceases to decline; you'll encounter a long line of cars at any location, day or night, but it's worth the wait.

### Eat at the Farmers Market

Located at 3rd and Fairfax, the Farmers Market is one of L.A.'s few communal outdoor spaces. People come here on lunch breaks or weekends to eat, drink, and, most importantly, people-watch.

Founded by a collective of farmers in 1934, the Farmers Market now houses more than 85 shops and restaurants—you can find everything from a Brazilian grill to a French *crêperie* to a Lebanese kebab stand in the open-air bazaar ringed by stalls and stands.

The Farmers Market and the adjacent shopping area, The Grove, are also low-key places to spot celebrities.

### Try a Taco Truck

Everyone in Los Angeles has a taco truck that they swear by. Typically, these stands on wheels have a regular corner and semi-regular hours. The only reliable way to find a good one is to ask a local, or follow elusive trucks on Twitter.

Not all taco trucks are created equal, but most share these qualities: they are tasty, cheap, and authentic.

### See a Show at the Hollywood Bowl

No doubt you've seen the iconic dome in movies, but nothing compares to spending a summer evening in a bleacher seat (or, better yet, one of the coveted boxes) at the Hollywood Bowl. For the ultimate Hollywood Bowl experience, pack a picnic complete with bottle of wine and wicker basket, and don't be afraid to share goodies with your neighbors.

Performances range from reggae night to rock concerts to Los Angeles Philharmonic performances. But as most Angelenos would agree, the experience is as much about sitting outside under the night sky as it is about the music.

### Hike Griffith Park

Extremely accessible from the city, this park offers a 53-mile network of trails, roads, and bridle paths. One of the most popular routes is up Mount Hollywood, which boasts panoramic views of the Los

Angeles basin, the Griffith Observatory, and the Hollywood sign along the way.

Don't feel like working up a sweat? Although riders must stay on specially marked trails, much of the park can be seen on horseback. Private stables are located in the park's northwest and southwest boundaries.

## Stop at a Seafood Shack

There may be nothing that epitomizes Los Angeles more than a drive down the scenic Pacific Coast Highway, or PCH, as locals call it. After taking in the sweeping views and turquoise waters, stop at a seafood shack, such as Malibu Seafood or the Reel Inn, for some ahi burgers or fish-and-chips.

Afterwards, check out one of Malibu's most beautiful beaches: Topanga State Beach, Zuma Beach, or the small and secluded La Piedra, El Pescador, and El Matador beaches.

## Go to a Dodgers or Lakers Game

One way to blend in with the locals is to surround yourself with them.

Get out to Dodger Stadium for a baseball game, and don't forget to dress in all blue and eat a Dodger Dog while you're there. Unless it's a big game, tickets are easy to come by—especially if you're willing to sit in the cheap bleacher seats. You can also spend a bit more to sit in one of the special sections, such as the All-You-Can-Eat Pavilion.

It's much harder to procure Lakers tickets when they play at Staples Center, but if you plan ahead, a Lakers game is a surefire way to see big celebrities and even bigger feats of aerodynamics.

## Catch a Movie at the ArcLight

It would be an understatement to say that Angelenos take their movies seriously, especially considering that the entertainment industry is many locals' bread and butter. Look no further than the ArcLight in Hollywood for a signature L.A. movie-going experience. This theater has all the fixin's: stadium seating, gourmet food, and authentic costumes from favorite films on display in the lobby.

But what sets the ArcLight above the rest is that each movie is introduced by a staff member well versed in film trivia. If you're lucky, you might catch the directors as they frequently make appearances here to discuss their work.

If you truly want to live like a local, catch a flick in the afternoon—remember: Angelenos have plenty of sunny days to burn.

# IF YOU LIKE

## Hitting the Road

Considering that the greater L.A. area sprawls over more square mileage than some small countries, it comes as no surprise that residents clock a lot of road time. Contrary to popular belief, however, standstill freeway traffic is only part of the picture. In Los Angeles, the popular 1950s-era pastime of cruising is still alive and well.

One of the premier ways to see the L.A. hot spots so often captured on the silver screen is to take a drive down **Sunset Boulevard.** The famed thoroughfare runs from the **Pacific Coast Highway** in Malibu to Downtown Los Angeles, but the most well-known stretch is the **Sunset Strip** in West Hollywood.

Heading east on **Sunset Boulevard,** pass by legendary music venues including the Roxy, Whisky-A-Go-Go, and the Viper Room. Continue a little farther to glimpse movie star magnet of yesteryear the Sunset Tower Hotel (formerly the Argyle Hotel) and current celebrity hangout the Chateau Marmont.

The famous **Mulholland Drive** roadway snakes along the ridge separating L.A. from its suburban neighbor, the San Fernando Valley. Like Sunset Boulevard, Mulholland Drive starts at the ocean and extends all the way into Hollywood, but unlike its urban counterpart, Mulholland forgoes street scenes for mountain views, and traffic lights for unpaved stretches of road.

Another not-to-be-missed scenic stretch is the winding road that climbs through Laurel Canyon, a nexus of the 1960s music scene and former home to rockers Joni Mitchell and Neil Young among many others. At its apex, **Laurel Canyon Boulevard** meets up with Mulholland Drive, so be sure to fuel up before you start the climb.

## The Outdoors

Although Los Angeles's car culture is well publicized, its bike culture is a little more under-the-radar, but that is not to say there isn't a healthy cycling scene. With seemingly endless days of summer, Angelenos love to spend time outdoors.

One of the quintessential L.A. activities is to rent an old-school beach cruiser and bike along the 22-mile-long **Strand,** which stretches from Santa Monica's **Will Rogers State Beach** to **Torrance County Beach** in Venice.

If you are an outdoor enthusiast, don't forget to pack your hiking boots alongside your stiletto heels so that you can hike the **Santa Monica Mountains.** Popular routes include the Backbone Trail, a 43-mile stretch of chaparral-covered hillsides, oak woodlands, and creeks that links Will Rogers State Historic Park to Point Mugu, anchored in the middle by **Malibu Creek State Park** and **Topanga State Park.** The highly accessible **Griffith Park,** just north of Hollywood, is technically part of this mountain chain as well.

For some solitude and rural terrain, visit **Angeles National Forest,** in the northern reaches of L.A. County. The mostly flat and shaded Gabrielino Trail along the upper Arroyo Seco is a favorite of mountain bikers, runners, birders, and horseback riders. To get there, exit the 210 Freeway at Arroyo Boulevard–Windsor Avenue in Altadena. Drive three-quarters of a mile north and look for the small parking lot just before you reach Ventura Avenue.

## Seeing Stars

A surefire way to see stars (or at least the constellation they call home) is by **purchasing a star map** from vendors on street corners around the city. You can also sign up to be a part of a live audience and **watch a taping of a TV show.** If you haven't planned in advance, you can always **take a studio tour.**

In Los Angeles, moviegoing is elevated to an art form. Instead of seeing a flick at the multiplex, catch what's showing at the **Hollywood Forever Cemetery** (aka the "Resting Place of Hollywood's Immortals"), surrounded by the graves of Cecil B. DeMille, Jayne Mansfield, Rudolph Valentino, Douglas Fairbanks, and hundreds of other screen legends.

## Eye-Popping Views

Perch yourself high above Hollywood Hills and have a picnic at the **Hollywood Bowl.** Choose your sound track from a lineup of rock concerts sponsored by local radio station KCRW or time it with a Los Angeles Philharmonic concert.

Top off any trip to Los Angeles—literally—by taking in the view from the **Griffith Observatory.** Located on the southern slope of Mount Hollywood in Griffith Park, the 75-year-old icon offers stellar views of the heavens thanks to the observatory's original 12-inch Zeiss refracting telescope as well as a trio of solar telescopes.

Griffith Observatory is one of the best vantage points to see the **Hollywood sign.** For a view of the sign from the ground, walk, run, or bike around the **Hollywood Reservoir Trail.** The 4-mile walk around also offers great views of hillside mansions. The reservoir was built by the god of Los Angeles water, William Mulholland; its dam has a memorable movie cameo in Roman Polanski's *Chinatown.*

Seemingly floating above Downtown Los Angeles like a Jetsons-age oasis, the rooftop bar at the **Standard Hotel** attracts everyone from buttoned-up office workers, who flock to the space for happy hour drinks, to the swanked-out, late-night crowd. It's a great place to take in the surrounding scenery.

Get a bird's-eye view of the city from the **Getty Center** in Brentwood. Wander among the stunning, travertine marble–clad pavilions, see artwork like European paintings and antique French furniture, and explore the gardens. It'll be hard to tear your eyes from the view, especially at sunset. Dine in nearby Brentwood, West Hollywood, or back in Beverly Hills—Spago, anyone?

# FREE AND ALMOST FREE

Even in this town—where money seems to ooze from every hill and corner—there are plenty of fun things to do that are free and appeal to everyone, from kids to art lovers to film buffs. These are some of our top picks.

**Hang out at the Broad.** This museum's free admission and immersive exhibitions have made it one of the hottest places to spend a day in Los Angeles. Yayoi Kusama's "Infinity Mirrored Room" is a must-see. You'll need to make a reservation once you arrive at the museum; it's the only way to get into the sparkly chamber that has been dominating Instagram feeds across the Southland.

**Check out Freebies at Museums.** Though high-profile Angelenos have elevated conspicuous consumption to an art, you can still spend time here without dropping a dime. Culture vultures will be relieved to learn the Getty Center and Getty Villa offer complimentary admission. Just about all the other major museums in Los Angeles have free days, including the Geffen Contemporary and the Museum of Contemporary Art. Several museums stay open as late as 9 pm some nights.

**Be Part of the Audience.** Feel like you're a part of the Industry by sitting in on a taping of a live televison show. **Audiences Unlimited** (✉ *100 Universal City Plaza, Bldg. 153, Universal City* ☎ *818/260–0041* ⊕ *www.tvtickets.com*) helps fill seats for television programs (and sometimes for televised award shows). The free tickets are distributed on a first-come, first-served basis to those 16 and older.

**See the Great Grunion Runs.** The most popular and most unusual form of fishing in the L.A. area involves no hooks, bait, or poles, and is absolutely free. The grunion runs, which take place from March through July, occur when hundreds of thousands of small silver fish called grunion wash up on Southern California beaches to lay their eggs in the sand. The fish can be picked up by hand while they are briefly stranded on the beach. All that's required is a fishing license and a willingness to get your toes wet.

**Spend the Evening on the Griffith Observatory's Rooftop Observation Deck.** Known for stunning and famous views of Los Angeles, this rooftop deck is open until 10 pm every night except Monday.

**Watch Rehearsals at the Hollywood Bowl.** There's no charge to visit the Hollywood Bowl and the grounds that surround it, but an even better tip is that in the summer, from 9 am to noon on Tuesday, Thursday, and Friday, you can watch rehearsals for free. Take a snack and enjoy the view. If you can't make a rehearsal, seeing the stark white amphitheater with the Hollywood sign set against the mountains in the background is worth the trip alone.

**Walk in Famous Footsteps.** Frugal movie fans can experience Hollywood Boulevard's star-paved Walk of Fame or in the forecourt of TCL Chinese Theatre where celebs have been pressing hands, feet, and other body parts into cement since 1927 (time it right and you may catch a premiere, too). Music buffs can view memorabilia from past headliners at the free Hollywood Bowl Museum.

**Visit the Hollywood Forever Cemetery.** Inside the Hollywood Memorial Park right in the center of Hollywood, the Hollywood Forever Cemetery is where several of the film industry's famous are buried. Pick up a free map when you walk in for a self-guided tour.

# TOP MUSEUMS

Despite its long-standing reputation as a second-rate art capital when compared to New York, Los Angeles easily vies for the top spot when it comes to its museum exhibitions and gallery shows. Unlike in many other cultural capitals, the art here isn't concentrated in one area of the city. No matter where you are, there's likely to be a top-notch museum within driving distance.

Four major epicenters—Chinatown, Culver City, Santa Monica, and West Hollywood—boast hundreds of art spaces. In Downtown sits the largest concentration of galleries, Gallery Row, with approximately 30 galleries and museums within a short walk of one another.

## Must-See Museums

On a busy stretch of Wilshire Boulevard in Westwood, the **UCLA Hammer Museum** (✉ *10899 Wilshire Blvd., Westwood* ☎ *310/443–7000* ⊕ *www.hammer.ucla. edu*) is known for cutting-edge exhibitions with a special emphasis on "the art of our time," as they put it. The Hammer is also known for its extensive library dedicated to the study of video art.

In a modernist compound of rough-hewn Italian travertine on a hilltop in the Santa Monica Mountains, the Richard Meier–designed **Getty Center** (✉ *1200 Getty Center Dr., Los Angeles* ☎ *310/440–7300* ⊕ *www.getty.edu*) has fabulous views of the Pacific Ocean and the San Gabriel Mountains, as well as an extensive garden designed by Robert Irwin.

Claiming the crown of the largest art museum in the western United States, the **Los Angeles County Museum of Art** (✉ *5905 Wilshire Blvd., Miracle Mile* ☎ *323/857–6000* ⊕ *www.lacma.org*) is a complex of seven buildings with more than 100,000 objects dating from ancient times to the present.

LACMA may be the biggest museum in the West, but the **Museum of Contemporary Art** is certainly in the running in the best category, and is *the* place to see blockbuster exhibits. It has three buildings: the MOCA Grand Avenue (✉ *250 S. Grand Ave., Downtown* ☎ *213/626–6222* ⊕ *www.moca.org*) and the Geffen Contemporary (✉ *152 N. Central Ave., Little Tokyo* ☎ *213/626–6222* ⊕ *www.moca.org*) are located in Downtown, while the Pacific Design Center (✉ *8687 Melrose Ave., West Hollywood* ☎ *213/626–6222* ⊕ *www.moca.org*) is in West Hollywood.

Newer to Los Angeles but quickly gaining renown, **The Broad** museum (✉ *221 S. Grand Ave., Downtown* ☎ *213/232–6200* ⊕ *www.thebroad.org*) was opened by philanthropists Eli and Edythe Broad, and houses a massive collection of postwar to contemporary art in its honeycomb structure.

## Other Great Museums

Don't miss the **Getty Villa** (✉ *17985 Pacific Coast Hwy., Pacific Palisades* ☎ *310/440–7300* ⊕ *www.getty.edu*) in Pacific Palisades for Greek, Roman, and Etruscan antiquities.

If you're traveling with kids, check out the **California Science Center** (✉ *700 State Dr., Exposition Park* ☎ *213/744–7400* ⊕ *www.casciencectr.org*). Kids can explore space or see a live exhibit like the kelp forest dive show. Another favorite among younger patrons and adults alike is the **Natural History Museum of Los Angeles County** (✉ *900 Exposition Blvd.* ☎ *213/763–3466* ⊕ *www.nhm.org*), with its stunning Dinosaur Hall, and "Dinosaur Encounters," featuring life-sized puppets operated by performers.

# LOS ANGELES WITH KIDS

With seemingly endless sunny days, Angeleno kids almost never have to play indoors. There are a few things to keep in mind, however, when navigating the city with little ones: if possible, avoid the freeways by exploring no more than one neighborhood each day, and remember that you can never have too much sunscreen—L.A. parents don't leave home without the stuff.

Of course, the top reason many families comes to the L.A. area is to visit Disneyland. Experience all the classic attractions that you may recall from your own childhood visit, such as the "It's a Small World" ride, a meet-and-greet with Tinkerbell, or a Mickey Mouse home tour, who, unlike less amenable celebrities, makes a daily appearance for fans. But there's plenty more to see and do.

## Head Under the Sea

Head down to the **Aquarium of the Pacific** in Long Beach to learn tons of interesting facts about the Pacific Ocean. On display are shimmering schools of fish, a swaying kelp forest, a shark lagoon featuring more than 150 varieties, and a tropical reef habitat filled with zebra sharks, porcupine puffers, and a large blue Napoleon wrasse.

## Commune with Nature

Don't miss your chance to test-ride a high-wire bicycle or catch a film at the seven-story IMAX theater at the **California Science Center.** Just down the road is the **Natural History Museum,** where kids can explore everything from diamonds to its new dinosaur hall. In spring, don't miss the outdoor butterfly habitat, fittingly named the Pavilion of Wings, which makes way for the Spider Pavilion come fall.

## Walk in the Park

**Griffith Park** is the largest municipal park and urban wilderness area in the United States, and the kids will go wild for the pony rides and the classic 1926 merry-go-round. But the pièce de résistance is the Griffith Park and Southern Railroad, a circa-1940s miniature train that travels through an old Western town and a Native American village. Other highlights are the Los Angeles Zoo and the Griffith Observatory, an L.A. icon in its own right.

## Learn By Doing

Little ones can pan for gold in a small creek, play Spider-Man on a weblike climber, or race around a trike track at the **Kidspace Children's Museum.** Indoor activities include a walk-through kaleidoscope, two climbing towers—one mimicking raindrops, the other modeled after a wisteria vine, a bug diner (think banana worm bread and roasted cricket pizza), and a contraption that lets kids generate their very own earthquake.

## Hit the Beach

The best way to check out **Santa Monica Beach** is by renting bikes or roller skates at any one of the shacks on the Strand (a stretch of concrete boardwalk that snakes along the beach toward Venice). Some must-sees along the way: the roller dancers of Venice Beach, the bodybuilders of Muscle Beach, and the Santa Monica Pier, a 100-year-old structure that's home to a vintage 1920s carousel, an oversize Ferris wheel, and old-time amusement park games. After hitting the beach, drive over to the pedestrian-only Third Street Promenade to grab a bite and do some shopping.

# LOS ANGELES SPORTS ACTION

Famed Dodgers sportscaster Vin Scully may have recently retired, but his name lives on: in 2016 Elysian Park Avenue officially became Vin Scully Avenue—just one example of how sports are deeply woven into L.A. culture. It's an understatement to say the city takes pride in its professional sports.

## Baseball

**The Dodgers.** The Dodgers take on their National League rivals at one of major league baseball's most comfortable ballparks, Dodger Stadium. ⊠ *Dodger Stadium, 1000 Elysian Park Ave., exit off I–110, Pasadena Fwy.* ☎ *323/224–1507* ⊕ *www.dodgers.com.*

**Los Angeles Angels of Anaheim.** The Angels often contend for the top slot in the Western Division of pro baseball's American League. ⊠ *Angel Stadium of Anaheim, 2000 E. Gene Autry Way, Anaheim* ☎ *714/940–2000* ⊕ *www.angelsbaseball.com.*

## Basketball

**Los Angeles Clippers.** L.A.'s "other" pro basketball team, the Clippers, was formerly an easy ticket, but these days the club routinely sells out its home games. ⊠ *Staples Center, 1111 S. Figueroa St.* ☎ *213/742–7100* ⊕ *www.nba.com/clippers.*

**Los Angeles Lakers.** The team of pro-basketball champions Magic and Kareem, and Shaq and Kobe has slipped in recent years, but games still are still intense, especially if the Lakers are playing a rival team. ⊠ *Staples Center, 1111 S. Figueroa St., Downtown* ☎ *310/426–6000* ⊕ *www.nba.com/lakers.*

**Los Angeles Sparks.** The women's pro basketball team has made it to the WNBA playoffs more than a dozen times in the past two decades. ⊠ *Staples Center, 1111 S. Figueroa St.* ☎ *310/426–6031* ⊕ *www.wnba.com/sparks.*

**University of California at Los Angeles.** The University of California at Los Angeles Bruins play at Pauley Pavilion on the UCLA campus. ⊠ *Pauley Pavilion, 405 Hilgard Ave.* ☎ *310/825–2101* ⊕ *www.uclabruins.collegesports.com.*

**University of Southern California.** The Trojans of the University of Southern California play at the Galen Center. ⊠ *Galen Center, 3400 S. Figueroa St.* ☎ *213/740–4672* ⊕ *www.usctrojans.com.*

## Football

The Los Angeles Rams began playing home games at the L.A. Memorial Coliseum in 2016. The Los Angeles Chargers are scheduled to join them in 2019.

**UCLA Bruins.** The UCLA Bruins pack 'em in at the Rose Bowl. ⊠ *Rose Bowl, 1010 Rose Bowl, Pasadena* ☎ *626/577–3100* ⊕ *www.uclabruins.collegesports.com.*

**USC Trojans.** The USC Trojans play at the L.A. Memorial Coliseum, both a state and federal historic landmark. ⊠ *L.A. Memorial Coliseum, 3939 S. Figueroa St., Downtown* ☎ *213/740–4672* ⊕ *www.usctrojans.collegesports.com.*

## Hockey

**Anaheim Ducks.** The Anaheim Ducks push the puck at Honda Center. It became the first Southern California team to win the Stanley Cup in 2007. ⊠ *Honda Center, 2695 E. Katella Ave* ☎ *877/945–3946* ⊕ *www.nhl.com/ducks.*

**L.A. Kings.** The National Hockey League's L.A. Kings clinched the Stanley Cup for the first time in 2012, and in 2014 they won it again against the New York Rangers. ⊠ *Staples Center, 1111 S. Figueroa St.* ☎ *213/742–7100* ⊕ *www.lakings.com.*

# GREAT ARCHITECTURE

Sorry, New York, you may offer the best of the best in other categories, but when it comes to groundbreaking new architecture, Los Angeles takes the prize (the Pritzker, that is).

Amid the patchwork of California bungalows and stucco Caliterraneans that dot the cityscape dwell some of the last century's most notable architectural feats, many of them carefully restored and lovingly tended.

Here are a few examples that no architecture buff should miss.

## Classic Architecture

A stone's throw from the blaring ranchero music of South Broadway, the circa 1880s **Bradbury Building** (✉ *304 S. Broadway, Downtown*) designed by George H. Wyman lays testament to Downtown's halcyon days. This Victorian-style office building, best known for the intricate cast iron metalwork that details its soaring, light-filled atrium, is a mecca for architecture students. Don't be surprised if you see a few artsy types soaking up the ambience.

A fine example of Frank Lloyd Wright's work, the '20s-era **Hollyhock House** (✉ *4800 Hollywood Blvd., Los Feliz* ☎ *323/644–6269* ⊕ *www.hollyhockhouse.net*) can be found in Barnsdall Art Park. The park is adjacent to a grittier part of the Loz Feliz neighborhood, so be alert if you go here at night. Make sure to see the interior of the Hollyhock House, which has some of the master's lovely stained-glass windows and a huge stone fireplace.

Home to countless examples of the California Craftsman, Pasadena lays claim to the quintessential example, Charles and Henry Greene's **Gamble House** (✉ *4 Westmoreland Pl., Pasadena* ☎ *626/793–3334*

⊕ *www.gamblehouse.org*). Built in 1908, the house is heavy on stained glass and teak woodwork.

If the Gamble House doesn't satiate your appetite for all things Greene and Greene, check out the **Castle Green** (✉ *99 S. Raymond Ave., Pasadena* ☎ *626/793–0359* ⊕ *www.castlegreen.com*), a seven-story Moorish Colonial and Spanish-style building on a palm tree–lined site in Old Town Pasadena.

## Modern Masterpieces

Join the horde of photographers snapping photos on Grand Avenue. No, it's not a celebrity-fueled paparazzi gathering, just the day's usual crowd of people snapping photos of Frank Gehry's **Walt Disney Concert Hall** (✉ *111 S. Grand Ave., Downtown* ☎ *323/850–2000* ⊕ *www.laphil.com*). Wrapped in curving stainless steel, the music hall possesses a clothlike quality reminiscent of a ship's sails billowing in the wind.

And then there's L.A.'s other major Gehry favorite, the **Geffen Contemporary** (✉ *152 N. Central Ave., Downtown* ☎ *213/626–6222* ⊕ *www.moca.org*), which opened in the early 1980s as a temporary space for works housed inside the Museum of Contemporary Art.

In South Los Angeles, Simon Rodia's **Watts Towers** (✉ *1761–1765 E. 107th St., Watts* ⊕ *www.wattstowers.us*) consist of 17 sculptures constructed of steel and covered with a mosaic of broken glass, seashells, and pieces of 20th-century American ceramics.

## DID YOU KNOW?

Many films, including *Blade Runner* (1982), were filmed in the Bradbury Building, DTLA's architectural gem. Upper floors are offices, but visitors are permitted in the lobby.

# CRUISING THE SUNSET STRIP

For more than half a century, Hollywood's night owls have headed for the 1¾-mile stretch of Sunset Boulevard between Crescent Heights Boulevard on the east and Doheny Drive on the west, known as the Sunset Strip. The experience of driving it from end to end gives you a sampling of everything that makes L.A. what it is, with all its glamour and grit, and its history of those who rose fast and fell faster.

Left and top right, two views of Sunset Boulevard. Bottom right, Mel's Drive-in Diner.

In the 1930s and '40s, stars such as Errol Flynn and Rita Hayworth came for wild evenings of dancing and drinking at nightclubs like Trocadero, Ciro's, and Mocambo.

The Strip's image as Tinseltown's glamorous nighttime playground began to die in the '50s, and by the mid-'60s it was the center of L.A.'s raucous music-and-nightlife scene. Bands like the Doors and the Byrds played the Whisky a Go Go, and the city's counterculture clashed with police in the famous Sunset Strip curfew riots in the summer of 1966.

In the '70s, the Strip was all about glam rock, with David Bowie, T. Rex, and Queen hitting the venues. But this was when it began a decline that would last almost two decades, until it became a seedy section of the city where hookers hung out on every corner.

It's only been in the last decade that the Strip has seen a true revitalization, with new hotels, restaurants, and bars opening that have become haunts for celebs and A-listers. It retains its rough-and-tumble image in some sections but overall is a much classier spot to spend a night out.

# A CLASSIC DRIVE THROUGH L.A.

Depending on the time of day, driving the Strip is a different experience. In the afternoon grab lunch at a hotel and hobnob with industry types. At night, drive with the top down and come to hear music, hit a club, or have cocktails at a rooftop bar. Either way, it's good to park the car and walk (yes, walk!).

## WHERE TO EAT & DRINK

See and be seen at **Skybar at the Mondrian Hotel** (✉ 8440 Sunset Blvd. ☎ 323/848–6025), the luxe outdoor lounge and pool deck. The bar opens to the public at 8 pm daily. Come early to enjoy sweeping views of the city before turning your gaze inward to the beautiful people milling around.

Go to **Greenblatt's Deli** (✉ 8017 Sunset Blvd. ☎ 323/656-0606) for some of the best roast beef you'll ever have. Around since 1926, this casual deli has free parking in the back, and you can order picnic basket dinners to take to the Hollywood Bowl.

## TIPS FOR PARKING

Parking and traffic around the Strip can be tough on weekends. Although there's some parking on side streets, it may be worth it to park in a lot and pay $10-$25. Most of the hotels have garages as well.

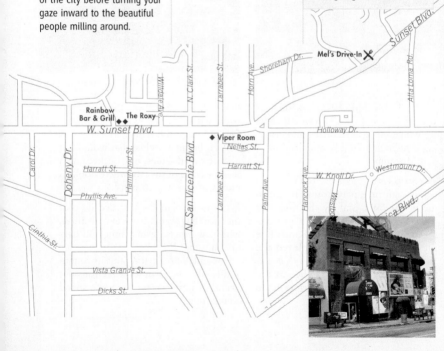

The Roxy

The Chateau Marmont

Andaz West Hollywood

Map labels:
- Selma Ave.
- N. Fairfax Ave.
- Laurel Canyon Blvd.
- Selma Dr.
- Greenblatt's Deli
- The Chateau Marmont
- Sunset Blvd.
- N. Havenhurst Dr.
- Heights Blvd.
- N. Crescent Heights Blvd.
- N. Harper Ave.
- Andaz West Hollywood ("Riot Hyatt")
- N. Kings Rd.
- Carney's
- Standard Hotel's Cactus Lounge
- Saddle Ranch Chop House
- Comedy Store
- Sunset Tower Hotel
- use of Blues
- De Longpre Ave.
- N. Olive
- bar at the rian Hotel
- Fountain Ave.
- N. Fl.

Stop in for a burger and shake at **Mel's Drive-In** (✉ 8585 Sunset Blvd. ☎ 310/854–7201), open 24 hours a day. The iconic 1950s-inspired diner in the heart of the Strip is a fun place to people-watch, day or night.

For the city's best hot dogs, chili fries, and frozen chocolate-dipped bananas, head to **Carney's** (✉ 8351 Sunset Blvd. ☎ 323/654-8300), a popular spot for a quick bite. You can't miss it—look for the yellow railcar.

## SIGHTS TO SEE

**The Chateau Marmont** (✉ 8221 West Sunset Boulevard). Greta Garbo once called this castle-like hotel home. It's also where John Belushi died.

**Comedy Store** (✉ 8433 Sunset Boulevard). David Letterman and Robin Williams rose to fame here.

**Andaz West Hollywood ("Riot Hyatt")** (✉ 8401 Sunset Boulevard). Led Zeppelin, the Rolling Stones, and the Who stayed and played here when they hit town.

**Rainbow Bar & Grill** (✉ 9015 Sunset Boulevard). Jimi Hendrix and Bob Marley began their climb to the top of the charts here.

**The Roxy** (✉ 9009 Sunset Boulevard). Neil Young was the opening act here in 1973; it's been a Strip anchor and front-runner in revitalization.

**The Viper Room** (✉ 8852 Sunset Blvd.) This always popular, always booked venue was where River Phoenix OD'd in 1993.

**Saddle Ranch Chop House** (✉ 8371 Sunset Boulevard). Originally the Thunder Roadhouse (co-owned by Dennis Hopper and Peter Fonda), this raucous steakhouse has a mechanical bull featured on many a TV show, including Sex and the City.

# A DRIVE BEYOND THE STRIP

California's Pacific Coast Highway at dusk

There's more to see along Sunset Boulevard than just the Strip. For a other classic L.A. drive, just before dusk, continue west on Sunset un you reach the Pacific Coast Highway (PCH) in Pacific Palisades, rig along the ocean, and you'll understand how the boulevard got its name

### WHEN TO GO

Time it right so you can catch that famous L.A. sunset, or drive down Sunset Boulevard late morning after rush hour and arrive just in time for lunch at a waterfront restaurant or a picnic on the beach.

The PCH is also known for its fresh seafood shacks along the roadside. For a classic local-favorite try **Reel Inn Restaurant,** (✉ *18661 Pacific Coast Hwy*), less than 10 minutes up the road from where Sunset hits the PCH.

### TRIP TIPS

While it's hard to tear your eyes awa from sites along the way, there are ha pin turns on the Boulevard, and drivi can be a challenge. Stop-and-go traffic especially along the Strip—means lo of fender benders, so be careful ar keep a safe distance.

# DOWNTOWN
# LOS ANGELES

# GETTING ORIENTED

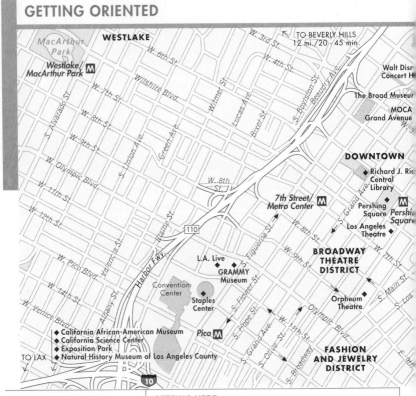

## DRIVING TIMES AND DISTANCES

Minimum times represent little to no traffic; maximum times assume the worst. Adjust accordingly taking rush hour and peak weekend travel time into account.

■ **From LAX:** 30–75 mins/ 19 miles

■ **From Hollywood:** 15–30 mins/7 miles

■ **From Beverly Hills:** 20–45 mins/12 miles

■ **From Pasadena:** 15–25 mins/12 miles

■ **From Santa Monica:** 22–45 mins/15 miles

## GETTING HERE

### Driving Strategy

The good news is that Freeways 5, 101, 110, and 10 all get you there; the bad news is that the traffic can delay your travels. If you're coming from the Hollywood area, skip the freeways altogether and take Sunset Boulevard, which turns into César Chávez Boulevard. Make a right on South Grand Avenue, and after a few blocks you'll be in the heart of Downtown. If you're coming directly from LAX, take the 105 E to the 110 N exit to the 6th Street/9th Street exit toward Downtown/Convention Center/Figueroa Street.

### Parking

If staying at a hotel in Downtown with a garage, keeping your car there and getting around by foot, rideshare, or even the Metro is a better option than driving. If you prefer to take your own car, there are several options including lots and street parking, the latter of which is more affordable, but harder to find.

2

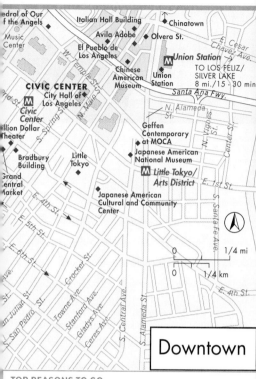

## PLANNING YOUR TIME

Visit weekdays during the day, when the area is bustling and restaurants are open for lunch. It's easy to find street parking on weekends, but with the exception of Chinatown, L.A. Live, Olvera Street, and destination bars such as the Edison, the area shuts down at night.

Seeing everything in one day is possible, but it's best to spread it out over two. For art lovers, the Museum of Contemporary Art, MOCA at the Geffen Contemporary, the African American Museum, the Japanese American Museum, and the Chinese American Museum are worthy of more than just a pass-through.

Plan your visits around specific areas you can walk to in one circuit. Parking lots run $9 to $20, so if you're on a budget you don't want to be moving your car around too much.

The entertainment industry loves to use Downtown for movie backdrops, so when film crews take over entire blocks for shooting, traffic jams up in every direction.

## TOP REASONS TO GO

**Visit Frank Gehry's Walt Disney Concert Hall.** Be wowed by the genius architecture and grab tickets for a Los Angeles Philharmonic performance led by passionate conductor Gustavo Dudamel.

**See a Lakers or Clippers Game.** Catch the action at the Staples Center and possibly rub elbows with stars such as Jack Nicholson, Billy Crystal, and Leonardo DiCaprio.

**Get Interactive at the GRAMMY Museum.** Set your inner rock god free playing virtual drums, or learn about folk music from Bob Dylan at this highly interactive museum.

**Take a Historic Walking Tour.** The L.A. Conservancy offers several tours, such as of Olvera Street, where you can see traditional Mexican culture and shop for handmade goods.

**Dine in at the Grand Central Market.** Check out the newly revitalized Grand Central Market, where you can grab bites from artisanal food vendors.

Sightseeing
★★★★★
Nightlife
★★★★
Dining
★★★★
Lodging
★★★
Shopping
★★★

If there's one thing Angelenos love, it's a makeover, and city planners have put the wheels in motion for a dramatic revitalization. Downtown is both glamorous and gritty and is an example of Los Angeles's complexity as a whole. There's a dizzying variety of experiences not to be missed here if you're curious about the artistic, historic, ethnic, or sports-loving sides of L.A.

Updated by
Clarissa Wei

Downtown Los Angeles isn't just one neighborhood: it's a cluster of pedestrian-friendly enclaves where you can sample an eclectic mix of flavors, wander through world-class museums, and enjoy great live performances or sports events.

As you venture into the different neighborhoods of Downtown—**Chinatown, Little Tokyo,** and **El Pueblo de Los Angeles**—take advantage of the tastes, sounds, and sights. Eat roast duck in Chinatown, red bean cakes in Little Tokyo, or pickled cactus on Olvera Street. Spend time browsing at the **Grand Central Market,** where stalls are filled with colorful locally grown produce and homemade treats such as tamales and olive bread. The market recently received a makeover, and is now offering everything from Texan barbecue to Thai-style chicken over rice. For art lovers, the **Geffen Contemporary at MOCA** has one of the most important modern and contemporary art collections, and those who are fans of architecture should make a point to see another Gehry creation, the **Walt Disney Concert Hall,** or the massive, geometrically designed **Cathedral of Our Lady for the Angels.**

To see the glory of Broadway's golden years, look up above the storefront signs, and you'll find the marvelous architecture and theater marquees of the majestic buildings they reside in. From the late 19th century to the 1950s—before malls and freeways—**Broadway** glittered with the finest shops and the highest number of luxurious theaters in the world, making it a rich, cultural haven. Though it remains the main road through Downtown's Historic District, the area has changed dramatically over the years. Currently bustling with businesses catering

*Tulips* by Jeff Koons at The Broad Museum

to mostly Mexican and Central American immigrants, between 1st and 9th streets you can find mariachi and *banda* music blaring from electronics-store speakers, street-food vendors hawking sliced papaya sprinkled with chili powder, and fancy dresses for a girl's *quinceañera* (15th birthday).

## TOP ATTRACTIONS

Fodor's Choice
★

**The Broad Museum.** The talk of the Los Angeles art world when it opened in 2015, this museum in an intriguing, honeycomb-looking building created by philanthropists Eli and Edythe Broad (rhymes with "road") to showcase their stunning private collection of contemporary art, amassed over five decades and still growing. With upward of 2,000 pieces by more than 200 artists, the collection has in-depth representations of the work of such prominent names as Jean Michel Basquiat, Jeff Koons, Ed Ruscha, Cindy Sherman, Cy Twombly, Kara Walker, and Christopher Wool. The "veil and vault" design of the main building integrates gallery space and storage space (visitors can glimpse the latter through a window in the stairwell): the veil refers to the fiberglass, concrete, and steel exterior; the vault is the concrete base. Temporary exhibits and works from the permanent collection are arranged in the small first-floor rooms and in the more expansive third floor of the museum, so you can explore everything in a few hours. Next door to The Broad is a small plaza with olive trees and seating, as well as the museum restaurant, Otium. Admission to the museum is free, but book timed tickets in advance to guarantee entry. ⊠ *221 S. Grand Ave., Downtown* ☎ *213/232–6200* ⊕ *www.thebroad.org* ☑ *Free* ☾ *Closed Mon.*

FAMILY    **California Science Center.** You're bound to see excited kids running up to the dozens of interactive exhibits here that illustrate the prevalence of science in everyday life. Clustered in different "worlds," the center keeps young guests busy for hours. They can design their own buildings and learn how to make them earthquake-proof; watch Tess, the dramatic 50-foot animatronic star of the exhibit "Body Works," demonstrate how the body's organs work together; and ride a bike across a trapeze wire three stories high in the air. One of the exhibits in the Air & Space section shows how astronauts Pete Conrad and Dick Gordon made it to outer space in the Gemini 11 capsule in 1966; also here is NASA's massive space shuttle *Endeavor*, located in the Samuel Oschin Pavilion, for which a timed ticket is needed to visit. The IMAX theater screens science-related large-format films. ⊠ *700 Exposition Park Dr., Exposition Park* ☎ *213/744–7400, 323/724–3623* ⊕ *www.californiasciencecenter.org* ⊠ *Free to permanent exhibitions; fees for some attractions, special exhibitions, and IMAX screenings vary.*

Fodor'sChoice    **Cathedral of Our Lady of the Angels.** A half block from Frank Gehry's cur-
★    vaceous Walt Disney Concert Hall sits the austere Cathedral of Our Lady of the Angels—a spiritual draw as well as an architectural attraction. Controversy surrounded Spanish architect José Rafael Moneo's unconventional design for the seat of the Archdiocese of Los Angeles. But judging from the swarms of visitors and the standing-room-only holiday masses, the church has carved out a niche for itself in Downtown L.A.

The plaza in front is glaringly bright on sunny days, though a children's play garden with bronze animals mitigates the starkness somewhat. Head underground to wander the mausoleum's mazelike white-marble corridors. Free guided tours start at the entrance fountain at 1 pm on weekdays. ■TIP➔ **There's plenty of underground visitors parking; the vehicle entrance is on Hill Street.** ⊠ *555 W. Temple St., Downtown* ☎ *213/680–5200* ⊕ *www.olacathedral.org* ⊠ *Free, parking $4 every 15 mins, $19 maximum.*

**El Pueblo de Los Angeles.** The oldest section of the city, known as El Pueblo de Los Angeles, represents the rich Mexican heritage of L.A. It had a close shave with disintegration in the early 20th century, but key buildings were preserved, and eventually **Olvera Street,** the district's heart, was transformed into a Mexican-American marketplace. Today vendors still sell puppets, leather goods, sandals, and woolen shawls from stalls lining the narrow street. You can find everything from salt and pepper shakers shaped like donkeys, to gorgeous glassware and pottery.

At the beginning of Olvera Street is the Plaza, a Mexican-style park with plenty of benches and walkways shaded by a huge Moreton Bay fig tree. On weekends, mariachi bands and folkloric dance groups perform. Nearby places worth investigating include the historic Avila Adobe, the Chinese American Museum, the Plaza Firehouse Museum, and the America Tropical Interpretive Center. Exhibits at the Italian American Museum of Los Angeles chronicle the area's formerly heavy Italian presence. ⊠ *Avila Adobe/Olvera Street Visitors Center, E-10 Olvera St., Downtown* ☎ *213/628–1274* ⊕ *www.elpueblo.lacity.org* ⊠ *Free for Olvera St. and guided tours, fees at some museums.*

Olvera Street, at the heart of the city's oldest neighborhood, is the place to experience many aspects of L.A.'s Mexican-American culture.

**Geffen Contemporary at MOCA.** The Geffen Contemporary is one of architect Frank Gehry's boldest creations. The largest of the three MOCA branches, with 40,000 square feet of exhibition space, it was once used as a police car warehouse. Works from the museum's permanent collection on display here include the artists Willem de Kooning, Franz Kline, Jackson Pollock, Mark Rothko, and Cindy Sherman. ✉ *152 N. Central Ave., Downtown* ☎ *213/626–6222* ⊕ *www.moca.org/exhibitions* ✉ *$12; free Thurs. 5 pm–8 pm* ☉ *Closed Tues.*

**GRAMMY Museum.** The interactive GRAMMY Museum brings the music industry's history to life. Throughout 30,000 square feet of space, the museum shows rare footage of GRAMMY performances, plus rotating exhibits on award-winning musicians. ✉ *800 W. Olympic Blvd., Downtown* ☎ *213/765–6800* ⊕ *www.grammymuseum.org* ✉ *$12.95.*

**Grand Central Market.** Handmade white-corn tamales, warm olive bread, dried figs, Mexican fruit drinks. Hungry yet? This mouthwatering gathering place is the city's largest and most active food market. Treated to a makeover in 2013, Grand Central Market is now the home to various artisanal food vendors. The spot bustles nonstop with locals and visitors surveying the butcher shop's display of everything from lambs' heads to pigs' tails. Produce stalls are piled high with locally grown avocados and heirloom tomatoes. Stop by **Chiles Secos** at stall C12 for a remarkable selection of rare chilies and spices, or **Sticky Rice** at stall C-5, for fantastic Thai-style chicken. Even if you don't plan on buying anything, it's a great place to browse and people-watch. ✉ *317 S. Broadway, Downtown* ☎ *213/624–2378* ⊕ *www.grandcentralmarket.com* ✉ *Free.*

Frank Gehry's Walt Disney Concert Hall was an instant L.A. icon.

**L.A. Live.** The mammoth L.A. Live stadium was built when there were few other arenas in Los Angeles. The first things you'll notice as you emerge from the parking lot are the giant LED screens and sparkling lights, and the buzz of crowds as they head out to dinner before or after a sporting event, awards ceremony, or concert at the Nokia Theater. There are dozens of restaurants and eateries here, including Los Angeles favorite Katsuya, the spot for sizzling Kobe beef platters and excellent sushi (the crab rolls are not to be missed). ⊠ *800 W. Olympic Blvd., Downtown* ☎ *213/763–6030* ⊕ *www.nokiatheatrelalive.com.*

**MOCA Grand Avenue.** The main branch of the Museum of Contemporary Art, designed by Arata Isozaki, contains underground galleries and presents elegant exhibitions. A huge Nancy Rubins sculpture fashioned from used airplane parts graces the museum's front plaza. ■ **TIP→ Take advantage of the free audio tour.** ⊠ *250 S. Grand Ave., Downtown* ☎ *213/626–6222* ⊕ *www.moca.org* 🖃 *$12; free Thurs. 5 pm–8 pm* ☉ *Closed Tues.*

**Fodor'sChoice**
★
**Walt Disney Concert Hall.** One of the architectural wonders of Los Angeles, the 2,265-seat hall is a sculptural monument of gleaming, curved steel designed by Frank Gehry. It's part of a complex that includes a public park, gardens, shops, and two outdoor amphitheaters, one of them atop the concert hall. The acoustically superlative venue is the home of the city's premier orchestra, the Los Angeles Philharmonic, whose music director, Gustavo Dudamel, is an international celebrity in his own right. The orchestra's season runs from late September to early June, before they head to the Hollywood Bowl for the summer. The highly praised Los Angeles Master Chorale also performs here. Look for

## BEST SPOTS FOR STAR-SIGHTING

■ **Courtside seats at a Lakers game during the playoffs.** Best way to see Kobe up close? Be a celebrity, know a celebrity, or be a celebrity's agent. Having an in at one of the big Downtown law firms that often buy season tickets is also a winning strategy. Otherwise, hire a private concierge service and be prepared to pay—a lot. Whatever you do, don't buy tickets off the street.

■ **Opening night galas.** Try for the Walt Disney Concert Hall or preview opening parties at the Museum of Contemporary Art. Celebrities support their fellow artists in Los Angeles and often entry to these fêtes is as easy as paying for the ticket to get in.

■ **The rooftop bar at the Standard.** The place still has enough buzz to attract the occasional celebrity. Booking a room is the surest way to gain access to the rooftop bar and pool. Word of advice: Never name-drop in Los Angeles. People who are truly connected here don't have to.

big-name acts such as Pink Martini during the off-season, and special holiday events like the Deck the Hall Holiday Sing-Along. ■ TIP➔ Free 60-minute guided tours are offered on most days, and there are self-guided audio tours. ✉ *111 S. Grand Ave., Downtown* ☎ *323/850–2000* ⊕ *www.laphil.org* ✒ *Tours free.*

## WORTH NOTING

**Avila Adobe.** Built as a private home for cattle rancher Francisco Avila in 1818, this museum preserves 7 of what were originally 18 rooms in the city's oldest standing residence. This graceful structure features 3-foot-thick walls made of adobe brick over cottonwood timbers, a traditional interior courtyard, and 1840s-era furnishings that bring to life an era when the city was still part of Mexico. The museum is open daily from 9 to 4. ✉ *E-10 Olvera St., Downtown* ☎ *213/485–6855* ⊕ *www.elpueblo. lacity.org/sightssounds/historicstructures/theavilaadobe.*

**Bradbury Building.** Stunning wrought-iron railings, ornate plaster moldings, pink marble staircases, a birdcage elevator, and a skylighted atrium that rises almost 50 feet—it's easy to see why the Bradbury Building leaves visitors awestruck. Designed in 1893 by a novice architect who drew his inspiration from a science-fiction story and a conversation with his dead brother via Ouija board, the office building was originally the site of turn-of-the-20th-century sweatshops, but now it houses a variety of businesses. Scenes from *Blade Runner* and *Chinatown* were filmed here, which means there's often a barrage of tourists snapping photos. Visits are limited to the lobby and the first-floor landing. ✉ *304 S. Broadway, at 3rd St., Downtown* ☎ *213/626–1893.*

**California African American Museum.** With more than 3,500 historical artifacts, this museum showcases contemporary art of the African diaspora. Artists represented here include Betye Saar, Charles Haywood, and June Edmonds. The museum has a research library with more than 20,000 books available for public use. ■ TIP➔ If possible, visit on a Sunday, when there's almost always a diverse lineup of speakers and performances. ✉ *600 State Dr., Exposition Park* ☎ *213/744–7432* ⊕ *www. caamuseum.org* 🎫 *Free* ☉ *Closed Mon.*

**Chinatown.** Smaller than San Francisco's Chinatown, this neighborhood near Union Station still represents a slice of Southeast Asian life. Sidewalks are usually jammed with tourists, locals, and, of course, Asian residents hustling from shop to shop picking up goods, spices, and trinkets from small shops and mini-plazas that line the street. Although some longtime establishments have closed in recent years, the area still pulses with its founding culture. During Chinese New Year, giant dragons snake down the street. And, of course, there are the many restaurants and quick-bite cafés specializing in Chinese feasts. In recent years, a slew of hip eateries like Baohaus and Chego located at Far East Plaza have injected the area with vibrancy.

An influx of local artists has added a spark to the neighborhood by taking up empty spaces and opening galleries along Chung King Road, a faded pedestrian passage behind the West Plaza shopping center between Hill and Yale. Also look for galleries along a little side street called Gin Ling Way on the east side of Broadway. Chinatown has its main action on North Broadway. There are several garages available for parking here that range $5–$10 per day. ✉ *Bordered by Yale, Bernard, Ord, and Alameda Sts., Los Angeles.*

**Chinese American Museum.** Since it's in El Pueblo Plaza, you might assume that this museum features Mexican-American art. It's actually the last surviving structure of L.A.'s original Chinatown. Three floors of exhibits reveal the different cultures that have called this area home, as well as how the original residents paved the way for what is now a vibrant and varied Chinatown. Rotating exhibits feature the work of Chinese-American artists. ✉ *425 N. Los Angeles St., Downtown* ☎ *213/485–8567* ⊕ *www.camla.org* 🎫 *$3* ☉ *Closed Mon.*

**City Hall of Los Angeles.** This gorgeous 1928 landmark building is a TV star—it was in the opening scenes of *Dragnet* and served as the Daily Planet building in the original *Adventures of Superman*. During extensive renovations, the original Lindburg Beacon was put back in action atop the hall's 13th-story tower. The revolving spotlight, inaugurated by President Calvin Coolidge from the White House via a telegraph key, was used from 1928 to 1941 to guide pilots into the Los Angeles airport. The observation deck, located on the 27th floor, is free to the public and has a stellar view of the greater Los Angeles area. ✉ *200 N. Spring St., Downtown* ☎ *213/485–2121* ⊕ *www.lacity. org* ☉ *Closed weekends.*

**Exposition Park.** Originally developed in 1880 as an open-air farmers' market, this 114-acre park has a lovely sunken rose garden and three museums—the California African American Museum, the California Science Center, and the Natural History Museum of Los Angeles County—as well as an IMAX theater. There's also the Los Angeles Memorial Coliseum and Sports Arena, where Olympic festivities were held in 1932 and 1984 and where USC games are now played. Good news for commuters: The Metro Expo Line, which connects the

L.A.'s Chinatown has its share of Chinese restaurants, shops, and cultural institutions, but you'll also find a growing community of artists and galleries.

Westside to Downtown Los Angeles, has a stop at Exposition Park. ⚠ Note that the park and neighborhood are sketchy at night. ⊠ *Between Exposition and Martin Luther King Jr. Blvds., Exposition Park*.

**Italian Hall Building.** This landmark is noteworthy because its south wall bears an infamous mural. Famed Mexican muralist David Alfaro Siqueiros shocked his patrons in the 1930s by depicting an oppressed worker of Latin America being crucified on a cross topped by a menacing American eagle. The anti-imperialist mural was promptly whitewashed but was later restored by the Getty Museum. It can be seen on the Italian Hall building today. Today the site functions as a museum and has seven color-coded exhibits on the history of Italian Americans. ⊠ *650 N. Main St., Downtown* ☎ *213/485–8432* ⊕ *www. italianhall.org*.

**Japanese American Cultural and Community Center.** Plenty of traditional and contemporary cultural events make this center well worth the trip. Founded in 1980, JACCC is home to a number of civic and arts organizations. Through the center's basement you reach the James Irvine Garden, a serene sunken space where local plants mix with bamboo, Japanese wisteria, and Japanese maples. The main floor of the museum houses the George J. Doizaki Gallery, which has 2,000 square feet of exhibition space and has housed everything from national treasures of Japan to the Bugaku costumes from the Kasuga Grand Shrine in Nara. ⊠ *244 S. San Pedro St., Downtown* ☎ *213/628–2725* ⊕ *www. jaccc.org* ⊗ *Doizaki Gallery closed Mon. and Tues.; Japanese garden closed Sat.–Mon.*

## THE ARTFUL LOS ANGELES METRO

Long ago, Los Angeles had an enviable public transportation system known as the Pacific Electric Red Cars, trolleys that made it possible to get around this sprawling city without an automobile. In the mid-1900s, the last of the Red Cars disappeared, and L.A. lost itself in the car culture.

That culture is here to stay, but in recent years, a new rail system has emerged. You can now take the subway through parts of Downtown, Hollywood, Pasadena, and North Hollywood. The Red Line starts at Downtown's Union Station, then curves northwest to Hollywood and on to Universal City and North Hollywood. The Blue and Green light rail lines are designed for commuters. The Gold Line goes from Union Station up to Azusa, stopping in Pasadena. Take the Expo Line from Downtown to Santa Monica, or the Purple Line from Union Station to Koreatown.

When convenient, taking the Metro can save you time and money. If you're worried about being caught in the subway during an earthquake, keep in mind that stations and tunnels were built with reinforced steel and were engineered to withstand a magnitude 8 earthquake.

The Metro Rail stations are worth exploring themselves, and you can sign up for a free docent-led MTA Art Moves tour (☎ 213/922–2738 ⊕ www.metro.net/about/art), which departs from the entrances to the Hollywood & Highland and Union stations. You'll receive a free day pass to ride the rails as you visit the colorful murals, sculptures, and architectural elements that illustrate themes of Los Angeles history.

The Universal City station is next to the site of the Campo de Caheunga, where Mexico relinquished control of California to the United States in 1847. The station features a time line of the area's past done in the traditional style of colorful Mexican folk art.

The North Hollywood station also celebrates local history, including native Gabrielino culture, many immigrant communities, Amelia Earhart (a local), Western wear designer Nudie, and the history of transportation in L.A. County.

There are film reels on the ceiling of the Hollywood and Vine station as well as original Paramount Pictures film projectors from the 1930s, and floor paving modeled after the yellow brick road from *The Wizard of Oz*. Imposing, glass-clad columns juxtaposed with rock formations can be seen at the Vermont and Beverly station. The old Red Car trolley makes an appearance in the Hollywood and Western station.

**Japanese American National Museum.** What was it like to grow up on a sugar plantation in Hawaii? How difficult was life for Japanese Americans interned in concentration camps during World War II? These questions are addressed by changing exhibitions at this museum in Little Tokyo that also include fun tributes to anime and Hello Kitty. Volunteer docents are on hand to share their own stories and experiences. The museum occupies its original site in a renovated 1925 Buddhist temple and an 85,000-square-foot adjacent pavilion. ⊠ *100 N. Central Ave., off E. 1st St., Downtown* ☎ *213/625–0414* ⊕ *www.janm.org* 🎟 *$10* ☉ *Closed Mon.*

Diners at the Wexler's Deli counter inside Grand Central Market

**Little Tokyo.** One of three official Japantowns in the country—all of which are in California—Little Tokyo is blossoming again thanks to the next generation of Japanese Americans setting up small businesses. Besides dozens of sushi bars, tempura restaurants, and karaoke bars, there's a lovely garden at the Japanese American Cultural and Community Center and a renovated 1925 Buddhist temple with an ornate entrance at the Japanese American National Museum.

On 1st Street you'll find a strip of buildings from the early 1900s. Look down when you get near San Pedro Street to see the art installation called *Omoide no Shotokyo* ("Remembering Old Little Tokyo"). Embedded in the sidewalk are brass inscriptions naming the original businesses, quoted reminiscences from residents, and steel time lines of Japanese-American history up to World War II. Nisei Week (a *nisei* is a second-generation Japanese American) is celebrated every August with traditional drums, dancing, a carnival, and a huge parade. ⊠ *Bounded by 1st, San Pedro, 3rd, and Central Sts., Downtown* ⊕ *www.visitlittletokyo.com.*

**Los Angeles Theatre.** Built in 1931, the Los Angeles Theatre opened with the premiere of Charlie Chaplin's classic *City Lights*. Full of glorious French Baroque–inspired details, the six-story lobby is awe-inspiring with its dramatic staircase, enormous fountain, grandiose chandeliers, and ornate gold detailing. You can occasionally witness the old Hollywood glamour by catching a special movie screening. ⊠ *615 Broadway, Downtown* ☎ *213/629–2939* ⊕ *www.losangelestheatre.com.*

**Million Dollar Theater.** The Million Dollar Theater opened in 1918 as part of Sid Grauman's famed chain of movie theaters. This Spanish Baroque–style venue had the special feature of having its own organ.

Film stars such as Gloria Swanson, Rudolph Valentino, and a young Judy Garland frequently made appearances. In the '40s, the venue swung with jazz and big band performers including Billie Holiday. The theater is open for special events and is worth a stop if you're walking past to inspect the lavish exterior with entertainment figures carved into the molding. ⊠ *307 S. Broadway, Downtown* ☎ *213/617–3600* ⊕ *www.milliondollar.la.*

FAMILY **Natural History Museum of Los Angeles County.** The hot ticket at this beaux arts–style museum completed in 1913 is the Dinosaur Hall, whose more than 300 fossils include adult, juvenile, and baby skeletons of the fearsome Tyrannosaurus rex. The Discovery Center lets kids and curious grown-ups touch real animal pelts, and the Insect Zoo gets everyone up close and personal with the white-eyed assassin bug and other creepy crawlers. A massive hall displays dioramas of animals in their natural habitats. Also look for pre-Columbian artifacts and crafts from the South Pacific. Outdoors, the 3½-acre Nature Gardens shelter native plant and insect species and contain an expansive edible garden. ⊠ *900 Exposition Blvd., off I–110, near Vermont Ave., Exposition Park* ☎ *213/763–3466* ⊕ *www.nhm.org* ⊠ *$12.*

**Orpheum Theatre.** Opened in 1926, the opulent Orpheum Theatre played host to live attractions including classic comedians, burlesque dancers, jazz greats like Lena Horne, Ella Fitzgerald, and Duke Ellington, and later on rock-and-roll performers such as Little Richard. After extensive restorations, the Orpheum once again revealed a stunning white marble lobby, majestic auditorium with fleur-de-lis panels, and two dazzling chandeliers. A thick red velvet and gold-trimmed curtain opens at showtime, and a white Wurlitzer pipe organ (one of the last remaining organs of its kind from the silent movie era) is at the ready. The original 1926 rooftop neon sign again shines brightly, signaling a new era for this theater. ⊠ *842 S. Broadway, Downtown* ☎ *877/677–4386* ⊕ *www.laorpheum.com.*

**Pershing Square.** The city's cultures come together in one of its oldest parks, named in honor of World War I General John J. Pershing. Opened in 1866, the park was renovated in the 1990s by architect Ricardo Legorreta and landscape architect Laurie Olin with colorful walls, fountains, and towers. Although the massive block-and-sphere architecture looks somewhat dated, Pershing remains an icon of Downtown L.A. Nearby office workers utilize the area for a stroll or lunch break. Free yoga classes are held at the community room. From mid-November to mid-January, the place attracts ice skaters to an outdoor rink. ⊠ *Bordered by 5th, 6th, Hill, and Olive Sts., Los Angeles* ☎ *213/847–4970* ⊕ *www.laparks.org/pershingsquare* ⊠ *Free.*

**Richard J. Riordan Central Library.** The nation's third-largest public library, the handsome Richard J. Riordan Central Library was designed in 1926 by Bertram Goodhue. Restored to their pristine condition, a pyramid tower and a torch symbolizing the "light of learning" crown the building. The Cook rotunda on the second floor features murals by Dean Cornwell depicting the history of California, and the Tom Bradley Wing, named for another mayor, has a soaring eight-story atrium.

The library offers frequent special exhibits, plus a small café where you can refuel. Don't ignore the gift shop, which is loaded with unique items for readers and writers. Free docent walking tours are offered Monday through Friday at 12:30 pm, Saturday at 11 am and 2 pm, and Sunday at 2 pm. A self-guided tour map is also available on the library's website. ⊠ *630 W. 5th St., at Flower St., Downtown* ☎ *213/228–7000* ⊕ *www.lapl.org* ✉ *Free.*

**Staples Center.** Home to the Lakers, the Clippers, the Sparks, and the ice hockey team the Los Angeles Kings, the Staples Center is Downtown's top sports destination. It's also the preferred venue for superstars like Bruce Springsteen, Madonna, and Justin Timberlake. Though not open for visits except for during events, the saucer-shaped building is eye-catching. ⊠ *1111 S. Figueroa St., Downtown* ☎ *213/742–7100* ⊕ *www.staplescenter.com.*

**Union Station.** Even if you don't plan on traveling by train anywhere, head here to soak up the ambience of a great rail station. Envisioned by John and Donald Parkinson, the architects who also designed the grand City Hall, the 1939 masterpiece combines Spanish Colonial Revival and art deco elements that have retained their classic warmth and quality. The waiting hall's commanding scale and enormous chandeliers have provided the backdrop for countless scenes in films, TV shows, and music videos. ⊠ *800 N. Alameda St., Downtown* ⊕ *www. unionstationla.com.*

# HOLLYWOOD AND THE STUDIOS

with Los Feliz, Silver Lake, and Echo Park

Visit Fodors.com for advice, updates, and bookings

# GETTING ORIENTED

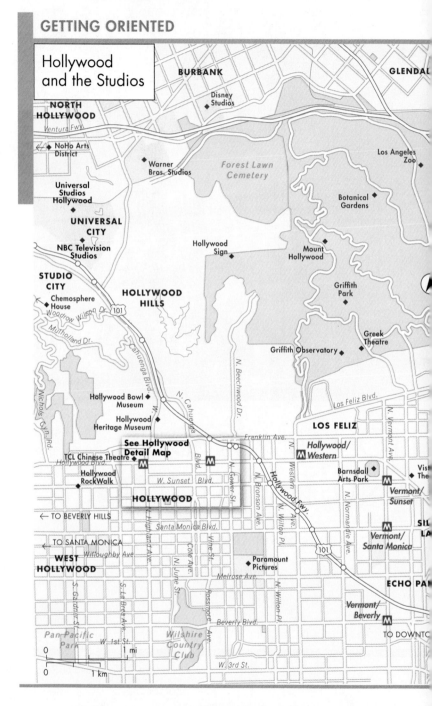

Hollywood
and the Studios

BURBANK

GLENDAL

NORTH
HOLLYWOOD

Disney
Studios

*Ventura Fwy.*

NoHo Arts
District

Los Angeles
Zoo

Warner
Bros. Studios

*Forest Lawn
Cemetery*

Universal
Studios
Hollywood

Botanical
Gardens

UNIVERSAL
CITY

NBC Television
Studios

Hollywood
Sign

Mount
Hollywood

STUDIO
CITY

Chemosphere
House

*Woodrow Wilson Dr.* 101

HOLLYWOOD
HILLS

Griffith
Park

*Mulholland Dr.*

Greek
Theatre

*Nichols Cyn. Rd.*

*Cahuenga Blvd.*

Griffith Observatory

*N. Beechwood Dr.*

Hollywood Bowl
Museum

*Los Feliz Blvd.*

Hollywood
Heritage Museum

*N. Cahuenga Blvd.*

Franklin Ave.

LOS FELIZ

*N. Vermont Ave.*

See Hollywood
Detail Map

TCL Chinese Theatre

Hollywood/
Western

*Hollywood Blvd.*

Hollywood
RockWalk

W. Sunset Blvd.

*N. Gower St.*

*N. Bronson Ave.*

*Hollywood Fwy.*

*Western Ave.*

Barnsdall
Arts Park

Vis
The

Vermont/
Sunset

HOLLYWOOD

← TO BEVERLY HILLS

Santa Monica Blvd.

*N. Highland Ave.*

*N. Wilton Pl.*

*N. Normandie Ave.*

Vermont/
Santa Monica

SIL
LA

← TO SANTA MONICA

Willoughby Ave.

*Hine St.*

WEST
HOLLYWOOD

*S. Gardner St.*

*S. La Brea Ave.*

*N. June St.*

*Cole Ave.*

Paramount
Pictures

Melrose Ave.

*N. Wilton Pl.*

ECHO PA

*Rossmore Ave.*

Beverly Blvd.

Vermont/
Beverly

TO DOWNTO

Pan Pacific
Park

W. 1st St.

*Wilshire
Country
Club*

W. 3rd St.

0    1 mi

0    1 km

## TOP REASONS TO GO

**See the Studios.** Catch a glimpse of movie magic in action at Paramount Pictures, Warner Bros. Studios, Universal Studios Hollywood, and NBC Television Studios.

**Walk in Famous Footsteps.** Outside the TCL Chinese Theatre are footprints of more than 200 of the silver screen's biggest stars, and the Hollywood Walk of Fame, on Hollywood Boulevard and Vine Street, has stars honoring more than 2,500 of the entertainment industry's most famous on its sidewalks.

**Picnic at the Hollywood Bowl.** Even if you don't get tickets for a show, stop at this L.A. landmark just north of Hollywood Boulevard for a great outdoor meal.

**Get up to Griffith Park.** The largest municipal park and urban wilderness in the country has a zoo, miles of trails to hike, an observatory, and one of L.A.'s best views.

**Check Out the Best Hollywood Memorabilia.** The Hollywood Museum has an incredible collection of Tinseltown's most glamorous costumes, photos, and more.

## GETTING HERE

### Driving Strategy
During rush hour, traffic jams on the Hollywood Freeway (U.S. 101/Highway 170), San Diego Freeway (I-405), and Ventura Freeway (U.S. 101/Highway 134) can make for lengthy trips to or from the Valley.

The best way to get from Hollywood to Burbank is to skip the freeways altogether and take Hollywood Boulevard to Cahuenga Boulevard heading north, and take a right on Barham Boulevard straight into Burbank.

Los Angeles Metro's Red Line subway makes two stops in the heart of Hollywood: the Hollywood/Vine Station and the Hollywood/Highland Station. This is by far the easiest way to get to the Valley or to Downtown Los Angeles.

## PLANNING YOUR TIME

Plan to spend the better part of a morning or afternoon taking in central Hollywood, where you can see the TCL Chinese Theatre and the Hollywood Walk of Fame.

Hollywood Boulevard is known for its underlying (and sometimes highly apparent) grit. Families might prefer a daytime walk.

Later in the evening, you can return to Hollywood for a movie at El Capitan or the fabulous ArcLight, or a summertime concert at the Hollywood Bowl.

Expect to spend most of a day at Universal Studios Hollywood and CityWalk; studio tours at Paramount and Warner Bros. last up to two hours.

## DRIVING TIMES AND DISTANCES

Minimum times listed below represent little to no traffic; maximum times assume the worst. Adjust accordingly, taking rush hour and peak weekend travel time into account.

■ **LAX to Hollywood:** 30–60 mins/25 miles

■ **Beverly Hills to Hollywood:** 15–45 mins/5 miles

■ **Hollywood to Burbank:** 20–40 mins/7 miles

■ **Santa Monica to Hollywood:** 30–90 mins/20 miles

# A DAY AT GRIFFITH PARK

The 4,100-acre Griffith Park (the largest municipal park and urban wilderness area in the United States) stands out as an oasis in a city covered in cement and asphalt.

(above) On the trail in Griffith Park (lower right) A resident of the park's zoo (upper right) The Griffith Observatory

On warm weekends, there are parties, barbecues, mariachi bands, and strolling vendors selling fresh fruit. Joggers, cyclists, and walkers course its roadways. There are also top attractions within the park, including the Griffith Observatory and the Los Angeles Zoo.

The park was named after Col. Griffith J. Griffith, a mining tycoon who donated 3,000 acres of land to the city for the park in 1896. It has been used as a film and television location since the early days of motion pictures. One early Hollywood producer advised, "A tree is a tree, a rock is a rock, shoot it in Griffith Park."

## GETTING HERE

The park has several entrances: off Los Feliz Boulevard at Western Canyon Avenue, Vermont Avenue, Crystal Springs Drive, and Riverside Drive; from the Ventura/134 Freeway at Victory Boulevard, Zoo Drive, or Forest Lawn Drive; from the Golden State Freeway (I–5) at Los Feliz Boulevard and Zoo Drive. The park is open from 6 am to 10 pm.

## TOP EXPERIENCES

### VISIT THE GRIFFITH OBSERVATORY

Griffith Observatory offers breathtaking panoramic views, and the structure itself, whose interior was recently renovated, is a pristinely maintained art deco spectacle. Visit during a scheduled talk or show at the Leonard Nimoy Event Horizon Theater, look through the Zeiss Telescope on a clear night, or check out the Samuel Oschin Planetarium and its incredible dome.

The expansive grounds are open to the public, and include a monument dedicated to James Dean; several scenes from *Rebel Without a Cause* were filmed here (if you've never seen the film, it's a definite must-watch before visiting). To see the lights of the city twinkle at night from above, stay late and head up to the Observatory Deck, open until 10 pm every evening except Monday.

### CLIMB MOUNT HOLLYWOOD

There are plenty of scenic routes throughout the park, but one of the best trails is to the top of Mount Hollywood. Park for free at the Griffith Observatory lot and pick up the trail from there. It's an easy half-hour hike to the top. On clear days you'll be able to see all the way to the Pacific Ocean and Catalina Island. About two-thirds of the way up is Dante's View, an area with benches where you can stop for a break or snack. You'll likely cross paths with horseback riders on the way.

An up-close view of the Hollywood sign from below means hiking a little more than 6 miles round-trip from the parking lot.

### CHECK OUT THE LOS ANGELES ZOO AND BOTANICAL GARDENS

In the northeast corner of the park, the zoo's highlights include a gorilla reserve, a Sumatran tiger, a snow leopard, and an acre dedicated to one of the largest troops of chimpanzees in the United States. In addition, the zoo claims to have more flamingoes than any other zoo worldwide.

### ENJOY A BIKE TOUR

There's a flat, family-friendly 4.7-mile path that runs along Crystal Springs Drive and Zoo Drive. Rentals are available inside the park at **Spokes n' Stuff Bike Shop** (✉ *4730 Crystal Springs Dr., at ranger station parking lot* ☎ *323/653–4099* ⊕ *www.spokes-n-stuff.com*).

### CATCH A CONCERT AT THE GREEK THEATRE

This 6,100-seat **Greek Theatre** (☎ *323/665–1927* ⊕ *www.greektheatrela.com*) is an outdoor venue where top artists such as Elton John and Paul Simon have performed.

Sightseeing
★★★★★
Nightlife
★★★★
Dining
★★★★
Lodging
★★★★★
Shopping
★★★

The Tinseltown mythology of Los Angeles was born in Hollywood, still one of the city's largest and most vibrant neighborhoods. In the Hollywood Hills to the north of Franklin Avenue sit some of the most marvelous mansions the moguls ever built; in the flats below Sunset and Santa Monica boulevards are the classic Hollywood bungalows where studio workers once resided. Reputation aside, though, it's mostly a workaday neighborhood without the glitz and glamour of places like Beverly Hills. The only major studio still located in Hollywood is Paramount; Warner Bros., Disney, and Universal Studios Hollywood are to the north in Burbank and Universal City.

Updated by
Clarissa Wei

Of course, the notion of Hollywood as a center of the entertainment industry can be expanded to include more than one neighborhood: to the north is Studio City, a thriving strip at the base of the Hollywood Hills which is home to many smaller film companies; Universal City, where you'll find Universal Studios Hollywood; and Burbank, home to several major studios. North Hollywood, a suburban enclave that's actually in the San Fernando Valley, has its own thriving arts district. Los Feliz, to the east, is where you'll find Griffith Park and the trendy Vermont Avenue area where you can shop, browse for books, or catch a movie at the independent theater. Even farther east you'll find the arty havens of Silver Lake and Echo Park.

There are more than 2,500 stars honored on the Hollywood Walk of Fame.

## HOLLYWOOD

Sure, Hollywood's top attractions are a bit touristy—but if it's your first time, you should at least make a brief stop here. Be sure to check out the Hollywood Walk of Fame and catch a movie in one of the neighborhood's opulent movie palaces, such as the TCL Chinese Theatre or El Capitan.

Like Downtown L.A., Hollywood continues to undergo a transformation designed to lure a hip, younger crowd and big money back into the fold. New sleek clubs and restaurants seem to pop up every month drawing in celebrities, scenesters, and starry-eyed newcomers to create a colorful nighttime landscape (and some parking headaches).

Many daytime attractions can be found on foot around the home of the Academy Awards at the **Dolby Theatre,** part of the Hollywood & Highland entertainment complex. The adjacent **TCL Chinese Theatre** delivers silver screen magic with its iconic facade and ornate interiors from a bygone era. A shining example of a successful Hollywood revival can be seen and experienced just across Hollywood Boulevard at the 1926 **El Capitan Theatre,** which offers live stage shows and a Wurlitzer organ concert before select movie engagements.

Walk the renowned **Hollywood Walk of Fame** to find your favorite celebrities and you can encounter derelict diversions literally screaming for your attention (and dollar), numerous panhandlers, and an occasional costumed superhero not sanctioned by Marvel Comics. At Sunset and Vine, a developer-interpreted revival with sushi, stars, and swank condos promises to continue the ongoing renovations of the area. In summer, visit the crown jewel of Hollywood, the **Hollywood Bowl**, which features shows by the Los Angeles Philharmonic and many guest stars.

The San Fernando Valley is only a couple of miles north of the Hollywood Bowl, yet some say it's worlds away. Over the hill from the notably trendier areas of Downtown and Hollywood, "The Valley" gets a bad rap. But all snickering aside, this area is home to many of the places that have made Los Angeles famous: **Disney Studios, Warner Bros. Studios,** and **Universal Studios Hollywood.**

For newcomers, it's hard to resist the allure of the sound stages and back lots of Tinseltown's studios. Studio tours are the best way for mere mortals to get close to where celebs work. Most tours last at least a couple of hours, and allow you to see where hit television shows are filmed, spot actors on the lot, and visit movie sound stages—some directors even permit visitors on the set while shooting.

## TOP ATTRACTIONS

**Dolby Theatre.** The interior design of the theater that hosts the Academy Awards was inspired by European opera houses, but underneath all the trimmings the space has one of the finest technical systems in the world. A tour of the Dolby, which debuted in 2001 as the Kodak Theatre, is a worthwhile expense for movie buffs who just can't get enough insider information. Tour guides share plenty of behind-the-scenes tidbits about Oscar ceremonies as they escort you through the theater. You'll get to step into the VIP lounge where celebrities mingle on the big night and get a bird's-eye view from the balcony seating. ■TIP➜ If you have the Go Los Angeles Card, the tour is included. ⊠ *6801 Hollywood Blvd., Hollywood* ☎ *323/308–6300* ⊕ *www.dolbytheatre.com* ✆ *Tour $22.*

**El Capitan Theatre.** This theater—where Orson Welles debuted *Citizen Kane*—originally opened in 1926 as a playhouse and was remodeled in the 1940s into a movie palace. Restored to its former grandeur by the Walt Disney Company, the palatial venue features soaring ceilings and a lavish East Indian motif. Movies are often preceded by live stage or music events. ⊠ *6838 Hollywood Blvd., Hollywood* ☎ *323/467–7674* ⊕ *www.elcapitan.go.com.*

**Hollywood Bowl Museum.** Before the concert, or during the day, visit the Hollywood Bowl Museum for a time-capsule version of the Hollywood Bowl's history. The microphone used during Frank Sinatra's 1943 performance is just one of the pieces of rare memorabilia on display. Throughout the gallery, drawers open to reveal vintage programs or letters written by fans tracing their fondest memories of going to the Hollywood Bowl. Headphones let you listen to recordings of such great Bowl performers as Amelita Galli-Curci, Ella Fitzgerald, and Paul McCartney, and videos give you a tantalizing look at performances by everyone from the Beatles to Esa-Pekka Salonen. Be sure to pick up a map and take the "Bowl Walk" to explore the grounds. In the summer, the store stays open until showtime. ⊠ *2301 N. Highland Ave., Hollywood* ☎ *323/850–2058* ⊕ *www.hollywoodbowl.com/visit/hollywood-bowl-museum* ✆ *Free* ☉ *Closed Mon. in summer; closed Sun. and Mon. during off-season.*

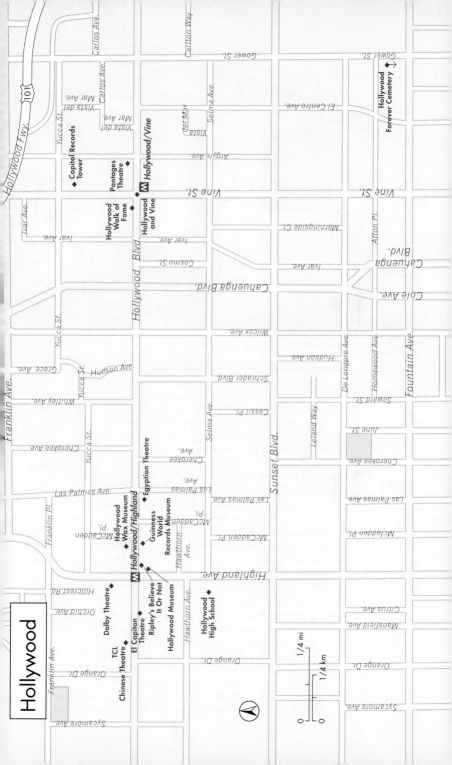

# Hollywood

- Hollywood Fwy. 101
- Carlos Ave.
- Carlton Way
- Gower St.
- Gower St.
- Yucca St.
- Vista del Mar Ave.
- Carlos Ave.
- El Centro Ave.
- Selma Ave.
- **Capitol Records Tower** ♦
- **Pantages Theatre** ♦
- Vista del Mar
- Argyle Ave.
- **Ⓜ** *Hollywood/Vine*
- **Hollywood Forever Cemetery** ♦ →
- Ivar Ave.
- **Hollywood Walk of Fame**
- **Ⓜ** *Hollywood and Vine*
- Vine St.
- Ivar Ave.
- Vine St.
- Ivar Ave.
- Cosmo St.
- Morningside Ct.
- Afton Pl.
- Hollywood Blvd.
- *Cahuenga Blvd.*
- Cahuenga Blvd.
- Cole Ave.
- Grace Ave.
- Yucca St.
- Hudson Ave.
- Wilcox Ave.
- Hudson Ave.
- De Longpre Ave.
- Homewood Ave.
- Fountain Ave.
- Franklin Ave.
- Whitley Ave.
- Schrader Blvd.
- Seward St.
- Cherokee Ave.
- Yucca St.
- Selma Ave.
- Cassil Pl.
- Sunset Blvd.
- Leland Way
- June St.
- Cherokee Ave.
- **Egyptian Theatre** ♦
- Cherokee Ave.
- Las Palmas Ave.
- Las Palmas Ave.
- Las Palmas Ave.
- McFadden Pl.
- **Hollywood Wax Museum** ♦
- **Guinness World Records Museum** ♦
- McCadden Pl.
- McCadden Pl.
- Hawthorn Ave.
- Franklin Pl.
- **Ⓜ** *Hollywood/Highland*
- Highland Ave.
- Hillcrest Rd.
- Orchid Ave.
- **Dolby Theatre** ♦
- **Ripley's Believe It Or Not** ♦
- **Hollywood Museum**
- **TCL Chinese Theatre** ♦
- **El Capitan Theatre** ♦
- Hawthorn Ave.
- **Hollywood High School** ♦
- Franklin Ave.
- Orange Dr.
- Orange Dr.
- Citrus Ave.
- Mansfield Ave.
- Sycamore Ave.
- Sycamore Ave.
- 1/4 mi
- 1/4 km
- 0
- 0

Take a tour of this classic Hollywood studio.

**Hollywood Forever Cemetery.** Leave it to Hollywood to have a graveyard that feels more V.I.P. than R.I.P. With its revived grounds and media-genic approach, this celebrity-filled cemetery (formerly the Hollywood Memorial Park) is well worth a visit. The lush gardens, lovely lakes, and spectacular views of the Hollywood sign and Griffith Observatory (whose founder, Griffith J. Griffith, is buried here) make it a good spot for an afternoon walk; you can pick up a map of the grounds in the gift shop. Among the graves are those of Cecil B. DeMille, Douglas Fairbanks Sr., and Mel Blanc, voice of many Warner Bros. cartoon characters, whose headstone reads, "That's all, folks!"

Film and music fans flock here to find their dearly departed idols, including King Kong's love, Fay Wray, and punk rockers Johnny Ramone and Dee Dee Ramone (buried under his given name, Douglas Glenn Colvin). The large Grecian tomb in the center of the lake belongs to philanthropist William A. Clark Jr., founder of the Los Angeles Philharmonic. Inside the Cathedral Mausoleum is Rudolph Valentino's crypt, stained red from many lipstick kisses. For years, a mysterious "Lady in Black" visited Valentino's tomb on the anniversary of his death.

In the summer, the cemetery hosts events including film screenings starring Valentino and other interred residents on the mausoleum's outer wall, and guests congregate on the grounds to enjoy a picnic while watching the movie. The cemetery also hosts Dia De Los Muertos in October, a Mexican festival celebrating the dead with colorful costumes, art, and music. When planning a visit, even for a festive event, maintain a respectful attitude. The cemetery still performs burials and proper etiquette is expected. Don't miss the concerts at the on-site Masonic Lodge, a stunning high-ceilinged building that uses candles as lighting. ⊠ *6000 Santa Monica Blvd., Hollywood* 📞 *323/469–1181* ⊕ *www.hollywoodforever.com* 🎫 *Free; check online for film screenings.*

**Fodor'sChoice** **Hollywood Museum.** Lovers of Tinseltown's glamorous past may find
★ themselves humming "Hooray for Hollywood" as they tour this gem of cinema history inside the Max Factor Building. For years, Factor's famous makeup was manufactured on the top floors, and on the ground floor was a salon. After an extensive renovation, this art deco landmark that Factor purchased in 1928 now holds this museum with more than 10,000 bits of film memorabilia.

Exhibits include sections dedicated to Marilyn Monroe, Michael Jackson, and Bob Hope, and to costumes and props from such films as *Moulin Rouge, The Silence of the Lambs,* and *Planet of the Apes.* There's also an impressive gallery of photos showing movie stars frolicking at the Brown Derby, Ciro's, the Trocadero, the Mocambo, and other fabled venues.

Hallway walls are covered with the autograph collection of ultimate fan Joe Ackerman; aspiring filmmakers may want to check out the early film equipment. The museum's showpiece is the Max Factor exhibit, where separate dressing rooms are dedicated to Factor's "color harmony," which created distinct looks for "brownettes" (Factor's term), redheads, and, of course, bombshell blondes. You can practically smell the peroxide of Marilyn Monroe getting her trademark platinum look here. Also worth a peek are makeup cases owned by Lucille Ball, Lana Turner, Ginger Rogers, Bette Davis, Rita Hayworth, and others who made Max Factor makeup popular. ⊠ *1660 N. Highland Ave., at Hollywood Blvd., Hollywood* 📞 *323/464–7776* ⊕ *www.thehollywoodmuseum.com* 🎫 *$15* 🕐 *Closed Mon. and Tues.*

**Hollywood Walk of Fame.** Along Hollywood Boulevard (and part of Vine Street) runs a trail of affirmations for entertainment-industry overachievers. On this mile-long stretch of sidewalk, inspired by the concrete handprints in front of TLC Chinese Theatre, names are embossed in brass, each at the center of a pink star embedded in dark-gray terrazzo. They're not all screen deities; many stars commemorate people who worked in a technical field, such as sound or lighting. The first eight stars were unveiled in 1960 at the northwest corner of Highland Avenue and Hollywood Boulevard: Olive Borden, Ronald Colman, Louise Fazenda, Preston Foster, Burt Lancaster, Edward Sedgwick, Ernest Torrence, and Joanne Woodward (some of these names have stood the test of time better than others). Since then, more than 2,000 others have been immortalized, though that honor doesn't come cheap—upon selection by a special committee, the personality in question (or more likely his or her movie studio or record company) pays about $30,000 for the privilege. To aid you in spotting celebrities you're looking for, stars are identified by one of five icons: a motion-picture camera, a radio microphone, a television set, a record, or a theatrical mask. ⊠ *Hollywood Blvd. and Vine St., Hollywood* 📞 *323/469–8311* ⊕ *www.walkoffame.com.*

**DID YOU KNOW?**

At the top of the Capitol Records Tower, a blinking light spells out "Hollywood" in Morse code.

Fodor's Choice  **Paramount Pictures.** With a history dating to the early 1920s, the Para-
★ mount lot was home to some of Hollywood's most luminous stars, including Mary Pickford, Rudolph Valentino, Mae West, Marlene Dietrich, and Bing Crosby. Director Cecil B. DeMille's base of operations for decades, Paramount offers probably the most authentic studio tour, giving you a real sense of the film industry's history. This is the only major studio from film's golden age left in Hollywood—all the others are in Burbank, Universal City, or Culver City.

Memorable movies and TV shows with scenes shot here include *Sunset Boulevard, Forrest Gump,* and *Titanic.* Many of the *Star Trek* movies and TV series were shot entirely or in part here, and several seasons of *I Love Lucy* were shot on the portion of the lot Paramount acquired in 1967 from Lucille Ball. You can take a 2-hour studio tour or a 4½-hour VIP tour, led by guides who walk and trolley you around the back lots. As well as gleaning some gossipy history, you'll spot the sets of TV and film shoots in progress. Reserve ahead for tours, which are for those ages 10 and up. ■TIP➜ You can be part of the audience for live TV tapings (tickets are free), but you must book ahead. ✉ *5555 Melrose Ave., Hollywood* ☎ *323/956–1777* ⊕ *www.paramountstudiotour.com* ✉ *$55 regular tour, $178 VIP tour.*

**TCL Chinese Theatre.** The stylized Chinese pagodas and temples of the former Grauman's Chinese Theatre have become a shrine both to stardom and the combination of glamour and flamboyance that inspire the phrase "only in Hollywood." Although you have to buy a movie ticket to appreciate the interior trappings, the courtyard is open to the public. The main theater itself is worth visiting, if only to see a film in the same setting as hundreds of celebrities who have attended big premieres here.

And then, of course, outside in front are the oh-so-famous cement hand- and footprints. This tradition is said to have begun at the theater's opening in 1927, with the premiere of Cecil B. DeMille's *King of Kings,* when actress Norma Talmadge just happened to step in wet cement. Now more than 160 celebrities have contributed imprints for posterity, including some oddball specimens, such as casts of Whoopi Goldberg's dreadlocks. ✉ *6925 Hollywood Blvd., Hollywood* ☎ *323/461–3331* ⊕ *www.tclchinesetheatres.com* ✉ *Tour $15.*

**WORTH NOTING**

**Capitol Records Tower.** According to legend, singer Nat King Cole and songwriter Johnny Mercer suggested that the record company's headquarters be shaped like a stack of 45s, influencing the design of this now iconic '50s structure. Or so the story goes. Architect Welton Becket claimed he just wanted to design a structure that economized space, and in so doing, he created the world's first cylindrical office building.

On its south wall, L.A. artist Richard Wyatt's mural *Hollywood Jazz, 1945–1972* immortalizes musical greats Duke Ellington, Billie Holiday, Ella Fitzgerald, and Miles Davis. Pop icons the Beatles are commemorated in stunning photos near the Vine Street entrance, and John Lennon's star on the Hollywood Walk of Fame out front is a popular gathering spot for fans on his birthday.

The recording studios are beneath the parking lot; all kinds of major artists, including Frank Sinatra, the Beatles, and Radiohead, have filled these echo chambers with sound. At the top of the tower, a blinking light spells out "Hollywood" in Morse code. The building is not open to the public. ☒ *1750 N. Vine St., Hollywood* ⊕ *www.capitolrecords. com* ☞ *Check website for events.*

**OFF THE
BEATEN
PATH**

**Chemosphere House.** Shaped like a flying saucer from a '60s film, the Chemosphere House sits perched high up off Mulholland Drive overlooking the Valley, and is a must-see for architecture fans of the mod era. It was designed by the late architect John Lautner, a student of Frank Lloyd Wright. To get here, head north up Laurel Canyon, then turn right on Mulholland, and right on Torreyson Place. Turn left up the narrow unmarked road where the private home sits at the top. ☒ *7776 Torreyson Dr., Hollywood.*

**Egyptian Theatre.** Hieroglyphics in Hollywood? Why not? Impresario Sid Grauman built Hollywood's first movie palace in 1922; the Egyptian-theme theater hosted many premieres in its early heyday. In 1992 it closed—with an uncertain future. Six years later it reopened with its Tinseltown shine restored.

The nonprofit American Cinematheque now hosts special screenings and discussions with notable filmmakers, and on weekends you can watch a documentary called *Forever Hollywood* ($7). Walk past giant palm trees to the theater's forecourt and entrance. Backstage tours, which detail the theater's Old Hollywood legacy, take place once a month. Films, primarily classics and independents, are shown in the evening. ☒ *6712 Hollywood Blvd., Hollywood* ☎ *323/466–3456* ⊕ *www. americancinemathequecalendar.com* ☞ *Check website for tickets.*

**QUICK
BITES**

**Pig 'n Whistle.** During Hollywood's heyday, the Pig 'n Whistle was the place to stop for a bite before or after seeing a movie in the neighboring Egyptian Theatre. You can expect overstuffed booths, dramatic paneled ceilings, and attentive service. ☒ *6714 Hollywood Blvd., Hollywood* ☎ *323/463–0000* ⊕ *www.pignwhistlehollywood.com.*

**Guinness World Records Museum.** The namesake of the world-famous book, this museum exhibits replicas and photographs of record-breakers, like the most-tattooed person and the world's heaviest man. An interactive theater with moving, vibrating seats lets you experience the force of a record being broken. You can also attempt the world's longest jump, or compare your height with the world's tallest man. ☒ *6764 Hollywood Blvd., Hollywood* ☎ *323/463–6433* ⊕ *www.guin- nessmuseumhollywood.com* ☒ *$20.*

**QUICK
BITES**

**25 Degrees.** Proudly serving its signature burgers, fries, and shakes, 25 Degrees has won awards for having one of the best burgers in town. At street level, the round-the-clock eatery exudes a bit of the old Hollywood glamour while putting a modern spin on the classic burger joint. ☒ *Holly- wood Roosevelt Hotel, 7000 Hollywood Blvd., Hollywood* ☎ *323/466–7000* ⊕ *www.25degreesrestaurant.com/los-angeles.*

**Hollywood and Vine.** The mere mention of this intersection inspires images of a street corner bustling with movie stars, hopefuls, and moguls arriving on foot or in a Duesenberg or a Rolls-Royce. In the old days this was the hub of the radio and movie industry: film stars like Gable and Garbo hustled in and out of their agents' office buildings (some now converted to luxury condos) at these fabled cross streets. Even the Red Line Metro station here keeps up the Hollywood theme, with a *Wizard of Oz*–style yellow brick road, vintage movie projectors, and old film reels on permanent display. Sights visible from this intersection include the Capitol Records Building, the Avalon Hollywood nightclub, Pantages Theater, and the W Hollywood Hotel. ⊠ *Hollywood Ave. and Vine St., Hollywood.*

**Hollywood Heritage Museum.** This unassuming building across from the Hollywood Bowl is a treasure trove of memorabilia from the earliest days of Hollywood filmmaking, including a thorough look back at Cecil B. DeMille's starry career. Large sections of the original stone statues from *The Ten Commandments* lay like fallen giants among smaller items in glass cases around the perimeter of this modest museum. A documentary tracking Hollywood's golden era is worth taking in.

The building itself is the restored Lasky-DeMille Barn, designated a California State Historic Landmark in 1956. ⊠ *2100 N. Highland Ave., Hollywood* ☎ *323/874–4005* ⊕ *www.hollywoodheritage.org* ☎ *$7* ⊙ *Closed Mon.–Thurs.*

**Hollywood High School.** This mid-century modern building has seen its fair share of Hollywood royalty in its classrooms, and many productions have been shot in its halls. Surely no other high school has such a shining alumni list—such names as Carol Burnett, Carole Lombard, John Ritter, Lana Turner, and Sarah Jessica Parker call HHS their alma mater. You can't enter the school grounds, but you can take in the star-studded mural, *Portrait of Hollywood,* by famed local painter Eloy Torrez, on the exterior of the auditorium on the Highland Avenue side. ⊠ *1521 N. Highland Ave., Hollywood* ⊕ *www. hollywoodhighschool.net.*

**Hollywood RockWalk.** Providing equipment for countless Los Angeles bands since the 1960s, Guitar Center pays tribute to its rock-star clientele with the Hollywood RockWalk in front of the building. The concrete slabs are imprinted with the talented hands of Van Halen, Bonnie Raitt, Chuck Berry, Dick Dale, Def Leppard, Carlos Santana, KISS, and others. Two standouts are Joey Ramone's upside-down hand and Lemmy of Motörhead's "middle finger salute." The store's mini-museum displays signed sheet music and memorabilia like Bob Dylan's hat and harmonica. ⊠ *Guitar Center, 7425 Sunset Blvd., Hollywood* ☎ *323/874–1060* ⊕ *www.rockwalk.com* ☎ *Free.*

**Hollywood Sign.** With letters 50 feet tall, Hollywood's trademark sign can be spotted from miles away. The icon, which originally read "Hollywoodland," was erected in the Hollywood Hills in 1923 to advertise a segregated housing development and was outfitted with 4,000 light bulbs. In 1949 the "land" portion of the sign was taken down. By 1973 the sign had earned landmark status, but since the

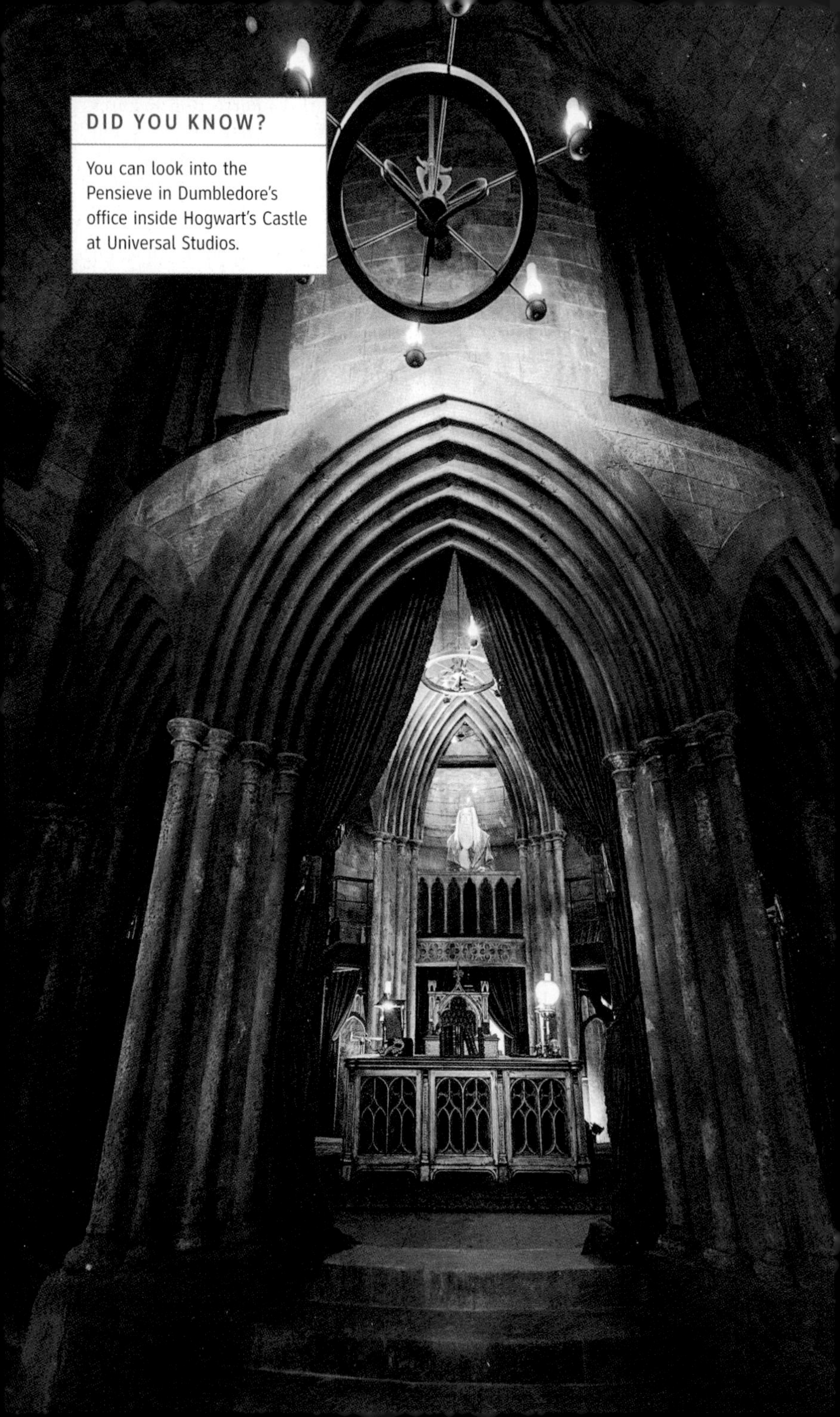

### DID YOU KNOW?

You can look into the Pensieve in Dumbledore's office inside Hogwart's Castle at Universal Studios.

letters were made of wood, its longevity came into question. A make-over project was launched and the letters were auctioned off (rocker Alice Cooper bought the "o" and singing cowboy Gene Autry sponsored an "l") to make way for a new sign made of sheet metal. Inevitably, the sign has drawn pranksters who have altered it over the years, albeit temporarily, to spell out "Hollyweed" (in the 1970s, to push for more lenient marijuana laws), "Go Navy" (before a Rose Bowl game), and "Perotwood" (during businessman Ross Perot's 1992 presidential bid). A fence and surveillance equipment have since been installed to deter intruders, but another vandal managed to pull the "Hollyweed" prank once again in 2017 after Californians voted to make recreational use of marijuana legal statewide. ■ TIP→ **Use caution if driving up to the sign on residential streets; many cars speed around the blind corners.** ⊠ *Griffith Park, Mt. Lee Dr., Hollywood* ⊕ *www.hollywoodsign.org.*

**Hollywood Wax Museum.** If a walk through Hollywood hasn't yielded any star-spotting, head over to this venerable icon of a museum, which has been open continuously since 1965. Get up close and personal with Drew Barrymore, Cameron Diaz, and Lucy Liu, or pose with a dapper, lifelike Samuel L. Jackson. Vignettes from classic films re-create well-known scenes, such as Katharine Hepburn and Humphrey Bogart in *The African Queen* or Tom Hanks in *Forrest Gump*, as well as the figures from the *Wizard of Oz*. There's an homage to Heath Ledger in *The Dark Knight,* alongside older icons such as John Wayne and Charlie Chaplin. Be sure to walk the red carpet with the latest Oscar stars and, if you're so inclined, creep along the dimly lit "horror chamber" where scenes from popular films of fright are reconstructed. The effect is heightened at night when fewer visitors are around. ⊠ *6767 Hollywood Blvd., Hollywood* ☎ *323/462–5991* ⊕ *www.hollywoodwaxmuseum.com/hollywood* ⊡ *$20.*

**Pantages Theatre.** Just steps from the fabled intersection of Hollywood and Vine, this Hollywood Boulevard landmark is an art deco palace originally built as a vaudeville showcase in 1930. Once host of the Academy Awards, it's now home to such Broadway shows as *The Lion King, Hairspray, Wicked,* and *The Book of Mormon.* ⊠ *6233 Hollywood Blvd., Hollywood* ☎ *323/468–1770* ⊕ *www.hollywood-pantages.com.*

**Ripley's Believe It or Not.** The ticket prices may be a bit steep for these slightly faded relics of the bizarre and sometimes creepy, but where else can you see a bikini made of human hair, a sculpture of Marilyn Monroe made of shredded money, and animal freaks of nature? Whether you believe it or not, it's fun to marvel at the museum's wacky curiosities. ⊠ *6780 Hollywood Blvd., Hollywood* ☎ *323/466–6335* ⊕ *www.ripleys.com/hollywood* ⊡ *$23.*

## STUDIO CITY

Ventura Boulevard, the famed commercial strip, cuts through the lively neighborhood of Studio City. This area, located west of Universal City, is home to several smaller film and TV studios.

## UNIVERSAL CITY

Although it has its own zip code and subway station, Universal City, over the hill from Hollywood, is simply the name for the unincorporated area of Los Angeles where Universal Studios Hollywood and CityWalk are located.

### TOP ATTRACTIONS

FAMILY **Universal Studios Hollywood.** A theme park with classic attractions like roller coasters and thrill rides, Universal Studios also provides a tour of some beloved television and movie sets. A favorite attraction is the tram tour, during which you can experience the parting of the Red Sea; duck from dinosaurs in Jurassic Park; visit Dr. Seuss's Whoville; see the airplane wreckage of *War of the Worlds*; and get chills looking at the house from *Psycho*. ■TIP➡ The tram ride is usually the best place to begin your visit, because the lines become longer as the day goes on.

Most attractions are designed to give you a thrill in one form or another, including the spine-tingling Transformers: The Ride 3-D, or the bone-rattling roller coaster, Revenge of the Mummy. The Simpsons Ride takes you on a hair-raising animated journey through the clan's hometown of Springfield. Don't forget to indulge in magical moments at The Wizarding World of Harry Potter and try some Butterbeer in Hogsmeade. Geared more toward adults, CityWalk is a separate venue run by Universal Studios, where you'll find shops, restaurants, nightclubs, and movie theaters. ✉ *100 Universal City Pl., Universal City* ☎ *818/622–3801* ⊕ *www.universalstudioshollywood.com* 🎫 *$99.*

## BURBANK

Johnny Carson, host of *The Tonight Show,* used to ironically refer to downtown Burbank as "beautiful," but it's since become one of the area's most desirable suburbs. It's also home to Warner Bros. Studios, Disney Studios, and NBC Studios, and to Bob Hope Airport (BUR), one of the two major airports serving L.A.

### TOP ATTRACTIONS

**Warner Bros. Studios.** If you're looking for an authentic behind-the-scenes look at how films and TV shows are made, head to this major studio center, one of the world's busiest. After a short film on the studio's movies and TV shows, hop aboard a tram for a ride through the sets and soundstages of such favorites as *Casablanca* and *Rebel Without a Cause.* You'll see the bungalows where Marlon Brando, Bette Davis, and other icons relaxed between shots, and the current production offices for Clint Eastwood and George Clooney. You might even spot a celeb or see a shoot in action—tours change from day to day depending on the productions taking place on the lot.

Tours are given at least every hour, more frequently from May to September, and last 2 hours and 25 minutes. Reservations are required, and advance notice is needed for people with mobility issues. Children under eight are not admitted. A five-hour deluxe tour costing $295 includes lunch, and lets you spend more time exploring the sets. ✉ *3400 W. Riverside Dr., Burbank* ☎ *877/492–8687* ⊕ *www.wbstudiotour.com* 🎫 *$62, $295 for deluxe tour.*

## NORTH HOLLYWOOD

Originally called Lankershim after the family of ranchers and farmers who first settled here, this area took the name North Hollywood in the 1920s to capitalize on the popularity of the city just over the hill to the south. Today, the large and bustling neighborhood serves as the terminus of the Metro Red Line subway, around which the NoHo Arts District thrives.

### WORTH NOTING

**NoHo Arts District.** Don't let the name fool you—this West Coast enclave bears little resemblance to its New York namesake. In fact, the name *NoHo* was spawned when the city, desperate to reinvent this depressed area, abbreviated the region's North Hollywood name. A square mile at the intersection of Lankershim and Magnolia in North Hollywood, the NoHo Arts District has slowly tried to transform itself into a cultural hot spot that includes several theaters showcasing aspiring young actors, a comedy club, galleries, boutiques, and restaurants. ✉ *Lankershim and Magnolia Blvds., North Hollywood* ⊕ *www. nohoartsdistrict.com.*

## LOS FELIZ

In the rolling hills below the stunning Griffith Observatory, Los Feliz is one of L.A.'s most affluent neighborhoods. With Hollywood just a few miles west, its winding streets are lined with mansions belonging to some of the biggest celebrities. In recent years, both Vermont and Hillhurst avenues have come alive with hip restaurants, boutiques, and theaters.

### TOP ATTRACTIONS

**Griffith Observatory.** High on a hillside overlooking the city, Griffith Observatory is one of the area's most celebrated landmarks. Its interior is just as impressive as its exterior, thanks to a massive expansion and cosmic makeover completed a decade ago. Highlights of the building include the Foucault's pendulum hanging in the main lobby, the planet exhibitions on the lower level, and the playful wall display of galaxy-themed jewelry along the twisty indoor ramp.

In true L.A. style, the Leonard Nimoy Event Horizon Theater presents guest speakers and shows on space-related topics and discoveries. The Samuel Oschin Planetarium features an impressive dome, digital projection system, theatrical lighting, and a stellar sound system. Shows are $7.

CLOSE UP

# Laurel Canyon and Mulholland Drive

The hills that separate Hollywood from the Valley are more than a symbolic dividing line between the city slickers and the suburbanites; they have a community in their own right and a reputation as a hideaway for celebrities and wealthy creatives.

The 2002 movie *Laurel Canyon* showed the lifestyle of one kind of Canyon dweller—freethinking entertainment industry movers and shakers seeking peaceful refuge in their tree-shaded homes. By day they're churning out business deals and working on projects; by night they're living it up with private parties high above the bustle of the city streets. Landslides can cause road closures in Laurel Canyon, so do some research beforehand.

Drive through Laurel Canyon and you'll pass estates and party pads dating back to the silent film era. If you have time to cruise Mulholland Drive, expect breathtaking views that show the city's serene side.

Grab a meal at the Café at the End of the Universe, which serves up dishes created by celebrity chef Wolfgang Puck. ■TIP➔ For a fantastic view, come at sunset to watch the sky turn fiery shades of red with the city's skyline silhouetted. ⊠ *2800 E. Observatory Ave., Los Feliz* ☎ *213/473–0800* ⊕ *www.griffithobservatory.org* ☉ *Closed Mon.* ☞ *Observatory grounds and parking are open daily.*

**Griffith Park.** The country's largest municipal park, the 4,210-acre Griffith Park is a must for nature lovers, the perfect spot for respite from the hustle and bustle of the surrounding urban areas. Plants and animals native to Southern California can be found within the park's borders, including deer, coyotes, and even a reclusive mountain lion. Bronson Canyon (where the Batcave from the 1960s *Batman* TV series is located) and Crystal Springs are favorite picnic spots.

The park is named after Colonel Griffith J. Griffith, a mining tycoon who donated 3,000 acres to the city in 1896. As you might expect, the park has been used as a film and television location for at least a century. Here you'll find the Griffith Observatory, the Los Angeles Zoo, the Greek Theater, two golf courses, hiking and bridle trails, a swimming pool, a merry-go-round, and an outdoor train museum. ⊠ *4730 Crystal Springs Dr., Los Feliz* ☎ *323/913–4688* ⊕ *www.laparks.org/dos/parks/griffithpk* 🖆 *Free; attractions inside park have separate admission fees.*

FAMILY **Los Angeles Zoo.** A short drive from Downtown Los Angeles at the junction of the Ventura Freeway (Highway 134) and the Golden State Freeway (I–5) is the 80-acre Los Angeles Zoo. You'll need good walking shoes, as distances are compounded by plenty of construction detours. You'll see tigers, lions, and bears, along with a few endangered species such as the California condor and Sumatran tigers. "Elephants of Asia" opened to great acclaim with an elaborate enclosure of sand, grassy hills, and waterfalls. The Rainforest of the Americas exhibit is a must-visit for children and adults alike. ⊠ *5333 Zoo Dr., Los Feliz* ☎ *323/644–4200* ⊕ *www.lazoo.org* 🖆 *$20.*

## DID YOU KNOW?

Renovations to the Griffith Observatory have made its interior nearly as spectacular as the views of Hollywood from outside.

**Vista Theatre.** The Vista, around since 1923, is one of the few theaters still showing 35mm film. This single-screen gem shows brand-new releases, and features art deco fixtures and Egyptian-themed details. One of the most affordable theaters in the city, The Vista borders Los Feliz and Silver Lake, and is close to fun bars and restaurants for a pre- or post-show meal or cocktail. ⊠ *4473 Sunset Blvd, Los Feliz* ☎ *323/660–6639* ⊕ *www.vintagecinemas.com/vista.*

### WORTH NOTING

**Barnsdall Art Park.** The panoramic view of Hollywood alone is worth a trip to this hilltop cultural center. On the grounds you'll find the 1921 **Hollyhock House,** a masterpiece of modern design by architect Frank Lloyd Wright. It was commissioned by philanthropist Aline Barnsdall to be the centerpiece of an arts community. While Barnsdall's project didn't turn out the way she planned, the park now hosts the L.A. Municipal Art Gallery and Theatre, which provides exhibition space for visual and performance artists.

Wright dubbed this style "California Romanza" (*romanza* is a musical term meaning "to make one's own form"). Stylized depictions of Barnsdall's favorite flower, the hollyhock, appear throughout the house in its cement columns, roof line, and furnishings. The leaded-glass windows are expertly placed to make the most of both the surrounding gardens and the city views. On summer weekends, there are wildly popular wine tastings and outdoor movie screenings. Self-guided tours are available Thursday through Sunday from 11 am to 4 pm. With its proximity to a rougher Hollywood intersection, this area might not be the safest place to wander around at night. Travel in groups when possible. ⊠ *4800 Hollywood Blvd., Los Feliz* ☎ *323/644–6269* ⊕ *www.barnsdall.org* ⊡ *Free; house tours $7* ⊗ *House tours closed Mon.–Wed.*

## SILVER LAKE

This hilly, mostly residential neighborhood sits southeast of Los Feliz and northwest of Echo Park. Regarded as a bohemian enclave since the 1930s, it was the site of the first large film studio built by Walt Disney. Silver Lake is known for cute boutiques, bougie coffee houses, and specialty restaurants along its stretch of Sunset Boulevard.

## ECHO PARK

Silver Lake's edgier older cousin and neighbor, Echo Park is centered on a beautifully restored lakefront park (you can even rent a paddleboat and experience the lake in all its glory). The first residential neighborhood northwest of Downtown Los Angeles, Echo Park has long been under scrutiny for gentrification, along with Highland Park and Silver Lake. This predominantly Latino and Mexican neighborhood has likewise experienced an influx of young artists and industry hopefuls, as well as rent hikes, but it's not devoid of diversity or character. Film buffs take note: it was one of the principal locations of Roman Polanski's film, *Chinatown.*

4

# BEVERLY HILLS, WEST HOLLYWOOD, AND THE WESTSIDE

Visit Fodors.com for advice, updates, and bookings

# GETTING ORIENTED

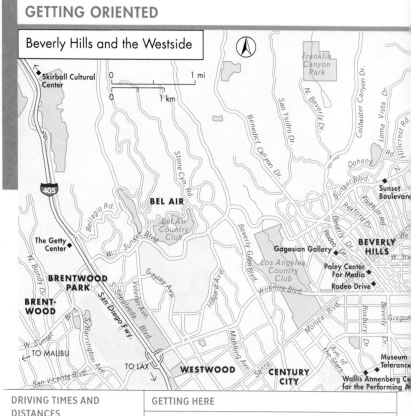

## Beverly Hills and the Westside

## DRIVING TIMES AND DISTANCES

Minimum times listed below represent little to no traffic; maximum times assume the worst.

Adjust accordingly taking rush hour and peak weekend travel time into account.

■ **From LAX:** 30–75 mins/15 miles

■ **From Downtown:** 20–45 mins/12 miles

■ **From Hollywood:** 20–25 mins/7 miles

■ **From Malibu:** 15–30 mins/8 miles

## GETTING HERE

### Driving Strategy

If Santa Monica is jammed up, try Pico or Olympic Boulevard, which run roughly parallel a bit farther south. Westwood Village and Brentwood's commercial district on San Vicente Boulevard come alive at night and on weekends, and the afternoon rush hour can add a lot of time to your trip— another good reason to plan museum trips early in the day or on Sunday.

### Parking

In Beverly Hills, you can park your car in one of several municipal lots (often free for the first hour or two), and spend as long as you like strolling along Rodeo Drive.

For street parking, bring quarters for the meter, or pay with a credit card. Parking on residential streets is by permit only.

4

## PLANNING YOUR TIME

Museums open between 10 am and noon. LACMA is open Monday but closed Wednesday and has extended hours into the evening. The other museums are closed on Monday (except for the Page).

Set aside a day to do this entire tour: an hour or two for the Farmers Market and The Grove, four hours for the museums, and an hour for the Wilshire Boulevard sights.

After a drive along Sunset Boulevard and a foray into the hills to see opulent homes, plan to arrive in the Golden Triangle of Beverly Hills midday. Most stores open by 10 or 11, with limited hours on Sunday. (Some close on Sunday or Monday.)

Advance reservations are not essential, but are recommended for visits to the Museum of Tolerance, closed Saturday, and the Getty Center, closed Monday. Each museum merits at least half a day.

## TOP REASONS TO GO

**Shop on Rodeo.** Even if it's window-shopping, it's a one-of-a-kind experience to watch the parade of diamonds, couture gowns, and Ferraris being fetishized.

**Explore the Grounds and Gallery at the Getty.** The galleries are fantastic, but go to enjoy the view, Richard Meier's architecture, and the Central Garden.

**Get Cultured at LACMA.** See Chris Burden's iconic "Urban Light" installation in front of the museum, and the plethora of collections inside.

**Feast at the Farmers Market.** Visit for a shopping respite or to take in and appreciate the Farmers Market's 75-year-old history and atmosphere.

**Drive down Sunset Boulevard to the Ocean.** The quintessential Los Angeles experience, it's best to start at La Cienega headed west on Sunset, which will take you through the Sunset Strip. Now may be a good time to test-drive that convertible.

Sightseeing
★★★★
Nightlife
★★★
Dining
★★★★
Lodging
★★★★
Shopping
★★★★★

The rumors are true: Beverly Hills delivers on a dramatic, cinematic scale of wealth and excess. A known celebrity haunt, come here to daydream, or to live like the rich and famous for a day. Window-shop or splurge at tony stores, and keep an eye out for filming locales; just walking around here will make you feel like you're on a movie set.

## BEVERLY HILLS

Updated by
Clarissa Wei

When visiting Beverly Hills for the first time, many people head for the boutiques and restaurants that line the palm tree–fringed sidewalks of **Rodeo Drive.** People tend to stroll, not rush. Shopping ranges from the accessible and familiar (Pottery Barn) to the unique, expensive, and architecturally stunning (Prada).

### TOP ATTRACTIONS

**Gagosian Gallery.** This contemporary art gallery, owned and directed by the legendary Larry Gagosian, has its roots in Los Angeles and branches in New York and around the world. Previous exhibitions here include works by Damien Hirst, Richard Avedon, Richard Serra, Jeff Koons, and Frank Gehry. During Oscar season the gallery is known for its celeb-filled openings. ⊠ *456 N. Camden Dr., Beverly Hills* ☎ *310/271–9400* ⊕ *www.gagosian.com.*

**Melrose Avenue.** Once a hangout for rebels scouring vintage clothing shops and record stores, Melrose Avenue has gone more mainstream with the addition of chain stores like Urban Outfitters. The farther west you go on Melrose, the tonier the selection. Here you can get your designer fix at such high-end shops as Marc Jacobs, Helmut Lang, Hérve Léger, Alexander McQueen, Agent Provocateur, Paul Smith, Diane von Furstenberg, Vera Wang, and Vivienne Westwood. Nearby Melrose Place (a small street that's only a few blocks long) houses Carolina Herrera, Monique Lhuillier, and other upscale shops. ⊠ *Melrose Ave., Beverly Hills.*

Window-shop and gawk at celebs at the famous and upscale Rodeo Drive.

QUICK
BITES
**Nate 'n' Al's.** A longtime refuge from California's lean cuisine, Nate 'n' Al's serves up steaming pastrami, matzo ball soup, and potato latkes. Media and entertainment insiders like newsman Larry King have been seen kibbitzing at this old-time East Coast–style establishment. ■ TIP➔ There can be a bit of a wait, so plan accordingly. ✉ *414 N. Beverly Dr., at Brighton Way, Beverly Hills* ☎ *310/274–0101* ⊕ *www.natenal.com.*

FAMILY **Museum of Tolerance.** This museum unflinchingly confronts bigotry and racism. One of the most affecting sections covers the Holocaust, with film footage of deportations and concentration camps. Upon entering, you are issued a "passport" bearing the name of a child whose life was dramatically changed by the Nazis; as you go through the exhibit, you learn the fate of that child. An exhibit called "Anne: The Life and Legacy of Anne Frank," brings her story to life through immersive environments, multimedia presentations, and interesting artifacts. Simon Wiesenthal's Vienna office is set exactly as the famous "Nazi hunter" had it while performing his research that brought more than 1,000 war criminals to justice.

Interactive exhibits include the Millennium Machine, which engages visitors in finding solutions to human rights abuses around the world; Globalhate.com, which examines hate on the Internet by exposing problematic sites via touch-screen computer terminals; and the Point of View Diner, a re-creation of a 1950s diner that "serves" a menu of controversial topics on video jukeboxes.

■TIP➜ Plan to spend at least three hours touring the museum; making a reservation is especially recommended for Friday, Sunday, and holiday visits. ⊠ *9786 W. Pico Blvd., south of Beverly Hills, Los Angeles* ☎ *310/772–2505 for reservations* ⊕ *www.museumoftolerance.com* 🖾 *$15.50.*

**Paley Center for Media.** Architect Richard Meier, also responsible for the Getty Center, designed this sleek stone-and-glass building that holds a world-class collection of television and radio programs. You can search for more than 150,000 of them, spanning eight decades, on an easy-to-use computer, then settle into comfortable seating and watch them on monitors. A visit here is a blissful way to while away the hours. Feel like watching a disco-infused, late-1970s episode of *Sesame Street?* It's here, along with award shows, radio serials, and hundreds of TV sitcoms. The library plays snippets of a variety of programs from a roast of Dean Martin to an interview with John Lennon. ■TIP➜ Free parking is available in the lot off Santa Monica Boulevard. ⊠ *465 N. Beverly Dr., Beverly Hills* ☎ *310/786–1000* ⊕ *www.paleycenter.org* 🖾 *Free* ⊙ *Closed Mon. and Tues.*

**Rodeo Drive.** The ultimate shopping indulgence, Rodeo Drive is one of Southern California's bona fide tourist attractions. The art of window-shopping is prime among the retail elite: Tiffany & Co., Gucci, Jimmy Choo, Valentino, Harry Winston, Prada—you get the picture. Several nearby restaurants have patios where you can sip a drink while watching shoppers saunter by with shopping bags stuffed with superfluous delights. Near the southern end of Rodeo Drive is Via Rodeo, a curvy cobblestone street designed to resemble a European shopping area, that makes the perfect backdrop to strike a pose for that glamour shot. To give your feet a rest, $5 trolley tours depart on the hour from 11 to 4 at the southeast corner of Rodeo Drive and Dayton Way. They're a terrific way to get an overview of the neighborhood. ⊠ *Rodeo Dr., Beverly Hills* ⊕ *www.rodeodrive-bh.com.*

**QUICK BITES**

**MILK.** This place is so popular that lines often spill out the door and onto the sidewalk. The Warm Ooey Gooey Chocolate Sundae and Milky Way Malted Milk Shakes are just a few of the homemade treats that will tempt your sweet tooth. ⊠ *7290 Beverly Blvd., Beverly Hills* ☎ *323/939–6455* ⊕ *www.themilkshop.com.*

**Wallis Annenberg Center for the Performing Arts.** Located in the heart of Beverly Hills, the Wallis Annenberg Center for the Performing Arts opened its doors in 2014. A breath of fresh air, this complex is centered on the 1934 Italianate-style Beverly Hills Post Office. The interior is gorgeous, with six Depression-era murals painted by California artist Charles Kassler depicting laborers and artisans. There's a new building holding the 500-seat Bram Goldsmith Theater and the 150-seat Lovelace Studio Theater. Affordable parking is available underneath the space. ⊠ *9390 N. Santa Monica Blvd., Beverly Hills* ☎ *310/246–3800* ⊕ *www.thewallis.org.*

In a ravine separating the museum and the Getty Research Institute, conceptual artist Robert Irwin created the playful Central Garden in stark contrast to Meier's mathematical architectural geometry. The garden's design is what Hollywood feuds are made of: Meier couldn't control Irwin's vision, and the two men sniped at each other during construction, with Irwin stirring the pot with every loose twist his garden path took. The result is a refreshing garden walk whose focal point is an azalea maze (some insist the Mickey Mouse shape is on purpose) in a reflecting pool.

Inside the pavilions are the galleries for the permanent collections of European paintings, drawings, sculpture, illuminated manuscripts, and decorative arts, as well as photographs gathered internationally. The Getty's collection of French furniture and decorative arts, especially from the early years of Louis XIV (1643–1715) to the end of the reign of Louis XVI (1774–92), is renowned for its quality and condition; you can see a pair of completely reconstructed salons. In the paintings galleries, a computerized system of louvered skylights allows natural light to filter in, creating a closer approximation of the conditions in which the artists painted. Notable among the paintings are Rembrandt's *The Abduction of Europa,* Van Gogh's *Irises,* Monet's *Wheatstack, Snow Effects,* and *Morning,* and James Ensor's *Christ's Entry into Brussels.*

If you want to start with a quick overview, pick up the brochure in the entrance hall that guides you to collection highlights. There's also an instructive audio tour (free, but you have to leave your ID) with commentaries by art historians and other experts. Art information rooms with multimedia computer stations contain more details about the collections. The Getty also presents lectures, films, concerts, and special programs for kids, families, and all-around culture lovers. The complex includes an upscale restaurant and downstairs cafeteria with panoramic window views. There are also outdoor coffee carts. ■ TIP➔ On-site parking is subject to availability and can fill up by midday on holidays and in the summer, so try to come early in the day or after lunch. A tram takes you from the street-level entrance to the top of the hill. Public buses (Metro Rapid Line 734) also serve the center and link to the Expo Rail extension. ⊠ *1200 Getty Center Dr., Brentwood* ☏ *310/440–7300* ⊕ *www.getty.edu* 🎟 *Free; parking $15* ☉ *Closed Mon.*

### WORTH NOTING

**Skirball Cultural Center.** The mission of this Jewish cultural institution in the beautiful Santa Monica Mountains is to explore the connections "between 4,000 years of Jewish heritage and the vitality of American democratic ideals." The extraordinary museum, featuring exhibits like "Visions and Values: Jewish Life from Antiquity to America," has a massive collection of Judaica—the third largest in the world. A big draw is the Noah's Ark interactive exhibition, where children are invited to re-create the famous tale using their own imagination. ⊠ *2701 N. Sepulveda Blvd., north of Brentwood, Los Angeles* ☏ *310/440–4500* ⊕ *www.skirball.org* 🎟 *$12; free Thurs.* ☉ *Closed Mon.*

The Annenberg Space for Photography

QUICK BITES

**Sprinkles Cupcakes.** The haute cupcake craze isn't going away, so expect lines that extend out the door and down the block. If you need an after-hours fix, not to worry: in 2012, Sprinkles debuted the world's first Cupcake (and cookie) ATM, open round the clock. ✉ *9635 S. Santa Monica Blvd., Beverly Hills* ☎ *310/274–8765* ⊕ *www.sprinkles.com.*

# BRENTWOOD

A wealthy residential enclave west of Beverly Hills, Brentwood is home to the world-class Getty Center.

### TOP ATTRACTIONS

FAMILY
Fodor's Choice
★

**The Getty Center.** With its curving walls and isolated hilltop perch, the Getty Center resembles a pristine fortified city of its own. You may have been lured here by the beautiful views of Los Angeles—on a clear day stretching all the way to the Pacific Ocean—but the amazing architecture, uncommon gardens, and fascinating art collections will be more than enough to capture and hold your attention. When the sun is out, the complex's rough-cut travertine marble skin seems to soak up the light.

Getting to the center involves a bit of anticipatory lead-up. At the base of the hill, a pavilion disguises the underground parking structure. From there you either walk or take a smooth, computer-driven tram up the steep slope, checking out the Bel Air estates across the humming 405 freeway. The five pavilions that house the museum surround a central courtyard and are bridged by walkways. From the courtyard, plazas, and walkways, you can survey the city from the San Gabriel Mountains to the ocean.

Chris Burden's iconic *Urban Light* sculpture sits at the entrance to LACMA.

## WEST HOLLYWOOD

West Hollywood is not a place to see things (like museums or movie studios) as much as it is a place to do things—like go to a nightclub, eat at a world-famous restaurant, or attend an art gallery opening. Since the end of Prohibition, the **Sunset Strip** has been Hollywood's nighttime playground, where stars headed to such glamorous nightclubs as the Trocadero, the Mocambo, and Ciro's. It's still going strong, with crowds still filing into well-established spots like Whiskey a Go Go and paparazzi staking out the members-only Soho House. But hedonism isn't all that drives West Hollywood. Also thriving is an important interior design and art gallery trade exemplified by the Cesar Pelli–designed **Pacific Design Center.**

West Hollywood has emerged as one of the most progressive cities in Southern California. It's also one of the most gay-friendly cities anywhere, with a large LGBTQ community. Its annual Gay Pride Parade is one of the largest in the nation, drawing tens of thousands of participants each June.

The historic **Farmers Market** and **The Grove** shopping mall are both great places to people-watch over breakfast.

### TOP ATTRACTIONS

**MOCA Pacific Design Center.** Located in the heart of West Hollywood, MOCA Pacific Design Center features rotating exhibitions of architecture, design, and contemporary art. Don't miss the MOCA Store for its avant-garde selections of mindfully curated gifts. ✉ *8687 Melrose Ave., West Hollywood* ☎ *310/657–0800* ⊕ *www.moca.org* ✉ *Free* ☽ *Closed Mon.*

**Pacific Design Center.** World-renowned architect Cesar Pelli's original vision for the Pacific Design Center was three buildings that together housed designer showrooms, office buildings, parking, and more—a sleek shrine to design. These architecturally intriguing buildings were built years apart: the building sheathed in blue glass (known as the Blue Whale) opened in 1975; the green building opened in 1988. The final "Red" building opened in 2013, completing Pelli's grand vision many years later. All together the 1.2-million-square-foot complex covers more than 14 acres, housing more than 120 design showrooms as well as 2,100 interior product lines. You'll also find restaurants such as Red Seven by Wolfgang Puck, the Silverscreen movie theater, and an outpost of the Museum of Contemporary Art. ⊠ *8687 Melrose Ave., West Hollywood* ☎ *310/657–0800* ⊕ *www. pacificdesigncenter.com.*

**Santa Monica Boulevard.** From La Cienega Boulevard in the east to Doheny Drive in the west, Santa Monica Boulevard is the commercial core of West Hollywood's gay community, with restaurants and cafés, bars and clubs, bookstores and galleries, and other establishments catering largely to the LGBTQ scene. Twice a year—during June's L.A. Pride and on Halloween—the boulevard becomes an open-air festival. ⊠ *Santa Monica Blvd., between La Cienega Blvd. and Doheny Dr., West Hollywood* ⊕ *weho.org.*

**Sunset Boulevard.** One of the most fabled avenues in the world, Sunset Boulevard began humbly enough in the 18th century as a route from El Pueblo de Los Angeles to the Pacific Ocean. Today, as it passes through West Hollywood, it becomes the sexy and seductive Sunset Strip, where rock and roll had its heyday and cocktail bars charge a premium for the views. It slips quietly into the tony environs of Beverly Hills and Bel Air, twisting and winding past gated estates and undulating vistas. ⊠ *Sunset Blvd., West Hollywood.*

**West Hollywood Library.** Across from the Pacific Design Center, this library, designed by architects Steve Johnson and James Favaro in 2011, is a welcome addition to the city. Replete with floor-to-ceiling glass, a modern and airy interior, a huge mural by Shepard Fairey, and other art by Kenny Scharf and Retna, this three-story building and the adjoining park are a great place to take a break from your tour of the city. They also have an impressive LGBT book collection. There's inexpensive parking and a café below. ⊠ *625 N. San Vicente Blvd., West Hollywood* ☎ *310/652–5340* ⊕ *www.colapublib.org/libs/whollywood.*

**WORTH NOTING**

**Sunset Plaza.** With a profusion of sidewalk cafés, Sunset Plaza is one of the best people-watching spots in town. Sunny weekends reach the highest pitch, when people flock to this stretch of Sunset Boulevard for brunch or lunch and to browse in the trendy shops that offer a range of price points. There's free parking in the lot behind the shops. ⊠ *8600 block of Sunset Blvd., a few blocks west of La Cienega Blvd., West Hollywood.*

## BEST SPOTS FOR STAR SIGHTING

■ **Hit Hotel Bars and Spas.** Waiting for your car at the valet stand at any of the big, insider hotels during Awards Season, most likely at the Beverly Wilshire Beverly Hills (a Four Seasons Hotel), Chateau Marmont, and Sunset Tower. You don't have to book a room in the hotel to valet your car here, you can stop in for a meal or cocktail, as all three hotels have restaurants and bars.

■ **Stroll Along Robertson Boulevard.** The paparazzi-filled street of Robertson in West Hollywood, especially coming in and out of the iconic restaurant, the Ivy.

■ **Eat at Industry Restaurants.** There are those certain places filmmakers and celebs love—whether it's for the special treatment there or simply the food—such as Mr. Chow in Beverly Hills and Dan Tana's on Sunset in West Hollywood.

**QUICK BITES**

**Urth Caffé.** The ultra-trendy Urth Caffé is full of beautiful people refueling on organic coffee and tea with a range of health-conscious sandwiches, salads, and juices. The outdoor patio is a great place to take in the scene or spot celebrities. ⊠ *8565 Melrose Ave., West Hollywood* ☎ *310/659–0628,* ⊕ *www.urthcaffe.com.*

**West Hollywood Design District.** More than 200 businesses—art galleries, antiques shops, fashion outlets (including Rag & Bone and Christian Louboutin), and interior design stores—are found in the design district. There are also about 40 restaurants, including the famous paparazzi magnet, The Ivy. All are clustered within walking distance of each other—rare for L.A. ⊠ *Melrose Ave. and Robertson and Beverly Blvds., West Hollywood* ☎ *310/289–2534* ⊕ *wehodesigndistrict.com.*

### MID-WILSHIRE AND MIRACLE MILE

The 1.5-mile strip of Wilshire Boulevard between La Brea and Fairfax avenues was bought up by developers in the 1920s, and they created a commercial district that catered to automobile traffic. Nobody thought the venture could be successful, so the burgeoning strip became known as Miracle Mile. It was the world's first linear downtown, with building designs incorporating wide store windows to attract attention from passing cars. As L.A.'s art deco buildings have come to be appreciated, preserved, and restored over the years, the area's exemplary architecture is a highlight. The surrounding Mid-Wilshire area encompassing Miracle Mile includes the notable **Petersen Automotive Museum** which got a $90-million upgrade in 2015. Clad in steel ribbons, it sits as a beacon on the Mid-Wilshire section of Museum Row.

#### TOP ATTRACTIONS

FAMILY **La Brea Tar Pits Museum.** Show your kids where Ice Age fossils come from by taking them to the stickiest park in town. The area formed when deposits of oil rose to the earth's surface, collected in shallow pools, and coagulated into asphalt. In the early 20th century geologists discovered that all that goo contained the largest collection of Pleistocene (Ice Age) fossils ever found at one location: more than 600 species of birds, mammals, plants, reptiles, and insects. Roughly 100 tons of fossil bones have been removed in excavations during the last 100 years, making this one of the world's most famous fossil sites. You can see most of the pits through chain-link fences, and the new Excavator Tour gets you as close as possible to the action.

Pit 91 and Project 23 are ongoing excavation projects; tours are offered, and you can volunteer to help with the excavations in the summer. Several pits are scattered around Hancock Park and the surrounding neighborhood; construction in the area has often had to accommodate them, and in nearby streets and along sidewalks, little bits of tar occasionally ooze up. The museum displays fossils from the tar pits and has a glass-walled laboratory that allows visitors to view paleontologists and volunteers as they work on specimens. ⊠ *5801 Wilshire Blvd., West Hollywood* ☎ *323/857–6300* ⊕ *www.tarpits.org* 🖂 *$12; parking $12.*

**Fodor's**Choice   **Los Angeles County Museum of Art (LACMA).** Without a doubt, this is the
★           focal point of the museum district that runs along Wilshire Boulevard. Chris Burden's *Urban Light* sculpture, composed of more than 220 restored cast-iron antique street lamps, elegantly marks the location. Inside you'll find one of the country's most comprehensive art collections, with more than 120,000 objects dating from ancient times to the present. The museum, which opened in 1965, now includes numerous buildings that cover more than 20 acres.

The permanent collection's strengths include works by prominent Southern California artists; Latin American artists such as Diego Rivera and Frida Kahlo; Islamic and European art; paintings by Henri Matisse, Rene Magritte, Paul Klee, and Wassily Kandinsky; art representing the ancient civilizations of Egypt, the Near East, Greece, and Rome; and costumes and textiles dating back to the 16th century.

The Broad Contemporary Art Museum, designed by Renzo Piano, opened in 2008 and impresses with three vast floors. BCAM presents contemporary art from LACMA's collection in addition to temporary exhibitions that explore the interplay between the present and the past.

LACMA's other spaces include the Ahmanson Building, a showcase for Art of the Pacific, European, Middle Eastern, South and Southeast Asian collections; the Robert Gore Rifkind Center for German Expressionist Studies; the Art of the Americas Building; the Pavilion for Japanese Art, featuring scrolls, screens, drawings, paintings, textiles, and decorative arts from Japan; the Bing Center, a research library, resource center, and theater; and the Boone Children's Gallery, located in the Hammer Building, where story time and art lessons are among the activities offered.

■TIP→ Temporary exhibits sometimes require tickets purchased in advance. ⊠ *5905 Wilshire Blvd., West Hollywood* ☎ *323/857–6000* ⊕ *www.lacma.org* 🖂 *$15.*

FAMILY   **Petersen Automotive Museum.** L.A. is a mecca for car lovers, which explains the popularity of this museum with a collection of more than 300 automobiles and other motorized vehicles. But you don't have to

be a gearhead to appreciate the Petersen; there's plenty of fascinating history here for all to enjoy. Learn how Los Angeles grew up around its freeways, how cars evolve from the design phase to the production line, and how automobiles have influenced film and television. To see how the vehicles, many of them quite rare, are preserved and maintained, take the 90-minute tour of the basement-level Vault (young kids aren't permitted in the Vault, but they'll find plenty to keep them occupied throughout the museum). ⊠ *6060 Wilshire Blvd., Mid-Wilshire* ☎ *323/930–2277* ⊕ *www.petersen.org* ⊠ *$15.*

## WORTH NOTING

**Craft and Folk Art Museum.** This small but important cultural landmark pioneered support for traditional folk arts. The two-story space has a global outlook, embracing social movements and long-established trends. It mounts rotating exhibitions where you might see anything from costumes of carnival celebrations around the world to handmade quilts. The courtyard area is a tranquil space often used for opening receptions. The ground-level gift shop stocks a unique collection of handcrafts, jewelry, ceramics, books, and textiles. ⊠ *5814 Wilshire Blvd., Mid-Wilshire* ☎ *323/937–4230* ⊕ *www.cafam.org* ⊠ *$7* ⊙ *Closed Mon.*

**Los Angeles Museum of the Holocaust.** A museum dedicated solely to the Holocaust, it uses its extensive collections of photos and artifacts as well as award-winning audio tours and interactive tools to evoke European Jewish life in the 20th century. The mission is to commemorate the lives of those who perished and those who survived the Holocaust. The building is itself a marvel, having won two awards from the American Institute of Architects. ⊠ *100 S. The Grove Dr., Los Angeles* ☎ *323/651–3704* ⊕ *www.lamoth.org* ⊠ *Free.*

# SANTA MONICA
# AND THE BEACHES

# GETTING ORIENTED

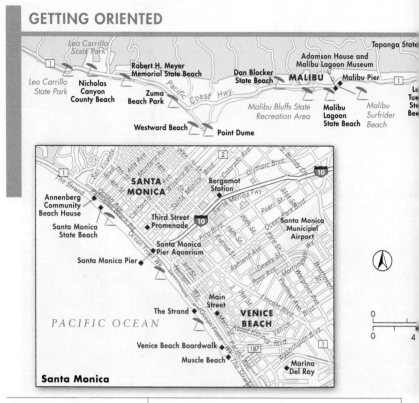

Santa Monica

## DRIVING TIMES AND DISTANCES

Minimum times listed below represent little to no traffic; maximum times assume the worst. Adjust accordingly taking rush hour and peak weekend travel time into account.

■ **LAX to Santa Monica:** 20–60 mins/18 miles

■ **Santa Monica to Malibu:** 30–75 mins/22 miles

■ **Santa Monica to Venice Beach:** 10–15 mins/3 miles

■ **Venice Beach to Redondo Beach:** 25–40 mins/13 miles

## GETTING HERE

### Driving Strategy

From Downtown, the easiest way to hit the coast is by taking the Santa Monica Freeway (I–10) due west. Once you reach the end of the freeway, I–10 runs into the famous Highway 1. Better known as the Pacific Coast Highway, or PCH, Highway 1 continues north to Sonoma County and south to San Diego. MTA buses run from Downtown along Pico, Olympic, Santa Monica, Sunset, and Wilshire boulevards westward to the coast. Driving along the coast is a quintessential L.A. experience—so is sitting in beach traffic. Avoid driving to Malibu during rush hour when traffic along PCH moves at a snail's pace.

### Parking

Public parking is usually available at beaches, though fees can range anywhere from $8 to $20; in some areas, it's possible to find free street and highway parking.

Will Rogers State
Historic Park and Museum

**PACIFIC
PALISADES**

TO BEVERLY HILLS →

Villa Malibu

apanga
State
Beach

Will Rogers
State Beach

**CULVER
CITY**

Santa Monica
State Beach

**SANTA
MONICA**

**VENICE
BEACH**

See Detail Map

**MARINA
DEL REY**

**PLAYA
DEL REY**

Los Angeles
International
Airport

*PACIFIC OCEAN*

**EL
SEGUNDO**

**MANHATTAN
BEACH**

Manhattan Beach

**HERMOSA
BEACH**

Hermosa Beach

4 mi

**REDONDO
BEACH**

Redondo Beach

# Santa Monica and the Beaches

## TOP REASONS TO GO

**Bike along The Strand.** Spend the day on this 22-mile paved path, also known as the South Bay Bike Trail, which stretches from Santa Monica to Redondo Beach.

**Watch the Sun Set over the Pacific in Malibu.** Whether you watch it cliff-side or parked on a beach blanket, the view will stay fixed in your mind as a trip highlight.

**Spend the Day at Santa Monica Pier.** See concerts here in the summer, or bring your family for a stroll during the day and enjoy classic fair food.

**Catch the Mellow Vibe in Venice Beach.** Walk along the canals, shop, and grab an all-organic lunch on Abbot Kinney, or watch tanned locals in tie-dye toting longboards.

**Take a Surfing Lesson.** The sport is said to have started on Redondo Beach in the early 1900s—learn how to hang ten from several great schools along the coast.

## PLANNING YOUR TIME

**5**

If you've got the time, break your coastal visit into two excursions: Santa Monica and Venice in one excursion, and Malibu for another.

The best way to tour L.A.'s coastal communities is to park your car and walk, cycle, or skate along the bike path, known as The Strand.

For this, of course, a sunny day is best; on all but the hottest days, when millions of Angelenos flock to the beaches, get started in the morning, either before or after rush hour.

Places like Santa Monica Pier, Main Street, and the Venice Boarwalk are more interesting to observe as the day progresses. Late afternoon to sunset is the liveliest time on the pier.

Try to avoid the boardwalk, beach, and backstreets of Santa Monica and Venice at night, when the crowds dissipate.

| | |
|---|---|
| Sightseeing ★★★ | L.A.'s beaches are an iconic and integral part of Southern |
| Nightlife ★★★ | California, and getting some sand on the floor of your |
| Dining ★★★★ | car is a rite of passage. Hugging the Santa Monica Bay |
| Lodging ★★★ | in an arch, the desirable communities of Malibu, Santa |
| Shopping ★★★★ | Monica, and Venice move from ultrarich to ultracasual |

to bohemian. Continuing south to L.A.'s three beach cities, Manhattan Beach, Hermosa, and Redondo, the scene shifts from posh to working class, but the sand remains the center of the action.

## SANTA MONICA

Updated by
Clarissa Wei

This pedestrian-friendly little city, about 8.3 square miles, has a dynamic population of artists and writers, entertainment folks, educators, and retired people; its left-wing politics have earned it the nickname of the People's Republic of Santa Monica (just like Berkeley in Northern California). Mature trees, Mediterranean-style architecture, and strict zoning have helped create a sense of place often missing from L.A.'s residential neighborhoods, and its cooler, sometimes-foggy climate is another draw. Being a desirable neighborhood, real estate here isn't cheap.

### TOP ATTRACTIONS

FAMILY **Main Street.** This thoroughfare is a great spot for star sightings or for strolling among the laid-back California crowd. Streets are lined with old-fashioned, colorful, and cozy boutiques that stock everything from high-end garments to bohemian favorites. There's also a standard crop of shopping mall outposts plus a good selection of casual restaurants and cafés. ⊠ *Between Pacific St. and Rose Ave., and Santa Monica and Venice Blvds., Santa Monica* ⊕ *www.mainstreetsm.com.*

The three-block Third Street Promenade is great for shopping and for pedestrians only.

NEED A BREAK **Mariasol Cocina Mexican.** Soak up the atmosphere inside this fun-loving eatery at the very end of Santa Monica Pier. Sip oversize margaritas and devour plates of nachos before rejoining the crowds outside. ⊠ *401 Santa Monica Pier, Santa Monica* ☎ *310/917–5050* ⊕ *www.mariasol.com.*

NEED A BREAK **Shutters on the Beach.** Escape busy Santa Monica State Beach at this unfussy oceanfront hotel and its casual café and bar, Coach, where white wood walls and blue striped seating offset wood and wicker furnishings. Head here at sunset for sophisticated, fruity cocktails and fresh seafood, like oysters and Dungeness crab, one block from Santa Monica Pier. ⊠ *1 Pico Blvd., Santa Monica* ☎ *310/458–0030* ⊕ *www.shuttersonthebeach.com.*

FAMILY **Santa Monica Pier.** Souvenir shops, carnival games, arcades, eateries, an outdoor trapeze school, a small amusement park, and an aquarium all contribute to the festive atmosphere of this truncated pier at the foot of Colorado Boulevard below Palisades Park. The pier's trademark 46-horse Looff Carousel, built in 1922, has appeared in several films, including *The Sting.* The Soda Jerks ice cream fountain (named for the motion the attendant makes when pulling the machine's arm) inside the carousel building is a pier staple. Free concerts are held on the pier in the summer. ⊠ *Colorado Ave. and the ocean, Santa Monica* ☎ *310/458–8901* ⊕ *www.santamonicapier.org.*

FAMILY **Santa Monica Pier Aquarium.** Run by beach conservation group Heal the Bay, this live marine life menagerie contains more than 100 species of marine animals and plants, all found in Santa Monica Bay. The Dorothy Green Room features live and interactive exhibits about local watersheds, and short educational films on the weekends. The Kid's Corner provides books, games, and a puppet show. Don't miss this chance to learn about the area's ecology and staggering evidence of how pollution is affecting ocean life. The Aquarium can be tricky to find—look for it tucked under the eastern end of the Santa Monica Pier bridge along Ocean Front Walk. Follow the colorful seascape murals that cover the outside walls. ⊠ *1600 Ocean Front Walk, Santa Monica* 🕾 *310/393–6149* ⊕ *www.healthebay.org/aquarium* 🖃 *$5* ⊗ *Closed Mon.*

**Third Street Promenade.** Stretch your legs along this pedestrians-only three-block stretch of 3rd Street, close to the Pacific, lined with jacaranda trees, ivy-topiary dinosaur fountains, strings of lights, and branches of nearly every major U.S. retail chain. Outdoor cafés, street vendors, movie theaters, and a rich nightlife make this a main gathering spot for locals, visitors, street musicians, and performance artists. Plan a night just to take it all in or take an afternoon for a long people-watching stroll. There's plenty of parking in city structures on the streets flanking the promenade. **Santa Monica Place,** at the south end of the promenade, is a sleek outdoor mall and foodie haven. Its three stories are home to Bloomingdale's, Louis Vuitton, Coach, and other upscale retailers. Don't miss the ocean views from the rooftop food court. ⊠ *Third St., between Colorado and Wilshire Blvds., Santa Monica* ⊕ *www.downtownsm.com.*

## WORTH NOTING

**Annenberg Community Beach House.** This beachfront property was originally developed in the 1920s by William Randolph Hearst as a palatial private residence and a gathering spot for Hollywood's megastars. In 1947 it was converted into a members-only beach club; the state of California bought and renamed the club in 1959, but it took the earthquake of 2004 for the state to reconceive the property as a public place. With the help of the Annenberg foundation, it reopened as a community beach house in 2009. Feel like a millionaire lounging by the pool on one of the beachside chairs, or lunch at the café while enjoying uninterrupted ocean views. The house's Beach=Culture events series includes a variety of classes (yoga, beach volleyball), readings, and exhibits; check the website for the calendar. Hours are subject to change, so call to confirm hours and book in advance. ⊠ *415 Pacific Coast Hwy., Santa Monica* 🕾 *310/458–4904* ⊕ *www. annenbergbeachhouse.com* 🖃 *Free; pool $10.*

**Bergamot Station.** Named after a stop on the Red Trolley line that once shuttled between Downtown and the Santa Monica Pier, Bergamot Station is now a depot for intriguing art. The industrial facades house more than 30 art galleries, shops, a café, and a museum. The galleries cover many kinds of media: photography, jewelry, and paintings from somber to lurid. ⊠ *2525 Michigan Ave., Santa Monica* 🕾 *310/453–7535* ⊕ *www.bergamotstation.com* ⊗ *Closed Sun. and Mon.*

**Santa Monica State Beach.** The first beach you'll hit after the Santa Monica Freeway (I–10) runs into the Pacific Coast Highway, wide

## FOR THE ADVENTURER

**Legends Beach Bike Tours.** Those who like a little history with their vacations should take a guided tour with Legends, part of Perry's Café and Rentals. A tour takes you through the unique enclaves of Santa Monica and Venice Beach, and you can learn their role in the history of surf and skate in Southern California. Bike tours are offered daily at 11 am from May through September, last two hours (plus one hour of free riding), and cost $59. ⊠ 930 Palisades Beach Rd., Santa Monica ☎ 310/939-0000 ⊕ www. perryscafe.com.

**Trapeze School of New York.** Get a different view of the energetic scene by taking a trapeze class right on the Santa Monica Pier. Launch off from a platform 23 feet high and sail above the crowds and waves. Beginners are welcome. Classes are held daily, but times vary, so check the website and make reservations in advance. ⊠ 370 Santa Monica Pier, Santa Monica ☎ 310/394-5800 ⊕ www.trapezeschool.com.

**Venice Beach Skate Plaza.** Watch skateboarders displaying a wide range of ability levels as they careen around this concrete park, situated between the beach and the boardwalk in Venice. There's also an impressive crew of disco roller skaters, and drum circles that gravitate toward the middle of the boardwalk. ⊠ 1800 Ocean Front Walk, off E. Market St., Venice ⊕ www.veniceskatepark.com.

and sandy Santa Monica is *the* place for sunning and socializing. Be prepared for a mob scene on summer weekends, when parking becomes an expensive ordeal. Swimming is fine (with the usual post-storm pollution caveat); for surfing, go elsewhere. For a memorable view, climb up the stairway over the PCH to Palisades Park, at the top of the bluffs. Free summer-evening concerts are held on the pier on Thursday nights. **Amenities:** food and drink; lifeguards; parking; showers; toilets; water sports. **Best for:** partiers; sunset; surfing; swimming; walking. ⊠ 1642 Promenade, PCH at California Incline, Santa Monica ☎ 310/458-8573 ⊕ www.smgov.net/portals/beach 🅿 $10 parking.

# PACIFIC PALISADES

Stunning ocean views, glamorous homes, and dusty canyons define this affluent area, snug between Santa Monica and Malibu. Although there is a downtown village of sorts south of Sunset Boulevard, natural terrain is the main draw here, luring visitors to hiking trails or along the Palisades' winding roads.

### TOP ATTRACTIONS

Fodor'sChoice ★ **Getty Villa Malibu.** Feeding off the cultures of ancient Rome, Greece, and Etruria, the villa exhibits astounding antiquities, though on a first visit even they take a backseat to their environment. This mega-mansion sits on some of the most valuable coastal property in the world. Modeled after an Italian country home, the Villa dei Papiri in Herculaneum, the Getty Villa includes beautifully manicured gardens, reflecting pools, and statuary. The structures blend thoughtfully into the rolling terrain and significantly improve the public spaces, such as the new outdoor amphitheater, gift store, café, and entry arcade. Talks and educational programs are offered at an indoor theater. ■ TIP➔ An advance timed entry ticket is required for admission. Tickets are free and may be ordered from the museum's website or by phone. ⊠ *17985 Pacific Coast Hwy., Pacific Palisades* ☎ *310/440–7300* ⊕ *www.getty. edu* ⊠ *Free, tickets required; parking $15* ⊙ *Closed Tues.*

**Will Rogers State Historic Park and Museum.** A humorist, actor, and rambling cowboy, Will Rogers lived on this site in the 1920s and 1930s. His ranch house, a folksy blend of Navajo rugs and Mission-style furniture, has become a museum of Rogers memorabilia. A short film shown in the visitor center highlights Rogers's roping technique and homey words of wisdom. Open for docent-led tours, the ranch house features Rogers' stuffed practice calf and the high ceiling he raised so he could practice his famed roping style indoors.

Rogers was a polo enthusiast, and in the 1930s his front-yard polo field attracted such friends as Douglas Fairbanks Sr. for weekend games. Today the park's broad lawns are excellent for picnicking, and there are miles of eucalyptus-lined trails for hiking. Free weekend games are scheduled from April through October, weather permitting.

Also part of the park is **Inspiration Point Trail.** Who knows how many of Will Rogers's famed witticisms came to him while he and his wife hiked or rode horses along this trail from their ranch. The point is on a detour off the lovely 2-mile loop, which you can join near the riding stables beyond the parking lot. The panorama is one of L.A.'s widest and most wow-inducing, from the peaks of the San Gabriel Mountains in the east, to the Oz-like cluster of downtown skyscrapers, to Catalina Island looming off the coast to the southwest. If you're looking for a longer trip, the top of the loop meets up with the 65-mile Backbone Trail, which connects to Topanga State Park. ⊠ *1501 Will Rogers State Park Rd., Pacific Palisades* ☎ *310/454–8212* ⊠ *Free; parking $12.*

## WORTH NOTING

**Will Rogers State Beach.** This clean, sandy, 3-mile beach, with a dozen volleyball nets, gymnastics equipment, and a playground for kids, is an all-around favorite. The surf is gentle, perfect for swimmers and beginning surfers. However, it's best to avoid the beach after a storm, when untreated water flows from storm drains into the sea. **Amenities:** food and drink; lifeguards; parking; showers; toilets. **Best for:** sunset; swimming; walking. ⊠ *17700 PCH, 2 miles north of Santa Monica Pier, Pacific Palisades* ☎ *310/305–9503* ⊕ *www.parks.ca.gov* ⊠ *$15 parking.*

# VENICE

From the resident musicians and roving hippies of the boardwalk, to the hipster boutiques and farm-to-table cafés of Abbot Kinney Boulevard, Venice is not easily defined—which is what makes this creative-minded neighborhood so fun to explore.

Considering all of the dreamers who flock here today, it makes sense that Venice was a turn-of-the-20th-century fantasy that never quite came to be. Abbot Kinney, a wealthy Los Angeles businessman, envisioned this little piece of real estate as a romantic replica of Venice, Italy. He developed an incredible 16 miles of canals, floated gondolas on them, and built scaled-down versions of the Doge's Palace and other Venetian landmarks. Some canals were rebuilt in 1996, but they don't reflect the old-world connection quite as well as they could.

Ever since Kinney first planned his project, it was plagued by ongoing engineering problems and drifted into disrepair. Today only a few small canals and bridges remain. On nearby **Abbot Kinney Boulevard** there's a wealth of design and home decor shops and chic cafés—plus great people-watching.

## TOP ATTRACTIONS

**Venice Beach Boardwalk.** The surf and sand of Venice are fine, but the main attraction here is the boardwalk scene, which is a cosmos all its own. Go on weekend afternoons for the best people-watching experience. You can also swim, fish, surf, and skateboard, or play racquetball, handball, shuffleboard, and basketball (the boardwalk is the site of hotly contested pickup games). You can rent a bike or in-line skates and hit The Strand bike path, then pull up a seat at a sidewalk café and watch the action unfold. ⊠ *1800 Ocean Front Walk, west of Pacific Ave., Venice* ☎ *310/392–4687* ⊕ *www.venicebeach.com.*

**NEED A BREAK**

**The Cow's End Cafe.** Stop at this two-story locals' favorite for coffee and pastries, or choose from a long list of sandwiches for something more substantial. Sit out front and watch the crowds drifting in off the beach, or get cozy upstairs in one of the comfortable reading chairs. ⊠ *34 Washington Blvd., Venice* ☎ *310/574–1080* ⊕ *www.thecowsendcafe.com.*

**NEED A BREAK**

**Venice Whaler.** This beachfront bar boasts an amazing view and serves tasty pub food with a basic selection of beers. Be prepared for rowdy crowds of sports fans and beachgoers at happy hour and on weekends. They also serve a great brunch. ⊠ *10 W. Washington Blvd., Venice* ☎ *310/821–8737* ⊕ *www.venicewhaler.com.*

## WORTH NOTING

**Marina del Rey.** Just south of Venice, this condo-laden, chain restaurant–lined development is a good place to grab brunch (but watch for price gougers), walk, or ride bikes along the waterfront. A number of places, such as **Hornblower Cruises and Events** (⊠ *13755 Fiji Way* ☎ *888/467–6256* ⊕ *www.hornblower.com*) in Fisherman's Village, rent boats for romantic dinner or party cruises around the marina. There are a few man-made beaches, but you're better off hitting the larger (and cleaner) beaches up the coast. ⊠ *Fisherman's Village, 1375 Fiji Way, Los Angeles.*

*Continued on page 99*

# ALONG
# THE STRAND
## L.A.'S COASTAL
## BIKE PATH

Cycling along the Strand

Venice Beach graffiti

On the Waterfront Cafe

Santa Monica Beach

Venice Beach café

When L.A. wants to get out and play by the water, people hit the Strand for the afternoon. This paved 22-mile path hugs the coastline and loops through tourist-packed stretches and sleepy beach towns. Quirky cafés, loads of souvenir stands, a family-packed amusement park on a pier, and spots for gazing at the Pacific are just a few things to see along the way.

The path extends from Santa Monica's Will Rogers State Beach to Torrance County Beach in South Redondo. It's primarily flat—aside from a few hills you encounter as you head toward Playa del Rey—and it's a terrific way for people of all fitness levels to experience L.A.'s beaches not far from Hollywood or Beverly Hills. You can explore at your own pace.

The hardest part of the journey isn't tackling the path itself—it's trying to get through it all without being distracted by the surrounding activity. With colorful graffitied murals, surfers and sailboats, weightlifters and tattoo par-

lors, local characters in carnivalesque costumes, volleyball games and skateboarders, there are almost too many things to busy youself with.

Santa Monica amusement park

## KEY

| | |
|---|---|
| **P** | Restaurants |
| **P** | Paid Parking |
| **P** | Street Parking |
| | Food and Drink |

Pacific Coast Hwy.

Montana Ave.          SANTA
MONICA
Wilshire Ave.
Santa Monica Blvd.

Santa Monica State Beach

Santa Monica Fwy.    10

Santa Monica Pier →

Santa Monica
Amusement Park

Pico Blvd.

THE STRAND

Ocean Park Blvd.

405

Rose Ave.

0 ——— 1 mi
0 ——— 1 km

Venice State Beach

Muscle Beach

Lincoln Blvd.

Venice Blvd.

VENICE
BEACH

Washington Blvd.

Venice Fishing Pier •

MARINA
DEL REY

Marina del Rey Beach

Pacific Ave.

Culver Blvd.

90

Jefferson Blvd.

PLAYA DEL REY

Pacific Ocean

Pershing Dr.

Manchest

Vista del Mar

Los Angeles
International Airport

1

Imperial Hwy.

El Porto Beach

THE STRAND

EL SEGUNDO

Sepulveda Blvd.

## GETTING HERE AND AROUND

### ITINERARY BASICS

❶ Santa Monica is an ideal place to start your trip; if you're biking, rent here. On the way back, stop for dinner at one of the many restaurants along and near the Third Street Promenade.

Take a break when you get to Venice Beach to soak up the scene on the ❷ Venice Ocean Boardwalk. Grab some fresh-squeezed lemonade from a stand or snag a table at a café.

If you're dedicating only a half-day to explore the Strand, ❸ Marina del Rey is a good spot to turn around; with more time and energy, follow signs for the slight detour here and continue to the second half, known as the South Bay Bike Trail.

❹ Manhattan Beach Manhattan Beach wins for being one of the best for kids, with its wide stretch of sand and good swimming.

The pier at ❺ Redondo Beach, lined with restaurants and shops, makes stopping here well worthwhile.

### PARKING, RENTALS & TOURS

If you're driving to any of the ocean beaches, expect to pay $5 to $12 for parking, depending on the time of year, day of week, and location.

Those who like a little history with their vacation should take a guided tour from Legends Bike Tours (part of Perry's Rental's) with a Santa Monica Beach Sherpa who will tour you through the unique enclaves of Santa Monica, Venice Beach, and their role in the history of surf and skate in Southern California. ✉ 930 Palisades Beach Rd., Santa Monica ☎ 310/939-0000.

Rosecrans Ave.

Manhattan Beach

Highland Ave.

MANHATTAN
BEACH

Manhattan Beach Pier •

Manhattan
Beach Blvd.

HERMOSA
BEACH

Hermosa City Beach

Hermosa Ave.

Artesia Blvd.

91

Hermosa Beach Pier •

PCH

REDONDO
BEACH

Redondo Beach Pier •

Redondo Beach ❺

1

**Muscle Beach.** Bronzed young men bench-pressing five girls at once, weight lifters doing tricks on the sand—the Muscle Beach facility fired up the country's imagination from the get-go. There are actually two spots known as Muscle Beach. The original Muscle Beach, just south of the Santa Monica Pier, is where bodybuilders Jack LaLanne and Vic and Armand Tanny used to work out in the 1950s. When it was closed in 1959, the bodybuilders moved south along the beach to Venice, to a city-run facility known as "the Pen," and the Venice Beach spot inherited the Muscle Beach moniker. The spot is probably best known now as a place where a young Arnold Schwarzenegger first came to flex his muscles in the late '60s and began his rise to fame. The area now hosts a variety of sports and gymnastic events, and the occasional "beach babe" beauty contests that always draw a crowd. ⊠ *1800 Ocean Front Walk, Venice* ⊕ *www.musclebeach.net.*

## PLAYA DEL REY

5

Hills built by ancient sand dunes run parallel to the ocean, lending a secluded feeling to this easygoing coastal community. When night falls, the hillside homes sparkle high above the water, and the cluster of dive bars on Culver Boulevard fill with local characters. Jetties have dulled the waves that drew surfers here in the 1950s and '60s, leaving the neighborhood with a slightly romantic, forgotten vibe.

## MALIBU

North of Santa Monica, up the Pacific Coast Highway, past rock slides, rollerbladers, and cliff-side estates, Malibu is home to blockbuster names like Spielberg, Hanks, and Streisand. This ecologically fragile 23-mile stretch of coastline is a world of its own, with its slopes slipping dramatically into the ocean.

In the public imagination Malibu is synonymous with beaches and wealth—but in the past couple of years there's been some friction between these two signature elements. Some property owners, such as billionaire music producer David Geffen, have come under attack for blocking public access to the beaches in front of their homes. All beaches are technically public, though; if you stay below the mean high-tide mark you're in the clear.

### TOP ATTRACTIONS

**Adamson House and Malibu Lagoon Museum.** With spectacular views of Surfrider Beach and lush garden grounds, this Moorish Spanish–style house epitomizes all the reasons to live in Malibu. It was built in 1929 by the Rindge family, who owned much of the Malibu area in the early part of the 20th century. The Rindges had an enviable Malibu lifestyle, decades before the area was trendy. In the 1920s, Malibu was quite isolated; in fact all visitors and some of the supplies arrived by boat at the nearby Malibu Pier. (The town becomes isolated today whenever rock slides close the highway.) The house, covered with magnificent tile work in rich blues, greens, yellows, and oranges

The Getty Villa: a gorgeous setting for a spectacular collection of ancient art

from the now-defunct Malibu Potteries, is right on the beach—high chain-link fences keep out curious beachgoers. Even an outside dog bathtub near the servants' door is a tiled gem. Docent-led tours provide insights on family life here as well as the history of Malibu and its real estate. Signs posted around the grounds outside direct you on a self-guided tour, but you can't go inside the house without a guide. Guided tours take place on Fridays and Saturdays at 11 am. There's pay parking in the adjacent county lot or in the lot at PCH and Cross Creek Road. ⌂ *23200 Pacific Coast Hwy., Malibu* ☎ *310/456–8432* ⊕ *www.adamsonhouse.org* ▭ *$7* ⊙ *Check website for closing times.*

**Malibu Lagoon State Beach.** Bird-watchers, take note: in this 5-acre marshy area near Malibu Beach Inn you can spot egrets, blue herons, avocets, and gulls. (You need to stay on the boardwalks so as not to disturb their habitats.) The path leads out to a rocky stretch of Surfrider Beach, and makes for a pleasant stroll. The sand is soft, clean, and white, and you're also likely to spot a variety of marine life. Look for the signs to help identify these sometimes exotic-looking creatures. The lagoon is particularly enjoyable in the early morning and at sunset—and even more so now, thanks to a restoration effort that improved the lagoon's scent. The parking lot has limited hours, but street-side parking is usually available at off-peak times. Close by are shops and a theater. **Amenities:** lifeguards; parking (fee); showers; toilets. **Best for:** sunset; walking. ⌂ *23200 Pacific Coast Hwy., Malibu* ☎ *310/457–8143* ⊕ *www.parks. ca.gov* ▭ *$12 parking.*

**Malibu Pier.** This 780-foot fishing dock is a great place to drink in the sunset, take in some coastal views, or to watch local fishermen reel up a catch. Some tours also leave from here. A pier has jutted out here since the early 1900s; storms destroyed the last one in 1995, and it was rebuilt in 2001. The pier's landing was damaged in 2011 and is undergoing repair. Over the years, private developers have worked with the state to refurbish the pier, which now yields a gift shop, water-sport rentals, a burger joint, and a wonderful farm-to-table restaurant with stunning views. ⊠ *Pacific Coast Hwy. at Cross Creek Rd., Malibu* ⊕ *www.malibupier.com.*

Fodor'sChoice ★ **Robert H. Meyer Memorial State Beach.** Part of Malibu's most beautiful coastal area, this beach is made up of three minibeaches—El Pescador, La Piedra, and El Matador—each with the same spectacular view. Scramble down the steps to the rocky coves via steep, steep stairways; all food and water needs to be toted in, as there are no services. Portable toilets at the trailhead are the only restrooms. "El Mat" has a series of caves, Piedra some nifty rock formations, and Pescador a secluded feel, but they're all picturesque and fairly private. ⚠ **Keep track of the incoming tide so you won't get trapped between those otherwise scenic boulders. Amenities:** parking (fee); toilets. **Best for:** snorkeling; solitude; sunset; surfing; walking; windsurfing. ⊠ *32350, 32700, and 32900 Pacific Coast Hwy., Malibu* ☎ *818/880–0363* ⊕ *www.parks.ca.gov.*

**Topanga State Park.** This is another way into Santa Monica via the Trippet Ranch entrance, which gives you several options: a ½-mile nature loop, a 7-mile round-trip excursion to the Parker Mesa Overlook—breathtaking on a clear day—or a 10-mile trek to the Will Rogers park. Parking is $10 per vehicle. (Exit U.S. 101 onto Topanga Canyon Boulevard in Woodland Hills and head south until you can turn left onto Entrada; if going north on PCH, turn onto Topanga Canyon Boulevard—a bit past Sunset Boulevard—and go north until you can turn right onto Entrada.) ⊠ *20829 Entrada Rd., Malibu* ☎ *310/574–2488* ⊕ *www.parks.ca.gov.*

**Zuma Beach Park.** This 2-mile stretch of white sand, usually dotted with tanning teenagers, has it all: from fishing and kitesurfing to swings and volleyball courts. Beachgoers looking for quiet or privacy should head elsewhere. Stay alert in the water: the surf is rough and inconsistent. **Amenities:** food and drink; lifeguards; parking; showers; toilets. **Best for:** partiers; sunset; swimming; walking. ⊠ *30000 Pacific Coast Hwy., Malibu* ☎ *310/305–9522* ⊕ *www.zuma-beach. com* 🚾 *$10 parking.*

## WORTH NOTING

**Dan Blocker State Beach** (*Corral Beach*). The narrow stretch of fine sand and rocks here make this little beach great for walking, light swimming, kayaking, and scuba diving. Clustered boulders create cozy spots for couples and picnickers, and because of the limited parking available along PCH, it's rarely crowded. Originally owned by the star of the *Bonanza* TV series, the beach was donated to the state after Blocker (who played Hoss) died in 1972. Locals still know this as Corral Beach. **Amenities:** lifeguards; toilets. **Best for:** solitude; walking; swimming; snorkeling. ⊠ *26000 Pacific Coast Hwy., at Corral Canyon Rd., Malibu* ☎ *310/305–9503.*

5

The boardwalk of Venice Beach

**Las Tunas State Beach.** This small beach known for its groins (metal gates constructed in 1929 to protect against erosion) has good swimming, diving, and fishing conditions, and a rocky coastline that wraps elegantly around the Pacific Coast Highway. Watch out for high tides. **Amenities:** food and drink; lifeguards. **Best for:** solitude; swimming. ⊠ *19444 Pacific Coast Hwy., Malibu* ☎ *310/305–9545.*

**Nicholas Canyon County Beach.** Sandier and less private than most of the rocky beaches surrounding it, this little beach is great for picnics. You can sit at a picnic table high up on a bluff overlooking the ocean, or cast out a fishing line. Surfers call it Zero Beach because the waves take the shape of a hollow tube when winter swells peel off the reef. **Amenities:** lifeguards; parking (fee); showers; toilets. **Best for:** solitude; surfing; walking; windsurfing. ⊠ *33805 Pacific Coast Hwy., Malibu* ☎ *310/305–9503.*

**Topanga State Beach.** The beginning of miles of public beach, Topanga has good surfing at the western end, the mouth of the canyon. Close to a busy section of the PCH and rather narrow, the beach here is more lively, as groups of teenagers often zip over Topanga Canyon Boulevard from the Valley. There are swing sets on-site, as well as spots for fishing. **Amenities:** food and drink; lifeguards; parking (fee); toilets; showers. **Best for:** surfing. ⊠ *18700 block of Pacific Coast Hwy., Malibu* ☎ *310/305–9503.*

**Westward Beach–Point Dume.** Go tide-pooling, fishing, snorkeling, or bird-watching (prime time is late winter–early spring). Hike to the top of the sandstone cliffs at Point Dume to whale-watch—their migrations can be seen between December and April—and take in dramatic coastal views.

Westward is a favorite surfing beach, but the steep surf isn't for novices. The Sunset restaurant is between Westward and Point Dume (at 6800 Westward Beach Road). Bring your own food, since the nearest concession is a long hike away. **Amenities:** food and drink; lifeguards; parking (fee); toilets; showers. **Best for:** surfing; walking. ✉ *71030 Westward Beach Rd., Malibu* ☎ *310/305–9503* 🅿 *Parking $14.*

QUICK
BITES

**The Sunset Restaurant and Bar.** This local secret is as close to the beach as you can get for a meal without getting sand in your drink. Stop in for a cocktail at the friendly bar, a light meal of grilled fish tacos, or one of their unique salads. ✉ *Off Pacific Coast Hwy., just north of Zuma Beach, 6800 Westward Beach Rd., Malibu* ☎ *310/589–1007* ⊕ *www.thesunsetrestaurant.com.*

# MANHATTAN BEACH

5

Chic boutiques, multimillion-dollar homes, and some of the best restaurants in Los Angeles dot the hilly downtown streets of this tiny community. While the glamour and exclusivity are palpable, with attractive residents making deals over cocktails, this is still a beach town. Annual volleyball and surfing tournaments, crisp ocean breezes, and a very clean walking and biking path invite all visitors.

## WORTH NOTING

**Manhattan Beach.** A wide, sandy strip with good swimming and rows of volleyball courts, Manhattan Beach is the preferred destination of muscled, tanned young professionals and dedicated bikini-watchers. There are also such amenities as a bike path, a playground, a bait shop, fishing equipment for rent, and a sizable fishing pier. **Amenities:** food and drink; lifeguards; parking (fee); toilets; showers. **Best for:** swimming; walking. ✉ *Manhattan Beach Blvd. at N. Ocean Dr., Manhattan Beach* ☎ *310/372–2166* 🅿 *Metered parking; there are long-term and short-term lots.*

# HERMOSA BEACH

This energetic beach city boasts some of the priciest real estate in the country. But down by the sand, the vibe is decidedly casual, with plenty of pubs and ambling young couples. Volleyball courts line the wide beach, drawing many amateur and pro tournaments. The walkable 300-meter pier features dramatic views of the coastline winding southward.

## WORTH NOTING

**Hermosa Beach.** South of Manhattan Beach, Hermosa Beach has all the amenities of its neighbor but attracts a rowdier crowd. Swimming takes a backseat to the volleyball games and parties on the pier and boardwalk, but the water here is consistently clean and inviting. **Amenities:** food and drink; lifeguards; parking (fee); showers; toilets. **Best for:** partiers; surfing; swimming. ✉ *1201 The Strand, Hermosa Ave. at 33rd St., Hermosa Beach* ☎ *310/372–2166* 🅿 *Parking (metered) at 11th St. and Hermosa Ave., and 13th St. and Hermosa Ave.*

# REDONDO BEACH

With its worn-in pier and cozy beach, Redondo is a refreshingly unglamorous counterpoint to neighboring beach cities. This was the first port in Los Angeles County in the early 1890s, before business shifted south to San Pedro Harbor, and the community still retains a working-class persona. The best way to soak up the scene these days is with a stroll along the sprawling pier, which features shops, casual restaurants, a live fish market, and fantastic sunset views.

## WORTH NOTING

**Redondo Beach.** The pier here marks the starting point of this wide, busy beach along a heavily developed shoreline community. Restaurants and shops flourish along the pier, excursion boats and privately owned crafts depart from launching ramps, and a reef formed by a sunken ship creates prime fishing and snorkeling conditions. If you're adventurous, you might try to kayak out to the buoys and hobnob with pelicans and sea lions. A series of free rock and jazz concerts takes place at the pier every summer. **Amenities:** food and drink; lifeguards; parking; showers; toilets; water sports. **Best for:** snorkeling; sunset; swimming; walking. ⊠ *Torrance Blvd. at Catalina Ave., Redondo Beach* ☎ *310/372–2166.*

# 6

# PASADENA

# GETTING ORIENTED

## Pasadena and Environs

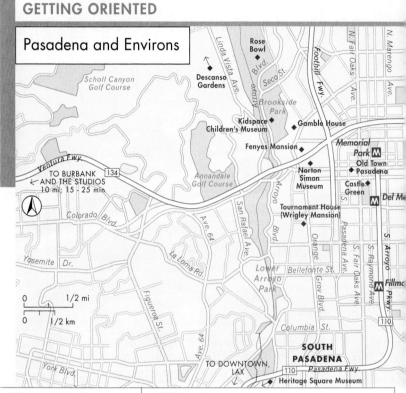

## DRIVING TIMES AND DISTANCES

Minimum times listed below represent little to no traffic; maximum times assume the worst.

Adjust accordingly taking rush hour and peak weekend travel time into account.

- **From LAX:** 30–90 mins/28 miles

- **From Los Feliz/Silver Lake:** 20–30 mins/13 miles

- **From Beverly Hills:** 30–60 mins/19 miles

- **From Burbank:** 15–25 mins/12 miles

## GETTING HERE

**Driving Strategy**

To reach Pasadena from Downtown Los Angeles, drive north on the Pasadena Freeway (I–110).

From Hollywood and the San Fernando Valley, use the Ventura Freeway (Highway 134, east), which cuts through Glendale, skirting the foothills, before arriving in Pasadena.

**Parking**

There are several city lots located in Old Town Pasadena with low rates, all close to Colorado Boulevard, the main drag. On-street parking here is also widely available with few restrictions.

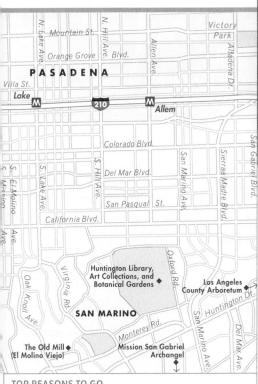

## PLANNING YOUR TIME

With its lush lawns, intricate gardens, and elegant buildings, the Huntington Library should command most of your time. Just be sure to keep the summer heat in mind when you visit—the gardens are more pleasant during the cooler morning hours.

A stop at the beautiful Gamble House shouldn't take more than an hour, leaving plenty of time for an afternoon visit to the Norton Simon Museum, one of the area's best spots to enjoy world-class art. Unless you're planning on seeing a game or hitting the flea market, you will probably want to skip the Rose Bowl.

After visiting the Huntington, take in the prime architectural offerings dotting the city. Head to Old Pasadena in the evening, when the wide boulevards and leafy side streets come to life. Shops, restaurants, and craft beer pubs stay open late in this relatively safe neighborhood, and it's easy to find affordable parking in nearby garages.

## TOP REASONS TO GO

**Visit the Huntington Library.** In addition to a collection of 18th-century British art, this library has 4 million manuscripts and 700,000 books, including the Gutenberg Bible.

**Walk through the Huntington's Botanical Gardens.** Set aside a couple of hours to enjoy the expansive lawns and stately trees surrounding the Huntington Library.

**See American Craftsmanship at the Gamble House.** The teak staircase and cabinetry are just a few of the highlights at this home, built in 1908.

**Check Out the Norton Simon Museum.** This small museum's fine collection features works by Renoir, Degas, Gauguin, and others.

**Hang Out in Old Town Pasadena.** Spend the afternoon walking around this 12-block historic town filled with cafés, restaurants, and shops.

Sightseeing
★★★★
Nightlife
★
Dining
★★
Lodging
★★
Shopping
★★

Although seemingly absorbed into the general Los Angeles sprawl, Pasadena is a separate and distinct city. It's best known for the Tournament of Roses, or more commonly, the Rose Bowl, seen around the world every New Year's Day. But the city has sites worth seeing year-round—from gorgeous Craftsman homes to exceptional museums, particularly the Norton Simon and the Huntington Library, Art Collections, and Botanical Gardens. Note that the Huntington and the Old Mill reside in San Marino, a wealthy, 4-square-mile residential area just over the Pasadena line.

Updated by
Clarissa Wei

First-time visitors to L.A. only here for a short time might find it hard to get out to Pasadena. However, if you've had your fill of city life and are looking for a nearby escape that feels much farther away than it is, with open space and fresher air, it's the perfect trip.

Start at the **Botanical Gardens,** then spend the afternoon strolling around **Old Town Pasadena,** with shops and restaurants filling its 19th-century brick buildings. Art and architecture lovers shouldn't miss the city's top site, the **Norton Simon Museum,** most noted for its excellent collection of Degas, as well as works by Rembrandt, Goya, and Picasso. The **Gamble House** is an immense three-story house and one of the country's shining examples of American Arts and Crafts bungalow architecture. The thing that might surprise you the most about visiting Pasadena is that even the drive here—on the freeway, though not during rush hour—is a scenic one. The Pasadena Freeway follows the curves of the *arroyo* (creek bed), lined with old sycamores. It was the main road north during the early days of Los Angeles, when horses and buggies made their way through the countryside to the small town of Pasadena. In 1939 the road became the Arroyo Seco Parkway, the first freeway in Los Angeles.

# TOP ATTRACTIONS

**Gamble House.** Built by Charles and Henry Greene in 1908, this American Arts and Crafts bungalow illustrates the incredible craftsmanship that went into early L.A. architecture. The term *bungalow* can be misleading, since the Gamble House is a huge three-story home. To wealthy Easterners such as the Gambles (as in Procter & Gamble), this type of vacation home seemed informal compared with their mansions back home. Admirers swoon over the teak staircase and cabinetry, the Greene and Greene–designed furniture, and an Emil Lange glass door. The dark exterior has broad eaves, with sleeping porches on the second floor. An hour-long, docent-led tour of the Gamble's interior will draw your eye to the exquisite details. For those who want to see more of the Greene and Greene homes, there are guided walks around the historic Arroyo Terrace neighborhood. Advance tickets are highly recommended. ⊠ *4 Westmoreland Pl., Pasadena* ☎ *626/793–3334* ⊕ *www.gamblehouse.org* ✍ *$15.*

**Fodor's Choice**
★ **Huntington Library, Art Collections, and Botanical Gardens.** If you have time for just one stop in the Pasadena area, be sure to see this sprawling estate built for railroad tycoon Henry E. Huntington in the early 1900s. Henry and his wife, Arabella (who was also his aunt by marriage), voraciously collected rare books and manuscripts, botanical specimens, and 18th-century British art. The institution they established became one of the most extraordinary cultural complexes in the world.

The library contains more than 700,000 books and 4 million manuscripts, including one of the world's biggest history of science collections.

Don't resist being lured outside into the Botanical Gardens, which extend out from the main building. The 10-acre Desert Garden has one of the world's largest groups of mature cacti and other succulents (visit on a cool morning or late afternoon). The Shakespeare Garden, meanwhile, blooms with plants mentioned in Shakespeare's works. The Japanese Garden features an authentic ceremonial teahouse built in Kyoto in the 1960s. A waterfall flows from the teahouse to the ponds below. In the Rose Garden Tea Room, afternoon tea is served (reserve in advance). The Chinese Garden, which is among the largest outside of China, sinews around waveless pools.

The Bing Children's Garden lets tiny tots explore the ancient elements of water, fire, air, and earth. A 1¼-hour guided tour of the Botanical Gardens is led by docents at posted times, and a free brochure with a map and property highlights is available in the entrance pavilion. ⊠ *1151 Oxford Rd., San Marino* ☎ *626/405–2100* ⊕ *www.huntington. org* ✍ *$20 weekdays, $23 weekends* ۞ *Closed Tues.*

**Fodor's Choice**
★ **Norton Simon Museum.** As seen in the New Year's Day Tournament of Roses Parade, this low-profile brown building is one of the finest midsize museums anywhere, with a collection that spans more than 2,000 years of Western and Asian art. It all began in the 1950s when Norton Simon (Hunt-Wesson Foods, McCalls Corporation, and Canada Dry) started collecting works by Degas, Renoir, Gauguin, and Cézanne. His collection grew to include old masters, impressionists, and modern works from Europe, as well as Indian and Southeast Asian art.

Today the Norton Simon Museum is richest in works by Rembrandt, Picasso, and, most of all, Degas—this is one of the only two U.S. institutions (the other is New York's Metropolitan Museum of Art) to hold nearly all of the artist's model bronzes.

Head down to the bottom floor to see temporary exhibits and phenomenal Southeast Asian and Indian sculptures and artifacts, where pieces like a Ban Chiang blackware vessel date back to well before 1000 BC. Don't miss a living artwork outdoors: the garden, conceived by noted Southern California landscape designer Nancy Goslee Power. The tranquil pond was inspired by Monet's gardens at Giverny. ⊠ *411 W. Colorado Blvd., Pasadena* ☎ *626/449–6840* ⊕ *www.nortonsimon. org* ⊠ *$12, free 1st Fri. of month 5–8 pm* ☉ *Closed Tues.*

**Old Town Pasadena.** This 22-block historic district contains a vibrant mix of restored 19th-century brick buildings interspersed with contemporary architecture. Chain stores have muscled in, but there are still some homegrown shops, plenty of tempting cafés and restaurants, and a bustling beer scene. In recent years, a vibrant Asian food scene has popped up in the vicinity as well. In the evening and on weekends, the streets are packed with people. Old Town's main action takes place on Colorado Boulevard between Pasadena Avenue and Arroyo Parkway. ⊠ *Pasadena.*

QUICK
BITES

**Green Zone.** It's no secret that the San Gabriel Valley where Pasadena is located has some of the best Chinese food outside of China. Green Zone is at the top of its class, serving out organic Chinese cuisine. ⊠ *34 S. Raymond Ave., Pasadena* ☎ *626/535–9700* ⊕ *www.greenzonerestaurant.com.*

## WORTH NOTING

**Castle Green.** One block south of Colorado Boulevard stands the one-time social center of Pasadena's elite. This Moorish building is the only remaining section of a turn-of-the-20th-century hotel complex. Today the often-filmed tower (see *The Sting, Edward Scissorhands, The Last Samurai, The Prestige*) is residential. The building is not open to the public on a daily basis, but it does organize a seasonal tour on the first Sunday of December. ⊠ *99 S. Raymond Ave., Pasadena* ☎ *626/385–7774* ⊕ *www.castlegreen.com.*

**Descanso Gardens.** Getting its name from the Spanish word for "rest," this 160-acre oasis is a respite from city life, shaded by massive oak trees. Known for being a smaller, mellower version of the nearby Huntington, Descanso Gardens features denser foliage, quaint dirt paths, and some hilly climbs that can make for good exercise. It's the perfect place to come in search of wonderful scents—between the lilacs, the acres of roses, and the forest of California redwoods, pines, and junipers, you can enjoy all sorts of fragrances. A forest of California live oak trees makes a dramatic backdrop for thousands of camellias, azaleas, and a breathtaking 5-acre International Rosarium holding 1,700 varieties of antique and modern roses. A small train ride draws families on weekends. There are also a child's train, a gift shop, and a café. ⊠ *1418 Descanso Dr., Pasadena* ☎ *818/949–4200* ⊕ *www.descansogardens.org* ⊠ *$9.*

The Desert Garden at the mesmerizing 120-acre Huntington Botanical Gardens

**Fenyes Mansion.** With its elegant dark-wood paneling and floors, curved staircases, and a theatrical stage in the parlor, it's easy to envision how this 1905 mansion along Pasadena's Millionaire's Row once served as gathering place for the city's elite (it also housed the Finnish Consulate until 1965). Most rooms on the ground and second floors are still fitted with original furniture; you can peek into these roped-off spaces, now home to mannequins dressed in period clothing, to get a sense of what life was like a century ago. You can visit the mansion (on your own or on a 90-minute tour), the adjacent Finnish Folk Art Museum, and the Historical Center Gallery, which has rotating exhibits dedicated to the art and culture of Pasadena. ⊠ *470 W. Walnut St., Pasadena* ☎ *626/577–1660* ⊕ *www.pasadenahistory.org* ✉ *$7; tours $15* ⊙ *Closed Mon. and Tues.*

**Heritage Square Museum.** Looking like a prop street set up by a film studio, Heritage Square resembles a row of bright dollhouses in the modest Highland Park neighborhood. Five 19th-century residences, a train station, a church, a carriage barn, and a 1909 boxcar that was originally part of the Southern Pacific Railroad, all built between the Civil War and World War I, were moved to this small park from various locations in Southern California to save them from the wrecking ball. The latest addition, a re-creation of a World War I–era drugstore, has a vintage soda fountain and traditional products. Docents dressed in period costume lead visitors through the lavish homes, giving an informative picture of Los Angeles in the early 1900s. Don't miss the unique 1893 Octagon House, one of just a handful of its kind built in California. ⊠ *3800 Homer St., off Ave. 43 exit, Highland Park* ☎ *323/225–2700* ⊕ *www.heritagesquare.org* ✉ *$10* ⊙ *Closed Mon.–Thurs.* ☞ *Tour included with admission price.*

FAMILY **Kidspace Children's Museum.** Straight out of a Looney Tunes cartoon, this activity-focused playground with oversize replicas of familiar objects offers lessons along with some fun. The whole family can gain tidbits of knowledge on earthquakes, animals, and insects. Explore gravity in the Physics Forest, which features 12 interactive experiences. In the sunny atrium, kids assume the role of ants on their daring ascent. Outside they can run and climb along a running river or take on a tricycle race. The museum is practically designed to wear out the little ones and give parents a much-needed break. ✉ *480 N. Arroyo Blvd., Pasadena* ☎ *626/449–9144* ⊕ *www.kidspacemuseum.org* 🖃 *$13* ⊘ *Closed Mon., unless promoted for special events.*

**Los Angeles County Arboretum.** Wander through a re-created tropical forest, a South Africa landscape, or the Australian outback at this arboretum. One highlight is the tropical greenhouse, with carnivorous-looking orchids and a pond full of brilliantly colored goldfish. The house and stables of the eccentric real-estate pioneer Lucky Baldwin are well preserved and worth a visit. Kids will love the many peacocks and waterfowl that roam the property. The most recent addition is a water-harvesting farm, where tall stalks of rainbow corn and vines of passion fruit grow in abundance. To get here, head east on I–210 just past Pasadena, exit in Arcadia on Baldwin Avenue and go south, and you will soon see the entrance. ✉ *301 N. Baldwin Ave., Arcadia* ☎ *626/821–3222* ⊕ *www.arboretum.org* 🖃 *$9.*

**The Old Mill (El Molino Viejo).** Built in 1816 as a gristmill for the San Gabriel Mission, the mill is one of the last remaining examples in Southern California of Spanish Mission architecture. The thick adobe walls and textured ceiling rafters give the interior a sense of quiet strength. Be sure to step into the back room, now a gallery with rotating quarterly exhibits. Outside, a chipped section of the mill's exterior reveals the layers of brick, ground seashell paste, and oxblood used to hold the structure together. The surrounding gardens are reason enough to visit, with a flower-decked arbor and old sycamores and oaks. In summer the California Philharmonic ensemble performs in the garden. ✉ *1120 Old Mill Rd., San Marino* ☎ *626/449–5458* ⊕ *www.old-mill.org* 🖃 *Free* ⊘ *Closed Mon.*

**Rose Bowl.** With an enormous rose on its exterior, this 100,000-plus-seat stadium, host of many Super Bowls and home to the UCLA Bruins, is impossible to miss. Set at the bottom of a wide arroyo in Brookside Park, the facility is closed except during games and special events like the monthly Rose Bowl Flea Market. ✉ *1001 Rose Bowl Dr., at Rosemont Ave., Pasadena* ☎ *626/577–3100* ⊕ *www.rosebowlstadium.com.*

**Rose Bowl Flea Market.** This massive flea market, held rain or shine on the second Sunday of each month, features antique and vintage finds along with new items from more than 2,500 vendors. Considered one of the best and most eclectic flea markets in the country, it draws hordes of fashion devotees and everyday bargain-seekers. Arrive early to beat the crowds, which tend to peak midday. Food and drink are readily available, and parking is free. Admission is $9 per person. ✉ *1001 Rose Bowl Dr., at Rosemont Ave., Pasadena* ☎ ⊕ *www.rgcshows.com/rosebowl.aspx* 🖃 *$8.*

DID YOU KNOW?

Raphael's Madonna and Child with Book is part of the wide-ranging collection of the Norton Simon Museum.

**Mission San Gabriel Archangel.** Established in 1771 as the fourth of 21 missions founded in California, this massive adobe complex was dedicated by Father Junípero Serra to St. Gabriel. Within the next 50 years, the San Gabriel Archangel became the wealthiest of all California missions. In 1833 the Mexican government confiscated the mission, allowing it to decline. The U.S. government returned the mission to the church in 1855, but by this time the Franciscans had departed. In 1908 the Claretian Missionaries took charge and poured much care into preserving the rich history. The cemetery here, the first in L.A. County, is said to contain approximately 6,000 Gabrieleno Indians. Tranquil grounds are lushly planted and filled with remnants of what life was like nearly two centuries ago. Public mass is held at the mission Sunday morning at 7 and 9:30, but call ahead as times are subject to change. If you're lucky, you'll hear the six bells that ring out during special services—a truly arresting experience. You can take a self-guided tour of the grounds here by purchasing a map in the gift shop. ⊠ *428 S. Mission Dr., San Gabriel* 🕾 *626/457–3048* ⊕ *www.sangabrielmission.org* 🗩 *$6.*

**Tournament House (Wrigley Mansion).** Chewing gum magnate William Wrigley purchased this white Italian Renaissance–style house in 1914. When his wife died in 1958, Wrigley donated the house to the city of Pasadena under the stipulation that it be used as the headquarters for the Tournament of Roses. The mansion features a green tile roof and manicured rose garden with 1,500 varieties. The interior provides a glimpse of the area's over-the-top style in the early 20th century. Tours of the house are every Thursday from 2 pm to 3 pm from February to August; fans of the Rose Parade can see the various crowns and tiaras worn by former Rose Queens, plus trophies and memorabilia. ⊠ *391 S. Orange Grove Blvd., Pasadena* 🕾 *626/449–4100* ⊕ *www.tournamentofroses.com* 🗩 *Free.*

# NIGHTLIFE

Los Angeles is not the city that never sleeps—instead it parties until 2 am (save for the secret after-hours parties at private clubs or warehouses), and wakes up to imbibe green juices and breakfast burritos as hangover cures, or to sweat it out in a yoga class. Whether you plan to test your limit at historic establishments Downtown, or take advantage of a cheap happy hour at a Hollywood dive, this city's nightlife has something for you.

A night out in Los Angeles can simultaneously surprise and impress. That unscheduled set by an A-list comedian at the stand-up comedy club, being talked into singing karaoke at the diviest place you've ever seen, dancing at a bar with no dance floor because, well, the DJ is just too good at his job—going out isn't always what you expect, but it certainly is never boring.

The focus of nightlife once centered on the Sunset Strip, with its multitude of bars, rock clubs, and dance spots, but more neighborhoods are competing with each other and forcing the nightlife scene to evolve. Although the Strip can be a worthwhile trip, other areas of the city are catching people's attention. Downtown Los Angeles, for instance, is becoming a destination in its own right, drawing cocktail connoisseurs at Seven Grand and rooftop revelers at the Standard.

Other areas foster more of a neighborhood vibe. Silver Lake and Los Feliz have both cultivated a relaxed environment where you can be drinking in a tiki bar so small you wind up talking with the person at the next stool over (Tiki-Ti) or bringing in a 45 to play on an old-fashioned record player (El Prado).

So if you find yourself disappointed with a rude bouncer, or drinks that are too watery, or a cover charge that just isn't worth it, try again. Eventually you'll find that perfect place where each time is the best time. If not, at least you'll walk away with a good story.

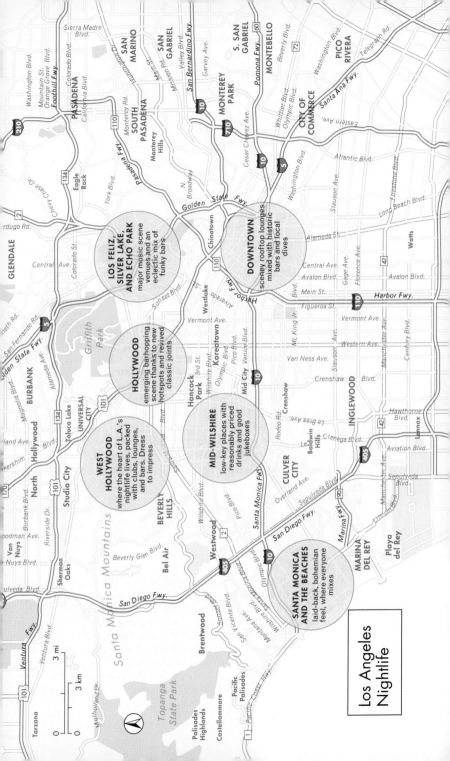

# Los Angeles Nightlife

**LOS FELIZ, SILVER LAKE, AND ECHO PARK** major music scene venues and an eclectic mix of funky bars

**DOWNTOWN** sceney rooftop lounges mixed with historic bars and local dives

**HOLLYWOOD** emerging barhopping scene thanks to new hotspots and revived classic joints

**WEST HOLLYWOOD** where the heart of L.A.'s nightlife lives, packed with clubs, lounges, and bars. Dress to impress

**MID-WILSHIRE** low-key places with reasonably priced drinks and good jukeboxes

**SANTA MONICA AND THE BEACHES** laid-back, bohemian feel, where everyone mixes

# PLANNING

### WHERE TO GET INFORMATION

Local publications like *LA Weekly* (⊕ *www.laweekly.com*) and LA Canvas (⊕ *www.lacanvas.com*) are great resources to discover what's happening in Los Angeles. Websites like DoLA (⊕ *www.dola.com*) and TimeOut LA (⊕ *www.timeout.com/los-angeles*) have listings of the latest events and recently opened bars and clubs.

### HOURS

Despite the high energy level of the L.A. nightlife crowd, don't expect to be partying until dawn—this is still an early-to-bed city. Bars close at 2 am, and it's safe to say that by this time, with the exception of a few after-hours venues, most clubs have closed for the night.

### PARKING

To avoid circling the block to look for a spot, we recommend using a ride service like Lyft or Uber to get to your destination. Garage or valet parking is available in most areas from $5 to $20. Most neighborhoods near party-heavy areas like West Hollywood require residential parking permits, so be sure to carefully read signs if you do decide to drive.

### BEST NIGHTLIFE EXPERIENCES

**Embrace another era.** Los Angeles is filled with historic buildings, and the bars inside them are using this as a selling point, creating truly interesting locations that can transport you to another time and place. Places like Cole's and Musso & Frank have long and interesting stories to tell, and upstarts like the Edison are aiming to re-create a bygone era, all of which adds up to an enjoyable drinking experience.

**Drink in the scenery.** The wonderful weather in Los Angeles makes for enjoyable nights outdoors, with plenty of spots offering rooftop pools or open-air patios where you can enjoy a cocktail: The Standard or the Ace Hotel in Downtown, or Yamashiro in Hollywood, to name a few.

**Rock (or laugh) the night away.** Los Angeles is the town that most wannabe entertainers run to so they can "make it," and you'd be missing out if you didn't try a rock show or comedy night while you're in town. Big-name performers command high ticket prices, but it's easy to find less expensive shows with up-and-coming acts. On Monday nights, the Satellite in Silverlake hosts monthlong residencies featuring performances by new artists, free of charge.

### LATE-NIGHT TRANSPORTATION

Uber and Lyft are both available in all areas of Los Angeles, and you won't have to wait more than a few minutes before your car arrives. If you happen to be partying in West Hollywood, the PickUp Line (⊕ *www.weho.org/business/weho-pickup*) is a free trolley that travels a 4-mile route through the neighborhood on Friday and Saturday evenings, and from 2 pm to 10 pm on Sundays. If you're strapped for cash, save money by taking the Metro, which runs until 2 am on Friday and Saturday nights. While the city is still in the midst of making trains more accessible, it's not the most efficient way to your destination, but it's worth looking into to save money.

**WHAT A NIGHT OUT COSTS**

Some high-profile clubs charge a $15 to $25 cover. Tipping the doorman to bypass the line is still a thing, but expect to drop more than $20 into the bouncer's hand to get anywhere. Most establishments have happy hour specials and cheap domestic beers, but cocktails cost anywhere from $12 to $18 at most bars.

# DOWNTOWN

With choice music venues, upscale bars, and divier clubs, Downtown is high on the list of after-dark options.

## BARS AND LOUNGES

Fodor's Choice
★ **BonaVista Lounge at the Westin Bonaventure.** Atop the Westin Bonaventure hotel, L.A.'s best-kept secret cocktail bar revolves 34 floors above the street. With glass walls and views of Downtown, snowcapped mountains, Hollywood, and beyond (on a clear day, you can spot the ocean), there isn't bad seat in the house. Don't eat the food. Drinks are great, if slightly overpriced, but hey, you're paying for a showstopping view. ⊠ *404 S. Figueroa St., Downtown* ☎ *213/624–1000* ⊕ *www.thebonaventure.com/bona-vista-lounge.*

**Broadway Bar.** This watering hole–meets–dive sits in a flourishing section of Broadway (neighbors include the swank Ace Hotel). Bartenders mix creative cocktails while DJs spin tunes nightly. The two-story space includes a smoking balcony overlooking the street. The crowd is often dressed to impress. ⊠ *830 S. Broadway, Downtown* ☎ *213/614–9909.*

**Edison.** The glitz and glam of the Roaring '20s is alive and well in the Edison, where the decor serves as tribute to the power plant that once occupied these premises. Black-and-white silent films are projected onto the walls, and tasty nibbles and artisanal cocktails are served (in a private room, if you prefer). There's live entertainment many nights, from jazz bands to burlesque shows. Closed Sunday–Tuesday. ⊠ *108 W. 2nd St., Downtown* ☎ *213/613–0000* ⊕ *www.edisondowntown.com.*

**El Dorado.** Though cavernous, you'll still be able to cozy up to your neighbor at the bar inside this Downtown lounge. The walls display boudoir art of women dressed for the 18th century, yet they have a '70s feel; it has all the trappings of a nouveau-speakeasy (it's in a basement, it has a pressed-tin ceiling), but feels like an unpretentious locals' joint. Regardless of the contrasts, the drinks are top notch—bartenders here have concocted a uniquely flavorful menu that doesn't skimp on the booze. ⊠ *416 Spring St., Downtown* ☎ *213/621–7710.*

Fodor's Choice
★ **Golden Gopher.** Craft cocktails, beers on tap, an outdoor smoking patio, and retro video games—this bar in the heart of Downtown is not to be missed. With one of the oldest liquor licenses in Los Angeles (issued in 1905), the Golden Gopher is the only bar in Los Angeles with an on-site liquor store for to-go orders—just in case you want to buy another bottle before you head home. ⊠ *417 W. 8th St., Downtown* ☎ *213/614–8001.*

7

**Fodor's**Choice
★

**Love Song Bar.** Lovers of T.S. Eliot and vinyl will find themselves instantly at home inside this cozy establishment named after Eliot's "The Love Song of J. Alfred Prufrock." When not pouring drinks, bartenders often act as DJs, playing records (the best of the '60s through the '80s) in their entirety. As it's housed inside the Regent Theater, the cozy nature of the place can be disrupted when there's a concert scheduled. For those with an appetite, fantastic food can be ordered from the pizza parlor next door—naturally, it's called Prufrock's. ⊠ *446 S. Main St., Downtown* ☎ *323/284-5661.*

**Redwood Bar & Grill.** If you're looking for a place with potent drinks and a good burger, this kitschy bar fits the bill perfectly. Known today as the "pirate bar" because of its nautical decor, the place dates back to the 1940s, when it was rumored to attract mobsters, politicians, and journalists due to its proximity to City Hall, the Hall of Justice, and the *Los Angeles Times.* There's nightly music from local rock bands, though it comes with a cover charge. ⊠ *316 W. 2nd St., Downtown* ☎ *213/680-2600* ⊕ *www.theredwoodbar.com.*

**Fodor's**Choice
★

**Resident.** Catch a lineup of indie tastemakers inside this converted industrial space, or hang outdoors in the beer garden while trying bites from on-site food truck KTCHN (on cooler evenings you can congregate around the fire pits). A wide variety of draft beers and a specially curated cocktail program are available inside at the bar, or at the trailer bar outside. ⊠ *428 S. Hewitt St., Downtown* ☎ *213/628-7503* ⊕ *www.residentdtla.com.*

**Seven Grand.** The hunting lodge vibe makes you feel like you need a whiskey in hand—luckily, this Downtown establishment stocks more than 700 of them. Attracting whiskey novices and connoisseurs, the bartenders here are more than willing to help you make a selection. Live jazz and blues bands play every night but Friday, so even if you're not a big drinker there's still some appeal (although you're definitely missing out). For a more intimate setting, try the on-site **Bar Jackalope,** a bar within a bar, which has a "whiskey tasting library" and seats only 24. ⊠ *515 W. 7th St., 2nd fl., Downtown* ☎ *213/614-0737* ⊕ *www.sevengrandbars.com.*

**Fodor's**Choice
★

**The Varnish.** Beeline through the dining room of Cole's to find an unassuming door that leads to this small, dimly lit bar-within-a-bar. Wooden booths line the walls, candles flicker, and live jazz is performed Sunday through Tuesday. The bartenders take their calling to heart, and shake and stir some of the finest cocktails in the city. Those who don't have a drink of choice can list their wants ("gin-based and sweet," "strong whiskey and herbaceous") and be served a custom cocktail. Be warned: Patrons requiring quick drinks will want to go elsewhere—perfection takes time. ⊠ *118 E. 6th St., Downtown* ☎ *213/265-7089* ⊕ *www.213hospitality.com/project/the-varnish.*

## CLUBS

**La Cita.** This dive bar may not look like much, but it more than makes up for it with an interesting mix of barflies, urban hipsters, and reasonable drink prices. Friday and Saturday nights, DJs mix Top 40 hits and a tiny dance floor packs in the crowd. For those more interested in drinking and socializing, head to the back patio where a TV plays local sports. ⌧ *336 S. Hill St., Downtown* ☎ *213/687–7111* ⊕ *www. lacitabar.com.*

## MUSIC

**Blue Whale.** This unassuming jazz club in Little Tokyo caters to a serious crowd, bringing progressive and modern jazz to the stage. Although the venue is focused on the music (yes, you may get shushed for talking—that's how small it is), there is a kitchen and bar for snacks and drinks. The club is on the third floor of Weller Court, and the cover runs around $10 to $20. ⌧ *123 Astronaut E. S. Onizuka St., Downtown* ☎ *213/620–0908* ⊕ *www.bluewhalemusic.com.*

# HOLLYWOOD AND THE STUDIOS

Hang out on the Eastside for a more affordable evening laden with L.A. realness. The nearby communities of Los Feliz, Echo Park, and Silver Lake are filled with drinking dens and after-dark destinations.

## HOLLYWOOD

Hollywood is no longer just a tourist magnet. With the renewed interest in discovering Hollywood history, this area is once again a nightlife destination for locals and visitors alike. Its blend of glitz and grime is reflected here in the after-hours scene.

### BARS AND LOUNGES

**Birds.** They call it your neighborhood bar, because even if you don't live in the neighborhood you'll feel at home at this Alfred Hitchcock–themed eatery. Located in Franklin Village, a block-long stretch of bars, cafés, and bookstores, come here for pub food or a cheap poultry-centric dinner. Weekend nights mean cheap beer and well drinks, crowds spilling onto the streets, and a few rounds of oversized Jenga. Right next to the UCB Theatre, you're likely to see a few comedians grabbing a drink here after their shows. ⌧ *5925 Franklin Ave., Hollywood* ☎ *323/465–0175* ⊕ *www.birdshollywood.com.*

**Burgundy Room.** Around since 1919, Burgundy Room attracts a fiercely loyal crowd of locals, as well as the occasional wandering tourists. The bar is supposedly haunted (check out the Ouija boards toward the back), but that just adds to its charm. Drinks aren't cheap, but the ambience makes it worth it. The jukebox plays classic 45s, and the attached gallery is worth taking a quick spin through if it's open. ⌧ *1621½ N. Cahuenga Blvd., Hollywood* ☎ *323/465–7530.*

**Good Times at Davey Wayne's.** It's a fridge; it's a door; it's the entrance to Davey Wayne's, a bar and lounge that pulls out all the stops to transport you back in time to the '70s. The interior is your living room; the outside is an ongoing backyard barbecue with all of your friends. Except, wait, I don't recognize anyone…who invited all these drunk people to my house?! On hot days, enjoy a boozy snow cone from the outdoor shed/bar. Inside, sip on a smoky/spicy cocktail called Enter the Dragon, and listen to a throwback rock band. Come early to beat the crowds or be prepared to get up close and personal with your neighbors. ⊠ *1611 N. El Centro Ave., Hollywood* ☎ *323/962–3804* ⊕ *www.goodtimesatdaveywaynes.com.*

FAMILY
Fodor's Choice
★

**Musso & Frank Grill.** The prim and proper vibe of this old-school steak house won't appeal to those looking for a raucous night out; instead, its appeal lies in its history and sturdy drinks. Established in 1919, its dark wood decor, red tuxedo–clad waiters, and highly skilled bartenders can easily shuttle you back to its Hollywood heyday when Marilyn Monroe, F. Scott Fitzgerald, and Greta Garbo once hung around and sipped martinis. ⊠ *6667 Hollywood Blvd., Hollywood* ☎ *323/467–7788* ⊕ *www. mussoandfrank.com.*

**No Vacancy.** Talk to the girl. Enter through the bedroom. This mysterious Hollywood speakeasy with a spacious patio regularly features a live DJ, burlesque dancers, and a tightrope walker. It gets busy, so plan your night accordingly. If the atmosphere doesn't take your breath away, the drinks will. ⊠ *1727 N. Hudson Ave., Hollywood* ☎ *323/465–1902* ⊕ *www.novacancyla.com.*

**Playhouse.** Reminiscent of Las Vegas, this splashy spot on Hollywood Boulevard has DJs spinning everything from house to '90s hip-hop. Guest artists like 50 Cent and Too Short drop in from time to time for live performances. Upscale dress is common. Expect to drop anywhere from $20 to $30 for the cover charge. ⊠ *6506 Hollywood Blvd., Hollywood* ☎ *323/656–4600* ⊕ *www.playhousenightclub.com.*

**The Room.** This place maintains its reputation as a hip-hop club, serving cool cocktails in a chill environment. Cherry Poppin' Wednesday is a local favorite, with funk, soul, and old-school hip-hop played all night long. The bar likes to maintain a Rat Pack vibe (check out the photo of Frank Sinatra by the bar). ⊠ *1626 N. Cahuenga Blvd., Hollywood* ☎ *323/462–7196* ⊕ *www.theroomhollywood.com.*

**Three Clubs.** Part martini lounge, part biker bar, this spot right on the corner of Santa Monica and Vine has plush leather booths and cozy bar seats. The focus is on fresh and local ingredients for all the cocktails, and they offer a daily happy hour. There's a small cover charge to watch bands, comedy, or burlesque shows on the stage in the back room. ⊠ *1123 Vine St., Hollywood* ☎ *323/462–6441* ⊕ *www.threeclubs.com.*

**Tropicana Bar.** This bar embodies the L.A. lifestyle—enjoying perfectly mixed cocktails beside a shimmering pool at the Hollywood Roosevelt Hotel while you're surrounded by beautiful people never seems to lose its appeal. You'll find loungers in the afternoon and evenings. There's never a cover charge, but the drinks can get pricey, and the lines are long on weekend nights. For something more low-key, try the Roosevelt's **Library Bar,** which serves drinks topped with ingredients from the farmers' markets. ⊠ *Hollywood Roosevelt Hotel, 7000 Hollywood Blvd., Hollywood* 🕾 *323/466–7000* ⊕ *www.hollywoodroosevelt.com.*

**Yamashiro Hollywood.** Modeled after a mansion in Kyoto, this Japanese place with a hillside perch has spectacular koi ponds and gardens, as well as sweeping views of Hollywood's twinkling lights. Additional lures here include the tasty, if pricey, food and delicious drinks. ∎ **TIP→ The mandatory valet parking costs $10.** ⊠ *1999 N. Sycamore Ave., Hollywood* 🕾 *323/466–5125* ⊕ *www.yamashirohollywood.com.*

## CLUBS

**Boardner's.** This neighborhood lounge has been around for decades, and its dim lighting and leather booths give it a well-worn feel. The adjoining open-air Club 52, with an ornate tiled fountain in the center, has its own cover charge and entrance, and often hosts burlesque shows or live bands. The long-running Saturday Goth night, Bar Sinister, remains popular here after 19 years. ⊠ *1652 N. Cherokee Ave., Hollywood* 🕾 *323/462–9621* ⊕ *www.boardners.com.*

## COMEDY

**iO West.** The Los Angeles branch of this theater troupe offers nightly shows featuring both seasoned and amateur improv groups. There's a bar in the waiting area—more common for comedy clubs than improv theaters—where performers and their friends congregate after hours. ⊠ *6366 Hollywood Blvd., Hollywood* 🕾 *323/962–7560* ⊕ *www.ioimprov.com/west.*

Fodor'sChoice ★ **Upright Citizens Brigade.** The L.A. offshoot of New York's famous troupe continues its tradition of sketch comedy and improv with weekly shows like "Facebook" (where the audience's online profiles are mined for material), and "Doug Loves Movies," where comedian Doug Benson invites three surprise guests (Zach Galifianakis and Sarah Silverman have both made appearances) to play a movie-themed game show with loose rules. Arrive early as space is limited. A second theater on Sunset Boulevard opened in 2014. ⊠ *5919 Franklin Ave., Hollywood* 🕾 *323/908–8702* ⊕ *www.ucbtheatre.com.*

## MUSIC

**Avalon.** This multitasking art deco venue offers both live music and club nights. The killer sound system, cavernous space, and multiple bars make it a perfect venue for both. The club is best known for its DJs, who often spin well past the 2 am cutoff for drinks. The crowd can be a mixed bag, depending on the night, but if you're looking to dance, you likely won't be disappointed. Upstairs is **Bardot,** which hosts a free Monday night showcase of up-and-coming artists called School Night! that's always a good time. Remember to RSVP online in advance; they'll be checking names at the door. ⊠ *1735 Vine St., Hollywood* 🕾 *323/462–8900* ⊕ *www.avalonhollywood.com.*

**Baked Potato.** Located in Hollywood-adjacent Studio City, this small club showcases contemporary jazz and blues every evening, along with regular Monday night jam sessions. The cover ranges from $10 to $20, on top of a two-drink minimum. True to its name, baked potatoes in every form make up the menu. ⊠ *3787 Cahuenga Blvd., North Hollywood* 🕾 *818/980–1615* ⊕ *www.thebakedpotato.com.*

**California Institute of Abnormalarts.** Better known as the CIA, this bar manages to make its circus theme seem kooky and fun (imagine Tim Burton directing *Pee-Wee's Big Adventure,* then add a David Lynch twist). The list of events varies, from magic shows to burlesque performances to the occasional film screening. Expect a $5–$10 cover, which isn't bad considering there's so much to look at and ogle. ✉ *11334 Burbank Ave., North Hollywood* ☎ *818/221–8065.*

Fodor's Choice ★ **El Floridita.** Although the exterior might not look like much, El Floridita is a popular live salsa music spot on Monday, Friday, and Saturday, with dancers ranging from enthusiasts to those just trying to keep up. There's a $15 cover to listen to the band, although admission is free with dinner. Reservations are recommended to guarantee a table. ✉ *1253 N. Vine St., Hollywood* ☎ *323/871–8612* ⊕ *www.elfloridita.com.*

**The Fonda Theatre.** Right on the edge of the Walk of Fame, this historic venue was one of the area's first theaters when it opened in the 1920s. The Spanish Colonial–style theater now hosts some of the biggest names in music, so scope out the calendar before coming to town. Expect to shell out around $20 to park in the adjacent lot, or take a ride-share to the venue. Drinks are pricey, so grab a cocktail on Hollywood Boulevard before the show. ✉ *6126 Hollywood Blvd., Hollywood* ☎ *323/464–0808* ⊕ *www.fondatheatre.com.*

**Genghis Cohen Cantina.** Chinese food and live music is not a pairing you see often, but the success of this place will make you wonder why it's not done all the time. A wide range of musicians plays here Monday through Saturday (many are singer-songwriter types), along with the occasional comedy show. ✉ *740 N. Fairfax Ave., Hollywood* ☎ *323/653–0640* ⊕ *www.genghiscohen.com.*

**Largo at the Coronet.** The welcoming vibe of this venue attracts big-name performers who treat its stage as their home away from home in Los Angeles. Standouts include musician and music producer Jon Brion, who often appears here with special drop-in guests (Fiona Apple and Andrew Bird have both been on the bill). Comedians Sarah Silverman and Patton Oswalt each host a monthly comedy show. Bring cash for drinks in the Little Room before the show. ✉ *366 N. La Cienega Blvd., Hollywood* ☎ *310/855–0350* ⊕ *www.largo-la.com.*

## LOS FELIZ

### BARS AND LOUNGES

Fodor's Choice ★ **Bigfoot Lodge.** Located on a strip among other hidden gems in Atwater Village, just over the Shakespeare Bridge from Los Feliz, the cabin-in-the-woods-style bar with taxidermy as art makes Bigfoot Lodge kitschy, but not absent of class. There's a variety of drinks, including both cheap and craft beer, and cocktails. DJs spin on certain nights. ✉ *3172 Los Feliz Blvd., Los Feliz* ☎ *323/662–9227.*

**Dresden Room.** This bar's 1940s lounge decor makes it a favorite with folks in Los Angeles. The long-running house band, Marty and Elayne, has entertained patrons for more than three decades. (They've found a new generation of fans, thanks to the film *Swingers.*) They also host an open-mike night on Tuesdays. There's never a cover, but expect a two-drink minimum if you want to stay for the entertainment. ✉ *1760 N. Vermont Ave., Los Feliz* ☎ *323/665–4294* ⊕ *www.thedresden.com.*

**Good Luck Bar.** Around for more than 20 years, this dimly lit Chinese-themed bar is a favorite with younger locals looking to pair up. Many dates have started (or ended) here, and that might have something to do with the place's most popular drink, the Potent Potion. DJs spin on weekends (despite the lack of dance floor). ✉ *1514 Hillhurst Ave., Los Feliz* ☎ *323/666–3524* ⊕ *www.goodluckbarla.com.*

## SILVER LAKE

Silver Lake's best bars can be found in one condensed area, Sunset Junction, the intersection of Sunset and Santa Monica boulevards. If you've spent your day shopping or dining here, return at night when coffee culture takes a breather and makes way for dark eclectic bars patronized by locals and L.A.'s transplant community.

### BARS AND LOUNGES

**Akbar.** This bar's welcoming feel is one of the reasons many people consider it their neighborhood bar, even if they don't live in the neighborhood. The crowd is friendly and inviting, and theme nights attract all sorts of folks, gay or straight. The comedy nights are favorites, as are weekends, when DJs get everyone on the dance floor. ✉ *4356 W. Sunset Blvd., Silver Lake* ☎ *323/665–6810* ⊕ *www.akbarsilverlake.com.*

**Cha Cha Lounge.** This place's decor—part tiki hut, part tacky party palace—shouldn't work, but it does. An import from Seattle, its cheap drinks, foosball tables, and jovial atmosphere make it a natural party scene. ✉ *2375 Glendale Blvd., Silver Lake* ☎ *323/660–7595* ⊕ *www.chachalounge.com.*

Fodor'sChoice ★ **4100.** With swaths of fabric draped from the ceiling, this low-lit bar with a bohemian vibe makes it perfect for dates. Groups of locals also come through for the night, making the crowd a plentiful mix of people. The bartenders know how to pour drinks that are both tasty and potent. There's plenty of seating at the tables and stools along the central bar, which gets crowded on the weekends. ✉ *4100 Sunset Blvd., Silver Lake* ☎ *323/666–4460.*

**Smog Cutter.** The exterior may seem sketchy and the interior not much better, but that doesn't detract from this dive bar's main attraction: nightly karaoke with a fun and rowdy (in a good way) crowd. You have to meet the two-drink minimum at this cash-only hole-in-the-wall. ✉ *864 N. Virgil Ave., Silver Lake.*

**Thirsty Crow.** This whiskey bar serves up seasonal cocktails in a fun, rustic environment. Though small, it manages to find space for live musicians and an open-mike night on Saturdays. Part of the same hospitality group as Bigfoot Lodge and Highland Park Bowl, this watering hole has a locals-only feel. As local L.A. musician Father John Misty once said, "nothing good ever happens at the goddamn Thirsty Crow," but we think you should go and see for yourself. ✉ *2939 W. Sunset Blvd., Silver Lake* ☎ *323/661–6007* ⊕ *www.thirstycrowbar.com.*

**Fodor'sChoice**
★   **Tiki-Ti.** The cozy feel of this Polynesian-theme bar is due in part to its small size—12 seats at the bar, plus a few tables along one side. Open since 1961, it serves strong drinks (92 to be exact), one of which will have the entire place yelling your order. Don't be surprised to find a line outside. ⊠ *4427 Sunset Blvd., Silver Lake* ☎ *323/669–9381* ⊕ *www.tiki-ti.com.*

## MUSIC

**Fodor'sChoice**
★   **The Satellite.** This venue hosts a variety of bands, mostly indie rock acts, as well as a popular DJ night, Dance Yourself Clean (with a great range of highly danceable jams), which is held every Saturday. Monday nights are free, and feature exciting up-and-coming acts. Cover charges on other days range from $8 to $15. ⊠ *1717 Silver Lake Blvd., Silver Lake* ☎ *323/661–4380* ⊕ *www.thesatellitela.com.*

**Silverlake Lounge.** Discover new indie, rock, and classical acts at this divey venue. Cheap beer and well drinks abound, with happy hour specials daily. Order delivery from one of the restaurants nearby and eat it at the bar. ⊠ *2906 Sunset Blvd., Silver Lake* ☎ *323/663–9636* ⊕ *www.thesilverlakelounge.com.*

# ECHO PARK

See an up-and-coming local band, bring your own records to the bar, or impress a date in this eclectic neighborhood that manages to maintain its cultural authenticity more so than its neighbor, Silver Lake.

## BARS AND LOUNGES

FAMILY   **Button Mash.** This naturally lit barcade offers pan-Asian fare from chef duo Nyugen and Thi Tran of Starry Kitchen, and many craft beers on tap. With brand-new pinball games, throwbacks like Mario and Donkey Kong, and classics like Ms. Pac-Man, it's good for kids and groups. Open from 5 pm to midnight Tuesday–Friday, and from 4 pm to midnight on Saturday and Sunday. ⊠ *Echo Park* ☎ *213/250–9903* ⊕ *www.buttonmashla.com.*

**El Prado.** A small selection of constantly rotating wine and beer ensures you'll get to try something new and interesting each time you visit. A record player serves as the main source of music—while the idea may seem twee, it's the heart of a popular Tuesday night record club, where patrons bring in their own vinyl. ⊠ *1805 W. Sunset Blvd., Echo Park* ☎ *213/484–6079* ⊕ *www.elpradobar.com.*

**Fodor'sChoice**
★   **Mohawk Bend.** Spacious and clean, Mohawk Bend is always bustling due its ample seating and excellent happy hour. Sit on the patio by the fireplace, reserve a booth, or join family-style bar seating—there's even a skylit atrium to enjoy. The bar boasts "pub fare," but this is still California; you'll find plenty of vegan and vegetarian options available. Go for a beer—there are 72 on tap. ⊠ *2141 Sunset Blvd., Echo Park* ☎ *213/483–2337* ⊕ *mohawk.la.*

**Short Stop.** Other than its brightly lit "Cocktails" sign, the plain exterior of this spot belies a raucous dance party inside. Named for its proximity to Dodger Stadium, some patrons stop here after a game, while others wait until Saturdays when DJs play Motown hits all night. Bartenders can be a bit caustic. ⊠ *1455 W. Sunset Blvd., Echo Park* ☎ *213/482–4942.*

**Fodor'sChoice**
★
**1642 Beer and Wine.** This romantically lit hole-in-the-wall is easy to miss. Perfect for first dates, come here to experiment with craft beers or to warm up with wine. On the first Thursday of every month, get a free tamale with your drink, and hear some live old-time fiddle tunes. ⊠ *1642 W. Temple St., Echo Park* ☎ *213/989–6836.*

### MUSIC

**Fodor'sChoice**
★
**The Echo.** A neighborhood staple, this beloved spot showcases up-and-coming indie bands that are soon to be big names, with soul or reggae dance nights and DJ mash-up sessions rounding out the calendar. ⊠ *1822 Sunset Blvd., Echo Park* ☎ *213/413–8200* ⊕ *www. theecho.com.*

**Echoplex.** It may surprise you that while this spot is in the basement of the Echo, you have to cross the street and walk under the bridge to access it. A larger space than its sister theater, the Echoplex books bigger national tours and events. Comedians like Marc Maron, and a slew of big names in indie rock have graced the stage. ⊠ *1154 Glendale Blvd., Echo Park* ☎ *213/413–8200* ⊕ *www.attheecho.com.*

**Highland Park Bowl.** Looking for something unique in L.A.'s fastest grow-ing Highland Park neighborhood (5 miles south of Pasadena)? How about a steam-punk bowling alley with Neapolitan pizzas and great music? HPB has roots dating back to the 1920s, and the refurbished establishment aims to maintain elements of its origins. The space fea-tures eight lanes and caters to a younger crowd (with deep pockets, though) who can be found washing down their pies with PBR and craft cocktails. Other menu items include burgers and fries, but the pizza and bowling combo is their raison d'être. ⊠ *5621 N. Figueroa St., Highland Park* ☎ *323/257–2695* ⊕ *www.highlandparkbowl.com.*

# WEST HOLLYWOOD

Gay or straight, head to West Hollywood if you're looking for a party-loving crowd. This town has plenty of bars and clubs within walking distance, so you can hop around easily. Santa Monica Boulevard has everything from low-key sports bars to trendy clubs with raised danc-ing platforms.

## BARS AND LOUNGES

**Bar Marmont.** Right at the start of the Sunset Strip in West Hollywood, Bar Marmont (part of the swanky hotel, Chateau Marmont), is a par-tygoer's staple. Get fancy and come here with a group; the DJ starts around 10 pm. Or, come here early when it's less packed, and make your date treat you to the expensive (and strong) cocktails. The kitchen serves a changing menu of classic French-style dishes. ⊠ *8171 W. Sun-set Blvd., West Hollywood* ☎ *323/656–1010* ⊕ *www.chateaumarmont. com/barmarmont.php.*

**Barney's Beanery.** Open since 1920, Barney's Beanery is an iconic spot that drew legendary regulars Janis Joplin and Jim Morrison (among others) to its doorstep. There's an extensive menu, but all anyone talks about is the famous chili and the list of more than 85 beers. There are plenty of distractions, including three pool tables, a foosball table, and arcade games. ✉ *8447 Santa Monica Blvd., West Hollywood* ☎ *323/654–2287* ⊕ *www.barneysbeanery.com.*

**The Dime.** Though in a tiny space, the Dime manages to pack in the drinking hordes on the weekend. There's a DJ, a daily happy hour, and an all-around good vibe. The music usually gets going by 10 pm and can span the decades. Come on Sunday night if you're looking for a more relaxed atmosphere. ✉ *442 N. Fairfax Ave., Fairfax District* ☎ *323/272–3397* ⊕ *www.thedimela.com.*

**Jones.** Italian food and serious cocktails are the mainstays at Jones. Whiskey is a popular choice for the classic cocktails, but the bartenders also do up martinis properly (read: strong). The Beggar's Banquet is their version of happy hour (10 pm to 2 am, Sunday through Thursday), with specials on drinks and pizza. ✉ *7205 Santa Monica Blvd., West Hollywood* ☎ *323/850–1726* ⊕ *www.joneshollywood.com.*

**Rainbow Bar & Grill.** Its location next door to a long-running music venue, the Roxy, helped cement this bar and restaurant's status as a legendary watering hole for musicians (as well as their entourages and groupies). The Who, Guns 'n Roses, Poison, Kiss, and many others have all passed through the doors. Expect a $5–$10 cover, but you'll get the money back in drink tickets or a food discount. ✉ *9015 W. Sunset Blvd., West Hollywood* ☎ *310/278–4232* ⊕ *www. rainbowbarandgrill.com.*

**Skybar.** This beautiful poolside bar is well worth a visit, but it can be a hassle to get into if you're not staying at the hotel, on the guest list, or know someone who can pull strings. The drinks are on the pricier side, but in this part of town that's to be expected. ✉ *Hotel Mondrian, 8440 Sunset Blvd., West Hollywood* ☎ *323/650–8999* ⊕ *www.mondrianhotel.com.*

**The Standard.** Weekend pool parties in the summer are downright notorious at the Standard Hollywood. Party on the pool deck with DJs, or hear acoustic sets in the Cactus Lodge on Wednesday evenings. Check the calendar for special events like film screenings. ✉ *The Standard Hollywood, 8300 Sunset Blvd., West Hollywood* ☎ *323/650–9090* ⊕ *www. standardhotels.com.*

**Trunks Bar.** At Trunks Bar, the drinks are strong and so are the bartenders; see for yourself as these shirtless muscly men pour your drinks. Open for more than 25 years, the space is welcoming and the staff is friendly. Although a DJ usually plays music after 10 pm, there's no dance floor to speak of. People also come here often to watch a game or play pool. ✉ *8809 California Rte. 2, West Hollywood* ☎ *310/652–1015* ⊕ *www.trunksbar.com.*

*Continued on page 133*

Cole's

# L.A. STORY
## THE CITY'S HISTORY THROUGH ITS BARS

Los Angeles is known as a place where dreams are realized, but it is also a place where pasts are forgotten. Despite what people say about L.A.'s lack of memory, however, there are quite a few noteworthy old-school bars that pay tribute to the city's vibrant past and its famous patrons.

Collectively, these eclectic watering holes have hosted everyone from ex-presidents to rock legends to famed authors and, of course, a continual stream of countless movie stars.

The bars are located in virtually every corner of the city—from Downtown to West Hollywood to Santa Monica.

In terms of character, they run the gamut from dive to dressy and serve everything from top-shelf whisky to bargain-basement beer.

While it's their differences that have kept people coming back through the decades, they all have something in common: Each has a story to tell.

## EIGHT OF L.A.'S BEST

Mixing at Cole's

Chez Jay

Cole's

Frolic Room

**CHEZ JAY RESTAURANT** (1959)
**Noteworthy for:** Located down the block from the Santa Monica Pier, this steak-and-seafood joint walks the line between celebrity hangout and dive bar.
**Signature drink:** Martini
**Celeb clientele:** Members of the Rat Pack, Leonard Nimoy, Sean Penn, Julia Roberts, Renée Zellweger, Owen Wilson, Drew Barrymore
**Don't miss:** The little booth in the back of the restaurant, known to insiders as Table 10, is a favorite celebrity hideout.
**Filmed here:** *A Single Man, Goliath*
**Join the crowd:** *1657 Ocean Ave., Santa Monica, 310/395–1741*

**COLE'S** (1908)
**Noteworthy for:** Found inside the Pacific Electric building, touted as Los Angeles's oldest public house, and once the epicenter of the Red Car railway network, this watering hole has its original glass lighting, penny-tile floors, and 40-foot mahogany bar.
**Signature drink:** Oldfashioned

**Celeb clientele:** The men's room boasts that Charles Bukowski and Mickey Cohen once relieved themselves here.
**Don't miss:** The Varnish at Cole's is an in-house speakeasy with 11 booths that can be accessed through a hidden door marked by a tiny framed picture of a cocktail glass.
**Filmed here:** *Forrest Gump, L.A. Confidential, Mad Men*
**Join the crowd:** *118 E. 6th St., Los Angeles, 213/622–4049*

**CLIFTON'S REPUBLIC** (1931)
**Noteworthy for:** This historical cafeteria/playground featuring a giant redwood tree in the center and intimidating wildlife taxidermy throughout, serves tasty comfort food and houses three lively bars: the Monarch, the Gothic, and the Pacific Seas.
**Signature drink:** The Mind Eraser at the Tiki bar; El Presidio at the Monarch; the Hyperion at The Gothic Bar (careful—this one's strong).
**Claim to fame:** Clifton's whimsical forest-themed dining area inspired Walt Disney to create Disneyland.

Chez Jay

Harvelle's

Kibitz Room

Dresden Restaurant

**Don't miss:** The 40's-era Tiki Bar. Located at the top of a secret stairway, it features deliciously strong drinks, dancing cigarette girls and the occasional appearance of a sequined mermaid.

### FROLIC ROOM (1935)
**Noteworthy for:** This Hollywood favorite next door to the famed Pantages Theater has served actors and writers from Elizabeth Short to Charles Bukowski.

**Signature drink:** Cheap Budweiser ($2.75 during happy hour)

**Celeb clientele:** Kiefer Sutherland

**Don't miss:** A bowl of popcorn from the old-fashioned machine; the Hirschfeld mural depicting Marilyn Monroe, Charlie Chaplin, Louis Armstrong, Frank Sinatra, and others.

**Filmed here:** *L.A. Confidential, Southland*

**Join the crowd:** *6245 Hollywood Blvd., Los Angeles, 323/462–5890*

### HARVELLE'S (1931)
**Noteworthy for:** Located one block off the Third Street Promenade, this dark and sexy jazz bar is said to be the oldest live music venue on the Westside.

**Signature drink:** The Deadly Sins martini menu offers house made mixes named after the seven sins, from Pride to Lust.

**Don't miss:** The Toledo Show is a pulse-quickening weekly burlesque-and-jazz performance on Sunday nights.

**Join the crowd:** *1432 4th St., Santa Monica, 310/395–1676.*

### THE KIBITZ ROOM AT CANTER'S DELI (1961)
**Noteworthy for:** Adjacent to the famous Canter's Deli, which opened in 1948, this Fairfax District nightspot is definitely a dive bar, but that doesn't keep the A-listers away. Joni Mitchell, Jakob Dylan, and Fiona Apple have all played here.

**Signature drink:** Cheap beer

**Celeb clientele:** Jim Morrison, Frank Zappa, Juliette Lewis, Julia Roberts, Javier Bardem, Penélope Cruz

In golden days

Pastrami at Canter's

La Dolce Vita

**Don't miss:** The decor is pure retro 1960s, including vinyl booths and a fall-leaf motif on the ceiling.
**Filmed here:** *I Ought to Be in Pictures, Entourage, Curb Your Enthusiasm, Sunset Strip, Enemy of the State, What's Eating Gilbert Grape*
**Join the crowd:** *419 N. Fairfax Ave., Los Angeles, 323/651–2030.*

### DOLCE VITA (1966)

**Noteworthy for:** Located in tony Beverly Hills, this staple for northern Italian has a classy clubhouse atmosphere, round leather booths, white tablecloths, and exposed-brick walls.
**Signature drink:** Martini
**Celeb clientele:** Members of the Rat Pack; several ex-presidents, including Ronald Reagan. The place prides itself on being a safe haven from pesky paparazzi.
**Don't miss:** The burgundy-hued round leather booths.
**Join the crowd:** *9785 Santa Monica Blvd., Los Angeles, 310/278–1845*

### MUSSO & FRANK GRILL (1919)

**Noteworthy for:** This swanky old-timer is called the oldest bar in Hollywood. While that title may spark jealousy among some of its Tinseltown counterparts, there is no doubt that this famed grill conjures Hollywood's halcyon days with its authentic '30s-era decor—and serves a mean martini.
**Signature drink:** The Mean Martini
**Celeb clientele:** Charlie Chaplin, Greta Garbo, Ernest Hemingway, F. Scott Fitzgerald, Marilyn Monroe
**Don't miss:** The red tuxedo-clad waiters are famous in their own right; some have been at the restaurant for more than 40 years.
**Filmed here:** *Ocean's Eleven, Charlie's Angels 2, Mad Men*
**Join the crowd:** *6667 Hollywood Blvd., Los Angeles, 323/467–7788*

## CLUBS

**Rage.** The various events at this gay bar and dance club draw different crowds—show queens for Broadway musical sing-alongs, drag queens (and more show queens) for the Dreamgirls Revue, half-nude chiseled-bodied men for Fetch Tuesdays and Thursday Night College Night. There's lots of eye candy, even more so on weekends. ✉ *8911 Santa Monica Blvd., West Hollywood* ☎ *310/652–7055* ⊕ *www.rage-nightclub.com.*

## COMEDY

**Comedy Store.** Three stages give seasoned and unseasoned comedians a place to perform and try out new material, with performers such as Louis C.K. and Sarah Silverman dropping by just for fun. The front bar along Sunset Boulevard is a popular hangout after or between shows, oftentimes with that night's comedians mingling with fans. ✉ *8433 Sunset Blvd., West Hollywood* ☎ *323/650–6268* ⊕ *www.thecomedystore.com.*

**Laugh Factory.** Top stand-up comics appear at this Sunset Boulevard mainstay, often working out the kinks in new material in advance of national tours. Stars such as Kevin Hart and Tim Allen sometimes drop by unannounced, and Kevin Nealon puts on a monthly show. Midnight Madness on the weekends is extremely popular, with comics performing more daring sets. ✉ *8001 W. Sunset Blvd., West Hollywood* ☎ *323/656–1336* ⊕ *www.laughfactory.com* ✉ *$20.*

## MUSIC

Fodor's Choice ★ **El Rey Theater.** This former movie house from the 1930s has been given a second life as a live music venue. Legends and rising stars grace the stage of El Rey. The Pixies and Ringo Starr have both stopped here while on tour. ✉ *5515 Wilshire Blvd., West Hollywood* ☎ *323/936–6400* ⊕ *www.theelrey.com.*

**The Troubadour.** The intimate vibe of the Troubadour helps make this club a favorite with music fans. Around since 1957, this venue has a storied past. These days, the eclectic lineup is still attracting the crowds, with the focus mostly on rock, indie, and folk music. Those looking for drinks can imbibe to their heart's content at the adjacent bar. ✉ *9081 Santa Monica Blvd., West Hollywood* ⊕ *www.troubadour.com.*

**Viper Room.** This rock club on the edge of the Sunset Strip has been around for more than 20 years and is famously known as the site of much controversial Hollywood history. Today the venue books rising alt-rock acts, and covers typically range from $5 to $10. ✉ *8852 W. Sunset Blvd., West Hollywood* ☎ *310/358–1881* ⊕ *www.viperroom.com.*

**Whisky A Go Go.** The hard-core metal and rock scene is alive and well at the legendary Whisky A Go Go (the full name includes the prefix "World Famous"), where Janis Joplin, Led Zeppelin, Alice Cooper, Van Halen, the Doors (they were the house band for a short stint), and Frank Zappa have all played. On the Strip for more than five decades, they book both underground acts, and huge names in rock. ☒ *8901 Sunset Blvd., West Hollywood* ☎ *310/652–4202* ⊕ *www.whiskyagogo.com.*

# KOREATOWN

Known primarily for its boundless Korean barbecue spots and karaoke, this segment of Central L.A. off the beaten path is also home to unique must-visit bars.

## BARS AND LOUNGES

**Dan Sung Sa.** Step through the curtained entrance and back in time to 1970s Korea at Dan Sung Sa, which gained wider popularity after Anthony Bourdain paid a visit. At this quirky time-capsule bar, wood-block menus feature roughly 100 small eats. You'll see much that looks familiar, but fortune favors the bold. Take a chance on corn cheese, or try the *makgeolli*: a boozy Korean rice drink you sip from a bowl. It pairs perfectly with good conversation and snacking all night long. ☒ *3317 W. 6th St.* ☎ *213/487–9100.*

Fodor's Choice
★ **HMS Bounty.** This super-kitschy nautical-themed bar in the heart of Koreatown offers drink specials and food at prices that will make you swoon. Make sure you speak to the grandmotherly Korean bartender—introduce yourself once and she'll never forget your name and order. ☒ *3357 Wilshire Blvd.* ☎ *213/385–7275* ⊕ *www.thehmsbounty.com.*

**The Prince.** *Mad Men* and *New Girl* both had multiple scenes filmed in this Old Hollywood relic, which dates back to the early 1900s. The Prince is trimmed with vintage fabric wallpaper and bedecked with a stately mahogany bar; the grand piano waits in the wings. Squire lamps punctuate red leather booths where you can enjoy Korean fare and standard cocktails, wine, and beer. ☒ *3198 W. 7th St.* ☎ *213/389–1586* ⊕ *theprincela.com.*

# SANTA MONICA AND THE BEACHES

In Santa Monica, the focus of nightlife shifts toward more live music, historic dives, and any space that has a view of the ocean.

## SANTA MONICA

### BARS AND LOUNGES

FAMILY **Chez Jay.** Around since 1959, this dive bar continues to be a well-loved place in Santa Monica. Everyone from the young to the old (including families) frequents this historical landmark. It's a charming place, from the well-worn booths with their red checkered tablecloths to the ship's wheel near the door. ✉ *1657 Ocean Ave., Santa Monica* ☎ *310/395–1741* ⊕ *www.chezjays.com.*

**The Galley.** Santa Monica's oldest restaurant and bar, The Galley's nautical theme is consistent inside and out: the boatlike exterior features wavy blue neon lights and porthole windows; inside, fishing nets and anchors adorn the walls, and the whole place is laglow with colorful string lights. Most patrons tend to crowd the center bar, with the more dinner-oriented folks frequenting the booths. ✉ *2442 Main St., Santa Monica* ☎ *310/452–1934.*

### MUSIC

**Harvelle's.** The focus of this bar and music club is on jazz, blues, and soul. The club is small, with an even smaller checkerboard dance floor. Reserve tables in advance at this Westside establishment; order a martini off the Deadly Sins menu, and catch a burlesque show on Sunday night. ✉ *1432 4th St., Santa Monica* ☎ *310/395–1676* ⊕ *www.harvelles.com.*

## VENICE

### BARS AND LOUNGES

**The Brig.** This charming bar has its pluses (interesting drinks, talented DJs) and minuses (ugh, parking), but is worth a look if you're in the area. There's always a food truck around, and the bar's fine with you bringing in outside food. ✉ *1515 Abbot Kinney Blvd., Venice* ☎ *310/399–7537* ⊕ *www.thebrig.com.*

**The Otheroom.** With a focus on craft beers and fine wines, this bar has become a favorite local hangout. The space is welcoming, especially with its large front windows thrown open on particularly gorgeous days. The bar doesn't serve food, but allows patrons to bring their own—a wise decision, given the number of food trucks in the area. ✉ *1201 Abbot Kinney Blvd., Venice* ☎ *310/396–6230* ⊕ *www.theotheroom.net.*

## MALIBU

### BARS AND LOUNGES

FAMILY **Duke's Barefoot Bar.** With a clear view of the horizon from almost everywhere, a sunset drink at Duke's Barefoot Bar is how most beachgoers like to end their day. The entertainment is in keeping with the bar's theme, with Hawaiian dancers as well as live music by Hawaiian artists occupying the calendar. The menu features Korean steak street tacos, and a buffet in the afternoon with locally grown Hawaiian produce. Just don't expect beach-bum prices. ✉ *21150 Pacific Coast Hwy., Malibu* ☎ *310/317–0777* ⊕ *www.dukesmalibu.com.*

**Moonshadows.** This outdoor lounge attracts customers with its modern look and views of the ocean. DJs are constantly spinning lounge music in the background, and there's never a cover charge. ✉ *20356 Pacific Coast Hwy., Malibu* ☎ *310/456–3010* ⊕ *www.moonshadowsmalibu.com.*

# HERMOSA BEACH

## BARS AND LOUNGES

**Lighthouse Cafe.** Featured in *La La Land*, the 2016 musical set in Los Angeles, this onetime jazz bistro now offers a wide range of live entertainment, adding reggae and karaoke (either backed by a DJ or a live band, depending on when you go), to the repertoire. There's a $5 cover charge on Friday and Saturday after 9 pm, and brunch and live music all day on Saturday and Sunday. ✉ *30 Pier Ave., Hermosa Beach* ☎ *310/376–9833* ⊕ *www.thelighthousecafe.net.*

**Underground Pub and Grill.** Throw darts, shoot pool, or play shuffleboard at this British pub (its name refers to London's subway system), or watch a game on one of the many monitors. ✉ *1334 Hermosa Ave., Hermosa Beach* ☎ *310/318–3818* ⊕ *www.undergroundpubandgrill.com.*

# PERFORMING
# ARTS

Updated by
Alene Dawson

The art scene in Los Angeles extends beyond the screen and onto the stage. A place of artistic innovation and history, one can discover new and challenging theatrical works across L.A. stages, while the city still maintains a respect for tradition with its restored theaters and classic plays. See live music at impeccably designed amphitheaters like the Hollywood Bowl; listen in on captivating lectures by authors and directors at various intimate spaces. An homage to its roots as a filmmaking mecca, you can also stumble across retrospectives and rare screenings in movie theaters all over the city, often followed by Q&As with the cast.

L.A.'s art scene is varied, and caters to all budgets and tastes. East West Players at the David Henry Hwang Theatre focuses on Asian-American-themed plays, and if an opera at the Dorothy Chandler Pavilion seems out of your price range, Actors' Gang in Culver City offers a free Shakespeare play in Media Park in the summer. The Independent Theatre Company hosts a free Shakespeare festival in Griffith Park, also during summer.

## PLANNER

### WHERE TO GET INFORMATION
To find up-to-date listings of noteworthy local events, ⊕ *www.la.com*, ⊕ *www.experiencela.com*, and ⊕ *www.discoverlosangeles.com* are all great resources. LAist (⊕ *laist.com*) offers a list of standout events throughout the week. The free alternative publication *LA Weekly* (⊕ *www.laweekly.com*) is issued every Thursday and has a full calendar of events.

## BEST PERFORMING ARTS EXPERIENCES

**Head Outdoors for a Summer Event.** Outdoor entertainment is what L.A. summers are all about, from concerts at the open-air Greek Theatre or Hollywood Bowl, to Friday Night Sing-Alongs in the outdoor garden of the Walt Disney Concert Hall at the Music Center, and picnics during a movie screening at Hollywood Forever Cemetery (⊕ *www.cinespia.org*).

**Watch a Classic Movie.** Theaters and venues throughout the city, like the New Beverly (owned by director Quentin Tarantino), show classic retrospectives all year long.

**Visit a Smaller Theater.** Although it's easy to be wowed by performances at large venues, like the Center Theatre Group, it's the smaller theaters that are getting braver and bolder with their original plays or reworked classics—oftentimes at a cheaper price, too.

# CONCERTS

Hear top-notch live musical performances at restored and new state-of-the-art concert halls across the city.

## MAJOR CONCERT HALLS

**Fodor's**Choice ★ **Dorothy Chandler Pavilion.** Though half a century old, this theater maintains the glamour of its early years, richly decorated with crystal chandeliers and classical theatrical drapes. Part of the Los Angeles Music Center, a large portion of programming is made up of dance and ballet performances, like Shen Yun Performing Arts, a large production showcasing classical Chinese dance and music. Ticket-holders can attend free talks that take place an hour before opera performances. ■ TIP→ Reservations for the talks aren't required, but it's wise to arrive early as space is limited. ⊠ *135 N. Grand Ave., Downtown* ☎ *213/972–7211* ⊕ *www.musiccenter.org.*

**Greek Theatre.** With a robust lineup from May through November, acts such as Beck, John Legend, and Chicago have all graced the stage at this scenic outdoor venue. The 5,900-capacity amphitheater is at the base of Griffith Park, and you may want to make a day of it by hiking or stargazing beforehand. There is usually slow, preshow traffic on concert nights, but it'll give you a chance to take in the beautiful park foliage and homes in the Hollywood Hills. Paid lots are available for parking, but wear comfortable shoes and expect to walk, as some lots are fairly far from the theater. Or, park and enjoy cocktails in the trendy and chic Los Feliz neighborhood below before a show, then walk up to the venue. ⊠ *2700 N. Vermont Ave., Los Feliz* ☎ *323/665–5857* ⊕ *www.greektheatrela.com.*

**Fodor's**Choice ★ **Hollywood Bowl.** For those seeking a quintessential Los Angeles experience, a concert on a summer night at the Bowl, the city's iconic outdoor venue, is unsurpassed. The Bowl has presented world-class performers since it opened in 1920. The L.A. Philharmonic plays here from June to September; its performances and other events draw large crowds. Parking is limited near the venue, but there are additional

8

remote parking locations serviced by shuttles. You can bring food and drink to any event, which Angelenos often do, though you can only bring alcohol when the LA Phil, as the orchestra is known, is performing. (Bars sell alcohol at all events, and there are dining options.) It's wise to bring a jacket even if daytime temperatures have been warm—the Bowl can get quite chilly at night. ■TIP➔ **Visitors can sometimes watch the LA Phil practice for free, usually on a weekday; call ahead for times.** ✉ *2301 Highland Ave., Hollywood* ☎ *323/850–2000* ⊕ *www. hollywoodbowl.com.*

**Microsoft Theatre.** Formerly known as the Nokia Theatre L.A., the Microsoft Theatre is host to a variety of concerts and big-name awards shows—the Emmys, American Music Awards, BET Awards, and the ESPYs—this theater and the surrounding L.A. Live complex are a draw for those looking for a fun night out. The building's emphasis on acoustics and versatile seating arrangements means that all the seats are good, whether you're at an intimate Neil Young concert or the People's Choice Awards. Outside, the L.A. Live complex hosts restaurants and attractions, including the Grammy Museum, to keep patrons entertained before and after shows (though it's open whether or not there's a performance). ✉ *777 Chick Hearn Ct., Downtown* ☎ *213/763–6030* ⊕ *www.nokiatheatrelalive.com.*

**Shrine Auditorium.** Since opening in 1926, the auditorium has hosted nearly every major awards show at one point or another. Today, the venue and adjacent Expo Hall hosts performers like Radiohead, and festivals, including Tenacious D's comedy/music extravaganza, Festival Supreme, in October. The Shrine's Moorish Revival–style architecture is a spectacle all its own. ✉ *665 W. Jefferson Blvd., Downtown* ☎ *213/748–5116* ⊕ *www.shrineauditorium.com.*

**Wiltern Theater.** Built in 1931, this historical art deco landmark, named for its location at the intersection of Wilshire Boulevard and Western Avenue, serves mainly as a space for music (it's a top destination for touring musicians), but other live entertainment can be seen here as well, including comedy and dance. The main floor is standing room only for most shows, but there are some seating areas available if desired. ✉ *3790 Wilshire Blvd.* ☎ *213/388–1400* ⊕ *www.wiltern.com.*

# FILM

Movie-watching is deeply embedded in L.A.'s culture, and here it's not just a pastime, it's an event. It's easy to find screenings that host post-film discussions with the actors or directors, even for big-budget films. A number of the theaters on this list are attractions themselves, with restorations that honor the history of the buildings. Whether it's a first-run film or a revival, your night out will be an elevated moviegoing experience that's unique to L.A.

The Los Angeles Master Chorale onstage at the Walt Disney Concert Hall

## ART AND REVIVAL HOUSES

**The American Cinemathèque at the Aero and Egyptian Theatres.** American Cinemathèque screens classic and independent films at two theaters, the Aero and the Egyptian. Expect everything from Hitchcock thrillers, to anime by Hayao Miyazaki, plus occasional Q&A sessions with directors and actors following film screenings. The Egyptian Theatre in Hollywood has the distinction of hosting the first-ever movie premiere when it opened back in 1922. Its ornate courtyard and columns have been restored to preserve the building's history. The Aero Theatre in Santa Monica opened in 1940. ✉ *6712 Hollywood Blvd., Hollywood* ☎ *323/466–3456* ⊕ *www.americancinematheque.com.*

**Cinefamily at The Silent Movie Theatre.** Although the name may imply that only silent movies are shown here, this theater also has a packed schedule of film screenings, from rare to indie to foreign. Regular events include Doug Benson's Movie Interruption, Haunted Hangovers (early matinees paired with coffee or mimosas on weekends leading up to Halloween), and The Silent Treatment—pre–sound era films that run on the second Saturday of every month (though it's best to check the calendar for changes). Also expect special guests, live music, dance parties, and potlucks. ✉ *611 N. Fairfax Ave., Fairfax District* ☎ *323/655–2510* ⊕ *www.cinefamily.org.*

**New Beverly Cinema.** When Oscar-winning filmmaker Quentin Tarantino became the owner and head programmer of the space, which originally opened in 1978, he ensured that the New Beverly would show only 35mm film. Classic films and '80s and '90s throwbacks are the draw here, along with a low admission price for daily double features. ✉ *7165 Beverly Blvd., Hollywood* ☎ *323/938–4038* ⊕ *www.thenewbev.com.*

**Nuart.** Foreign, indie, documentaries, classics, recent releases, Oscar short-film screenings—there's not much the Nuart doesn't show. Midnight showings, like the long-running *Rocky Horror Picture Show* with a live "shadow cast" on Saturday nights, continue to bring in locals. Q&A sessions with directors and actors also happen here from time to time. ⊠ *11272 Santa Monica Blvd., West L.A.* ☎ *310/473–8530* ⊕ *www.landmarktheatres.com/los-angeles/nuart-theatre.*

## ESSENTIAL LOS ANGELES CINEMAS

Fodor's Choice
★
**ArcLight.** This big multiplex includes the historic Cinerama Dome, that impossible-to-miss golf ball–looking structure on Sunset Boulevard, which was built in 1963. Like many L.A. theaters, the ArcLight has assigned seating (you will be asked to select seats when purchasing tickets). The complex is a one-stop shop with a parking garage, shopping area, restaurant, and in-house bar. The events calendar is worth paying attention to, as directors and actors often drop by to chat with audiences. Amy Adams and Samuel L. Jackson, for example, have both made time for post-screening Q&As. Movies here can be pricey (ranging from around $18–$25), but the theater shows just about every new release. ■TIP→ Evening shows on the weekend feature "21+" shows, during which moviegoers can bring alcoholic beverages into the screening rooms. ⊠ *6360 Sunset Blvd., Hollywood* ☎ *323/464–4226* ⊕ *www.arclightcinemas.com.*

FAMILY
**El Capitan Theatre.** The theater packs in as much preshow entertainment as it can, such as an immersive light-and-projection show before movies such as *Beauty and the Beast.* There's also an on-site organ player to entertain folks as they find their seats. VIP tickets are available, and include reserved seating, popcorn, and a drink. ⊠ *6838 Hollywood Blvd., Hollywood* ☎ *323/467–7674* ⊕ *elcapitan.go.com.*

**Vista Theater.** Beyond offering first-run films, this vintage theater established in 1923 features a unique, restored Egyptian-style interior—the hieroglyphic details, busts, and red velvet curtains all add to the atmosphere. Other bragging points include larger-than-usual legroom and affordable ticket prices; even shows at night and on weekends cost less than $10. Currently tickets are only available at the box office. Be sure to visit the Los Feliz 3, the Vista's sister theater, just down the road on Vermont Avenue. ⊠ *4473 Sunset Dr., Los Feliz* ☎ *323/660–6639* ⊕ *www.vintagecinemas.com/vista.*

# THEATER

The Los Angeles theater scene is still living under the shadow of Broadway, but places like Pantages Theatre in Hollywood rival even some of the best New York stages.

**LA Stage Tix.** LA Stage Alliance sells discounted tickets to performances all over the city, and you can read show descriptions on their website. ☎ *213/614–0556* ⊕ *www.lastagetix.com.*

## MAJOR THEATERS

**Ahmanson Theatre.** The largest of L.A.'s Center Group's three theaters, Ahmanson Theatre presents larger-scale classic revivals, dramas, musicals, and comedies like *Into the Woods,* that are either going to, or coming from Broadway and the West End. The ambience is a theater-lover's delight. ⊠ *135 N. Grand Ave., Downtown* ☎ *213/628–2772* ⊕ *www.centertheatregroup.org.*

**Center for the Art of Performance at UCLA.** An array of arresting events happens here, from the Los Angeles Chamber Orchestra, to storytelling series The Moth, to performances by activist artists Silencio Blanco, and more. The Los Angeles Ballet is one of the frequent guests here. ⊠ *Royce Hall, 340 Royce Dr.* ☎ *310/825–4401* ⊕ *cap.ucla.edu.*

**Center Theatre Group.** Celebrating their 50th anniversary, Center Theatre Group is comprised of three venues: The Ahmanson and the Taper (both at the Music Center campus Downtown), and the Kirk Douglas Theatre in Culver City. They show an array of productions, from the world premiere of newcomer Nigerian playwright Ngozi Anyanwu's *Good Grief,* to touring productions of Broadway hits like *Jersey Boys.* ⊠ *135 N. Grand Ave., Downtown* ☎ *213/972–7211* ⊕ *www.centertheatregroup.org.*

**Geffen Playhouse.** Well-known actors are often on the bill at the Geffen, and plays by established playwrights, such as Neil LaBute and Lynn Nottage, happen regularly. With two stages hosting world premieres and critically acclaimed works, there's always something compelling to watch. ■ TIP→ **Free events are frequently put on for ticket holders, including Wine Down Sundays, which features music and wine sampling before evening shows.** ⊠ *10886 Le Conte Ave., Westwood* ☎ *310/208–5454* ⊕ *www.geffenplayhouse.com.*

**Kirk Douglas Theatre.** This theater, located in a walkable Culver City neighborhood (close to cocktail bars and trendy restaurants), stages modern works and world premieres. The smallest venue of the group at 317 seats, the theater also hosts intimate workshops and readings. ⊠ *9820 W. Washington Blvd., Culver City* ☎ *213/628–2772* ⊕ *www.centertheatregroup.org.*

**Los Angeles Ballet.** Going on its 11th year presenting world-class productions, Los Angeles Ballet (LAB), the city's one and only professional classical ballet company, performs at a number of venues across the city, showcasing both classical and modern ballet. ☎ *310/998–7782* ⊕ *www.losangelesballet.org.*

**Mark Taper Forum.** Both dramas and comedies dominate the stage at the Mark Taper Forum, next door to the Ahmanson Theatre in Downtown. Plenty of shows that premiered here have gone on to Broadway and off-Broadway theaters (a number of Pulitzer Prize–winning plays have also been developed here). ⊠ *135 N. Grand Ave., Downtown* ☎ *213/628–2772* ⊕ *www.centertheatregroup.org.*

**Pantages Theatre.** For the grand-scale theatrics of a Broadway show, such as *Hamilton* and *The Book of Mormon,* the 2,703-seat Pantages Theatre (the last theater built by Greek-American vaudeville

8

producer Alexander Pantages), lights up Hollywood Boulevard on show nights, when lines of excited patrons extend down the block. ✉ *6233 Hollywood Blvd., Hollywood* ☎ *800/982–2787* ⊕ *www.hollywoodpantages.com.*

**Ricardo Montalbán Theatre.** Plays, musicals, and concerts all happen at this midsize theater, mostly focusing on Latin culture. When the weather warms up, they host the Rooftop Cinema Club, where you can watch a flick on the roof (they give out blankets on cold nights), indulge at the snack bar, and take in views of Hollywood. ✉ *1615 N. Vine St., Hollywood* ☎ *323/871–2420* ⊕ *www.themontalban.com.*

**Saban Theatre.** This historic art deco theater in Beverly Hills plays host to rock and soul artists and legends, as well as comedy shows. ✉ *8440 Wilshire Blvd., Beverly Hills* ☎ *323/655–0111* ⊕ *www.sabantheatre.org.*

## SMALLER THEATERS

**The Actors' Gang.** Socially conscious, unconventional, and politically themed shows are the focus here. Helmed by artistic director Tim Robbins (who was also one of its founders in 1981), the Actors' Gang also has educational and outreach programs to benefit local students and the community. Their Prison Project initiative, for example, conducts acting workshops at California state prisons. Famous actors are also known to make cameos at the theater. ■ TIP➔ In summer, the Actors' Gang offers adaptations of Shakespeare for free in Media Park. Call or check the website for the schedule. ✉ *9070 Venice Blvd., Culver City* ☎ *310/838–4264* ⊕ *www.theactorsgang.com.*

FAMILY **Bob Baker Marionette Theater.** Trained puppeteer and marionette manufacturer Bob Baker purchased this theater on the outer edges of Downtown Los Angeles (a brightly painted mural will catch your eye from the road) in 1961. Baker died at age 90 in 2014, but his memory lives on at this cultural landmark, and one of the country's longest-running puppet theaters. An annual carnival, as well as galas, screenings presented by Cinefamily, and of course marionette performances, are held throughout the year (they also host birthday parties). Purchase tickets online or over the phone. ✉ *1345 W. 1st St., at Glendale Blvd., Downtown* ☎ *213/250–9995* ⊕ *www.bobbakermarionettetheater.com.*

**David Henry Hwang Theatre at the Union Center for the Arts.** Plays at this Little Tokyo theater focus on the Asian-American experience and features an Asian-American cast. Their Theatre for Youth Program is a traveling production that promotes racial tolerance and understanding among students. It is also home to the David Henry Hwang Writers Institute. ✉ *120 Judge John Aiso St., Little Tokyo* ☎ *213/625–7000* ⊕ *www.eastwestplayers.org.*

**Deaf West Theatre.** All works at this theater, which is rapidly garnering critical attention (performers from their breakout production of *Spring Awakening* were even asked to perform at the 2016 Tony Awards), are simultaneously spoken (or sung) as well as signed by a sign-language interpreter. ✉ *5112 Lankershim Blvd., North Hollywood* ☎ *818/762–2998* ⊕ *www.deafwest.org.*

**Fountain Theatre.** The multiple award–winning (Los Angeles Drama Critics Circle, NAACP Theater Awards, Ovation Award, to name a few) Fountain Theatre is committed to multiethnic theater and dance. Although their 80-seat venue may be intimate, they are powerhouses at producing original plays in addition to revivals. ✉ *5060 Fountain Ave., Hollywood* ☎ *323/663–1525* ⊕ *www.fountaintheatre.com.*

**Fremont Centre Theatre.** This theater centers on original material and world premieres with professional actors year-round. The small venue is known for its dedication to diversity and its inclusive atmosphere, with "talkbacks" (Q&As between actors and audience members) after certain shows. Ray Bradbury regularly produced shows here for five years before his death in 2012, including a stage adaptation of *Fahrenheit 451.* ✉ *1000 Fremont Ave., South Pasadena* ☎ *626/441–5977* ⊕ *www.fremontcentretheatre.com.*

**Hudson Theatres.** This theater/café/art gallery hosts a variety of local and traveling companies, and shows span all genres. Nestled among a number of small-scale theaters on Theatre Row in Hollywood, awards and nominations include those from the Los Angeles Drama Critic's Circle, Ovations, NAACP, GLAADMEDIA, and DramaLogue. ✉ *6539 Santa Monica Blvd., Hollywood* ☎ *323/856–4249* ⊕ *www.hudsontheatre.com.*

**Odyssey Theatre.** Odyssey Theatre presents largely traditional dramas in an intimate space, typically with astute direction and powerful acting. They also produce contemporary, experimental plays (or thoughtful explorations of the classics) throughout the season. ✉ *2055 S. Sepulveda Blvd., West L.A.* ☎ *310/477–2055* ⊕ *www.odysseytheatre.com.*

**The Pasadena Playhouse.** Exceptional plays and musicals, occasionally featuring known TV and movie actors, are what this theater is mostly known for. Although not all of the plays are first-run works, their theater program, HOTHOUSE at The Playhouse, helps to develop original plays. The playhouse also holds the title of official state theater of California. Tours of the venue are available by appointment. ✉ *39 S. El Molino Ave., Pasadena* ☎ *626/356–7529* ⊕ *www.pasadenaplayhouse.org.*

**The REDCAT (Roy and Edna Disney/Cal Arts Theater).** Located inside the Walt Disney Concert Hall, this theater serves as a space for innovative performance and visual art. The gallery features changing art installations. Tickets are reasonably priced at $25 and under for most events. ✉ *631 W. 2nd St., Downtown* ☎ *213/237–2800* ⊕ *www.redcat.org.*

FAMILY **Santa Monica Playhouse.** Housing three theaters, this venue brings a number of original plays, touring companies, poetry readings, spoken word events, and revival shows to the stage. Their Family Theatre Musical Matinee Series features family-friendly reworked classic plays. A number of educational programs and workshops are available for all ages. ✉ *1211 4th St., Santa Monica* ☎ *310/394–9779* ⊕ *www.santamonicaplayhouse.com.*

**Theatre of NOTE.** With an emphasis on experimental plays by cutting-edge (albeit lesser-known) authors, this theater produces unique works and encourages new artists through its Young Writers Program, and NOTEworthy, a staged reading series where playwrights can get feedback about their material from the audience. ✉ *1517 N. Cahuenga Blvd., Hollywood* ☎ *323/856–8611* ⊕ *www.theatreofnote.com.*

FAMILY **Theatre West.** Performing classic plays and new works year-round, this theater co-op has been in operation since 1962 and has won awards for its work over the years. **Storybook Theatre** performs interactive plays for ages three through nine. ⊠ *3333 Cahuenga Blvd. W, Hollywood* ☎ *323/851–7977 Theatre West, 818/761–2203* ⊕ *www.theatrewest.org.*

## THEATER ENSEMBLES

**Billy Wilder Theater.** Specializing in restored archival film, the Billy Wilder Theater, home of the UCLA Film & Television Archive, presents a number of acclaimed screenings, including both silent and foreign films. The Hammer Museum produces its own events for the theater, including readings, lectures, and conversations with artists. Authors Jonathan Lethem and Roxane Gay, and director David Lynch have all made appearances. ■TIP➜ Hammer Museum programs are free; screenings by the UCLA Film & Television Archive have charged admission with a ticket. ⊠ *10899 Wilshire Blvd.* ☎ *310/206–8013 UCLA Film & Television Archive, 310/443–7074 Hammer Museum* ⊕ *www.cinema.ucla.edu.*

**Cornerstone Theater Company.** This traveling theater has various "cycles" or series, all designed to address and work towards solutions for socioeconomic issues in urban and rural communities. Their current "Hunger Cycle" presents world premiere plays throughout California over the course of six years, and examines everything from food equity to food addiction, while engaging members of the community. They perform in unconventional venues across the region, so check the website for locations. ⊠ *708 Traction Ave., Downtown* ☎ *213/613–1700* ⊕ *www. cornerstonetheater.org.*

Fodor's Choice ★ **Walt Disney Concert Hall.** One of the architectural wonders of Los Angeles, the 2,265-seat hall is a sculptural monument of gleaming, curved steel designed by Frank Gehry. It's part of a complex that includes a public park, gardens, shops, and two outdoor amphitheaters, one of them atop the concert hall. The acoustically superlative venue is the home of the city's premier orchestra, the Los Angeles Philharmonic, whose music director, Gustavo Dudamel, is an international celebrity in his own right. The orchestra's season runs from late September to early June, before they head to the Hollywood Bowl for the summer. The highly praised Los Angeles Master Chorale also performs here. Look for big-name acts such as Pink Martini during the off-season, and special holiday events like the Deck the Hall Holiday Sing-Along. ■TIP➜ Free 60-minute guided tours are offered on most days, and there are self-guided audio tours. ⊠ *111 S. Grand Ave., Downtown* ☎ *323/850–2000* ⊕ *www.laphil.org* ✉ *Tours free.*

9

# SHOPPING

Updated by
Ashley Tibbits

Los Angeles's close association to the rich and famous has long made it a major shopping destination, but in recent years the city has grown beyond just a locale for luxe clothing and accessories—although high-end goods will always be a cornerstone of L.A.'s retail scene. With a wealth of stellar vintage spots, purveyors of affordable on-the-pulse products, and an ever-growing number shops selling local, artisanal goods, there is truly something for every type of spender here.

No matter what it is you're shopping for, L.A.'s consistently sunny and warm weather also means you can often hunt for wares in the open air, whether it be at a flea market full of hidden treasures, or a street lined with boutiques to explore. As you stroll, good eateries are never too far away, and you can always find somewhere delicious to dine and covertly star-watch.

If in fact you are in the celebrity-studded city to catch a glimpse of a famous face or two, you may want to start at their mecca, Beverly Hills, where a bevy of major designers' outposts and impeccably curated stores cater to upcale clientele.

After getting your fix there, you can hop into your car and absorb the city's other varied offerings, including down-and-dirty bargains in Downtown, dozens of well-designed boutiques lining Venice's famed Abbot Kinney Boulevard, or mint-condition vintage fashions in Los Feliz.

## DOWNTOWN

Downtown L.A. is dotted with ethnic neighborhoods (Olvera Street, Chinatown, Koreatown, Little Tokyo) and several large, open-air shopping venues (the Fashion District, the Flower Market, Grand Central Market, the Toy District, and the Jewelry District).

## TOP SHOPPING EXPERIENCES

**3rd Street and The Grove.** Stores on 3rd Street range from independent designer boutiques to chic houseware havens. Just blocks away, The Grove, an open-air shopping area, has brand-name stores, restaurants, the adjoining Farmers Market, and celebrity sighting.

**Main Street, Santa Monica.** Three blocks away from the ocean, this is the choice for easy Sunday shopping after stopping at the Farmers Market or before heading to Santa Monica Pier. You'll also spot some impressive street performers.

**Melrose Avenue, Melrose Place, and Nearby Robertson.** Come to this trendy row of shops to browse or buy unique fashion-forward finds.

**Rodeo Drive.** There are a surprising variety of shops that are reasonably priced on the surrounding streets—but Rodeo Drive is not to be missed for the quintessential Beverly Hills experience, even if you're only window-shopping.

**Sunset Boulevard in Silver Lake.** If you have a penchant for perfectly worn jeans and a countercultural vibe, this laid-back locale will suit your tastes. With its fashionably rough edges and dirty-chic clientele, Silver Lake is the edgy counterpart to more upscale Los Feliz.

It offers an urban bargain hunter's dream shopping experience if you know precisely what you're looking for (like diamonds and gems from the Jewelry District) or if you're willing to be tempted by unexpected finds (piñatas from Olvera Street, slippers from Chinatown, or lacquered chopsticks from Little Tokyo).

## BOOKS

**Fodor'sChoice** ★ **The Last Bookstore.** California's largest used and new book and record shop is a favorite for both book lovers and fans of a good photo op, thanks to elements like an archway created from curving towers of books, a peephole carved into the stacks, and an in-store vault devoted to horror texts. Aside from the awesome aesthetics, shoppers will love to get lost in the store's collection of affordable books, art, and music. ⊠ *453 S. Spring St., ground fl., Downtown* ☎ *213/488–0599* ⊕ *www.lastbookstorela.com.*

## CLOTHING

**Alchemy Works.** This beautifully curated shop specializes in goods by local brands including hats by Janessa Leone, jewelry by Gabriela Artigas, and clothing by Vivian Chan, much of which is decidedly contemporary and minimal, but everything in this shop is made with exceptional attention to craftsmanship. There's also an in-store Warby Parker Glass House, where shoppers can try on different styles by the affordable eyewear brand. Besides wearables, Alchemy Works also offers housewares, apothecary items, books and magazines, and more must-haves for modern design lovers. ⊠ *826 E. 3rd St., Downtown* ☎ *323/487–1497* ⊕ *www.alchemyworks.us.*

**Fodor's Choice** **Shareen.** This vintage mecca is a must-stop for any vintage-loving lady
★ (sorry, men are strictly forbidden here). A favorite for fashionable
brides-to-be, the massive, two-level warehouse space stocks mostly
dresses organized into racks like day wear, cocktail frocks, prom
dresses, '20s and '80s sequined pieces, and vintage bridal, but you can
also shop the house line of vintage-inspired modern red carpet and
bridal looks, and accessorize with separates (fur coats, bell bottoms,
blouses), slips, scarves, and gloves. Shy types should be aware that there
are no changing rooms; sling your stuff on one of the decorated beds or
chairs and be ready to bare it all—but this is a safe space, so have no
fear. ⊠ *1721 N. Spring St., Downtown* ⊕ *www.shareen.com.*

## HOME FURNISHINGS

**Hammer & Spear.** This brilliantly decorated shop also acts as a showroom
for the owners' interior design business. With dim, moody lighting, luxurious objets d'art (marble bookends, handmade stoneware vessels and
sculptures), and a seamless mix of modern and vintage furniture and
textiles, the space is an interior design junkie's fantasy realized. ⊠ *255
S. Santa Fe Ave., Suite 101, Downtown* ☎ *213/928–0997* ⊕ *www.ham-
merandspear.com.*

**Museum of Contemporary Art Store.** Besides prints and books that coordinate with the museum's exhibitions and permanent collection, this
gift shop offers apothecary items, modernist ceramics, and even toys
and games for children to appease any art lover. ⊠ *250 S. Grand Ave.,
Downtown* ☎ *213/621–1710* ⊕ *www.moca.org.*

**Poketo.** Those in search of design-happy goods including handmade
ceramics, jute rugs, and hanging lamps will have plenty to pick from
at this colorful boutique where cool, contemporary, often locally made
wares are the specialty. ⊠ *820 E. 3rd St., Downtown* ☎ *213/537–0751*
⊕ *www.poketo.com.*

## SHOPPING STREETS AND DISTRICTS

**Fashion District.** With the influx of emerging designers in this pocket
of Downtown, it's become much more than just a wholesale market.
Besides containing the plant paradise that is the Flower District as well
as the Fabric District, the neighborhood now boasts a bevy of boutiques
and cool coffee shops, thanks in part to the opening of the stylish Ace
Hotel. ⊠ *Roughly between I–10 and 7th St., and S. San Pedro and S.
Main Sts., Downtown* ⊕ *www.fashiondistrict.org.*

**Jewelry District.** Filled with bargain hunters, these crowded sidewalks
resemble a slice of Manhattan. While you can save big on everything
from wedding bands to sparkling belt buckles, the neighborhood
also offers several more upscale vendors for those in search of super-
special pieces. ⊠ *Between Olive St. and Broadway from 5th to 8th
St., Downtown.*

**Fodor's Choice** **Olvera Street.** Historic buildings line this redbrick walkway overhung
★ with grape vines. At dozens of clapboard stalls you can browse south-
of-the-border goods—leather sandals, woven blankets, and devotional

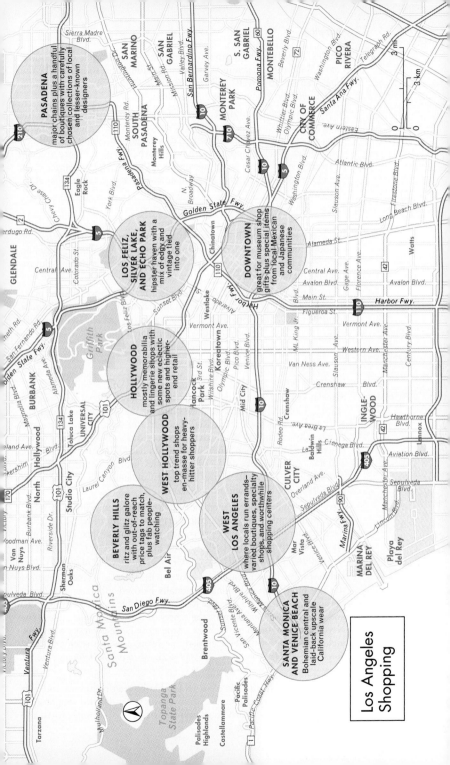

# Los Angeles Shopping

**PASADENA** major chains plus a handful of boutiques with carefully chosen collections of local and lesser-known designers

**LOS FELIZ, SILVER LAKE, AND ECHO PARK** hipster haven with a mix of edgy and vintage tied into one

**DOWNTOWN** great for museum shop gifts plus special items from local Mexican and Japanese communities

**HOLLYWOOD** mostly memorabilia and lingerie shops with some new eclectic spots and higher-end retail

**WEST HOLLYWOOD** top trend shops en-masse for heavy-hitter shoppers

**BEVERLY HILLS** ritz and glitz galore with out-of-reach price tags to match, plus fab people-watching

**WEST LOS ANGELES** where locals run errands—varied boutiques, specialty shops, and worthwhile shopping centers

**SANTA MONICA AND VENICE BEACH** Bohemian central and laid-back upscale California wear

candles, as well as cheap toys and souvenirs—and sample outstanding tacos. With the musicians and cafés providing the sound track, the area is constantly lively. ⊠ *Between Cesar Chavez Ave. and Arcadia St., Downtown* ⊕ *www.olvera-street.com.*

**Santee Alley.** Situated in the Fashion District, Santee Alley is known for back-alley deals on knock-offs of designer sunglasses, jewelry, handbags, shoes, and clothing. Be prepared to haggle, and don't lose sight of your wallet. Weekend crowds can be overwhelming, but there's plenty of street food to keep your energy up. ⊠ *Santee St. and Maple Ave. from Olympic Blvd. to 11th St., Downtown* ⊕ *www.thesanteealley.com.*

# HOLLYWOOD AND THE STUDIOS

Browsing Hollywood Boulevard, you'll find a mixed bag of offerings including lingerie, movie memorabilia, souvenirs, and wig shops, while the crowd-heavy Hollywood & Highland complex is home to more familiar retailers and eateries.

Outside the main drag, Hollywood has a few other pockets for picking up high-end goods, including La Brea Avenue, where you'll find a handful of design-happy shops. Take a leisurely stroll as you browse upscale clothing, antiques, and furniture stores.

## HOLLYWOOD

### BOOKS AND MUSIC

Fodor's Choice
★

**Amoeba Records.** Touted as the "World's Largest Independent Record Store," Amoeba is a playground for music-lovers, with a knowledgeable staff and a focus on local artists. Catch free in-store appearances and signings by artists and bands that play sold-out shows at venues down the road. There's a rich stock of new and used CDs and DVDs, LPs, and 45s, an impressive cache of collectibles, and walls filled with concert posters. ⊠ *6400 W. Sunset Blvd., at Cahuenga Blvd., Hollywood* ☎ *323/245–6400* ⊕ *www.amoeba.com.*

**Larry Edmunds Bookshop.** Cinephiles will love this iconic 70-plus-year-old shop that in addition to stocking tons of texts about motion picture history offers film fans the opportunity to pick up scripts, posters, and photographs from Hollywood's Golden Era to the present. ⊠ *6644 Hollywood Blvd., Hollywood* ☎ *323/463–3273* ⊕ *www.larryedmunds.com.*

**Meltdown.** The largest comic book store on the West Coast is a monument to titles ranging from the internationally beloved (*Batman, The Flash*) to the niche (*Snotgirl, Love and Rockets*). Graphic novels, toys, posters, and an art gallery supplement the scores of books and collectibles. The NerdMelt Showroom in the back of the store hosts a variety of events, including some of the best comedy performances in the city. ⊠ *7522 Sunset Blvd., Hollywood* ☎ *323/851–7223* ⊕ *www.meltcomics.com.*

### CLOTHING

**Jet Rag.** While Jet Rag is a go-to for Halloween costumes and TV/film wardrobes, it's also on local vintage-lovers' radars for sought-after items, like perfectly worn boots and leather jackets, denim cutoffs, and colorful cat-eye sunnies. The store takes its reasonable prices one step further on Sunday with an all-day parking lot sale where everything goes for $1; just be prepared to dig for the real finds. ✉ *825 N. La Brea Ave., Hollywood* ☎ *323/939–0528.*

**Lost & Found.** Specializing in emerging local and indie designers, this impeccably curated retailer keeps posh housewares such as lambswool throws, Brazilian soapstone cookware, and hand-thrown ceramics regularly in stock. But while you're there, don't sleep on the men's French shirting, modern bohemian clothing by Los Angeles' own Raquel Allegra, and luxurious baby blankets; there's something chic for everyone in the family. ✉ *6320 Yucca St., Hollywood* ☎ *323/856–5872* ⊕ *www.lostandfoundshop.com.*

### MALLS AND SHOPPING CENTERS

**Hollywood & Highland.** Full of designer shops (BCBGMaxAzria, Louis Vuitton) and chain stores (Victoria's Secret, Fossil, and Sephora), this entertainment complex is a huge tourist magnet. The design pays tribute to the city's film legacy, with a grand staircase leading up to a pair of three-story-tall stucco elephants, a nod to the 1916 movie *Intolerance*. Pause at the entrance arch, called Babylon Court, which frames a picture-perfect view of the Hollywood sign. On the second level, next to the Dolby Theatre, is a visitor information center with maps, brochures, and a multilingual staff. The streets nearby provide the setting for Sunday's Hollywood Farmers Market, where you're likely to spot a celebrity or two picking up fresh produce or stopping to pick up breakfast from the food vendors. ✉ *Hollywood Blvd. and Highland Ave., Hollywood* ☎ *323/817–0220* ⊕ *www.hollywoodandhighland.com.*

**Space 15 Twenty.** Trendy retailer Urban Outfitters' first concept store caters to creatives by combining a shopping experience with a cultural one by way of an adjacent space that regularly hosts art exhibitions, pop-ups featuring local makers, and other interactive events. The structure also houses popular eatery Umami Burger, a skate shop, an acclaimed hair salon, and more. ✉ *1520 N. Cahuenga Blvd., at Cahuenga Blvd., Hollywood* ☎ *323/465–1893* ⊕ *www.space15twenty.com.*

## STUDIO CITY

Although Studio City offers plenty of strip mall styles, this enclave not far from Hollywood gets a dose of sophistication from Tejunga Village, a leafy stretch between Tejunga Avenue and Moorpark Street filled with cafés and restaurants.

## BURBANK

It's not a major shopping destination, but Burbank has some offbeat shops that are well worth exploring. Given its close proximity to some major studios, the area has a few hidden gems for finding post-production castaways, like mint-condition designer and vintage clothing.

### CLOTHING

**It's a Wrap.** For nearly four decades, the wardrobe departments of movie and TV studios and production companies have been shipping clothes and props here daily. Besides scoring occasional gems from designers like Georgio Armani, Versace, Chanel, and more for between 35% and 95% off retail price, insiders flock here to get their hands on a piece of history. Good news for the serious collectors: your purchase includes the title and code from the production it was used on, so you can properly place each piece of memorabilia. ⊠ *3315 W. Magnolia Blvd., at California St., Burbank* ☎ *818/567–7366* ⊕ *www. itsawraphollywood.com.*

**Playclothes Vintage Fashions.** Productions including *Mad Men*, *Austin Powers*, and *Catch Me If You Can* (among many, many others) have turned to this vintage shop for mint-condition pieces from the 1930s through the 1980s. Ladies who love the pinup look will adore the selection of curve-hugging pencil skirts, cardigans, and lingerie, while men will have their pick of Hawaiian shirts, suits, and skinny ties. The time-warped interior also features decorative home accents and furniture from decades past. ⊠ *3100 W. Magnolia Blvd., Burbank* ☎ *818/557–8447* ⊕ *www.vintageplayclothes.com.*

## LOS FELIZ

Stroll past the mansions on Los Feliz Boulevard before hitting the vintage shops and sophisticated boutiques with old-school tendencies—think refurbished brick and classic decor.

### BOOKS

**Skylight Books.** A neighborhood bookstore through and through, Skylight has excellent sections devoted to kids, fiction, travel, food, and it even has a live-in cat. Be sure to browse the Staff Picks section, as the well-informed employees have the inside scoop on new or under-the-radar must-reads. The space also hosts book discussion groups, panels, and author readings with hip literati. Art-lovers can peruse texts on design and photography, graphic novels, and indie magazines at Skylight's annex a few doors down. ⊠ *1818 N. Vermont Ave., Los Feliz* ☎ *323/660–1175.*

### CLOTHING

FAMILY **La La Ling.** This isn't your average kids' clothing store; La La Ling offers pieces hip enough to be worn by the cool parents it counts as clientele. Shoppers can expect affordable finds like Wu-Tang onesies, rock band tees, and skinny jeans. The store also stocks supplies for the nursery and bath time, plus burp cloths, bibs, swaddlers, and other essentials new mommies and daddies need on the regular. ⊠ *1810 N. Vermont Ave., Los Feliz* ☎ *323/664–4400* ⊕ *www.lalaling.com.*

Fodor's Choice **SquaresVille.** A go-to shopping destination for the city's top stylists and ★ fashion insiders, this shop offers an affordable selection of funky finds from the '70s, '80s, and '90s. Besides a regular rotation of bohemian dresses, well-worn novelty tees, and chunky turquoise baubles, a rack of designer labels frequently features pieces by the likes of Moschino, Gucci, and Dolce & Gabbana. ⊠ *1800 N. Vermont Ave., Los Feliz* ☎ *323/669–8464* ⊕ *squaresvillevintage.tumblr.com.*

**Steven Alan Outpost.** Yes, this brick-and-mortar stocks a great selection of the designer's effortless and modern clothing collection, but what's really special about the Los Feliz outpost is the inclusion of L.A.-based indie brands like jewelry by Maya Brenner and Grace Lee, and candles from Maison Louis Marie. ✉ *1937 Hillhurst Ave., Los Feliz* ☎ *323/667–9500.*

**Vamp.** What this airy minimalist boutique may lack in quantity, it more than makes up for in quality. Since 2005, the shop has been serving its stylish Eastside clientele a selection of contemporary clogs, mules, pumps, boots, and more by labels including Rachel Comey, Ancient Greek, and Los Angeles's own Charlotte Stone. Inventory here also includes cool bags, hosiery, jewelry, and handcrafted ceramics. ✉ *1951 Hillhurst Ave., Los Feliz* ☎ *323/662–1150* ⊕ *www.vampshoeshop.com.*

### GIFTS AND SOUVENIRS

**Soap Plant/Wacko.** This pop-culture supermarket offers a wide range of items, including rows of books on art and design. But it's the novelty stock that makes the biggest impression, with ant farms, X-ray specs, and anime figurines. An adjacent gallery space, La Luz de Jesus, focuses on underground art. ✉ *4633 Hollywood Blvd., Los Feliz* ☎ *323/663–0122* ⊕ *www.soapplant.com.*

**Spitfire Girl.** When the person you're shopping for is the nontraditional type, count on this quirky boutique to provide unique goods including taxidermy, printed wood flasks, white magic spell kits, and cheeky socks, much of which is created by Spitfire Girl's own house label. ✉ *1939½ Hillhurst Ave., Los Feliz* ☎ *323/912–1977* ⊕ *www. spitfiregirl.com.*

## SILVER LAKE

The action here is concentrated along Sunset Boulevard, where the young and hip come to sip artisanal coffee and peruse the one-of-a-kind wares.

### BOOKS

**Secret Headquarters.** This could be the coolest comic-book store on the planet, with a selection to satisfy both the geekiest of collectors and those more interested in artistic and literary finds. Rich wood floors and a leather chair near the front window of this intimate space mark the sophisticated setting, which features wall displays neatly organized with new comics and filing cabinets marked DC and Marvel filled with old classics like *Superman* and newer favorites like *Buffy* and *Saga.* ✉ *3817 W. Sunset Blvd., Silver Lake* ☎ *323/666–2228* ⊕ *www.thesecretheadquarters.com.*

### CLOTHING

**Clare V.** Clare Vivier's chic handbags are classic French glamour by way of laid-back California, and her eponymous Silver Lake boutique follows the same aesthetic. Inside, find her full line of messenger bags, fold-over clutches, and iPad cases, all of them made locally in Los Angeles. ✉ *3339 Sunset Blvd., Silver Lake* ☎ *323/665–2476* ⊕ *www. clarevivier.com.*

**Lake.** Styles here are for the sophisticated Eastsider: contemporary and comfortably chic. Find clothing by Isabel Marant, 365 Cashmere, and Rachel Craven, plus the finest apothecary goods including local brand Arcona, candles from Le Feu de L'Eau, and indigo-dyed textiles ⊠ *1618½ Silver Lake Blvd., Silver Lake* ☎ *323/664–6522* ⊕ *www. lakeboutique.com.*

**Mohawk General Store.** Filled with a brilliant marriage of indie and established designers, this upscale boutique is a mainstay for the modern minimalist. Local favorites Black Crane and Jesse Kamm are some of the shop's best sellers, but you'll also find internationally loved labels like Acne Studios, Mansur Gavriel, and Levi's Vintage Clothing. While this address (Mohawk's original) is devoted to womens wear and accessories, men can shop similarly luxe pieces at the more recently opened space next door. ⊠ *4011 W. Sunset Blvd., Silver Lake* ☎ *323/669–1601* ⊕ *www.mohawkgeneralstore.com.*

## COSMETICS

**Le Pink & Co.** This unapologetically feminine beauty shop is decorated with vintage perfume bottles. In stock are cult beauty brands such as Dr. Hauschka, Rosebud Salve, and RMS Beauty, as well as such hard-to-find brands as Eminence Organics and Bella Freud fragrance. While you're here, you can treat yourself to a range of services including facials and waxing that are offered just behind the shop's retail area. ⊠ *3820 W. Sunset Blvd., Silver Lake* ☎ *323/661–7465* ⊕ *www.lovelepink.com.*

## FOOD AND WINE

**Silver Lake Wine.** Boutique wineries from around the world provide this shop with the vintages that fill the floor-to-ceiling racks. Looking unassuming in jeans and T-shirts, the knowledgeable staff can steer you to the right wine or spirits for any occasion. You can wet your whistle at tastings on Sunday, Monday, and Thursday. Summer social events are held at nearby Barnsdall Art Park. ⊠ *2395 Glendale Blvd., Silver Lake* ☎ *323/662–9024* ⊕ *www.silverlakewine.com.*

## HOUSEWARES

**Lawson Fenning.** Interior design lovers will want to move into this modern, Scandinavian-designed shop, which besides providing its customers with a range of contemporary housewares and furniture (including Entler lighting, Mineral Workshop dyed panels, and Ben Medansky ceramics), is peppered with vintage pieces in perfect condition. Though the store has some decidedly big-ticket items, those shopping for smaller gifts can find incense by Blackbird and small woven baskets that won't break the bank. ⊠ *1618 Silver Lake Blvd., Silver Lake* ☎ *323/660–1500* ⊕ *www.lawsonfenning.com.*

**Yolk.** Stocked with a little bit of everything you'll want to get or give, this shop has a spot-on selection of fresh designer goods. Look for Boy Smells candles, Nipomo Mexican blankets, and Marimekko dinnerware, as well as a back room with children's organic cotton clothing and bedding and nontoxic wood toys. You'll also find handcrafted jewelry and works by local artists. ⊠ *1626 Silver Lake Blvd., Silver Lake* ☎ *323/660–4315* ⊕ *www.shopyolk.com.*

# ECHO PARK

With a bit more edge than neighboring Silver Lake, this increasingly cool area has an artsy, do-it-yourself appeal. Secondhand stores squeeze in alongside vegan restaurants, hip dive bars, and friendly boutiques stocked with clothes by local designers.

## CLOTHING

**Myrtle.** A shopping paradise for ladies who love modern-yet-girlie goods, Myrtle prides itself on offering its patrons pieces by a laundry list of local and female designers including Jill Aiko Yee, Atelier Delphine, and Jujumade, and offsets these contemporary items with cherry-picked vintage ones. The made-in-L.A. theme is even carried through in the shop's apothecary and paper goods selection. ⊠ *2213 Sunset Blvd., Echo Park* ☎ *213/413–0004* ⊕ *myrtlela.com.*

**Tavin.** It comes as no surprise that shop owner Erin Tavin is a former actress and wardrobe stylist; there's a particular drama to nearly every piece in this vintage haven. Colorful caftans, eyelet maxi dresses, and weathered cowboy boots are some items you could find in the charmingly crowded shop. A favorite destination for the city's fashion insiders, Tavin also always has adorable offerings for little ones, like teeny Oshkosh B'Gosh overalls and Levi's denim jackets. ⊠ *1543 Echo Park Ave., Echo Park* ☎ *213/482–5832* ⊕ *www.tavinboutique.com.*

### JEWELRY/ACCESSORIES

**Esqueleto.** As this jewelry boutique's name, which is Spanish for "skeleton," may indicate, it presents its cool customers with just the right amount of macabre. But that doesn't mean the light, airy, contemporary shop is stereotypically Goth in style; both its design and the inventory it stocks are perfectly polished and selected with a discerning artistic eye. With a mix of excellent vintage finds and emerging designers (Melissa Joy Manning, Lauren Wolf, and Satomi Kawakita are favorites here) the shop has become a go-to destination for alternative brides' engagement rings and wedding bands. ⊠ *1928 W. Sunset Blvd., Echo Park* ☎ *213/947–3508* ⊕ *www.shopesqueleto.com.*

# BEVERLY HILLS AND THE WESTSIDE

## BEVERLY HILLS

### BOOKS

**Taschen.** Philippe Starck designed the Taschen space to evoke a cool 1920s Parisian salon—a perfect showcase for the publisher's design-forward coffee table books about architecture, travel, culture, and photography. A suspended glass cube gallery in back hosts art exhibits and features limited-edition books. ⊠ *354 N. Beverly Dr., Beverly Hills* ☎ *310/274–4300* ⊕ *www.taschen.com.*

## CLOTHING

**Agent Provocateur.** Garter belts, corsets, and pasties—oh my! Shoppers will find a playful mix of naughty and nice at this Beverly Hills outpost of the beloved lingerie brand. Yes, the boudoir items here range from lovely and lacy (slinky slips and plunging bras) to downright racy (handcuffs and body chains), but everything in the shop is without question beautifully made, which makes it a desirable shopping destination even for the shy set. ⊠ *242 N. Rodeo Dr., Beverly Hills* ☎ *310/888–0050* ⊕ *www.agentprovocateur.com.*

**AllSaints Spitalfields.** The British store invaded Robertson Boulevard, bringing with it a rock-and-roll edge mixed with a dash of Downton Abbey. Look for leather biker jackets, tough shoes, edgy prints, and long sweaters and cardigans, which, worn correctly, let them know you're with the band. ⊠ *100 N. Robertson Blvd., Beverly Hills* ☎ *310/432–8484* ⊕ *www.us.allsaints.com.*

**Alo Yoga.** In a city that takes its yoga seriously, it only makes sense that this locally designed activewear brand would take its very first Los Angeles storefront to the next level. For Alo Yoga's flagship, that means an 8,000-square-foot space complete with an organic coffee bar, kombucha on tap, and a rooftop deck that hosts occasional sweat-and-stretch sessions. As for the clothing, the model-favorite line offers stylish leggings, sports bras, tanks, and more pieces that look as cool outside the fitness studio as they do during downward dog. ⊠ *370 N. Canon Dr., Beverly Hills* ☎ *310/295–1860* ⊕ *www.aloyoga.com.*

**Anto Distinctive Shirt Maker.** A laundry list of Hollywood's leading men, including Ryan Gosling and Tom Cruise, have been wearing Anto's bespoke shirting both on- and offscreen since 1955. An expertly tailored, customized shirt from this iconic showroom is decidedly an investment piece (and you'll need to make an appointment for that service ahead of time), but you can also shop ready-made ties and button-downs here if you're just dropping by. ⊠ *258 N. Beverly Dr., Beverly Hills* ☎ *310/278–4500* ⊕ *www.antoshirt.com.*

**Carroll & Co.** Dapper is the name of the game at this long-standing traditional men's clothing store, which has dressed such icons as Cary Grant and Clark Gable. Nearly 70 years since opening, Carroll & Co. still offers quality goods, excellent service, and styles that endure. Gents can also get fitted for a made-to-measure shirt or suit during a visit here. ⊠ *425 N. Canon Dr., Beverly Hills* ☎ *310/273–9060* ⊕ *www.carrollandco.com.*

**Céline.** Under designer Phoebe Philo's creative direction, the Parisian brand practically pioneers the minimalist-cool trend in womenswear. At the Beverly Hills brick-and-mortar, fashion lovers and Francophiles will love the selection of the label's leather handbags, heels, and chic ready-to-wear clothing. ⊠ *319 N. Rodeo Dr., Beverly Hills* ☎ *310/888–0120* ⊕ *www.celine.com.*

**Chanel.** Fans of the ladylike label will by happy to find that the Beverly Hills flagship store stocks the brand's trademark pieces, like quilted leather bags, tweed jackets, and jewelry designed with the signature double C logo. Beyond those essentials are plenty of other pieces from Chanel's ready-to-wear collection. ✉ *400 N. Rodeo Dr., Beverly Hills* ☎ *310/278–5500* ⊕ *www.chanel.com.*

**Prada.** Prada's Rodeo Drive haven sits inside the incredibly cool Rem Koolhaas–designed Italian showcase space, which features 20-foot-wide staircases and funhouse curves. ✉ *343 N. Rodeo Dr., Beverly Hills* ☎ *310/278–8661* ⊕ *www.prada.com.*

**Saint Laurent.** Celebrities with the coolest, edgiest styles know they can head to the slick storefront to score the label's signature pieces, like moto jackets, skinny jeans, and platform pumps. A men's store with equally rock star–worthy clothing and accessories is just down the street. ✉ *326 N. Rodeo Dr., Beverly Hills* ☎ *310/271–5051* ⊕ *www.ysl.com.*

**Versace.** With its columned facade, temple dome ceiling, and recherché design, this is just the place for a dramatic red-carpet gown, bold bags, sunglasses, and accessories. It also stocks sleek menswear for fashion-forward fellows. ✉ *248 N. Rodeo Dr., Beverly Hills* ☎ *310/205–3921* ⊕ *us.versace.com.*

## DEPARTMENT STORES

**Barneys New York.** This is truly an impressive one-stop shop for high fashion. Deal hunters will appreciate the co-op section, which introduces indie designers before they make it big. Shop for beauty products, shoes, and accessories on the first floor, then wind your way up the staircase for couture. Keep your eyes peeled for fabulous and/or famous folks spearing salads at Fred's on the top floor. ✉ *9570 Wilshire Blvd., Beverly Hills* ☎ *310/276–4400* ⊕ *www.barneys.com.*

**Neiman Marcus.** This is luxury shopping at its finest. The couture salon frequently trots out designer trunk shows, and most locals go right for the shoe department, which features high-end footwear favorites like Giuseppe Zanotti and Christian Louboutin ✉ *9700 Wilshire Blvd., Beverly Hills* ☎ *310/550–5900* ⊕ *www.neimanmarcus.com.*

## HOUSEWARES

**Gearys of Beverly Hills.** Since 1930, this has been the ultimate destination for those seeking the most exquisite fine china, crystal, silver, and jewelry, mostly from classic sources like Christofle, Baccarat, and Waterford. No wonder it's a favorite for registries of the rich and famous. ✉ *351 N. Beverly Dr., Beverly Hills* ☎ *310/273–4741* ⊕ *www.gearys.com.*

## JEWELRY AND ACCESSORIES

**Bulgari.** This luxe jewelry store's shimmering exterior is just a hint of the bold, contemporary Italian jewelry, watches, and other luxurious necessities that are the order of the day at Bulgari. ✉ *401 N. Rodeo Dr., Beverly Hills* ☎ *310/858–9216* ⊕ *us.bulgari.com.*

**Cartier.** Cartier has a bridal collection to sigh for in its chandeliered and respectfully hushed showroom, along with more playful pieces (chunky, diamond-encrusted Panther cocktail rings, for example), watches, and accessories. The stop itself feels like the ultimate playground for A-list clientele, complete with a red-carpeted spiral staircase. ✉ *370 N. Rodeo Dr., Beverly Hills* ☎ *310/275–4272* ⊕ *www.cartier.com.*

## DID YOU KNOW?

Rodeo Drive is the main drag of the chic shopping district bordered by Santa Monica Boulevard, Wilshire Boulevard, and Beverly Drive.

**Harry Winston.** Perhaps the most locally famous jeweler is Harry Winston, *the* source for Oscar-night jewelry. The three-level space, with a bronze sculptural facade, velvet-panel walls, private salons, and a rooftop patio, is as glamorous as the gems. ⊠ *310 N. Rodeo Dr., Beverly Hills* ☎ *310/271–8554* ⊕ *www.harrywinston.com.*

**Louis Vuitton.** Holding court on a prominent corner, Louis Vuitton carries its sought-after monogram (the ultimate symbol of luxury for many) on all manner of accessories and leather goods. ⊠ *295 N. Rodeo Dr., Beverly Hills* ☎ *310/859–0457* ⊕ *www.louisvuitton.com.*

**Tiffany & Co.** Who can resist a gift that comes in those iconic blue boxes? Discover three floors of classic and contemporary jewelry (including plenty of sparklers perfect for popping the question) as well as watches, crystal, and china. ⊠ *210 N. Rodeo Dr., Beverly Hills* ☎ *310/273–8880* ⊕ *www.tiffany.com.*

### SHOES

**Jimmy Choo.** This footwear designer is practically synonymous with flat-out sexy, sky-high stilettos. But there's also plenty more eye candy for fashionistas within the Rodeo Drive location's posh, monochromatic interior. ⊠ *240 N. Rodeo Dr., Beverly Hills* ☎ *310/860–9045* ⊕ *www. jimmychoo.com.*

## WEST HOLLYWOOD

West Hollywood is prime shopping real estate. And as they say with real estate, it's all about location, location, location. Here you can find art, design, and antiques stores, clothing boutiques for the ladies-who-lunch set, mega music stores, and specialty book vendors.

Melrose Avenue, for instance, is part bohemian-punk shopping district (from North Highland to Sweetzer) and part upscale art and design mecca (upper Melrose Avenue and Melrose Place). Discerning locals and celebs haunt the posh boutiques around Sunset Plaza (Sunset Boulevard at Sunset Plaza Drive), on Robertson Boulevard (between Beverly Boulevard and 3rd Street), and along upper Melrose Avenue.

The huge, blue Pacific Design Center, on Melrose at San Vicente Boulevard, is the focal point for this neighborhood's art- and interior design–related stores, including many on nearby Beverly Boulevard. The Beverly–La Brea neighborhood also claims a number of trendy clothing stores. Perched between Beverly Hills and West Hollywood, 3rd Street (between La Cienega Boulevard and Fairfax Avenue) is a magnet for small, friendly designer boutiques.

Melrose Place, not to be confused with the cheaper and trendier Melrose Avenue, is an in-the-know haven to savvy Los Angeles fashionistas and a charming anecdote to the city's addiction to strip malls and mega-shopping centers. This three-block-long strip, east of La Cienega and a block north of Melrose Avenue, lacks the pretentiousness of Rodeo. Reminiscent of the best of West Village shopping in New York, here haute couture meets pedestrian-friendly, tree-lined walkways.

9

Finally, the Fairfax District, along Fairfax Avenue below Melrose Avenue, encompasses the flamboyant, historic Farmers Market at Fairfax Avenue and 3rd Street; the adjacent shopping extravaganza, The Grove; and some excellent galleries around Museum Row at Fairfax Avenue and Wilshire Boulevard.

## ANTIQUES

**Blackman Cruz.** Not your grandmother's antiques shop, David Cruz and Adam Blackman's celebrity-loved shopping destination is known for selecting beautifully offbeat pieces (there's no shortage of ceremonial masks and animal figurines at any given time) as well as fine European and Asian furniture from the 18th to the mid-20th century. ⊠ *836 N. Highland Ave., West Hollywood* ☎ *310/657–9228* ⊕ *www.blackmancruz.com.*

## BOOKS AND MUSIC

**Book Soup.** One of the best independent bookstores in the country, Book Soup has been serving Angelenos since 1975. Given its Hollywood pedigree, it's especially deep in books about film, music, art, and photography. Fringe benefits include an international newsstand, a bargain-book section, and author readings several times a week. ⊠ *8818 Sunset Blvd., West Hollywood* ☎ *310/659–3110* ⊕ *www.booksoup.com.*

## CLOTHING

Fodor's Choice ★ **American Rag Cie.** Half the store features new clothing from established and emerging labels, while the other side is stocked with well-preserved vintage clothing organized by color and style. You'll also find plenty of shoes and accessories being picked over by the hippest of Angelenos. ⊠ *150 S. La Brea Ave., West Hollywood* ☎ *323/935–3154* ⊕ *www.amrag.com.*

**Decades.** A-listers scour these racks for dresses to wear during awards season. Owner Cameron Silver's stellar selection includes dresses by Pucci and Ossie Clark and bags by Hermès. On the street level, Decades Two resells contemporary designer and couture clothing and accessories. ⊠ *8214 Melrose Ave., West Hollywood* ☎ *323/655–1960* ⊕ *www.shopdecadesinc.com.*

Fodor's Choice ★ **Fred Segal.** The ivy-covered building and security guards in the parking lot might tip you off that this is *the* place to be. Visit during the lunch hour to stargaze at the super-trendy café. This L.A. landmark is subdivided into smaller boutiques purveying everything from couture clothing to skateboard wear. The entertainment industry's fashion fiends are addicted to these exclusive creations, many from cult designers just beginning to excite the masses. ⊠ *8100 Melrose Ave., West Hollywood* ☎ *323/651–4129* ⊕ *www.fredsegal.com.*

**H. Lorenzo.** Funky, high-end designer clothes (Ann Demeulemeester, Junya Watanabe, and Comme des Garcons, to name a few) attract a young Hollywood crowd that doesn't mind paying top dollar for such fresh finds. Next door, H. Men provides equally hot styles for guys. ⊠ *8660 Sunset Blvd., West Hollywood* ☎ *310/659–1432* ⊕ *shop.hlorenzo.com.*

**Isabel Marant.** Even before falling for the French designer's effortlessly cool clothing, footwear, and bags (think Paris meets Los Angeles), shoppers will already be enamored of the lush location on fashionable Melrose Place. Inside, the model-favorite destination has a modern rustic vibe, but the outside is a plant paradise, loaded with cacti and succulents. ✉ *8454 Melrose Pl., West Hollywood* ☎ *323/651–1493* ⊕ *www.isabelmarant.com.*

Fodor'sChoice ★ **Maxfield.** This modern concrete structure is one of L.A.'s most desirable destinations for ultimate high fashion. The space is stocked with sleek offerings from Chanel, Saint Laurent, Balmain, and Rick Owen, plus occasional pop-ups by fashion's labels-of-the-moment. For serious shoppers (or gawkers) only. ✉ *8825 Melrose Ave., at Robertson Blvd., West Hollywood* ☎ *310/274–8800* ⊕ *www.maxfieldla.com.*

**Reformation.** Local trendsetters flock here for the sexy, easy-to-wear silhouettes of Reformation's dresses (including a totally affordable bridal line), jumpsuits, and separates—it's a welcome bonus that the pieces here are sustainably manufactured using recycled materials. At the L.A.-based brand's first and only brick-and-mortar in California, customers can also shop a selection of leather bags, shoes, and beauty products by other indie brands. ✉ *8253 Melrose Ave., West Hollywood* ☎ *323/852–0005* ⊕ *www.thereformation.com.*

**Paul Smith.** You can't miss the massive, minimalist pink box that houses Paul Smith's fantastical collection of clothing, boots, hats, luggage, and objets d'art. Photos and art line the walls above shelves of books on pop culture, art, and Hollywood. As for the clothing here, expect the British brand's signature playfully preppy style, with vibrant colors and whimsical patterns mixed in with well-tailored closet staples. ✉ *8221 Melrose Ave., near West Hollywood* ☎ *323/951–4800* ⊕ *www.paulsmith.co.uk.*

**TenOverSix.** This indie designer haven houses the coolest clothing, accessories, and goods from on-the-verge brands including Apiece Apart, Jesse Kamm, and Building Block. Those shopping for something fresh and fashion-forward are sure to find it in this small but eclectic space. ✉ *8425 Melrose Ave., West Hollywood* ☎ *323/330–9355* ⊕ *shop.tenover6.com.*

**The Way We Wore.** Overlook the over-the-top vintage store furnishings to find one of the city's best selections of well-cared-for and one-of-a-kind items, with a focus on sequins and beads. Upstairs, couture from Halston, Dior, and Chanel can cost up to $20,000. ✉ *334 S. La Brea Ave., West Hollywood* ☎ *323/937–0878* ⊕ *www.thewaywewore.com.*

## HOUSEWARES

**Heath Ceramics.** This loft-like outpost of the beloved Sausalito-based ceramics company stocks everything from the Coupe Line (created by founder Edith Heath herself in the 1940s) to glass tumblers handblown in West Virginia. Also look for table linens, bud vases, and speciality foods like artisanal jams from Pasadena. ✉ *7525 Beverly Blvd., West Hollywood* ☎ *323/965–0800* ⊕ *www.heathceramics.com.*

**Jonathan Adler.** For fans of the whimsical NYC-based designer, this West Coast flagship store is the place to be. Mid-century and country-club styles get retooled in playful pottery, cheeky pillows, and graphic textiles. ✉ *8125 Melrose Ave., near West Hollywood* ☎ *323/658–8390* ⊕ *www.jonathanadler.com.*

**OK.** An über-gift shop, OK stocks the classy (such as Scandinavian stemware and vintage phones) and specializes in architecture and design books. There's also a second Silver Lake location. ⊠ *8303 W. 3rd St., West Hollywood* ☎ *323/653–3501* ⊕ *okthestore.com.*

## MALLS AND SHOPPING CENTERS

**Beverly Center.** In addition to luxury retailers like Bloomingdale's, Henri Bendel, and Dolce & Gabbana (which are always ideal for window-shopping if you don't have the means to splurge), this eight-level shopping center also offers plenty of outposts for more affordable brands including Aldo, H&M, and Uniqlo. ⊠ *8500 Beverly Blvd., West Hollywood* ☎ *310/854–0071* ⊕ *www.beverlycenter.com.*

**The Grove.** Come to this popular (and polarizing) outdoor mall for familiar names like Anthropologie, Nike, and Nordstrom; stay for the central fountain with "dancing" water and light shows, people-watching from the trolley, and, during the holiday season, artificial snowfall and a winter wonderland. Feel-good pop blasting over the loudspeakers aims to boost your mood while you spend. The adjacent Farmers Market offers tons of great dining options. ⊠ *189 The Grove Dr., West Hollywood* ☎ *323/900–8080* ⊕ *www.thegrovela.com.*

## MARKETS

**Melrose Trading Post.** Hollywood denizens love this hip market, where you're likely to find recycled rock T-shirts or some vinyl to complete your collection. Live music and fresh munchies entertain vintage hunters and collectors. The market is held 9 am to 5 pm every Sunday—rain or shine—in Fairfax High School's parking lot. ⊠ *Fairfax Blvd. and Melrose Ave., West Hollywood* ☎ *323/655–7679* ⊕ *www.melrosetradingpost.org.*

## SHOES

**Boot Star.** This huge selection of Western-style boots is heaven for urban cowboys and cowgirls. You can find materials ranging from calfskin to alligator, and most boots are handmade in Mexico and Texas. Custom sizing is available, for a guaranteed perfect fit. ⊠ *8493 Sunset Blvd., West Hollywood* ☎ *323/650–0475* ⊕ *www.bootstaronline.com.*

**Christian Louboutin.** You'll find more than the French designer's signature red-soled stilettos—coveted by the city's label-loving ladies—at this Robertson Boulevard outpost; chic leather handbags, sparkly sneakers, and even the brand's beauty line are just as worthy of a peek inside the store. Across the street male fashion aficionados can pick up dress shoes, embellished high-tops, and the lusted-after loafers. ⊠ *650 N. Robertson Blvd., West Hollywood* ☎ *310/247–9300* ⊕ *www.christianlouboutin.com.*

**Supreme.** The L.A. location for NYC's premier street-wear brand regularly sees crowds of sneakerheads and skaters, who know that this is the place to get the freshest urban gear around. Thursdays, when new merchandise drops in, lines can easily wrap around the block—but getting your hands on the goods (namely shoes, shirts, outerwear, hats, and backpacks) before anyone else just might be worth the trouble. ⊠ *439 N. Fairfax Ave., Beverly–La Brea* ☎ *323/655–6205* ⊕ *www.supremenewyork.com.*

# WEST L.A. AND CULVER CITY

This is L.A.'s errand central, where entertainment executives and industry types do their serious shopping. In general, it's more affordable than Beverly Hills.

A nascent art scene is blossoming in Culver City, along the intersection of La Cienega and Washington boulevards and the Santa Monica Freeway, and down side streets like Comey Avenue.

## WEST L.A.

### BOOKS AND STATIONERY

**Children's Book World.** One of the city's largest bookstores is as loved by parents as it is by kids. The Saturday morning storytelling series is a huge hit, and the knowledgeable staffers have an insatiable love for children's literature. Authors, including several celebrities, regularly stop by for meet-and-greets. ⊠ *10580½ W. Pico Blvd., West L.A.* ☎ *310/559–2665* ⊕ *www.childrensbookworld.com.*

### FOOD AND WINE

**Wally's Wine and Spirits.** It may be known as the wine store to the stars, but regular folks also delve into the vast selection of liquors and liqueurs, fine chocolates, and imported cheeses. The shop also offers regular tastings and other events wine aficionados won't want to miss. ⊠ *2107 Westwood Blvd., West L.A.* ☎ *310/475–0606* ⊕ *www. wallywine.com.*

## CULVER CITY

### FOOD AND WINE

**Surfas.** You're likely to rub elbows with area chefs in their work whites at this spacious and well-organized restaurant supply store. Find aisles of spices and jarred delicacies along with all the pots, pans, and appliances you'll need to be your own Top Chef. The adjoining café serves salads, sandwiches, and baked goods. ⊠ *8777 Washington Blvd., Culver City* ☎ *310/559–4770* ⊕ *www.surfasonline.com.*

### MALLS AND SHOPPING CENTERS

**Helms Bakery District.** The lovingly restored Helms Bakery, an art deco gem, has transformed into a major destination for modern furniture and design lovers. With outposts for H.D. Buttercup, Room & Board, and Kohler as well as plenty of great dining options—including a renowned burger-and-beer spot—this is a prime place to spend an afternoon dreaming up a makeover for your own home. ⊠ *8800 Venice Blvd., Culver City* ☎ *310/204–1865* ⊕ *www.helmsbakerydistrict.com.*

**Platform.** The neighborhood's newest retail complex is also its most experimental; with outposts for indie-cool labels (for several, this is their only brick-and-mortar), pop-ups, hip eateries, social events, and an ultramodern design complete with a technicolor mural by artist Jen Stark, it's quickly become a hot spot for the savvy shopper. ⊠ *8850 Washington Blvd., Culver City* ☎ *310/883–5138* ⊕ *www. platformla.com.*

9

# SANTA MONICA AND THE BEACHES

The breezy beachside communities of Santa Monica and Venice are ideal for leisurely shopping. Scores of tourists (and many locals) gravitate to the Third Street Promenade, a popular pedestrians-only shopping area that's within walking range of the beach and historic Santa Monica Pier. But there's more to the area than trendy chain stores; there's also a treasure trove of vintage goods and antiques to be found on Main Street and Ocean Park Boulevard, and Montana Avenue is home to retailers specializing in indie and artisanal wares.

In Venice, Abbot Kinney Boulevard is abuzz with spots to shop chic clothing, accessories, and housewares—including plenty of upscale outposts. The strip also has some of the city's best eateries, so it's easy to kill two birds with one stone. Nearby Lincoln and Rose avenues have also gained retail momentum in recent years, with many emerging brands choosing the area to open their first-ever storefronts. For those looking for the next big thing, this just might be the place to find it.

## SANTA MONICA

### CLOTHING

**The Levi's Store.** The beachside brick-and-mortar for America's classic denim brand is always a popular stop for those strolling down the Third Street Promenade. Besides stocking loads of the signature 501s and 511s, the store offers a slew of slim, slouchy, and stretchy styles of jeans, plus casual essentials like tees, sweats, and jackets for men, women, and little ones. ⊠ *1409 Third St. Promenade, Santa Monica* ☎ *310/393–4899* ⊕ *www.levi.com.*

**Planet Blue.** The beachy bohemian style is the focus here, with an abundance of jeans, breezy dresses, turquoise jewelry, bikinis, and other SoCal staples. ⊠ *800 14th St., Santa Monica* ☎ *310/394–0135* ⊕ *www. shopplanetblue.com.*

**Wasteland.** This vintage emporium, a block from the Third Street Promenade, sells gently used items for both women and men. You'll find everything from wide-lapeled polyester shirts to last year's Coach bag. There are also locations on Melrose Avenue and Ventura Boulevard. ⊠ *1330 4th St., between Arizona Ave. and Santa Monica Blvd., Santa Monica* ☎ *310/395–2620* ⊕ *www.shopwasteland.com.*

### MARKETS

**Brentwood Country Mart.** Among the dozens of stores within this family-friendly faux country market are Calypso St. Barth (for chic resort wear), Turpan (for luxury home goods), James Perse (for laid-back cotton knits), Jenni Kayne (for a curated mix of modern clothing, housewares, and gifts), and and Malia Mills (for American-made swimwear separates). Grab a chicken basket at Reddi Chik and chow down on the open-air patio. ⊠ *225 26th St., at San Vicente Blvd., Santa Monica* ☎ *310/451–9877* ⊕ *www.brentwoodcountrymart.com.*

**Third Street Promenade.** There is no shortage of spots to shop everything from sporting goods to trendy fashions on this pedestrian-friendly strip. Outposts here are mainly of the chain variety and in between splurging on books, clothing, sneakers, and more, shoppers can pop into one of many eateries to stay satiated, or even catch a movie at one of the theaters. Additionally, a chef-approved Farmers Market takes over twice a week, and with the beach just a few steps away, the destination is a quintessential California stop. ✉ *3rd St., between Broadway and Wilshire Blvd., Santa Monica.*

> ### PARKING TIPS
>
> Parking in Santa Monica is next to impossible on Wednesday, when some streets are blocked off for the Farmers Market, but there are several parking structures with free one- to two-hour parking.
>
> There are several well-marked, free (for two hours) parking lots throughout the core shopping area around Beverly Hills.

### HOUSEWARES AND GIFTS

**Limonaia.** This charming and cozy neighborhood boutique has something for every kind of gift recipient; Ben's Garden goods (pillows, coasters, trays, etc.) decorated with inspirational words, lovely cards for all occasions, beaded jewelry, cookbooks, and an extensive puzzle section are just a few things shoppers can find here. ✉ *1325 Montana Ave., Santa Monica* 🕾 *310/458–1858* ⊕ *www.shoplimonaia.com.*

**rumba.** Interior designer Kimba Hills curated this collection of "soft modern design" which includes many mid-century furniture pieces, patterned textiles and pillows, vintage glassware and ceramics, and contemporary artwork from emerging artists. Though the space is set up as a showroom for Hills's prospective clients, every item in here is up for grabs. ✉ *1740 Ocean Park Blvd., Santa Monica* 🕾 *310/392–3103* ⊕ *www.kimbahills.com/rumba-store.*

### TOYS

FAMILY **The Acorn Store.** Remember when toys didn't require computer programming? This old-fashioned shop (for ages 10 and under) sparks childrens' imaginations with dress-up clothes, picture books, and hand-painted wooden toys by brands like Poan and Haba. ✉ *1220 5th St., near Wilshire Blvd., Santa Monica* 🕾 *310/451–5845* ⊕ *www. theacornstore.com.*

## VENICE

### BEAUTY

**Strange Invisible Perfumes.** Finding your signature fragrance at this sleek Abbot Kinney boutique won't come cheap, but perfumer Alexandra Balahoutis takes creating her scents as seriously as a seasoned winemaker—and they're just as nuanced as a well-balanced glass of vino. Essences for the perfumes are organic, wild-crafted, biodynamic, and bottled locally. Highlights from SI's core collection include the cacao-spiked Dimanche and leathery Black Rosette. ✉ *1138 Abbot Kinney Blvd., Venice* 🕾 *310/314–1505* ⊕ *www.siperfumes.com.*

## CLOTHING

**Christy Dawn.** The fact that designer/store owner (and occasional model) Christy Dawn is a native Californian shows throughout her modern bohemian dresses, rompers, separates, and outwear. Effortless with a decidedly feminine feel, the line is created using exclusively deadstock fabric (for less of an environmental impact) and made locally. Her Venice storefront also features many other sustainable goods, including organic and biodynamic chocolates by Zenbunni, vintage jeans, French work shirts, accessories, and vegan sneakers. ⊠ *1930 Lincoln Blvd., Venice* ☎ *310/450–7860* ⊕ *www.christydawn.com.*

**Heist.** Owner Nilou Ghodsi has admitted that she stocks her Westside shop like an extension of her own closet, which in her case means keeping the focus on modern-yet-classic pieces as opposed to trendy ones. The airy boutique offers elegantly edgy separates from American designers like Nili Lotan and Ulla Johnson, as well as hard-to-find French and Italian designers. ⊠ *1100 Abbot Kinney Blvd., Venice* ☎ *310/450–6531* ⊕ *www.shopheist.com.*

**LCD.** Anyone who's looking to get a leg up on the hottest new designers will want to make this Lincoln Boulevard boutique a stop on their Venice shopping spree. The clean, modern space features cool, contemporary clothing by the likes of Ryan Roche, Sandy Liang, and Veda, plus beauty loot from cult brand Grown Alchemist, bags and eyewear from beloved local labels, and so much more for fashion followers to fawn over. ⊠ *1919 S. Lincoln Blvd., Venice* ☎ *424/500–2552* ⊕ *www.shoplcd.co.*

## HOME FURNISHINGS AND GIFTS

**Flowerboy Project.** As the name implies, this sweet shop specializes in fresh, seasonal blooms, but those stopping by just for the flowers may find it hard to resist gift-perfect goods like crystals, pretty paper goods, minimalist leather handbags, and dainty jewelery. And since the space also functions as a coffee shop, you can fuel up with a lavender- or rose-spiked latte as you browse. ⊠ *824 Lincoln Blvd., Venice* ☎ *310/452–3900* ⊕ *www.flowerboyproject.com.*

**General Store.** Right at home in the beachy, bohemian neighborhood, this well-curated shop is a decidedly contemporary take on the concept of general stores. The very definition of "California cool," General Store offers beauty and bath products loaded with organic natural ingredients, handmade ceramics, linen tea towels, and a spot-on selection of art books. Featuring an impressive number of local makers and designers, the boutique also sells modern, minimal clothing and has a kids' section that will wow even the hippest moms and dads. ⊠ *1801 Lincoln Blvd., Venice* ☎ *310/751–6393* ⊕ *www.shop-generalstore.com.*

# MALIBU

## MALLS AND SHOPPING CENTERS

**Malibu Country Mart.** Have the quintessential beachside shopping experience complete with browsing designer clothing (Curve, Ron Herman, or Madison) and mix-and-match bikinis (Letarte), picking up body-boosting wellness goodies at Sunlife Organics, and finishing the day off with dinner at iconic eatery, Mr. Chow. If you can squeeze in a workout, there's a Pure Barre and 5 Point Yoga to choose from, plus tarot readings at metaphysical outpost Malibu Shaman, and Eastern medicine treatments at Malibu Acupuncture. ✉ *3835 Cross Creek Rd., Malibu* ☎ *310/456–7300* ⊕ *www.malibu-countrymart.com.*

**Malibu Lumber Yard.** Emblematic Malibu lifestyle stores in this shopping complex include James Perse, Maxfield, and a too-chic J. Crew outpost. The playground and alfresco dining area make this an ideal weekend destination for families. ✉ *3939 Cross Creek Rd., Malibu* ⊕ *www.the-malibulumberyard.com.*

# PASADENA

The stretch of Colorado Boulevard between Pasadena Avenue and Arroyo Parkway, known as Old Town, is a popular pedestrian shopping destination in Pasadena, with retailers such as Crate & Barrel, H&M, and Tiffany's, which sits a block away from Forever 21. A few blocks east on Colorado, the open-air "urban village" known as Paseo Colorado mixes residential, retail, dining, and entertainment spaces along Colorado Boulevard between Los Robles and Marengo avenues. Enter on Colorado or Marengo for free parking.

# BOOKS

**Vroman's Bookstore.** Southern California's oldest and largest independent bookseller is justly famous for its great service. A newsstand, café, and stationery store add to the appeal. A regular rotation of events including trivia night, kids' storytime, author meet-and-greets, crafting sessions, discussions, and more get the community actively involved. ✉ *695 E. Colorado Blvd., Pasadena* ☎ *626/449–5320* ⊕ *www.vromansbookstore.com.*

# CLOTHING

**Elisa B.** This small but well-edited shop stocks casual wear from established basics brands like Michael Stars and J. Brand alongside high-end designer finds by labels including Opening Ceremony and A.L.C. ✉ *16 E. Holly St., Pasadena* ☎ *626/397–4770* ⊕ *www.elisab.com.*

## HOUSEWARES AND GIFTS

**Gold Bug.** Antiques, animal specimens, crystals, and other unique oddities for the eccentric giftees on your list are all found inside this offbeat boutique located just around the corner from bustling Colorado Boulevard, but the main draw here is the jewelry. Funky, whimsical finds like a black beaded bracelet with a diamond-flecked snake head clasp or a fur-and-chain-mail cuff are stocked alongside more minimal (yet still nature-inspired) pieces, all of which are created by independent designers and made of fine materials like gold or silver and semiprecious stones. ⊠ *22 E. Union St., Pasadena* ☎ *626/744–9963* ⊕ *www. goldbugpasadena.com.*

## MARKETS

**Pasadena City College Flea Market.** For bargain hunting, head to the Pasadena City College Flea Market on the first Sunday of each month. With 500 vendors, this is a great source for records, collectibles, furniture, and clothing at prices that won't break the bank. ⊠ *1570 E. Colorado Blvd., at Hill Ave., Pasadena* ☎ *626/585–7906.*

Fodor's Choice ★ **Rose Bowl Flea Market.** This massively popular flea market, which happens the second Sunday of each month (rain or shine), deservedly draws crowds that come for deals on goods including mid-century furniture, vintage clothing, pop culture collectibles, books, and music. Food and drink options are on hand to keep shoppers satiated, and general admission is just $9, but VIP/early-bird options are available for a little extra dough. Bring cash to avoid an inevitable line at the ATM, and feel free to try your hand at haggling. ⊠ *1001 Rose Bowl Dr., Pasadena* ☎ *323/560–7469* ⊕ *www.rgcshows.com.*

# WHERE TO EAT

# SOUTH-OF-THE-BORDER FLAVOR

From Cal-Mex burritos to Mexico City–style tacos, Southern California is a top stateside destination for experiencing Mexico's myriad culinary styles.

Many Americans are surprised to learn that the Mexican menu goes far beyond Tex-Mex (or Cal-Mex) favorites like burritos, chimichangas, enchiladas, fajitas, and nachos—many of which were created or popularized stateside. Indeed, Mexico has rich, regional food styles, like the complex mole sauces of Puebla and Oaxaca, and the fresh ceviches of Veracruz, as well as the trademark snack of Mexico City: tacos.

In Southern California, tacos are an obsession, with numerous blogs and websites dedicated to the quest for the perfect taco. They're everywhere—in ramshackle taco stands, roving taco trucks, and strip-mall *taquerias*. Whether you're looking for a cheap snack or lunch on the go, SoCal's taco selection can't be beat. But be forewarned: there may not be an English menu. Here we've noted unfamiliar taco terms, along with other potentially new-to-you items from the Mexican menu.

## THIRST QUENCHERS

Spanish for "fresh water," *agua fresca* is a nonalcoholic Mexican drink made from fruit, rice, or seeds that are blended with sugar and water. Fruit flavors like lemon, lime, and watermelon are common. Other varieties include *agua de Jamaica*, flavored with red hibiscus petals; *agua de horchata*, a cinnamon-scented rice milk; and *agua de tamarindo*, a bittersweet variety flavored with tamarind. If you're looking for something with a little more kick, try a *michelada*, a beer enhanced with lime juice, chili sauce, and other ingredients. It's served in a salt-rimmed glass with ice.

## DECODING THE MENU

**Ceviche**—Citrus-marinated seafood appetizer from the Gulf shores of Veracruz. Often eaten with tortilla chips.

**Chili relleno**—Roasted poblano pepper that is stuffed with ingredients like ground meat or cheese, then dipped in egg batter, fried, and served in tomato sauce.

**Clayuda**—A Oaxacan dish similar to pizza. Large corn tortillas are baked until hard, then topped with ingredients like refried beans, cheese, and salsa.

**Fish taco**—A specialty in Southern California, the fish taco is a soft corn tortilla stuffed with grilled or fried white fish (mahimahi or wahoo), pico de gallo, and shredded cabbage.

**Gordita**—"Little fat one" in Spanish, this dish is like a taco, but the cornmeal shell is thicker, similar to pita bread.

**Mole**—A complex, sweet sauce with Aztec roots made from more than 20 ingredients, including chilies, cinnamon, cumin, anise, black pepper, sesame seeds, and Mexican chocolate. There are many types of mole using various chilies and ingredient combinations, but the most common is *mole poblano* from the Puebla region.

**Quesadilla**—A snack made from a fresh tortilla that is folded over and stuffed with simple fillings like cheese, then toasted on a griddle. Elevated versions

of the quesadilla may be stuffed with sautéed *flor de calabaza* (squash blossoms) or *huitlacoche* (corn mushrooms).

**Salsa**—A class of cooked or raw sauces made from chilies, tomatoes, and other ingredients. Popular salsas include *pico de gallo,* a fresh sauce made from chopped tomatoes, onions, chilies, cilantro, and lime; *salsa verde,* made with tomatillos instead of tomatoes; and *salsa roja,* a cooked sauce made with chilies, tomatoes, onion, garlic, and cilantro.

**Sopes**—A small, fried corn cake topped with ingredients like refried beans, shredded chicken, and salsa.

**Taco**—Tacos are made from soft, palm-size corn tortillas filled with meat, chopped onion, cilantro, and salsa. Common taco fillings include *al pastor* (spiced pork), *barbacoa* (braised beef), *carnitas* (roasted pork), *cecina* (chili-coated pork), *carne asada* (roasted, chopped beef), *chorizo* (spicy sausage), *lengua* (beef tongue), *sesos* (cow brain), and *tasajo* (spiced, grilled beef).

**Tamales**—Sweet or savory corn cakes that are steamed, and may be filled with cheese, roasted chilies, shredded meat, or other fillings.

**Torta**—A Mexican sandwich served on a crusty sandwich roll. Fillings include meat, refried beans, and cheese.

**10**

Updated by
Paul Feinstein

Los Angeles may be known for its beach living and celebrity-infused backdrop, but it was once a farm town. The hillsides were covered in citrus orchards and dairy farms, and agriculture was a major industry. Today, even as L.A. is urbanized, the city's culinary landscape has re-embraced a local, sustainable, and seasonal philosophy at many levels—from fine dining to street snacks.

With a growing interest in farm-to-fork, the city's farmers' market scene has exploded, becoming popular at big-name restaurants and small eateries alike. In Hollywood and Santa Monica you can often find high-profile chefs scouring farm stands for fresh produce.

Yet the status of the celebrity chef continues to carry weight around this town. People follow the culinary zeitgeist with the same fervor as celebrity gossip. You can queue up with the hungry hordes at **Mozza** or try and snag a reservation to the ever-popular **Trois Mec** that's much like getting a golden ticket these days. Elsewhere, the seasonally driven bakery and insanely popular **Huckleberry** in Santa Monica has been given a Brentwood counterpart with the rustically sweet **Milo & Olive** created by the same owners. In Culver City, a run-down International House of Pancakes has been turned into the ski chalet–inspired **A-Frame Tavern**. The Ace Hotel opened an L.A. chapter Downtown, creating a hip haven when you can enjoy cocktails and locally sourced menu items poolside or in the restaurant.

Ethnic eats continue to be a backbone to the L.A. dining scene. People head to the San Gabriel Valley for dim sum, ramen, and unassuming taco lounges; Koreatown for epic Korean cooking and late-night coffeehouses; and West L.A. and "the Valley" for phenomenal sushi. Latin food is well represented in the city, making it tough to choose between Guatemalan eateries, Peruvian restaurants, nouveau Mexican bistros, and Tijuana-style taco trucks. With so many dining options, sometimes the best strategy is simply to drive and explore.

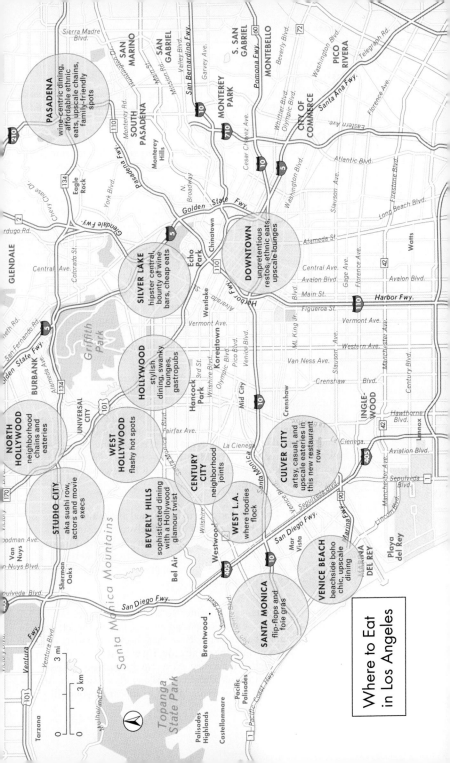

Sierra Madre Blvd.

**PASADENA**
wine-centric dining, affordable ethnic eats, upscale chains, family-friendly spots

SAN MARINO

SAN GABRIEL

SOUTH PASADENA

Monterey Hills

MONTEREY PARK

S. SAN GABRIEL

MONTEBELLO

CITY OF COMMERCE

PICO RIVERA

210

GLENDALE

Eagle Rock

Chinatown

Echo Park

**DOWNTOWN**
unpretentious restos, ethnic eats, upscale lounges

Watts

Golden State Fwy.

Harbor Fwy.

Atlanta Blvd.

**SILVER LAKE**
hipster central, bounty of wine bars, cheap eats

Westlake

Koreatown

Mid City

Griffith Park

BURBANK

**HOLLYWOOD**
stylish dining, swanky lounges, gastropubs

Hancock Park

**NORTH HOLLYWOOD**
neighborhood chains and eateries

UNIVERSAL CITY

**WEST HOLLYWOOD**
flashy hot spots

La Cienega

**CULVER CITY**
artsy, casual, and upscale eateries in this new restaurant row

INGLEWOOD

**STUDIO CITY**
aka sushi row, actors and movie execs

**CENTURY CITY**
neighborhood joints

**BEVERLY HILLS**
sophisticated dining with a Hollywood glamour twist

**WEST L.A.**
where foodies flock

Bel Air

Westwood

Mar Vista

**VENICE BEACH**
beachside boho chic, upscale dining

MARINA DEL REY

Playa del Rey

Santa Monica Mountains

**SANTA MONICA**
flip-flops and foie gras

Brentwood

San Diego Fwy.

Sherman Oaks

Pacific Palisades

Palisades Highlands

Castellammare

Topanga State Park

3 mi

3 km

Tarzana

Ventura Fwy.

Mulholland Dr.

## Where to Eat in Los Angeles

# PLANNER

### CHILDREN

Although it's unusual to see children in the dining rooms of L.A.'s most elite restaurants, dining with youngsters here does not have to mean culinary exile.

### SMOKING

Smokers should keep in mind that California law forbids smoking in all enclosed areas, including bars.

### RESERVATIONS

You'll be happy to hear it's getting easier to snag a desired reservation, but it's still a good idea to plan ahead. Some renowned restaurants are booked weeks or even months in advance. If that's the case, you can get lucky at the last minute if you're flexible—and friendly. Most restaurants keep a few tables open for walk-ins and VIPs. Show up for dinner early (6 pm) or late (after 9 pm) and politely inquire about any last-minute vacancies or cancellations.

Occasionally, an eatery may ask you to call the day before your scheduled meal to reconfirm: don't forget or you could lose out. While making your reservation, also inquire about parking. You'll find most places, except small mom-and-pop establishments, provide valet parking at dinner for reasonable rates (often around $6, plus tip).

### DINING HOURS

Despite its veneer of decadence, L.A. is not a particularly late-night city for eating. (The reenergized Hollywood dining scene is emerging as a notable exception.) The peak dinner times are from 7 to 9, and most restaurants won't take reservations after 10 pm. Unless otherwise noted, the restaurants listed in this guide are open daily for lunch and dinner. Generally speaking, restaurants are closed either Sunday or Monday; a few are shuttered both days. Most places—even the upscale spots—are open for lunch on weekdays, since many of Hollywood megadeals are conceived at that time.

### WHAT TO WEAR

Dining out in Los Angeles tends to be a casual affair, and even at some of the most expensive restaurants you're likely to see customers in jeans (although this is not necessarily considered in good taste). It's extremely rare for L.A. restaurants to actually require a jacket and tie, but all of the city's more formal establishments appreciate a gentleman who dons a jacket—let your good judgment be your guide.

### TIPPING AND TAXES

In most restaurants, tip the waiter 16%–20%. (To figure out a 20% tip quickly, just move the decimal point one place to the left on your total and double that amount.) Note that checks for parties of six or more sometimes include the tip already. Tip at least $1 per drink at the bar, and $1 for each coat checked. Never tip the maître d' unless you're out to impress your guests or expect to pay another visit soon. Also, be prepared for a sales tax of around 9.5% to appear on your bill.

## PRICES

If you're watching your budget, be sure to ask the price of daily specials recited by the waiter. The charge for specials at some restaurants is noticeably out of line with the other prices on the menu. Beware of the $10 bottle of water; ask for tap water instead.

If you eat early or late, you may be able to take advantage of a prix-fixe deal not offered at peak hours. Most upscale restaurants are offering great lunch deals with special menus at cut-rate prices designed to give customers a true taste of the place.

Credit cards are accepted unless otherwise noted in the review. While many restaurants do accept credit cards, some smaller places accept only cash. If you plan to use a credit card it's a good idea to double-check its acceptability when making reservations or before sitting down to eat.

| WHAT IT COSTS | | | | |
|---|---|---|---|---|
| | $ | $$ | $$$ | $$$$ |
| Restaurants | under $14 | $14–$22 | $23–$31 | over $31 |

Prices in the restaurant reviews are the average cost of a main course at dinner or, if dinner is not served, at lunch.

# RESTAURANT REVIEWS

*Listed alphabetically within neighborhoods; use the coordinate (✛ 1:B2) at the end of each listing to locate a site on the corresponding map. Restaurant reviews have been shortened. For full information, visit Fodors.com.*

## DOWNTOWN

The Eastside is home to L.A.'s Arts District, Financial District, Chinatown, Little Tokyo, the Theater District, and everything in between. The neighborhood, still dodgy in places, has experienced a culinary renaissance that has rippled through the area, making it a popular dining destination where people come in search of edgy and creative menus that celebrate its eclectic nature. Here you'll find plenty of cozy wine bars, quaint bistros, historical landmarks, ethnic eats, and upscale restaurants that lack pretension.

**$$** ✕ **Badmaash.** This laid-back Indian gastro-pub is beloved for its bound-
INDIAN ary-pushing menu, irreverent posters of Gandhi, and Bollywood movies projected onto the soaring white walls. True to its name (Badmaash is "hooligan" in Urdo), the restaurant challenges the formality of Indian cuisine, and makes eating curry very cool. **Known for:** indulgent tikka poutine; delicious short-rib samosas; decadent chili cheese naan. $ *Average main: $16* ✉ *108 W. 2nd St. #104, Downtown* ☎ *213/221–7466* ⊕ *www.badmaashla.com* ☽ *No lunch weekends* ✛ *1:C2.*

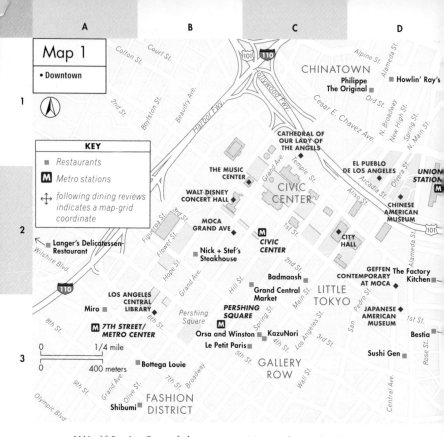

Map 1
• Downtown

A    B    C    D

1

KEY

■ *Restaurants*
Ⓜ *Metro stations*
✛ *following dining reviews indicates a map-grid coordinate*

← Langer's Delicatessen-Restaurant

2

3

0 ──── 1/4 mile
0 ──── 400 meters

CHINATOWN
Philippe The Original ■
■ Howlin' Ray's

CATHEDRAL OF OUR LADY OF THE ANGELS

EL PUEBLO DE LOS ANGELES

UNION STATION Ⓜ

THE MUSIC CENTER ■

WALT DISNEY CONCERT HALL ■

CIVIC CENTER

CHINESE AMERICAN MUSEUM

MOCA GRAND AVE ■

Ⓜ CIVIC CENTER

CITY HALL

Nick + Stef's Steakhouse ■

Badmaash ■

GEFFEN CONTEMPORARY AT MOCA ■

The Factory Kitchen ■

LOS ANGELES CENTRAL LIBRARY ■

Grand Central Market ■

LITTLE TOKYO

JAPANESE AMERICAN MUSEUM ■

Miro ■

Pershing Square

PERSHING SQUARE

Bestia ■

Ⓜ 7TH STREET/ METRO CENTER

Ⓜ Orsa and Winston ■ ■ KazuNori

Le Petit Paris ■

Sushi Gen ■

Bottega Louie ■

GALLERY ROW

FASHION DISTRICT

Shibumi ■

$$$$
ITALIAN

✕ **Bestia.** One of the most exciting and popular Italian restaurants in L.A. is housed inside a converted warehouse in the Arts District Downtown. Thirtysomethings flock to this hot spot with an ever-bustling bar and patio. **Known for:** Alla'nduja Pizza; homemade prosciutto; upscale modern decor. $ *Average main: $35* ✉ *2121 E. 7th Pl., Downtown* ☏ *213/514–5724* ⊕ *www.bestiala.com* ☾ *No lunch* ✛ *1:D3.*

$$$
ITALIAN

✕ **Bottega Louie.** A Downtown dining staple, this lively Italian restaurant and gourmet market features open spaces, stark white walls, and majestic floor-to-ceiling windows. If the wait is too long at this no-reservations eatery, you can sip on prosecco and nibble on pastries at the bar. **Known for:** mouthwatering crab beignets; one-of-a-kind portobello fries. $ *Average main: $25* ✉ *700 S. Grand Ave., Downtown* ☏ *213/802–1470* ⊕ *www.bottegalouie.com* ✛ *1:A3.*

$$$$
ITALIAN

✕ **The Factory Kitchen.** The homemade pasta, kneaded from imported Italian flour, is what dreams are made of. The large Arts District spot is carved from a converted warehouse and is held up inside by towering pillars. **Known for:** focaccina calda di recco al formaggio; cannoli. $ *Average main: $32* ✉ *1300 Factory Pl., Downtown* ☏ *213/996–6000* ⊕ *www.thefactorykitchen.com* ☾ *No lunch weekends* ✛ *1:D2.*

$ ECLECTIC Fodor's Choice ★ 🍴 **Grand Central Market.** In continuous operation since 1917, Grand Central Market has always been a hub for ethnic eats from Jewish delis and Asian fishmongers to Italian butchers and Latino farmers. While the vendors have changed over time, the market continues to feature an ever-evolving array of all-day dining choices, like Wexler's Deli for the best lox in L.A., or Madcapra for inventive falafel. **Known for:** breakfast at Eggslut; fast casual dining; popular lunch destination. [$] *Average main: $12* ✉ *317 S. Broadway, Downtown* ☎ *213/624–2378* 🌐 *www.grandcentralmarket.com* ✣ *1:C2.*

$$ SOUTHERN FAMILY Fodor's Choice ★ 🍴 **Howlin' Ray's.** Don't let the hour-long waits deter you—if you want the best Nashville fried chicken in L.A., Howlin' Ray's is worth the effort. Right in the middle of Chinatown, this tiny chicken joint consists of a few bar seats, a few side tables, and a kitchen that sizzles as staff yell out "yes, chef" with each incoming order. **Known for:** spicy dishes; classic Southern sides. [$] *Average main: $15* ✉ *727 N. Broadway, Suite 128, Downtown* ☎ *213/935–8399* 🌐 *www.howlinrays.com* ⏲ *Closed Mon. and Tues.* ✣ *1:D1.*

$$ JAPANESE 🍴 **KazuNori.** Part of the Sugarfish family (a chain of exceptional sushi restaurants), KazuNori is strictly about hand rolls. Inside, there's a horseshoe bar where diners line up to order from the set menu of three, four, five, or six hand rolls. **Known for:** must-try blue crab; commitment to quality; late-night eats. [$] *Average main: $19* ✉ *421 S. Main St., Downtown* ☎ *213/493–6956* 🌐 *www.kazunorisushi.com* ✣ *1:C3.*

$ DELI FAMILY 🍴 **Langer's Delicatessen-Restaurant.** This James Beard Award–winner not only has the look and feel of a no-frills Jewish deli from New York, it also has the food to match. The draw here is the hand-cut pastrami: lean, peppery, robust—and with a reputation for being the best in town. **Known for:** #19; matzo ball soup; rugelach. [$] *Average main: $13* ✉ *704 S. Alvarado St., Downtown* ☎ *213/483–8050* 🌐 *www.langersdeli.com* ⏲ *Closed Sun. No dinner* ✣ *1:A2.*

$$$$ FRENCH 🍴 **Le Petit Paris.** Housed in the historic El Dorado Building and keeping its original tile, this stunning Cannes transplant has multiple bars, a dog-friendly patio, majestic staircases, and the food to match. Lunch meetings progress over filet mignon carpaccio with truffle mousse, while dinner dates devour sirloins dripping with béarnaise. **Known for:** asparagus with hollandaise; croque-monsieur; perfect macarons. [$] *Average main: $35* ✉ *418 S. Spring St., Downtown* ☎ *213/217–4445* 🌐 *www.lepetitparisla.com* ✣ *1:C3.*

$$$ MEDITERRANEAN FAMILY 🍴 **Miro.** What looks like a museum in the heart of Downtown, this Spanish/North African/Italian hybrid is sating workers on lunch breaks during the day and a pre-theater crowd at night. The plates are meant to be shared, from grandiose charcuterie to homemade pastas. **Known for:** rare whiskey; homemade pastas; shared plates. [$] *Average main: $30* ✉ *888 Wilshire Blvd., Downtown* ☎ *213/988–8880* 🌐 *www.mirorestaurant.com* ⏲ *Closed Sun. No dinner Sun.–Fri.* ✣ *1:A3.*

$$$$ STEAKHOUSE 🍴 **Nick + Stef's Steakhouse.** A Downtown gem, Nick + Stef's by famed chef Joachim Splichal mixes all the trappings of a classic steak house with a sleek, modern aesthetic. Red-leather booths are filled with pre-museum

goers enjoying table-side Caesars and USDA prime steaks. **Known for:** California red wine; cheap happy hour. [$] *Average main: $35* ✉ *330 S. Hope St., Downtown* ☎ *213/680–0330* 🌐 *www.nickandstefssteakhouse.com* ⏲ *No lunch weekends* ✥ *1:B2.*

$$$$ JAPANESE FUSION

🍴 **Orsa and Winston.** Order from the tasting menu at this Japanese/Italian fusion restaurant to explore everything this hybrid cuisine has to offer. The space is tiny, with only nine tables and a few bar seats, and the decor is minimal. **Known for:** squid ink spaghettini; Maine lobster tail; hen egg omelet with Molise truffle. [$] *Average main: $85* ✉ *122 W. 4th St., Downtown* ☎ *213/687–0300* 🌐 *www.orsaandwinston.com* ⏲ *Closed Sun. and Mon.* ✥ *1:C3.*

$ AMERICAN FAMILY Fodor's Choice ★

🍴 **Philippe the Original.** First opened in 1908, Philippe's is one of L.A.'s oldest restaurants and claims to be the originator of the French dip sandwich. While the debate continues around the city, one thing is certain: the dips made with beef, pork, ham, lamb, or turkey on a freshly baked roll stand the test of time. **Known for:** $0.50 coffee; communal tables; post–Dodgers game eats. [$] *Average main: $8* ✉ *1001 N. Alameda St., Downtown* ☎ *213/628–3781* 🌐 *www.philippes.com* ✥ *1:D1.*

$$$ JAPANESE Fodor's Choice ★

🍴 **Shibumi.** This *kappo ryori* (fine dining) restaurant in the middle of Downtown is offering up some of the most inventive raw, steamed, grilled, and fried Japanese dishes you'll ever try. Chef David Schlosser serves you personally from the 400-year-old cypress bar. **Known for:** sea bream sashimi; chicken leg with matsutake mushrooms. [$] *Average main: $25* ✉ *815 Hill St., Downtown* ☎ *213/265–7923* 🌐 *www.shibumidtla.com* ⏲ *Closed Mon.* ✥ *1:A3.*

$$ JAPANESE

🍴 **Sushi Gen.** Consistently rated one of the top sushi spots in L.A., Sushi Gen continues to dole out the freshest and tastiest fish in town. Sit at the elongated bar and get to know the sushi masters while they prepare your lunch. **Known for:** chef recommendations; limited seating. [$] *Average main: $20* ✉ *422 E. 2nd St., Downtown* ☎ *213/617–0552* 🌐 *www.sushigen-dtla.com* ⏲ *Closed Sun. and Mon. No lunch Sat.* ✥ *1:D3.*

## HOLLYWOOD AND THE STUDIOS

### HOLLYWOOD

Hollywood has two faces; while it's a hub for tourists who come here to take photos along the Hollywood Walk of Fame, it is still in touch with its irreverent rock-and-roll roots. The result is a complex dining scene made up of cheap fast food, upscale eateries, and provocative hot spots helmed by celebrity chefs.

$ ASIAN FUSION

🍴 **Baroo.** This nondescript strip mall spot (there's no sign out front) serves healthy portions of Korean/Italian hybrids at reasonable prices. There are only eight items on the chalkboard menu, but you haven't lived until you've devoured their kimchi fried rice served with a 63-degree egg. **Known for:** homemade pasta; dishes served in alms bowls. [$] *Average main: $13* ✉ *5706 Santa Monica Blvd., Hollywood* ☎ *323/929–9288* 🌐 *www.baroola.strikingly.com* ⏲ *Closed Sun. and Mon.* ✥ *2:G2.*

$ MEXICAN FAMILY

🍴 **Cactus Taqueria #1.** A humble taco shack on the side of the road, Cactus offers up $2 tacos with all types of meat you could imagine, like tongue, pork skin, and beef head. They also have carne asada and chicken for the less adventurous. **Known for:** cash-only; classic Mexican dishes. $ *Average main: $6* ⊠ *950 Vine St., Hollywood* ☎ *323/464–5865* ▭ *No credit cards* ✛ *2:F2.*

$$
**✕ Café Gratitude.** This café prides itself on being a 100% organic plant-based establishment supporting sustainability. The space features a large, heated patio and sweeping windows that keep a permanent brightness to the proceedings. **Known for:** vegan; Indian curry bowl; eggplant Parmesan panini. $ *Average main: $16* ⊠ *639 N. Larchmont Blvd., Hollywood* ☎ *323/580–6383* ⊕ *www.cafegratitude.com* ✛ *2:F3.*

VEGETARIAN
FAMILY

$$$
**✕ Jitlada.** Some of the most authentic (and spiciest) Thai food can be found in a strip mall in East Hollywood. Inside, red chilies are waiting to set your mouth on fire. **Known for:** mango sticky rice; always packed; crying tiger beef. $ *Average main: $25* ⊠ *5233 W. Sunset Blvd., Hollywood* ☎ *323/667–9809* ⊕ *www.jitladala.wordpress.com* ☻ *Closed Mon.* ✛ *2:G2.*

THAI

$
**✕ Pink's Hot Dogs.** Since 1939, Angelenos and tourists alike have been lining up at this roadside hot dog joint. Open until 3 am on weekends, the chili dogs are the main draw, but don't shy away from themed and celebrity-inspired specials like the Emeril Legasse Bam Dog, the Lord of the Rings Dog, or the Giada De Laurentiis Dog. **Known for:** long lines; outside seating. $ *Average main: $6* ⊠ *709 N. La Brea Ave., Hollywood* ☎ *323/931–4223* ⊕ *www.pinkshollywood.com* ✛ *2:E2.*

AMERICAN
FAMILY

$$
**✕ Pizzeria Mozza.** Mario Batali and Nancy Silverton own this upscale pizza and antipasti eatery. The pies—thin-crusted delights with golden, blistered edges—are more Campania than California, and are served piping hot daily. **Known for:** affordable Italian-only wines; walk-ins welcome at bar. $ *Average main: $19* ⊠ *641 N. Highland Ave., Hollywood* ☎ *323/297–0101* ⊕ *www.pizzeriamozza.com* ✛ *2:E3.*

ITALIAN

$$$$
**✕ Providence.** Widely considered one of the best seafood restaurants in the country, chef-owner Michael Cimarusti and co-owner Donato Poto elevate sustainably driven fine dining to an art form. The elegant space is the perfect spot to sample exquisite seafood with the chef's signature application of French technique, traditional American themes, and Asian accents. **Known for:** pastries by chef Jessie Liu; Friday lunch special. $ *Average main: $120* ⊠ *5955 Melrose Ave., Hollywood* ☎ *323/460–4170* ⊕ *www.providencela.com* ☻ *No lunch Mon.–Thurs. and weekends* ✛ *2:F3.*

SEAFOOD
Fodor's Choice
★

**10**

$$
**✕ Roscoe's House of Chicken 'n Waffles.** Roscoe's is *the* place for down-home Southern cooking in Southern California. Just ask the patrons who drive from all over L.A. for bargain-priced fried chicken and waffles. The name of this casual eatery honors a late-night combo popularized in Harlem jazz clubs. **Known for:** busy; late-night eats; lemonade. $ *Average main: $15* ⊠ *1514 N. Gower St., Hollywood* ☎ *323/466–7453* ⊕ *www.roscoeschickenandwaffles.com* ✛ *2:F2.*

SOUTHERN
FAMILY

$$$$
**✕ Trois Mec.** Housed in an old Raffalo's Pizza spot (the sign is still there), this French haven features seven bar seats and a few tables lining the back wall. In order to eat here, you need to purchase tickets well in advance, which include a five-course tasting menu with items like raw scallops or lobster and pineapple. **Known for:** rotating menu; dumplings. $ *Average main: $85* ⊠ *716 Highland Ave., Hollywood* ⊕ *www.troismec.com* ☻ *Closed weekends* ✛ *2:E3.*

FRENCH

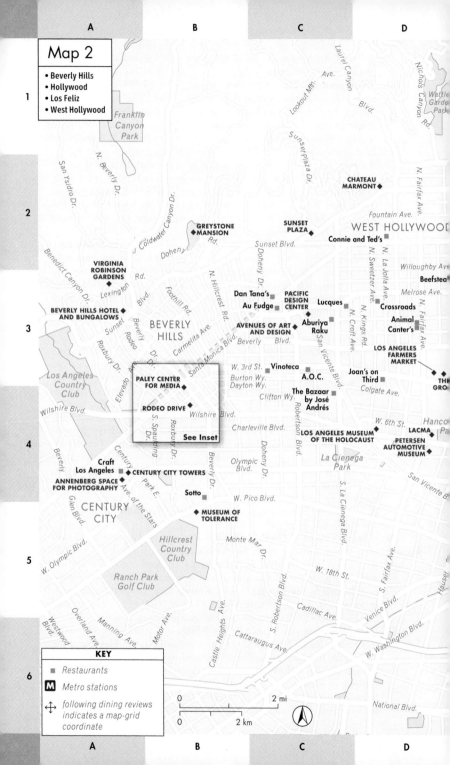

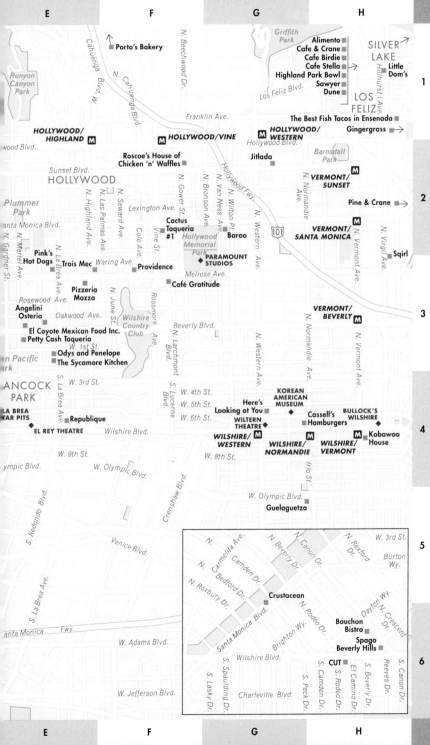

## KOREATOWN

Home to the largest and densest Korean population outside of Korea, Koreatown is also an ethnically diverse neighborhood. While Korean cuisine is ubiquitous here, like most of L.A., you can find incredible Asian fusion and even classic burger joints.

$ | ✕ **Cassell's Hamburgers.** Since 1948, Cassell's has been grilling up some
DINER | of the city's best burgers and remains on just about every top burger
FAMILY | list in town. The simple diner features bar stools, a dozen or so tables, and large windows looking out onto the street. **Known for:** perfectly cooked burgers and fries; no-frills dining; late-night eats. $ *Average main: $10* ✉ *3600 W. 6th St.* ☎ *213/387–5502* ⊕ *www.cassellshamburgers.com* ✛ *2:G4.*

$$ | ✕ **Guelaguetza.** A classic L.A. Mexican eatery, Guelaguetza serves the
MEXICAN | complex but not overpoweringly spicy cooking of Oaxaca, one of Mex-
FAMILY | ico's most renowned culinary capitals. Inside, you'll find a largely Spanish-speaking clientele bobbing their heads to nightly jazz and marimba while wolfing down the restaurant's specialty: the moles. **Known for:** salsa-covered chorizo; chili-marinated pork; family-owned restaurant. $ *Average main: $15* ✉ *3014 W. Olympic Blvd* ☎ *213/427–0608* ⊕ *www.ilovemole.com* ✛ *2:G4.*

$$$ | ✕ **Here's Looking At You.** Hawaiian and Asian-inspired dishes can be found
ECLECTIC | on this menu featuring veggie, meat, poultry, and seafood. The environment
Fodor'sChoice | is eclectic, as is the food, with signature dishes like stracciatella cheese on
★ | charred bread and Japanese saba with marigolds. **Known for:** pie; exceptional cocktails. $ *Average main: $25* ✉ *3901 W. 6th St.* ☎ *213/568–3573* ⊕ *www.hereslookingatyoula.com* ⊙ *Closed Tues.* ✛ *2:G4.*

$$ | ✕ **Kobawoo House.** Nestled into a dingy strip mall, this Korean power-
KOREAN | house is given away by the lines of locals waiting outside. Once inside,
FAMILY | scents of grilled meats and kimchi immediately fill your nostrils. **Known for:** kalbi beef; long lines; cheap eats. $ *Average main: $17* ✉ *698 S. Vermont Ave.* ☎ *213/389–7300* ⊕ *www.kobawoola.com* ✛ *2:H4.*

## BURBANK

Home to movie and television studios, there's a quiet sophistication to this part of town. Great restaurants are tucked away in strip malls and side streets.

$ | ✕ **Porto's Bakery.** Waiting in line at Porto's is as much a part of the experi-
CUBAN | ence as is indulging in a roasted pork sandwich or a chocolate-dipped crois-
FAMILY | sant. This Cuban bakery and café has been an L.A. staple for more than 50 years, often bustling during lunch. **Known for:** counter service; potato balls; roasted pork sandwiches. $ *Average main: $10* ✉ *3614 W. Magnolia Blvd., Burbank* ☎ *818/846–9100* ⊕ *www.portosbakery.com* ✛ *2:F1.*

$$$$ | ✕ **Scratch|Bar and Kitchen.** Forget everything you think you know about
MODERN | infamous *Top Chef* alum Phillip Lee and come to his restaurant for
AMERICAN | a one-of-a-kind experience, about 25 minutes outside of Burbank in
Fodor'sChoice | Encino. Sit at the bar as individual chefs showcase the 30 ingredients
★ | on the menu that month and make everything from scratch before your eyes. **Known for:** prix-fixe menu; inventive dishes. $ *Average main: $75* ✉ *16101 Ventura Blvd., Suite 255, Encino* ☎ *818/646–6085* ⊕ *www.scratchbarla.com* ✛ *3:B1.*

## LOS FELIZ

This affluent hillside community has a laid-back dining scene. Wine bars, burger joints, and taco stands are among the options for a family night out.

$ MEXICAN FAMILY 🍴 **The Best Fish Taco In Ensenada.** There's nothing fancy about this nautical-themed spot; there's a colorful patio, a few tables inside, and only two items on the menu: shrimp and fish tacos. Lightly battered and fried to perfection, the tacos come with ample choices of toppings that go great with the house-made horchata. **Known for:** lunch for under $10; lives up to its name. [$] *Average main: $6* ✉ *1650 Hillhurst Ave., Los Feliz* ☎ *323/466–5552* 🌐 *www.bestfishtacoinensenada.com* ✣ *2:H1.*

$ MEDITERRANEAN FAMILY 🍴 **Dune.** Simple, small, and understated, it's easy to miss the best falafel spot in town, squeezed into a retail row in Atwater Village, right next to Los Feliz. The tacos are crunchy outside, moist inside, and they're garnished to perfection with hummus, house pickles, and marinated cabbage. **Known for:** shawarma; tabbouleh. [$] *Average main: $11* ✉ *3143 Glendale Blvd., Los Feliz* ☎ *323/486–7073* 🌐 *www.dune.kitchen* ✣ *2:H1.*

$$ ITALIAN 🍴 **Little Dom's.** With a vintage bar and dapper barkeep who mixes up seasonally inspired retro cocktails, an attached Italian deli where you can pick up a pork-cheek sub, and an $18 Monday-night supper, it's not surprising that Little Dom's is a neighborhood gem. Cozy and inviting, with big leather booths you can sink into for the night, the restaurant puts a modern spin on classic Italian dishes such as wild-boar meatballs, almond-milk ricotta agnolotti, and grilled steak slathered in Parmesan. **Known for:** spaghetti and meatballs; outdoor seating; brunch. [$] *Average main: $20* ✉ *2128 Hillhurst Ave., Los Feliz* ☎ *323/661–0055* 🌐 *www.littledoms.com* ✣ *2:H1.*

## SILVER LAKE

With plenty of hipster appeal, the eateries of Silver Lake draw an eclectic crowd to its neighborhood hangouts.

$$$ ITALIAN Fodor's Choice ★ 🍴 **Alimento.** Chef Zach Pollack helms the best Italian restaurant in Silver Lake. The *escolar crudo* with eggplant puree makes you rethink your life; the *radiatori* with braised pork is fit for the gods; and the squid ink *strozzapreti* will have you booking a flight to Italy. **Known for:** house-made sourdough; intimate space; full bar. [$] *Average main: $25* ✉ *1710 Silver Lake Blvd., Silver Lake* ☎ *323/928–2888* 🌐 *www.alimentola.com* ⏲ *Closed Mon. No lunch* ✣ *2:H1.*

$$ MEDITERRANEAN 🍴 **Cafe Birdie.** Also located on the east side in Highland Park (about 20 minutes north of Silver Lake), come to Cafe Birdie for the ambience, and to try the mushroom toast with chanterelles and crème fraîche, or the butcher's pasta with veal, lamb, and ricotta. A full illuminated bar hugs one wall and oversees the smattering of copper-topped tables and large street-side windows. **Known for:** lemon panna cotta; full bar; floor to ceiling windows add great natural light. [$] *Average main: $19* ✉ *5631 N. Figueroa St., Highland Park* ☎ *323/739–6928* 🌐 *www.cafebirdiela.com* ⏲ *Brunch weekends only* ✣ *2:H1.*

$$$$ FRENCH 🍴 **Cafe Stella.** Quite possibly the best date spot in L.A., Stella delivers a French experience that rivals Paris. Start dinner off with some escargot,

and meatballs with tomato gravy and Parmesan. **Known for:** moules frites; traditional "French" service; outdoor seating. $ *Average main: $34* ⊠ *3932 Sunset Blvd., Silver Lake* ☏ *323/666–0265* ⊕ *www.cafestella.com* ☾ *No brunch Mon.* ✛ *2:H1.*

**$$**
VIETNAMESE
FAMILY

✕ **Gingergrass.** With minimalist decor marked by tropical wood banquettes, Silver Lake's bohemian past and über-trendy present converge at Gingergrass. Traditional Vietnamese favorites emerge from this café's open kitchen, sometimes with a California twist. **Known for:** pho; bánh mì; imperial rolls. $ *Average main: $15* ⊠ *2396 Glendale Blvd., Silver Lake* ☏ *323/644–1600* ⊕ *www.gingergrass.com* ✛ *2:H1.*

**$**
TAIWANESE
FAMILY

✕ **Pine and Crane.** P&C is a fast-casual Taiwanese hot spot in Silver Lake. The interior features wooden benches and banquettes where you can sit and slurp dan dan noodles with sesame-peanut sauce and cucumbers, or three cup Jidori chicken with rice, Chinese basil, and soy sauce. **Known for:** long lines; straightforward but flavorful dishes. $ *Average main: $12* ⊠ *1521 Griffith Park Blvd., Silver Lake* ☏ *323/668–1128* ⊕ *www.pineandcrane.com* ☾ *Closed Tues.* ✛ *2:H2.*

**$$$**
SEAFOOD

✕ **Sawyer.** This Silver Lake seafood spot features high ceilings, exposed brick, a hip crowd, and incredible fish. The lobster roll that comes with Kennebec fries is second to none, and the P.E.I. Black Mussels with Italian sausage will have you ordering extra bread for dipping. **Known for:** chocolate mousse; cocktail program; great wine selection. $ *Average main: $23* ⊠ *3709 Sunset Blvd., Silver Lake* ☏ *323/641–3709* ⊕ *www.sawyerlosangeles.com* ☾ *No brunch weekdays* ✛ *2:H1.*

**$$**
CAFÉ
FAMILY

✕ **Sqirl.** A small place that packs a big punch, Sqirl has graduated from a jam-and-toast spot to the busiest breakfast and lunch café in L.A. A line can always be found wrapping around the block, as patrons await their caffeine fixes and sorrel pesto rice bowls (the best item on the menu). **Known for:** homemade jams; knockout ricotta toast. $ *Average main: $14* ⊠ *720 N. Virgil Ave., Suite 4, Silver Lake* ☏ *323/284–8147* ⊕ *www.sqirlla.com* ✛ *2:H2.*

## BEVERLY HILLS AND THE WESTSIDE

Never short on sophistication, Beverly Hills, West Hollywood, and the Westside are known for their high-profile eateries that often have paparazzi camped outside.

### BEVERLY HILLS

Dining in the 90210 is always an elegant experience, especially when you're leaving your car with the valet at one of the hot new restaurants along Wilshire Boulevard. But meals here don't always break the bank; there are plenty of casual and affordable eateries here worth a visit.

**$$$$**
SPANISH

✕ **The Bazaar by José Andrés.** Celebrity Spanish chef José Andrés has conquered L.A. with this colorful and opulent Beverly Hills spot, which features a bar stocked with liquid nitrogen and a super-flashy patisserie. Pore over a menu of items like Spanish tapas (with a twist) and "liquid" olives (created through a technique called spherification). **Known for:** molecular gastronomy; foie gras cotton candy. $ *Average main: $65* ⊠ *SLS Hotel at Beverly Hills, 465 S. La Cienega Blvd., Beverly Hills* ☏ *310/246–5555* ⊕ *slshotels.com/beverlyhills/bazaar* ☾ *No lunch* ✛ *2:C4.*

CLOSE UP

## Local Chains Worth Indulging In

It's said that the drive-in burger joint was invented in L.A., probably to meet the demands of an ever-mobile car culture. Burger aficionados line up at all hours outside **In-N-Out Burger** (🌐 *www.in-n-out.com, multiple locations*), still a family-owned operation whose terrific made-to-order burgers are revered by Angelenos. Visitors may recognize the chain as the infamous spot where Paris Hilton got nabbed for drunk driving, but locals are more concerned with getting their burger fix off the "secret" menu, with variations like "Animal Style" (mustard-grilled patty with grilled onions and extra spread), a "4 x 4" (four burger patties and four cheese slices, for big eaters) or the bun-less "Protein Style" that comes wrapped in a bib of lettuce. Go online for a list of every "secret" menu item.

**Tommy's** is best known for their delightfully sloppy chili burger. Visit their no-frills original location (✉ *2575 Beverly Blvd., Los Angeles* ☎ *213/389–9060*)—a culinary landmark. For rotisserie chicken that will make you forget the Colonel altogether, head to **Zankou Chicken** (✉ *5065 Sunset Blvd., Hollywood* ☎ *323/665–7845* 🌐 *www.zankouchicken.com*), a small chain noted for its golden crispy-skinned birds, potent garlic sauce, and Armenian specialties. One-of-a-kind-sausage lovers will appreciate **Wurstküche** (✉ *800 E. 3rd St., Downtown* ☎ *213/687–4444* 🌐 *www.jerrysfamousdeli.com*), where the menu includes items like rattlesnake and rabbit or pheasant with Herbs de Provence. With a lively bar scene, the occasional celebrity sighting, and a spot directly across from the beach, **BOA Steakhouse** (✉ *101 Santa Monica Blvd., Santa Monica* ☎ *310/899–4466* 🌐 *www.hillstone.com*) is a popular hangout, while **Lemonade** (✉ *9001 Beverly Blvd., West Hollywood* ☎ *310/247–2500* 🌐 *www.senorfish.net*) is known for its healthy seasonally driven menu, pulled straight from L.A.'s farmers' markets.

10

$$$$ FRENCH FAMILY Fodor's Choice ★ 🍴 **Bouchon Bistro.** Chef Thomas Keller of Napa Valley's The French Laundry fame is at the head of this majestic bistro in Beverly Hills. Start with the classic onion soup that arrives with a bubbling lid of cheese, or the salmon rillettes, which are big enough to share. **Known for:** tasty steak frites; sumptuous croque madame; sweet profiteroles for dessert. [$] *Average main: $35* ✉ *235 N. Canon Dr., Beverly Hills* ☎ *310/271–9910* 🌐 *www.thomaskeller.com/bouchonbeverlyhills* ✣ *2:H6.*

$$$$ VIETNAMESE 🍴 **Crustacean.** At Crustacean, exotic fish swim through a glass-topped tank sunk into the marble floor which leads to the bar. Peruse the French-influenced Southeast Asian menu, which includes filet mignon with a ponzu glaze, and a ginger, basil, and lime Jidori chicken. **Known for:** sake-simmered dishes; colossal tiger prawns. [$] *Average main: $36* ✉ *9646 Santa Monica Blvd., Beverly Hills* ☎ *310/205–8990* 🌐 *www.houseofan.com/crustaceanbh* ⏲ *No lunch weekends* ✣ *2:G5.*

$$$$ STEAKHOUSE 🍴 **CUT.** In a true collision of artistic titans, celebrity chef Wolfgang Puck presents his take on steak houses in a space designed by Getty Center architect Richard Meier. Playful dishes like bone-marrow flan take center stage, while dry-age and seared hunks of Nebraskan sirloin prove the

Austrian-born chef understands America's love affair with beef. **Known for:** decadent dark chocolate soufflé; "Louis" cocktail. [$] *Average main: $36* ✉ *Beverly Wilshire (A Four Seasons Hotel), 9500 Wilshire Blvd., Beverly Hills* ☎ *310/276–8500* 🌐 *www.wolfgangpuck.com* ⏲ *Closed Sun. No lunch* ✥ *2:H6.*

$$$ ITALIAN 🍴 **Sotto.** You wouldn't know it from the outside, but this basement-level spot belies one of the best Italian restaurants in town. A 1,000-degree oven fires up Neapolitan pizzas as diners discuss entertainment news over bottles of Barolo. **Known for:** perfect cannoli; blistered little gems salad; scrumptious home-baked bread. [$] *Average main: $25* ✉ *9575 W. Pico Blvd., Beverly Hills* ☎ *310/277–0210* 🌐 *www.sottorestaurant.com* ✥ *2:B4.*

$$$$ MODERN AMERICAN Fodor's Choice ★ 🍴 **Spago Beverly Hills.** Wolfgang Puck's flagship restaurant is a modern L.A. classic. Spago centers on a buzzing red-bricked outdoor courtyard shaded by 100-year-old olive trees, and a daily-changing menu offers dishes like Cantonese-style striped bass, traditional Austrian specialties, or pizza with white truffles. **Known for:** great people-watching; magical mango soufflé. [$] *Average main: $32* ✉ *176 N. Cañon Dr., Beverly Hills* ☎ *310/385–0880* 🌐 *www.wolfgangpuck.com* ⏲ *No lunch Sun.* ✥ *2:H6.*

$$ ITALIAN 🍴 **Vinoteca.** If you're looking for an authentic Italian lunch experience, tuck into Vinoteca inside the Four Seasons Hotel in Beverly Hills. Specializing in Napoli street food, highlights include *arancino* (deep-fried rice bowls) with Sicilian salmon or *montanara* sandwiches with prosciutto and burrata. **Known for:** cozy space; laptop-friendly; heated patio. [$] *Average main: $15* ✉ *Four Seasons Los Angeles at Beverly Hills, 300 S. Doheny Dr., Beverly Hills* ☎ *310/273–2222* 🌐 *www.fourseasons.com/losangeles/dining/lounges/vinoteca* ⏲ *No lunch Sun.* ✥ *2:C3.*

## WEST HOLLYWOOD

Lively, stylish, and surrounded by the best restaurants and nightlife in Los Angeles, WeHo (as locals call it) is a magnet for celebrity sightings. There are great bakeries, well-regarded burger joints, and upscale bars serving couture cocktails.

$$ JAPANESE 🍴 **Aburiya Raku.** A small Japanese grill on one of L.A.'s busiest thoroughfares is pumping out late-night yakitori and sake to hungry foodies. Hot dishes run the gamut from Kobe beef to pork ears while foie gras bowls and yellowtail carpaccio round out the menu. **Known for:** cozy ambience; tasty homemade tofu. [$] *Average main: $15* ✉ *521 N. La Cienega Blvd., West Hollywood* ☎ *213/308–9393* 🌐 *www.aburiyarakula.wixsite.com/weho* ⏲ *Closed Sun.* ✥ *2:C3.*

$$$$ ITALIAN Fodor's Choice ★ 🍴 **Angelini Osteria.** Despite its modest, rather congested dining room, this is one of L.A.'s most celebrated Italian restaurants. The key is chef-owner Gino Angelini's consistently impressive dishes, like whole branzino, tender veal kidneys, or rich oxtail stew, as well as lasagna oozing with besciamella. **Known for:** large Italian wine selection; bold flavors. [$] *Average main: $40* ✉ *7313 Beverly Blvd., West Hollywood* ☎ *323/297–0070* 🌐 *www.angeliniosteria.com* ⏲ *Closed Mon. No lunch weekends* ✥ *2:E3.*

$$$
AMERICAN

✕**Animal.** Owned by Jon Shook and Vinny Dotolo of *Iron Chef* fame, this oft-packed James Beard Award–winning restaurant offers sharable plates with a focus on meat. Highlights include barbecue pork belly sandwiches, poutine with oxtail gravy, and foie gras *loco moco* (a hamburger topped with foie gras, quail egg, and Spam). **Known for:** bacon-chocolate crunch bar; a must for foodies. $ *Average main: $25* ✉ *435 N. Fairfax Ave., West Hollywood* ☎ *323/782–9225* ⊕ *www. animalrestaurant.com* ⊗ No lunch ✛ *2:D3.*

$$$$
MEDITERRANEAN

✕**A.O.C.** An acronym for Appellation d'Origine Contrôlée, the regulatory system that ensures the quality of local wines and cheeses in France, A.O.C. upholds this standard of excellence from shared plates to perfect wine pairings. Try the Spanish fried chicken, diver scallops with rapini pesto, or arroz negro with squid. **Known for:** amazing bacon-wrapped dates; quaint outdoor seating; fireplaces indoors. $ *Average main: $36* ✉ *8700 W. 3rd St., West Hollywood* ☎ *310/859–9859* ⊕ *www.aocwinebar.com* ⊗ No lunch weekends ✛ *2:C3.*

$$
AMERICAN
FAMILY
Fodor's Choice
★

✕**Au Fudge.** This WeHo hot spot owned by Jessica Biel is both kid- and parent-friendly, with kids' playrooms (complete with on-site au pairs) that give mom and dad a break while they dine. Food consists of chicken nuggets, burgers, and salads, all with healthy twists. **Known for:** fresh baked goods; on-site boutique. $ *Average main: $16* ✉ *9010 Melrose Ave., West Hollywood* ☎ *424/288–4268* ⊕ *www.aufudge.com* ✛ *2:C3.*

$$
VEGETARIAN
FAMILY

✕**Beefsteak.** *Top Chef* alum Marcel Vigneron brings his conscious plant-based cuisine to Melrose. The minimal restaurant features an array of vegetarian delights from bowls and wraps to smoothies and cakes. **Known for:** boozey smoothies; acclaimed kimchi; tasty vegan nachos. $ *Average main: $14* ✉ *7661 Melrose Ave., West Hollywood* ☎ *323/424–7443* ⊕ *www.beefsteakveg.com* ⊗ Closed Mon. ✛ *2:D3.*

$
DELI
FAMILY

✕**Canter's.** This granddaddy of L.A. delicatessens (it opened in 1931) cures its own corned beef and pastrami, and features delectable desserts from the in-house bakery. It's not the best (or friendliest) deli in town, but it's a classic. **Known for:** adjacent to Kibitz Room bar; plenty of seating means short wait times. $ *Average main: $12* ✉ *419 N. Fairfax Ave., Fairfax District* ☎ *323/651–2030* ⊕ *www.cantersdeli. com* ✛ *2:D3.*

$$$
SEAFOOD
FAMILY

✕**Connie and Ted's.** Inspired by the classic clam, oyster, and fish houses of New England, a well-heeled crowd can be found in this beautiful space (the roof is arched like a wave) dipping fried calamari or spooning up Jo's wicked good chowda'. Lobster rolls are insanely good, and you can never go wrong with the catch of the day. **Known for:** insane lobster rolls; catch of the day. $ *Average main: $28* ✉ *8171 Santa Monica Blvd., West Hollywood* ☎ *323/848–2722* ⊕ *www.connieandteds.com* ⊗ No brunch or lunch Mon. and Tues. ✛ *2:D2.*

$$$
VEGETARIAN
Fodor's Choice
★

✕**Crossroads.** From their famous Impossible Burger (you can't believe it's not meat) to their spicy meatball pizza, Crossroads's level of veggie inventiveness knows no bounds. The space itself is dimly lit, with red leather booths and a full bar illuminating its A-list clientele. **Known for:** great artichoke oysters; full bar; A-list clientele. $ *Average main: $24* ✉ *8284 Melrose Ave., West Hollywood* ☎ *323/782–9245* ⊕ *www. crossroadskitchen.com* ✛ *2:D3.*

**10**

$$$$ ITALIAN 🍴 **Dan Tana's.** If you're looking for an Italian vibe straight out of *Goodfellas*, your search ends here. Checkered tablecloths cover the tightly packed tables as Hollywood players dine on the city's best chicken and veal Parm, and down Scotches by the finger. **Known for:** elbow-room-only bar; lively atmosphere; long lines. [$] *Average main: $35* ✉ *9071 California Rte. 2, West Hollywood* ☎ *310/275–9444* 🌐 *www.dantanasrestaurant.com* ✥ *2:C3.*

$$ MEXICAN Fodor's Choice ★ 🍴 **El Coyote Mexican Food Inc.** Open since 1931, this landmark spot is perfect for those on a budget, or anyone after an authentic Mexican meal. The traditional fare is decadent and delicious; the margaritas are sweetened to perfection. **Known for:** affordable, quality cuisine; festive atmosphere; L.A. staple. [$] *Average main: $14* ✉ *7312 Beverly Blvd., Fairfax* ☎ *323/939–2255* 🌐 *www.elcoyotecafe.com* ✥ *2:E3.*

$$ CAFÉ FAMILY 🍴 **Joan's on Third.** Part restaurant, part bakery, part market, Joan's on Third has a little bit of everything. This roadside French-style café caters to families, the occasional local celebrity, and lovers of all things wholesome. **Known for:** crispy baguettes; fresh pastries; long lines. [$] *Average main: $16* ✉ *8350 W. 3rd St., West Hollywood* ☎ *323/655–2285* 🌐 *www.joansonthird.com* ✥ *2:D3.*

$$$$ MODERN AMERICAN 🍴 **Lucques.** Formerly the carriage house of silent film star Harold Lloyd, this ivy-laden, brick building has morphed into a chic restaurant that has elevated chef Suzanne Goin to national prominence. The California-inspired menu features seasonally changing dishes like grilled duck paillard and chanterelle lasagna, and staples like Goin's famous short ribs. **Known for:** stunning patio; James Beard Award–winning chef; famous short ribs. [$] *Average main: $35* ✉ *8474 Melrose Ave., West Hollywood* ☎ *323/655–6277* 🌐 *www.lucques.com* 🕒 *No lunch Sun. and Mon.* ✥ *2:C3.*

$$$ BRAZILIAN 🍴 **Odys and Penelope.** Named after the Greek mythological heroes, this purely South American restaurant features an open kitchen that blazes with beef, like Niman Ranch skirt steak and oak-grilled tri-tip. Veggies and sides are also phenomenal with a creamy cauliflower walnut pesto that will have you asking the Greek Gods how it was made. **Known for:** phenomenal warm cheese puffs; popular brunch spot. [$] *Average main: $30* ✉ *127 S. La Brea Ave., West Hollywood* ☎ *323/939–1033* 🌐 *www.odysandpenelope.com* 🕒 *Brunch weekends only* ✥ *2:E3.*

$$ MODERN MEXICAN FAMILY 🍴 **Petty Cash Taqueria.** A boisterous vibe permeates PCT as groups of twenty- and thirtysomethings feast on fresh guacamole under the graffitied walls. There are 10 or so tacos on the menu, from grilled octopus and Baja fish to pork belly and shrimp. **Known for:** house-made tortillas; delicious mescal cocktails. [$] *Average main: $15* ✉ *7360 Beverly Blvd., West Hollywood* ☎ *323/933–5300* 🌐 *www.pettycashtaqueria.com* 🕒 *No lunch Mon.–Thurs.* ✥ *2:E3.*

$$$$ FRENCH FAMILY Fodor's Choice ★ 🍴 **Republique.** This stunning expansive space, originally built for Charlie Chaplin back in the 1920s, serves French delicacies for breakfast, lunch, and dinner, every day of the week. The scent of homemade croissants waft through the building in the morning; steak frites can be enjoyed at night. **Known for:** classics like escargot; unbeatable pastries. [$] *Average main: $35* ✉ *624 S. La Brea Ave., West Hollywood* ☎ *310/362–6115* 🌐 *www.republiquela.com* ✥ *2:E4.*

$$ ✕ **The Sycamore Kitchen.** Sycamore Kitchen has one of the rarest fea-
AMERICAN tures in L.A.: a street-facing patio that's shielded from the traffic. Here,
FAMILY young families and local foodies dig into healthy breakfasts like butter-
milk rye pancakes or Jerusalem bowls with lentils and Zahtar chicken.
**Known for:** Rice Crispy cookie; healthy salads and sandwiches for
lunch. $ *Average main: $14* ✉ *143 S. La Brea Ave., West Hollywood*
☎ *323/939–0151* ⊕ *www.thesycamorekitchen.com* ✛ *2:E3.*

### BRENTWOOD

Everything from Asian fare to American comfort food can be found
throughout Brentwood's upscale dining scene.

$$$$ ✕ **Katsuya.** Highly regarded sushi chef Katsuya Uechi turns out spicy
JAPANESE tuna atop crispy rice, whimsical wonton cones filled with scoops of
silky crab and tuna tartare, and larger plates like miso-marinated black
cod. Don't neglect the plates from the robata bar, where skewers of
meats are grilled over hot coals. **Known for:** Philippe Starck–designed
space; delicious crispy rice. $ *Average main: $35* ✉ *11777 San Vicente
Blvd., Brentwood* ☎ *310/237–6174* ⊕ *www.katsuyarestaurant.com/
brentwood* ⊗ *No lunch weekends* ✛ *3:C2.*

### CENTURY CITY

This is the town where deals are made, ideas are discussed, and some
of the best meals can be discovered.

$$ ✕ **Clementine.** In fast-paced Century City, this quaint restaurant pays
CAFÉ homage to comfort food classics. Look for chicken potpie, macaroni
and cheese, roast beef sandwiches, and a slew of hearty salads.
**Known for:** family-owned neighborhood bakery; lunch to bring
to the beach. $ *Average main: $15* ✉ *1751 Ensley Ave., Century
City* ☎ *310/552–1080* ⊕ *www.clementineonline.com* ⊗ *Closed Sun.*
✛ *3:D2.*

$$$$ ✕ **Craft Los Angeles.** Accommodating Century City's growing legions of
MODERN agents and lawyers, Craft, around since 2007, is a major film indus-
AMERICAN try hangout. At the helm is *Top Chef* 's Tom Colicchio, who whips
up shared plates like roasted octopus and foie gras with apple butter.
**Known for:** house-made sorbet and ice cream; triple chocolate sun-
flower cookie; seasonal veggies. $ *Average main: $35* ✉ *10100 Constellation Blvd., Century City* ☎ *310/279–4180* ⊕ *www.craftlosangeles.
com* ⊗ *Closed Sun. No lunch Sat.* ✛ *2:A4.*

### CULVER CITY

Sandwiched between some of L.A.'s coolest neighborhoods, Culver City
has spent the past few years forming its own identity. A place for adventurous eaters, here you can find cuisines spanning the globe.

$$ ✕ **The Cannibal Beer and Butcher.** Don't mind the name: there's no human
AMERICAN on the menu, but meat lovers can rejoice in the various pork, cow, and
FAMILY chicken options. Try the cannibal burger, homemade jerky, or smoked
Carolina pork sausage while seated at wood tables in an Old West–chic
atmosphere. **Known for:** in-house butcher shop; brunch cocktails. $ *Av-
erage main: $18* ✉ *8850 Washington Blvd., Culver City* ☎ *310/838–
2783* ⊕ *www.thecanniballa.com* ✛ *3:F3.*

10

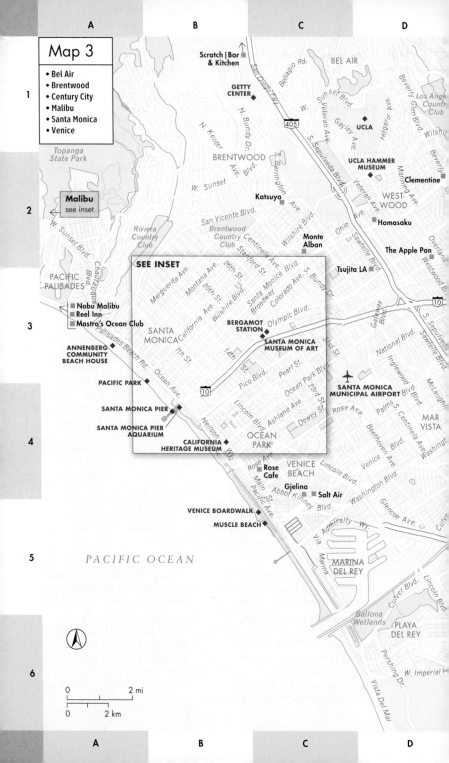

## Map 3

- Bel Air
- Brentwood
- Century City
- Malibu
- Santa Monica
- Venice

**A**     **B**     **C**     **D**

Scratch | Bar & Kitchen

GETTY CENTER

BEL AIR

Bellagio Rd.

Sunset Blvd.

N. Bundy Dr.

Beverly Glen Blvd.

Los Angeles Country Club

UCLA

Wilshire

UCLA HAMMER MUSEUM

Clementine

WESTWOOD

Hamasaku

The Apple Pan

Tsujita LA

Veteran Ave.

Gayley Ave.

Higard Ave.

Manning Ave.

S. Sepulveda Blvd.

Ohio

Sawtelle Blvd.

Overland

Westwood Bl.

405

Topanga State Park

Malibu
see inset

N. Kenter Ave.

BRENTWOOD

W. Sunset

S. Barrington Ave.

Katsuya

San Vicente Blvd.

Brentwood Country Club

Centinela Ave.

Wilshire Blvd.

Monte Alban

Riviera Country Club

W. Sunset Blvd.

Chautauqua Blvd.

PACIFIC PALISADES

Nobu Malibu
Reel Inn
Mastro's Ocean Club

ANNENBERG COMMUNITY BEACH HOUSE

PACIFIC PARK

SANTA MONICA PIER

SANTA MONICA PIER AQUARIUM

CALIFORNIA HERITAGE MUSEUM

Palisades Beach Rd.

Ocean Ave.

7th St.

Neilson Wy.

**SEE INSET**

Marguerita Ave.

Montana Ave.

California Ave.

20th St.

26th St.

Wilshire Blvd.

Santa Monica Blvd.

Broadway

Colorado Ave.

Stanford St.

S. Bundy Dr.

31st St.

SANTA MONICA

BERGAMOT STATION

Olympic Blvd.

SANTA MONICA MUSEUM OF ART

14th St.

Pico Blvd.

Pearl St.

Ocean Park Blvd.

Ashland Ave.

23rd St.

Dewey St.

Gateway Blvd.

National Blvd.

S. Sepulveda Blvd.

Sawtelle Blvd.

10

SANTA MONICA MUNICIPAL AIRPORT

Inglewood Blvd.

Palms Blvd.

S. Centinela Ave.

McLaughlin

MAR VISTA

Washington

Lincoln Blvd.

OCEAN PARK

Rose Ave.

Main St.

Pacific Ave.

VENICE BEACH

Rose Cafe

Gjelina

Salt Air

Abbot Kinney Blvd.

Beethoven Ave.

Venice Ave.

Washington Blvd.

Culver

VENICE BOARDWALK

MUSCLE BEACH

Via Marina

Admiralty Wy.

MARINA DEL REY

Glencoe Ave.

Culver Blvd.

Lincoln Blvd.

**PACIFIC OCEAN**

Ballona Wetlands

PLAYA DEL REY

Pershing Dr.

Vista Del Mar

W. Imperial H

0    2 mi

0    2 km

**A**     **B**     **C**     **D**

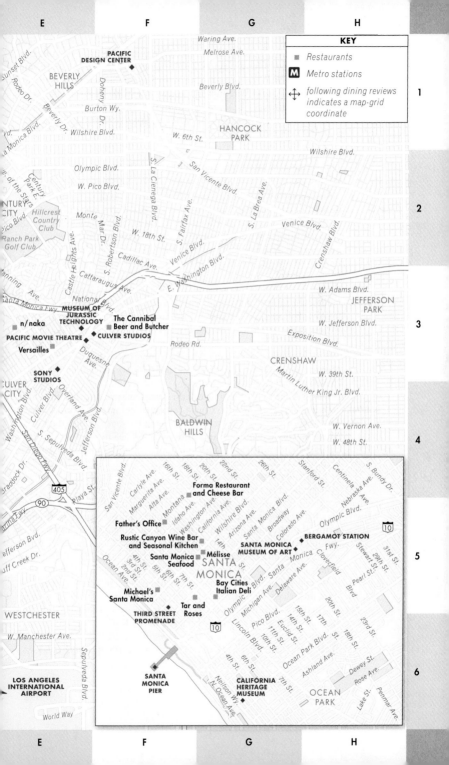

E    F    G    H

Waring Ave.
Melrose Ave.

**KEY**
■ Restaurants
Ⓜ Metro stations
⬌ following dining reviews
indicates a map-grid
coordinate

Sunset Blvd.
PACIFIC
DESIGN CENTER
BEVERLY
HILLS
Doheny Dr.
Beverly Blvd.
Burton Wy.
Rodeo Dr.
Beverly Dr.
Wilshire Blvd.
Monica Blvd.
W. 6th St.
HANCOCK
PARK
San Vicente Blvd.
Wilshire Blvd.

1

Olympic Blvd.
NTURY
CITY
Century
Park E.
Hillcrest
Country
Club
W. Pico Blvd.
Monte
Mar Dr.
S. La Cienega Blvd.
S. La Brea Ave.
Venice Blvd.
Crenshaw Blvd.

2

Pico Blvd.
Ranch Park
Golf Club
Castle Heights Ave.
S. Robertson Blvd.
Cadillac Ave.
W. 18th St.
S. Fairfax Ave.
Venice Blvd.
E. Washington Blvd.

anning    Ave.
Cattaraugus Ave.
National Blvd.
MUSEUM OF
JURASSIC
TECHNOLOGY
W. Adams Blvd.
JEFFERSON
PARK
Santa Monica Fwy.
n/naka
The Cannibal
Beer and Butcher
W. Jefferson Blvd.

3

PACIFIC MOVIE THEATRE
CULVER STUDIOS
Versailles
Duquesne
Ave.
Rodeo Rd.
Exposition Blvd.
CRENSHAW
W. 39th St.
Martin Luther King Jr. Blvd.

SONY
STUDIOS
CULVER
CITY
Culver Blvd.
Overland Ave.
Jefferson Blvd.
BALDWIN
HILLS
W. Vernon Ave.
W. 48th St.

4

Washington Blvd.
S. Sepulveda Blvd.
San Diego Fwy.
Braddock Dr.
405
90
arina Fwy.
San Vicente Blvd.
Carlyle Ave.
Marguerita Ave.
Alta Ave.
16th St.
18th St.
20th St.
22nd St.
26th St.
Forma Restaurant
and Cheese Bar
Stanford St.
Centinela Ave.
S. Bundy Dr.
Nebraska Ave.
Olympic Blvd.
31st St.
10

jefferson Blvd.
uff Creek Dr.
Father's Office
Rustic Canyon Wine Bar
and Seasonal Kitchen
Montana
Idaho Ave.
Washington Ave.
California Ave.
Wilshire Blvd.
Arizona Ave.
Santa Monica Blvd.
Broadway
Colorado Ave.
BERGAMOT STATION
Fwy.
Cloverfield
29th St.
Pearl St.
Stewart St.
30th St.

5

Santa Monica
Seafood
Mélisse
Ocean Ave.
4th St.
3rd St.
5th St.
7th St.
SANTA
MONICA
SANTA MONICA
MUSEUM OF ART
Olympic Blvd.
Santa Monica
Delaware Ave.
20th St.
17th St.
18th St.
23rd St.

WESTCHESTER
Michael's
Santa Monica
THIRD STREET
PROMENADE
Tar and
Roses
Bay Cities
Italian Deli
10
Michigan Ave.
Pico Blvd.
Lincoln Blvd.
15th St.
14th St.
11th St.
Euclid St.
Ocean Park Blvd.
Ashland Ave.
Dewey St.
Rose Ave.
Penmar Ave.

6

W. Manchester Ave.
Sepulveda Blvd.
LOS ANGELES
INTERNATIONAL
AIRPORT
World Way
SANTA
MONICA
PIER
Nielson Wy.
N. Ocean Ave.
4th St.
6th St.
CALIFORNIA
HERITAGE
MUSEUM
10th St.
7th St.
OCEAN
PARK
Lake St.

E    F    G    H

**$$$$** ✕ **n/naka.** *Chef's Table* star Niki Nakayama helms this *omakase*
JAPANESE (chef-selected) fine dining establishment. Small and intimate, any
Fodor's Choice given night will feature sashimi with kanpachi, sea bass with uni
★ butter, or Myazaki Wagyu beef. **Known for:** three-hour meals; excellent sake pairings. $ *Average main: $185* ✉ *3455 Overland Ave.,*
*Culver City* ☎ *310/836–6252* ⊕ *www.n-naka.com* ✆ *Closed Sun.*
*and Mon.* ✛ *3:E3.*

## WEST LOS ANGELES
The Westside has a cutting-edge dining scene that's slightly more family-
friendly, with primarily moderate and casual spots.

**$** ✕ **The Apple Pan.** A favorite since 1947, this unassuming joint with a
AMERICAN horseshoe-shaped counter—no tables here—turns out one heck of a
Fodor's Choice good burger. Try the cheeseburger with Tillamook cheddar, or the
★ hickory burger with barbecue sauce. **Known for:** indulgent apple
pie; perfect fries; Sanka coffee. $ *Average main: $8* ✉ *10801 W.*
*Pico Blvd., West L.A.* ☎ *310/475–3585* ▭ *No credit cards* ✆ *Closed*
*Mon.* ✛ *3:D2.*

**$$$** ✕ **Hamasaku.** A power lunch spot for Hollywood deal makers, this strip
JAPANESE mall sushi joint is decorated with fine art and serves up some of the
freshest fish in L.A. No one would fault you for getting a table, but
sitting at the bar and ordering directly from Chef Yoya Takahashi is
another experience altogether. **Known for:** celeb-inspired rolls; most
affordable omakase meal in town. $ *Average main: $25* ✉ *11043 Santa*
*Monica Blvd., West L.A.* ☎ *310/479–7636* ⊕ *www.hamasakula.com*
✆ *No lunch weekends* ✛ *3:D2.*

**$$** ✕ **Monte Alban.** This family-owned restaurant specializes in the subtle
MEXICAN cooking of one of Mexico's most respected culinary regions: Oaxaca.
FAMILY The flavors here are intense without being fiery, as families dine under
Mexican-themed murals and antique masks. **Known for:** signature
chiles rellenos; delicious sweet plantains; complex moles. $ *Average*
*main: $15* ✉ *11927 Santa Monica Blvd., West L.A.* ☎ *310/444–7736*
⊕ *montealbanrestaurante.com* ✛ *3:C2.*

**$** ✕ **Tsujita LA.** The crown prince of ramen in Los Angeles deserves every
JAPANESE accolade thrown at it. With lines wrapped around the block, patrons
FAMILY await *tonkotsu* (a pork broth that simmers for 60 hours) with tender
Fodor's Choice strips of pork, semi-hard noodles, wood ear mushrooms, and bamboo
★ shoots. **Known for:** spicy tuna; salmon bowls; long lines. $ *Average*
*main: $11* ✉ *2057 Sawtelle Blvd., West L.A.* ☎ *310/231–7373* ⊕ *www.*
*tsujita-la.com* ✛ *3:D3.*

**$** ✕ **Versailles.** Locals line up outside the door for Versailles's respectable,
CUBAN bargain-priced Cuban food. Diners go crazy over the citrusy mojo-
FAMILY marinated chicken seasoned with loads of garlic; others prefer flank
steak, paella, or *ropa vieja* (shredded beef). **Known for:** Cuban-style
flan; great for vegetarians. $ *Average main: $13* ✉ *10319 Venice Blvd.,*
*West L.A.* ☎ *310/558–3168* ⊕ *www.versaillescuban.com* ✛ *3:E3.*

## SANTA MONICA AND THE BEACHES

In these neighborhoods, choose from a diverse collection of eateries—from sandwich shops to upscale seafood houses—that cater to the healthy and active lifestyle of locals. But beware of overpriced eateries betting that an ocean view will help you forget about substandard value and quality. Fortunately, they're easy to avoid by sticking to our list here. As for budget eats, there are plenty of cafés, burger shacks, and casual chains that won't raise an eyebrow when you walk in with your sandy flip-flops.

### SANTA MONICA

This idyllic seaside town is a hotbed of culinary activity, with a dynamic farmers' market that attracts chefs from all over Los Angeles and local restaurants that celebrate seasonal dining.

$ DELI 🍴 **Bay Cities Italian Deli.** Part deli, part market, Bay Cities has been home to incredible Italian subs since 1925. This renowned counter service spot is always crowded (best to order ahead), but monster subs run the gamut from the mighty meatball, to their signature "Godmother" made with prosciutto, ham, capicola, mortadella, Genoa salami, and provolone. **Known for:** market with rare imports; excellent service. [$] *Average main: $10* ✉ *1517 Lincoln Blvd., Santa Monica* ☎ *310/395–8279* 🌐 *www.baycitiesitaliandeli.com* 🕒 *Closed Mon.* ✥ *3:G5.*

$$ AMERICAN 🍴 **Father's Office.** Distinguished by its vintage neon sign, this pub is famous for handcrafted beers and a brilliant signature burger. Topped with Gruyère and Maytag blue cheeses, arugula, caramelized onions, and applewood-smoked bacon compote, the "Office Burger" is a guilty pleasure worth waiting in line for, which is usually required. **Known for:** addictive sweet-potato fries; strict no-substitutions policy. [$] *Average main: $15* ✉ *1018 Montana Ave., Santa Monica* ☎ *310/736–2224* 🌐 *www.fathersoffice.com* 🕒 *No lunch weekdays* ✥ *3:F5.*

$$$ ITALIAN 🍴 **Forma Restaurant and Cheese Bar.** Pasta is served here "Dalla Forma," meaning it's cooked, then dipped into a cheese wheel and stirred up before serving. Catering to a higher-end crowd, Forma specializes in cheeses, pastas, and pizzas. **Known for:** generous happy hour; fresh mozzarella knots; Roman-style crispy artichokes. [$] *Average main: $28* ✉ *1610 Montana Ave., Santa Monica* ☎ *424/231–2868* 🌐 *www.formarestaurant.com* ✥ *3:F4.*

$$$ MODERN AMERICAN 🍴 **Michael's Santa Monica.** Michael's is a Santa Monica institution, and after a remodel, new chef, and menu, its reputation is secure. The New American shared-plates menu runs the gamut from a potatoes à la plancha (divine) to a duck breast (buttery) to a barbecued quail (sumptuous). **Known for:** stunning patio; incredible cheesecake. [$] *Average main: $30* ✉ *1147 3rd St., Santa Monica* ☎ *310/451–0843* 🌐 *www.michaelssantamonica.com* 🕒 *Closed Sun. No lunch* ✥ *3:F5.*

$$$$ FRENCH Fodor's Choice ★ 🍴 **Mélisse.** Chef-owner Josiah Citrin enhances his modern French cooking with seasonal California produce. The tasting menu might feature a white-corn ravioli in brown butter-truffle froth, lobster Bolognese, or elegant table-side presentations of Dover sole and stuffed rotisserie chicken. **Known for:** domestic and European cheese cart; contemporary/elegant decor. [$] *Average main: $135* ✉ *1104 Wilshire Blvd., Santa Monica* ☎ *310/395–0881* 🌐 *www.melisse.com* 🕒 *Closed Sun. and Mon. No lunch* ✥ *3:F5.*

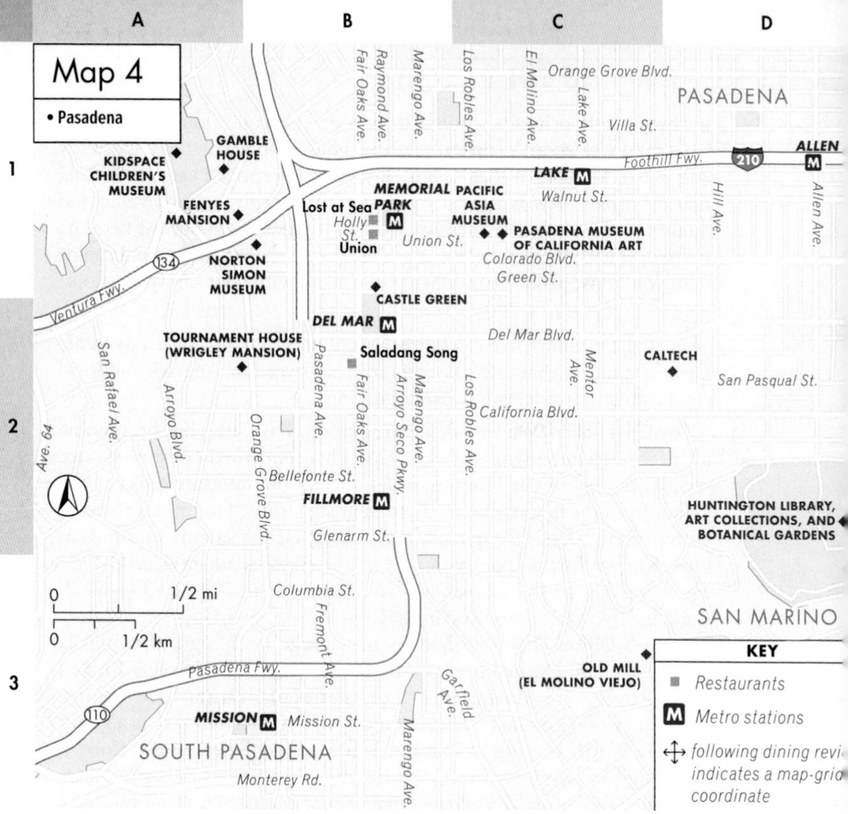
A
B
C
D
1
2
3
Map 4
• Pasadena
PASADENA
SAN MARINO
SOUTH PASADENA
Orange Grove Blvd.
Villa St.
Foothill Fwy.
210
ALLEN
LAKE
Walnut St.
Hill Ave.
Allen Ave.
Fair Oaks Ave.
Raymond Ave.
Marengo Ave.
Los Robles Ave.
El Molino Ave.
Lake Ave.
KIDSPACE CHILDREN'S MUSEUM
GAMBLE HOUSE
FENYES MANSION
NORTON SIMON MUSEUM
134
Ventura Fwy.
MEMORIAL PARK
PACIFIC ASIA MUSEUM
Lost at Sea
Holly St.
Union
Union St.
PASADENA MUSEUM OF CALIFORNIA ART
Colorado Blvd.
Green St.
CASTLE GREEN
DEL MAR
Del Mar Blvd.
TOURNAMENT HOUSE (WRIGLEY MANSION)
Saladang Song
Mentor Ave.
CALTECH
San Pasqual St.
San Rafael Ave.
Arroyo Blvd.
Orange Grove Blvd.
Pasadena Ave.
Fair Oaks Ave.
Arroyo Seco Pkwy.
Marengo Ave.
Los Robles Ave.
California Blvd.
Ave. 64
Bellefonte St.
FILLMORE
Glenarm St.
HUNTINGTON LIBRARY, ART COLLECTIONS, AND BOTANICAL GARDENS
0
1/2 mi
0
1/2 km
Columbia St.
Fremont Ave.
Pasadena Fwy.
OLD MILL (EL MOLINO VIEJO)
Garfield Ave.
110
MISSION
Mission St.
Monterey Rd.
Marengo Ave.
KEY
Restaurants
Metro stations
following dining revi
indicates a map-grid
coordinate

$$$$ MODERN AMERICAN 🍴 **Rustic Canyon Wine Bar and Seasonal Kitchen.** A Santa Monica mainstay, the seasonally changing menu at this California-inspired restaurant consistently upends norms. The homey, minimalist space offers sweeping views of Wilshire Boulevard, and on any given night the menu may include smoked duck pastrami with foie gras and truffles, or ricotta dumplings with butter beans. **Known for:** never-ending wine list; knowledgeable staff. [$] *Average main: $35* ✉ *1119 Wilshire Blvd., Santa Monica* ☎ *310/393–7050* 🌐 *www.rusticcanyonwinebar.com* ✥ *3:F5.*

$$ SEAFOOD FAMILY 🍴 **Santa Monica Seafood.** A Southern California favorite, this Italian seafood haven has been serving up fresh fish since 1939. Come for lunch or dinner, but make sure to take time to stroll around the market, read up on the history, and enjoy free tastings of the specials. **Known for:** deliciously seasoned rainbow trout; oyster bar; kids' meals. [$] *Average main: $20* ✉ *1000 Wilshire Blvd., Santa Monica* ☎ *310/393–5244* 🌐 *www.santamonicaseafood.com* ✥ *3:F5.*

$$$ MODERN AMERICAN 🍴 **Tar and Roses.** This small and dimly lit romantic spot in Santa Monica is full of adventurous options, like octopus and venison. The New American cuisine also features standouts like lamb tartare and drool-worthy strawberry tart for dessert. **Known for:** phenomenal oxtail dumplings; delicious hanger steak. [$] *Average main: $30* ✉ *602 Santa Monica Blvd., Santa Monica* ☎ *310/587–0700* 🌐 *www.tarandroses.com* ✥ *3:F5.*

## VENICE

A bit rough around the edges, this urban beach town is home to many of L.A.'s artists, skaters, and surfers. The dining scene continues to grow, but remains true to its cool and casual roots.

$$ ✕ **Gjelina.** Gjelina comes alive the minute you walk through the rustic
AMERICAN wooden door and into a softly lit dining room with long communal tables. The menu is seasonal, with outstanding small plates, charcuterie, pastas, and pizza. **Known for:** lively crowd on the patio; late-night menu; wild nettle pizza. Ⓢ *Average main: $20* ✉ *1429 Abbot Kinney Blvd., Venice* ☎ *310/450–1429* ⊕ *www.gjelina.com* ✛ *3:C4.*

$$$ ✕ **Rose Cafe.** This jaw-dropping restaurant serving mouthwatering
MODERN California cuisines features multiple patios, a full bar, and a bakery.
AMERICAN Creative types loiter for the Wi-Fi and sip espressos, while young fami-
FAMILY lies gather out back to nibble on yellowtail crudo and crispy brussels sprouts. **Known for:** sophisticated but unpretentious; in the heart of Venice. Ⓢ *Average main: $25* ✉ *220 Rose Ave., Venice* ☎ *310/399–0711* ⊕ *www.rosecafevenice.com* ◷ *Closed Mon.* ✛ *3:C4.*

$$$ ✕ **Salt Air.** A white marlin is camouflaged by the stark white walls in this
SEAFOOD hip Venice seafood spot. On trendy Abbot Kinney Boulevard, groups and daters pop in for lunch or dinner to shuck oysters by the dozen or enjoy tender grilled octopus by the tentacle. **Known for:** sumptuous monkey bread; freshest catch determines daily specials. Ⓢ *Average main: $30* ✉ *1616 Abbot Kinney Blvd., Venice* ☎ *310/396–9333* ⊕ *www.saltairvenice.com* ✛ *3:C4.*

## MALIBU

The beauty of the coastline makes every meal here taste like the best you've ever had. Here you'll find quaint family spots and extravagant hot spots.

$$$$ ✕ **Mastro's Ocean Club.** This steak house not only features the best views of
STEAKHOUSE the beach, it's also a great place to scope out A-listers. You may be paying for the ambience, but mouthwatering steaks, Dungeness crab, and lobster mashed potatoes just seem to taste better when the ocean is nipping at your feet. **Known for:** lively weekend brunch; live jazz nightly; reserve in advance. Ⓢ *Average main: $50* ✉ *18412 Pacific Coast Hwy., Malibu* ☎ *310/454–4357* ⊕ *www.mastrosrestaurants.com* ✛ *3:A3.*

$$$$ ✕ **Nobu Malibu.** At famous chef-restaurateur Nobu Matsuhisa's coastal
JAPANESE outpost, super-chic clientele sails in for morsels of the world's finest fish. It's hard not to be seduced by the oceanfront property, and stellar sushi and ingenious specialties match the upscale setting. **Known for:** exotic fish; toro with truffle teriyaki; bento box chocolate soufflé. Ⓢ *Average main: $35* ✉ *22706 Pacific Coast Hwy., Malibu* ☎ *310/317–9140* ⊕ *www.noburestaurants.com* ✛ *3:A3.*

$$ ✕ **Reel Inn.** Long wooden tables and booths are often filled with fish-
SEAFOOD loving families chowing down on mahi-mahi sandwiches and freshly
FAMILY caught swordfish. Outside, an expansive dog-friendly patio lets patrons enjoy the sounds and smells of the ocean across the street while washing down their conquests with ice cold brews and lemonade. **Known for:** easy-to-miss spot on the PCH; fresh catches. Ⓢ *Average main: $17* ✉ *18661 Pacific Coast Hwy., Malibu* ☎ *310/456–8221* ⊕ *www.reelinnmalibu.com* ✛ *3:A3.*

10

## PASADENA

With the revitalization of Old Town Pasadena, more people are discovering the beauty of Rose City. They mingle at bistros, upscale eateries, and taco trucks, but are also discovering the newer innovative dining spots that are giving Pasadena a hipper feel.

$$$$ SEAFOOD 🍴 **Lost at Sea.** A nautical-themed seafood restaurant is giving Pasadena couples another reason to go out at night. The seasonally changing menu might feature amberjack crudo or crostino with chopped octopus. **Known for:** perfectly cooked albacore tuna; always packed. [$] *Average main: $33* ✉ *57 Holly St., Pasadena* ☎ *626/385–7644* 🌐 *www.lostatseapas.com* ⏲ *Closed Mon.* ✣ *4:B1.*

$$ THAI 🍴 **Saladang Song.** With pierced steel paneled walls covered with fanciful designs, this tucked-away Thai palace has an extensive menu with all the SE Asian favorites, including satays, curries, and pad Thai. But consider the restaurant's other specialties, like the Thai omelet with ground chicken or the fried taro rolls served with a cucumber salad. **Known for:** mango and sweet sticky rice; secluded location. [$] *Average main: $15* ✉ *383 S. Fair Oaks Ave., Pasadena* ☎ *626/793–5200* 🌐 *www.saladang-thai.com* ✣ *4:B2.*

$$$ ITALIAN Fodor's Choice ★ 🍴 **Union.** There's a Michelin-quality Italian restaurant hiding in plain sight in Pasadena. The small and homey space is typically filled to the brim as diners await heaven-sent wild mushrooms with G&T polenta or the squid ink bombolotti with Maine lobster. **Known for:** superb wine list; great service. [$] *Average main: $31* ✉ *37 E. Union St., Pasadena* ☎ *626/795–5841* 🌐 *www.unionpasadena.com* ⏲ *No lunch* ✣ *4:B1.*

# WHERE TO STAY

Updated by
Michele Bigley

When it comes to finding a place to stay, travelers have never been more spoiled for choice than in today's Los Angeles. From luxurious digs in Beverly Hills and along the coast, to budget boutiques in Hollywood, hotels are stepping up service, upgrading amenities, and trying all-new concepts, like upscale hostels and retro-chic motels. Hotels in Los Angeles today are more than just a place to rest your head; they're a key part of the experience.

True to Hollywood's character, the city's ambitious makeover has all the paparazzi swooning. Over a dozen new properties have broken ground in L.A.'s heart, most notably the first American outpost of Mama Shelter and the upscale Dream Hollywood Hotel, while nearby, those with deep pockets will go gaga over the city's most buzzed about openings—The James West Hollywood and the deluxe Waldorf Astoria Beverly Hills.

If you have cash to spend, you'll find plenty of luxurious options in this edition. Nearly every major upscale hotel has a new look today, with the Mondrian, The London West Hollywood, Mosaic Hotel, and the Four Seasons at Beverly Hills leading the pack. For beachfront escapes, Terranea and Shutters on the Beach still remain at the top of Angelenos' lists as the best spots for staycations.

# PLANNER

### RESERVATIONS

Hotel reservations are an absolute necessity when planning your trip to Los Angeles—although rooms are easier to come by these days. Competition for clients also means properties undergo frequent improvements, so when booking ask about any renovations, lest you get a room within earshot of construction. In this ever-changing city travelers can find themselves without amenities like room service or spa access if their hotel is upgrading.

# WHERE SHOULD I STAY?

| | Neighborhood Vibe | Pros | Cons |
|---|---|---|---|
| Downtown | High-rises, office towers, commercial districts, and cultural institutions, with a growing residential scene. | Affordable hotels within walking distance of art museums, concert halls, and the L.A. Live complex. | Homeless encampments, with some sketchy areas at night. |
| Hollywood | Historic theaters and the Walk of Fame; L.A.'s Time Square. | Heart of the city's nightlife and see-and-be-seen spots, from lively nightclubs to popular eateries. | Steep parking fees, tourist trap, often crowded. |
| Studio City, Universal City, and North Hollywood | Residential and suburban feel, with some commercial (strip-mall) spots. | Safe, family-friendly, affordable accommodations, plentiful dining options. | Requires a car to get anywhere, even to a nearby coffee shop. |
| Beverly Hills | Upscale—one of the city's most sought-after addresses, with classy and elegant hotels. | Great shopping, celeb spotting, numerous restaurants all near quiet residential areas. | Big bucks to stay, dine, park, and shop here; limited diversity. |
| Culver City | Businesses mixed with residential buildings; centrally located. | Easy access to all points on the Westside; pedestrian-friendly strip in Culver City. | Some strictly office areas, no beach or ocean views. |
| Bel Air, West Hollywood, Westwood | Coveted neighborhood for elite; boutique hotels abound in West Hollywood. | Close proximity to Getty Center; ambitious restaurants and fun nightspots in West Hollywood. | Stuffy attitudes in Bel Air; spendy stays in West Hollywood. |
| LAX vicinity | Concentration of office towers and commercial buildings. | Convenient location near airport; incredibly affordable. | Little activity, dull nearby strip malls with restaurants and shopping. |
| Santa Monica and Malibu | Upscale beach towns with waterfront resorts, and hip boutique properties. | Ocean breezes, super-safe, family-friendly; walkable pockets with restaurants, cafés, and boutiques. | Some bars, but limited nightlife; steep prices for an ocean view. |
| Venice, Marina Del Rey, Manhattan, Hermosa, Long Beach | Edgy, artsy in Venice; residential in Manhattan Beach; sailing and biking in Marina del Rey. | Diverse neighborhoods but close to the ocean without Malibu's spendiness. Long Beach airport is a great alternative to LAX. | Mostly residential in some pockets; traffic along Highway 1 means long driving times. |
| Pasadena | Residential with walkable strip of shops and cafés. | Charming small-town feel, family-friendly, historic. | Removed from Westside and beaches; lengthy driving time into the city. |

### SERVICES
Most hotels have air-conditioning and flat-screen cable TV. Those in the moderate and expensive price ranges often have voice mail, coffeemakers, bathrobes, and hair dryers. Most also have high-speed Internet access in guest rooms, with a 24-hour use fee (though at a number of hotels, it's free). Wi-Fi is common even at budget properties. Southern California's emphasis on being in shape means most hotels have fitness facilities; if the one on-site is not to your liking, ask for a reference to a nearby sports club or gym.

### STAYING WITH KIDS
From Disneyland to the beach cities, laid-back Los Angeles definitely has a reputation as a family-friendly destination. Resorts and hotels along the coast, in particular, attract plenty of beach-going family vacationers looking for sun and sandcastles. Some properties provide such diversions as in-room movies, toys, and video games; others have suites with kitchenettes and foldout sofa beds. Hotels often provide cribs, rollaway beds, and references to babysitting services, but make arrangements when booking the room, not when you arrive. *Properties that are especially kid-friendly are marked FAMILY throughout the chapter.*

### PARKING
Exploring Los Angeles, a sprawling city of wide boulevards and five-lane freeways, requires a car. Though you might stroll Rodeo Drive on foot or amble along the Hollywood Walk of Fame, to get from one part of town to another, you'll need wheels. Thankfully, there's street parking in most areas (read signs carefully as some neighborhoods are by permit only) and many public parking lots are free for the first hour or two. Though a few hotels have free parking, most charge for the privilege, and some resorts only have valet parking, with fees as high as $50 per night.

### PRICES
Tax rates for the area will add 10%–14% to your bill depending on where in Los Angeles County you stay; some hoteliers tack on energy, service, or occupancy surcharges—ask about customary charges when you book your room.

When looking for a hotel, don't write off the pricier establishments immediately. Price categories here are determined by "rack rates"—the list price of a hotel room—which is often higher than those you'll find online or by calling the hotel directly. Specials abound, particularly in Downtown on the weekends. Many hotels have packages that include breakfast, theater tickets, spa services, or luxury rental cars. Pricing is competitive, so always check with the hotel for current special offers.

When making reservations, don't forget to check the hotel's website for exclusive online specials.

| WHAT IT COSTS | | | |
|---|---|---|---|
| $ | $$ | $$$ | $$$$ |
| Hotels | under $200 | $200–$300 | $301–$400 | over $400 |

Prices in the hotel reviews are the lowest cost of a standard double room in high season.

# HOTEL REVIEWS

*Use the coordinate (✥ 1:B2) at the end of each listing to locate a site on the corresponding map. Hotel reviews have been shortened. For full information, visit Fodors.com.*

## DOWNTOWN

An ongoing revitalization in Downtown, anchored around the L.A. Live complex, along with a thriving, hipster vibe in Koreatown and Echo Park make these areas a great place to see Los Angeles in transition: Think affordable accommodations rubbing elbows with business hotels, streets lined with coffeehouses, and edgy boutiques that can be explored on foot. If you're traveling alone, some parts of Downtown are better to drive rather than walk through after dark.

$$ HOTEL **Ace Hotel Downtown Los Angeles.** The L.A. edition of this bohemian-chic hipster haven is at once a hotel, theater, bar, and poolside lounge, housed in the gorgeous Spanish Gothic–style United Artists building in the heart of Downtown. **Pros:** lively rooftop lounge/pool area, aptly named Upstairs; gorgeous building and views; heart of Downtown. **Cons:** expensive parking rates compared to nightly rates ($36); some kinks in the service; compact rooms. [$] *Rooms from: $239* ✉ *929 S. Broadway, Downtown* ☎ *213/623–3233* 🌐 *www.acehotel.com/losangeles* 🛏 *183 rooms* 🍴 *No meals* ✥ *1:B3.*

$$ HOTEL **Hilton Checkers Los Angeles.** Opened as the Mayflower Hotel in 1927, Checkers combines its original character and period detail with contemporary luxuries such as pillow-top mattresses and high-speed Internet, and offers views of the L.A. Library and the Downtown skyline from its rooftop deck. **Pros:** historic charm; 24-hour room service; business-friendly. **Cons:** no on-street parking and valet is over $38.50; some rooms are compact. [$] *Rooms from: $229* ✉ *535 S. Grand Ave., Downtown* ☎ *213/624–0000, 800/445–8667* 🌐 *www.hilton.com* 🛏 *193 rooms* 🍴 *No meals* ✥ *1:B3.*

$ B&B/INN **The Inn at 657.** Proprietor Patsy Carter runs a homey, welcoming bed-and-breakfast near the University of Southern California that is decked out in period antiques with Far East accents, and offers a lavish breakfast and a private garden frequented by hummingbirds. **Pros:** vintage home and quiet garden; homemade treats; accessible innkeeper. **Cons:** low-tech stay; no elevator. [$] *Rooms from: $159* ✉ *657 W. 23rd St., Downtown* ☎ *213/741–2200* 🌐 *theinnat657la.com* 🛏 *6 rooms* 🍴 *Breakfast* ✥ *1:A3.*

$$ HOTEL FAMILY **JW Marriott Los Angeles at L.A. Live.** Set in a shimmering blue-glass tower, the 878-room convention center-adjacent hotel anchors the L.A. Live entertainment complex that's home to the Microsoft Theatre and more than a dozen bars, nightclubs, and eateries. **Pros:** higher floors have jetliner views; movie theaters, restaurants, and a pro sports arena are just out the door; excellent bacon burger at Ford's Filling Station. **Cons:** imposing and crowded lobby; expensive dining choices and valet ($45). [$] *Rooms from: $279* ✉ *900 W. Olympic Blvd., Downtown* ☎ *213/765–8600* 🌐 *www.lalivemarriott.com* 🛏 *888 rooms* 🍴 *No meals* ✥ *1:A3.*

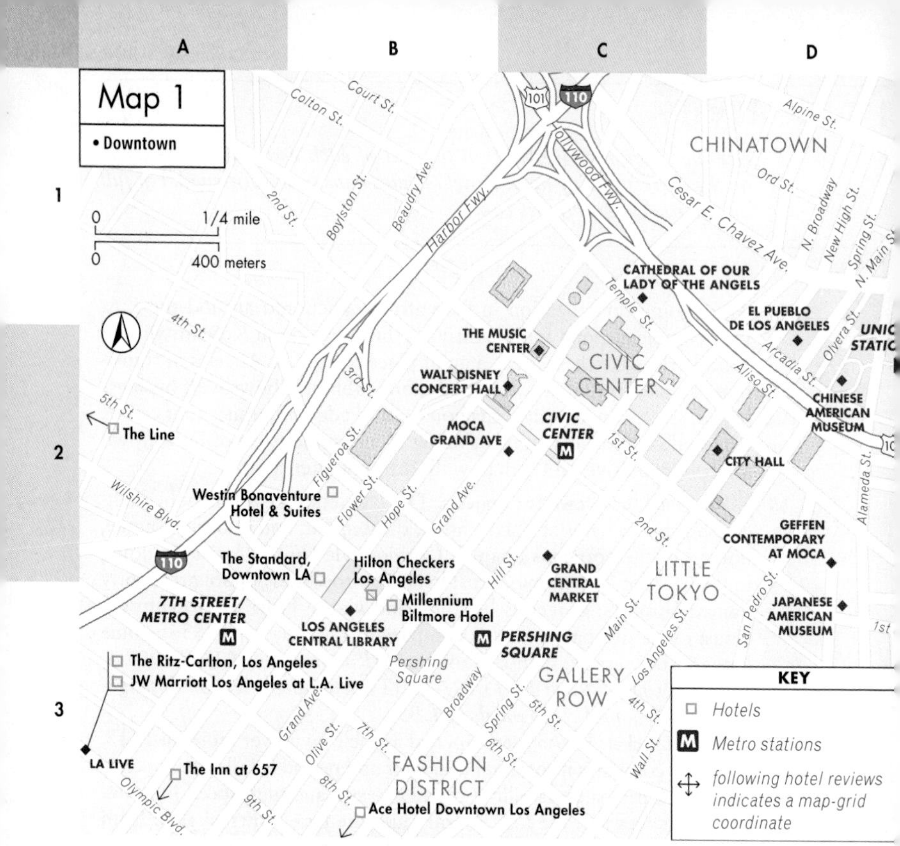
A
B
C
D
1
2
3
Map 1
• Downtown
0
1/4 mile
0
400 meters
Colton St.
Court St.
2nd St.
Boylston St.
Beaudry Ave.
Harbor Fwy.
Hollywood Fwy.
101
110
Alpine St.
CHINATOWN
Ord St.
Cesar E. Chavez Ave.
N. Broadway
New High St.
Spring St.
N. Main St.
4th St.
5th St.
3rd St.
CATHEDRAL OF OUR LADY OF THE ANGELS
Temple St.
EL PUEBLO DE LOS ANGELES
THE MUSIC CENTER
CIVIC CENTER
Arcadia St.
Olvera St.
UNION STATION
WALT DISNEY CONCERT HALL
Aliso St.
CHINESE AMERICAN MUSEUM
The Line
Figueroa St.
MOCA GRAND AVE
CIVIC CENTER
1st St.
CITY HALL
Alameda St.
Wilshire Blvd.
Westin Bonaventure Hotel & Suites
Flower St.
Hope St.
Grand Ave.
2nd St.
GEFFEN CONTEMPORARY AT MOCA
The Standard, Downtown LA
Hilton Checkers Los Angeles
Hill St.
GRAND CENTRAL MARKET
LITTLE TOKYO
San Pedro St.
Millennium Biltmore Hotel
7TH STREET/ METRO CENTER
JAPANESE AMERICAN MUSEUM
Main St.
Los Angeles St.
1st
LOS ANGELES CENTRAL LIBRARY
PERSHING SQUARE
The Ritz-Carlton, Los Angeles
Pershing Square
JW Marriott Los Angeles at L.A. Live
GALLERY ROW
KEY
Hotels
Metro stations
following hotel reviews indicates a map-grid coordinate
Broadway
Grand Ave.
Spring St.
5th St.
4th St.
Olive St.
7th St.
6th St.
Wall St.
LA LIVE
The Inn at 657
FASHION DISTRICT
Olympic Blvd.
9th St.
8th St.
Ace Hotel Downtown Los Angeles

$$$ HOTEL 🏨 **Millennium Biltmore Hotel.** As the local headquarters of John F. Kennedy's 1960 presidential campaign and the location of some of the earliest Academy Awards ceremonies, this Downtown treasure, with its gilded 1923 beaux-arts design, exudes ambience and history. **Pros:** 24-hour business center; tiled indoor pool and steam room; multimillion-dollar refurbishment in 2017. **Cons:** pricey valet parking ($45); standard rooms are compact. [$] *Rooms from: $349* ✉ *506 S. Grand Ave., Downtown* ☎ *213/624–1011, 866/866–8086* 🌐 *www.millenniumhotels.com* 🛏 *683 rooms* 🍴 *No meals* ✥ *1:B3.*

$$$ HOTEL 🏨 **The Ritz-Carlton, Los Angeles.** This citified Ritz-Carlton on the 23rd–26th floors of a 54-story tower within Downtown's L.A. Live entertainment complex features skyline views through expansive windows, blond woods, and smartened-up amenities such as flat-screen TVs (including one hidden in the bathroom mirror). **Pros:** designer spa *Jetsons*-esque relaxation room; rooftop pool; daily buffet of five light meals. **Cons:** expensive valet parking ($45); pricey room service. [$] *Rooms from: $379* ✉ *900 W. Olympic Blvd., Downtown* ☎ *213/742–6855* 🌐 *www.ritzcarlton.com* 🛏 *123 rooms* 🍴 *No meals* ✥ *1:A3.*

$$ HOTEL 🏨 **The Standard, Downtown L.A.** Built in 1955 as the headquarters of Standard Oil, the building was completely revamped in 2002 under the sharp eye of owner André Balazs, to become a sleek, cutting-edge hotel with spacious guest rooms. **Pros:** Rudy's barbershop on-site; 24/7 coffee

**CLOSE UP**

## Spa Specialists

Angelenos like to take their time. Here, there's a strong focus on wellness and finding ways to de-stress. Case in point, the ubiquitousness of spas in the city, where residents fit massages into their weekly routine.

When booking a massage, specify your preference for a male or female therapist. Give yourself time to arrive early and relax via steam, sauna, or Jacuzzi depending on the spa's selection. Tip at least 15% to 20%.

**Bliss at the W Hollywood.** Want that red-carpet glow? Bliss, tucked inside the W Hollywood Hotel, provides super-hydrating triple-oxygen-treatment facials that plump and reinvigorate. ⊠ *6250 Hollywood Blvd., Hollywood* ☎ *877/862–5477.*

**Chuan Spa at the Langham Huntington.** Chinese medicine–influenced therapies at the Huntington Spa help restore balance and harmony to the body via meditative breathing rituals and acupressure. ⊠ *1401 S. Oak Knoll Ave., Pasadena* ☎ *626/585–6414.*

**Hotel Bel-Air Spa by La Prairie.** This upscale spa in one of the city's most posh areas delivers anti-aging treatments in relaxing treatment rooms. Favorites include the caviar and the gold facials. ⊠ *701 Stone Canyon, Bel Air* ☎ *310/909–1681.*

**One Spa at Shutters on the Beach.** Treatments at Santa Monica's One aim to relax the body and mind. Body treatments here, such as the Moroccan Hammam, turn skin silky soft using all-natural tonics. ⊠ *Shutters on the Beach, 1 Pico Blvd., Santa Monica* ☎ *310/587–1712.*

**Peninsula Spa at the Peninsula Beverly Hills.** Rarefied treatments at this exclusive rooftop retreat include massages with oils laced with pulverized precious stones. ⊠ *9882 S. Santa Monica Blvd., Beverly Hills* ☎ *310/551–2888.*

**Spa at the Beverly Wilshire.** Rub elbows with celebs (or play out your *Pretty Woman* fantasies) at the Spa at the Beverly Wilshire with a mani-pedi, followed by an afternoon at the pool. Features include a fabulous rain shower (cascades vary from a cool mist to a brisk Atlantic storm); a mosaic-tile steam room; superstar facial treatments like hydra-facial and the Natura Bisse Diamond Collection; and oh-so-decadent massages. ⊠ *9500 Wilshire Blvd., Beverly Hills* ☎ *310/385–7023.*

**Spa at the Four Seasons, Beverly Hills.** Choose your own sound track in the deluxe treatment rooms at this spa that concentrates on traditional body treatments in small, seasonally scented private quarters. Try the fabulous inner peace immersion body treatment that begins with a scrub and massage, and ends with a Shirodhara treatment. ⊠ *300 S. Doheny Dr., Beverly Hills* ☎ *310/273–2222, 310/786–2229.*

**Spa Montage.** The Moroccan decor, ornate steam room, glass-walled sauna, co-ed mineral pool, and indoor Jacuzzi at this hidden Casbah of pampering will keep you relaxed for hours. ⊠ *225 N. Canon Dr., Beverly Hills* ☎ *310/860–7840.*

shop; lively rooftop lounge. **Cons:** disruptive party scene on weekends and holidays; street noise; pricey valet parking ($44). Ⓢ *Rooms from: $279* ✉ *550 S. Flower St., Downtown* ☎ *213/892–8080* ⊕ *www.standardhotels.com* ⇨ *207 rooms* ⦿|*No meals* ✛ *1:B2.*

$$$$    Ⓣ **Westin Bonaventure Hotel & Suites.** Step inside the futuristic lobby of
HOTEL    L.A.'s largest hotel to be greeted by fountains, an indoor lake and track,
FAMILY    and 12 glass elevators leading up to the historic rooms of this 35-story
property. **Pros:** spa with shiatsu massage; revolving rooftop lounge; many on-site restaurants. **Cons:** massive hotel might feel too corporate; mazelike lobby and public areas. Ⓢ *Rooms from: $489* ✉ *404 S. Figueroa St., Downtown* ☎ *213/624–1000, 866/716–8132* ⊕ *www. westin.com* ⇨ *1,489 rooms* ⦿|*No meals* ✛ *1:B2.*

## HOLLYWOOD AND THE STUDIOS

With easy access to the Walk of Fame and trendy nightlife, Hollywood caters to partygoers and action-seekers. Movie buffs may take days exploring the vicinity, but most travelers usually spend some time walking along Hollywood Boulevard, which is a congested strip of historic theaters, bars, restaurants, and kitschy (and sometimes tacky) shops. Many hotels in the area, however, offer great views of the Hollywood sign, and Universal Studios theme park is one or two Metro stops away. This area can be rough at night. Nearby in Los Feliz and Silver Lake, you'll find historic walkable neighborhoods packed with boutiques and cafés.

### HOLLYWOOD

$$    Ⓣ **Dream Hollywood.** Drawing from the city's color palette of blues,
HOTEL    whites, and oranges, this mid-century modern hotel is certainly dreamy,
with a rooftop pool and floor-to-ceiling windows in guest rooms displaying epic views of Hollywood. **Pros:** 24-hour room service; some rooms include private balcony; bath amenities from C.O. Bigelow. **Cons:** pricey; surrounding area can be sketchy at night. Ⓢ *Rooms from: $300* ✉ *6417 Selma Ave., Hollywood* ☎ *323/844–6417* ⊕ *www.dreamhotels. com/hollywood/default-en.html* ⇨ *178 rooms* ⦿|*No meals* ✛ *2:F2.*

$$$    Ⓣ **The Garland.** The Garland is the Valley's cool kid with a Hollywood
HOTEL    pedigree. **Pros:** large pool and play area; private balcony or patio in each
FAMILY    room; The Front Yard restaurant is a local fave for brunch. **Cons:** close
to the freeway; bar and restaurant close early. Ⓢ *Rooms from: $309* ✉ *4222 Vineland Ave., North Hollywood* ☎ *818/980–8000, 800/238– 3759* ⊕ *www.beverlygarland.com* ⇨ *255 rooms* ⦿|*No meals* ✛ *4:C1.*

$$$$    Ⓣ **Hollywood Roosevelt Hotel.** Poolside cabana rooms are adorned with
HOTEL    cow-skin rugs and marble bathrooms, while rooms in the main build-
**Fodor's Choice**    ing accentuate the property's history at this party-centric hotel in the
★    heart of Hollywood. **Pros:** Spare Room bowling alley on-site; pool is a popular weekend hangout; great burgers at the on-site 25 Degrees restaurant. **Cons:** reports of noise and staff attitude; stiff parking fees ($42). Ⓢ *Rooms from: $419* ✉ *7000 Hollywood Blvd., Hollywood* ☎ *323/466–7000, 800/950–7667* ⊕ *www.hollywoodroosevelt.com* ⇨ *353 rooms* ⦿|*No meals* ✛ *2:E2.*

$$$ HOTEL FAMILY **Loews Hollywood.** Part of the massive Hollywood and Highland shopping, dining, and entertainment complex, the 20-story Loews is at the center of Hollywood's action but manages to deliver a quiet night's sleep. **Pros:** large rooms with contemporary furniture; free Wi-Fi; Red Line Metro station adjacent. **Cons:** corporate feeling; very touristy; pricy parking ($50). [$] *Rooms from: $349* ✉ *1755 N. Highland Ave., Hollywood* ☎ *323/856–1200, 800/769–4774* 🌐 *www.loewshotels.com/en/hollywood-hotel* 🛏 *628 rooms* 🍴 *No meals* ✢ *2:E1.*

$ HOTEL FAMILY Fodor's Choice ★ **Magic Castle Hotel.** Guests at the hotel can secure advanced dinner reservations and attend magic shows at the Magic Castle, a private club in a 1908 mansion next door for magicians and their admirers. **Pros:** heated pool; near Hollywood and Highland; lush patio. **Cons:** strict dress code; no elevator; highly trafficked street. [$] *Rooms from: $199* ✉ *7025 Franklin Ave., Hollywood* ☎ *323/851–0800, 800/741–4915* 🌐 *magiccastlehotel.com* 🛏 *43 rooms* 🍴 *Breakfast* ✢ *2:E1.*

$ HOTEL Fodor's Choice ★ **Mama Shelter.** Even locals are just catching on to Hollywood's sexiest new property, complete with a rooftop bar populated with beautiful people lounging on loveseats, simple affordable rooms with quirky amenities like Bert and Ernie masks, and a down-home lobby restaurant that serves a mean Korean-style burrito. **Pros:** delicious food and cocktails on the property; affordable rooms don't skimp on style; foosball in lobby. **Cons:** spare and small rooms; creaky elevators. [$] *Rooms from: $159* ✉ *6500 Selma Ave., Hollywood* ☎ *323/785–6666* 🌐 *www.mamashelter.com/en/los-angeles* 🛏 *70 rooms* 🍴 *No meals* ✢ *2:F2.*

$ HOTEL **Moment Hotel.** Hollywood's best-value property housed in a former motor inn caters to young partygoers, who breeze in and out of the lobby (which doubles as a bar and breakfast lounge). **Pros:** suite comes with private balcony; on-site 24-hour rooms service ordered via in-room tablets; free Wi-Fi. **Cons:** street noise; not the safest neighborhood for walking at night. [$] *Rooms from: $180* ✉ *7370 Sunset Blvd., Hollywood* ☎ *323/822–5030* 🌐 *themomenthotel.com* 🛏 *39 rooms* 🍴 *No meals* ✢ *2:E2.*

$ HOTEL Fodor's Choice ★ **Palihotel.** Catering to young and hip budget travelers, who crave style over space, this design-centric boutique property on Melrose Avenue is in the heart of Hollywood's best shopping and dining including hot-spot The Hart and the Hunter. **Pros:** funky aesthetic; sweet corn hush puppies at The Hart and the Hunter restaurant are delish; fantastic location in a walkable neighborhood. **Cons:** small rooms; congested lobby; decor might not appeal to everyone. [$] *Rooms from: $190* ✉ *7950 Melrose Ave., Hollywood* ☎ *323/272–4588* 🌐 *www.pali-hotel.com* 🛏 *33 rooms* 🍴 *No meals* ✢ *2:D3.*

$$$ HOTEL Fodor's Choice ★ **The Redbury.** In the heart of Hollywood's nightlife, near the intersection of Hollywood and Vine, the Redbury is designed to appeal to guests' inner bohemian with paisley-patterned wallpaper, vibrant Persian rugs, and vintage rock posters. **Pros:** on-site kitchenettes and washer-dryer; excellent dining options; spacious suites. **Cons:** no pool or on-site gym; noisy on lower floors; some guests may find the Hollywood scene too chaotic. [$] *Rooms from: $329* ✉ *1717 Vine St., Hollywood* ☎ *323/962–1717, 977/962–1717* 🌐 *www.theredbury.com* 🛏 *57 suites* 🍴 *No meals* ✢ *2:F1.*

$$$$ HOTEL 🏨 **W Hollywood.** This centrally located, ultramodern it-location is outfitted for the wired traveler, and features a rooftop pool deck and popular on-site bars, like the Station Hollywood and the mod Living Room lobby bar. **Pros:** metro stop outside the front door; comes with in-room party necessities, from ice to cocktail glasses; comfy beds with petal-soft duvets. **Cons:** small pool; pricey dining and valet parking; in noisy part of Hollywood. [$] *Rooms from: $659* ✉ *6250 Hollywood Blvd., Hollywood* ☎ *323/798–1300, 888/625–4955* 🌐 *www.whotels.com/hollywood* 🛏 *305 rooms* 🍴 *No meals* ✥ *2:F2.*

## KOREATOWN

$$$ HOTEL 🏨 **The Line.** This boutique hotel pays homage to its Koreatown address (about 20 minutes from Downtown) with a dynamic dining concept by superstar chef Roy Choi, and a hidden karaoke speakeasy. **Pros:** on-site bikes to explore the area; cheery staff; houses the Houston Brothers' '80s-themed bar. **Cons:** expensive parking; lobby club crowds public spaces; far from parts of the city you may want to explore. [$] *Rooms from: $349* ✉ *3515 Wilshire Blvd.* ☎ *213/381–7411* 🌐 *www.thelinehotel.com* 🛏 *384 rooms* 🍴 *No meals* ✥ *1:A2.*

## BURBANK

$$ HOTEL 🏨 **Hotel Amarano Burbank.** Close to Burbank's TV and movie studios, the smartly designed Amarano feels like a Beverly Hills boutique hotel, complete with 24-hour room service, a homey on-site restaurant and lounge, and spiffy rooms. **Pros:** fireplace, cocktails, and tapas in lobby; penthouse with private gym; saltwater pool. **Cons:** street noise. [$] *Rooms from: $269* ✉ *322 N. Pass Ave., Burbank* ☎ *818/842–8887, 888/956–1900* 🌐 *www.hotelamarano.com* 🛏 *98 rooms, 34 suites* 🍴 *No meals* ✥ *4:D2.*

## UNIVERSAL CITY

$$ HOTEL FAMILY 🏨 **Sheraton Universal.** With large meeting spaces and a knowledgeable staff, this Sheraton buzzes year-round with business travelers and families, providing easy access to the free shuttle that takes guests to adjacent Universal Studios and CityWalk. **Pros:** pool area with cabanas and bar; oversize desks and office chairs in room. **Cons:** average in-house restaurant; touristy. [$] *Rooms from: $299* ✉ *333 Universal Hollywood Dr., Universal City* ☎ *818/980–1212, 888/627–7184* 🌐 *www.sheratonuniversal.com* 🛏 *457 rooms* 🍴 *No meals* ✥ *4:C2.*

## STUDIO CITY

$$ HOTELHOTEL FAMILY 🏨 **Sportsmen's Lodge.** This sprawling five-story hotel, a San Fernando Valley landmark just a short jaunt over the Hollywood Hills, has an updated contemporary look highlighted by the Olympic-size pool and summer patio with an outdoor bar. **Pros:** close to Ventura Boulevard restaurants; free shuttle to Universal Hollywood; quiet garden-view rooms worth asking for. **Cons:** pricey daily self-parking fee ($18); a distance from the city. [$] *Rooms from: $249* ✉ *12825 Ventura Blvd., Studio City* ☎ *818/769–4700, 800/821–8511* 🌐 *www.sportsmenslodge.com* 🛏 *190 rooms* 🍴 *No meals* ✥ *4:A2.*

## BEVERLY HILLS AND THE WESTSIDE

11

Beverly Hills, West Hollywood, and the Westside are central locations. From here you can easily drive to the beaches, the Getty Center, and mid-city. Hotels here, including the stylish Palihouse West Hollywood, come with a hefty price tag. The silver lining is walkable areas, so you'll spend less time in a car, and the access to the glittering coast.

### BEVERLY HILLS

**$$**
HOTEL

**Avalon.** Interior decorator Kelly Wearstler put her Midas touch on this mid-century Beverly Hills hotel, mixing classics by George Nelson and Charles Eames with her own chic designs. **Pros:** complimentary champagne at check-in; vintage hourglass pool; private cabanas. **Cons:** poolside social scene can be noisy. $ *Rooms from: $294* ⊠ *9400 W. Olympic Blvd., Beverly Hills* ☎ *310/277–5221, 800/670–6183* ⊕ *www. avalonbeverlyhills.com* ⤳ *86 rooms* ⦿ *No meals* ✢ *2:B4.*

**$$$$**
HOTEL
FAMILY

**Beverly Hills Hotel.** Nicknamed the "Pink Palace," this luxury spot with giant marble bathrooms and butler service continues to attract Hollywood's elite after more than 100 years. **Pros:** La Prairie day spa on-site; iconic Polo Lounge; retro Fountain Coffee room; massive 2017 restoration on bungalows lures the uberrich. **Cons:** pricey fare at the Polo Lounge; expensive valet parking ($48). $ *Rooms from: $525* ⊠ *9641 Sunset Blvd., Beverly Hills* ☎ *310/276–2251, 800/283–8885* ⊕ *www. beverlyhillshotel.com* ⤳ *208 rooms* ⦿ *No meals* ✢ *2:A3.*

**$$**
HOTEL

**Beverly Hills Plaza Hotel.** With a precious courtyard surrounding the pool, the well-maintained, all-suites Beverly Hills Plaza would be right at home in the south of France and has a price tag that makes the property accessible. **Pros:** amiable staff; adjacent to golf course. **Cons:** lowest-priced suites are accessible via stairs only; no services or restaurants close by, so car is a must. $ *Rooms from: $275* ⊠ *10300 Wilshire Blvd., Beverly Hills* ☎ *310/275–5575, 800/800–1234* ⊕ *www.beverly-hillsplazahotel.com* ⤳ *116 suites* ⦿ *No meals* ✢ *2:A4.*

**$$$$**
HOTEL
FAMILY

**Beverly Hilton.** Home to the Golden Globe Awards, The Beverly Hilton is glitzy and polished, offering spectacular views of Beverly Hills and sizeable balconies in many rooms. **Pros:** walking distance to Beverly Hills; complimentary car service; Trader Vic's indoor/outdoor tiki lounge on-site. **Cons:** somewhat corporate feel; valet parking adds $42 a night. $ *Rooms from: $425* ⊠ *9876 Wilshire Blvd., Beverly Hills* ☎ *310/274–7777, 877/414–8018* ⊕ *www.beverlyhilton.com* ⤳ *569 rooms* ⦿ *No meals* ✢ *2:A4.*

**$$$$**
HOTEL

**Beverly Wilshire, a Four Seasons Hotel.** Built in 1928, this Rodeo Drive–adjacent hotel is part Italian Renaissance (with elegant details like crystal chandeliers) and part contemporary. **Pros:** complimentary car service; Wolfgang Puck restaurant on-site; first-rate spa. **Cons:** small lobby; valet parking backs up at peak times; expensive dining options. $ *Rooms from: $845* ⊠ *9500 Wilshire Blvd., Beverly Hills* ☎ *310/275–5200, 800/427–4354* ⊕ *www.fourseasons.com/beverlywilshire* ⤳ *395 rooms* ⦿ *No meals* ✢ *2:B4.*

**$**
HOTEL
**Fodor's**Choice
★

**The Crescent Beverly Hills.** Built in 1926 as a dorm for silent-film actors, the Crescent is now a sleek boutique hotel with a great location—within the Beverly Hills shopping triangle—and with an even better price. **Pros:**

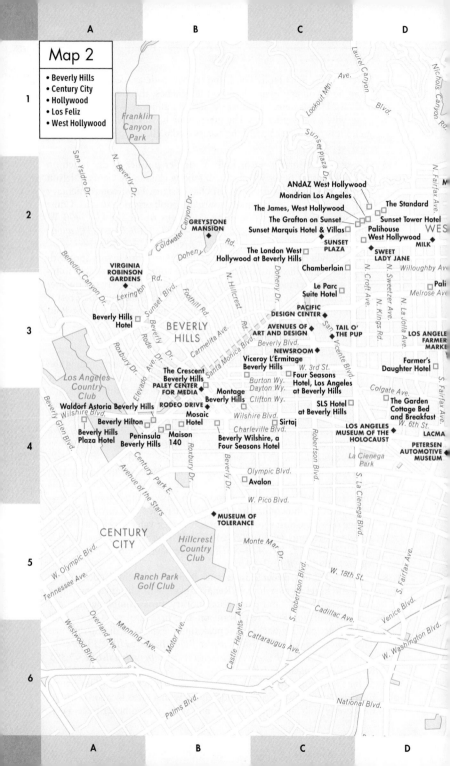

## Map 2

- Beverly Hills
- Century City
- Hollywood
- Los Feliz
- West Hollywood

Franklin Canyon Park

Lookout Mtn. Ave.

Laurel Canyon Blvd.

Nichols Canyon Rd.

N. Beverly Dr.

San Ysidro Dr.

N. Fairfax Ave.

Sunset Plaza Dr.

ANdAZ West Hollywood

Mondrian Los Angeles

The James, West Hollywood

The Standard

The Grafton on Sunset

Sunset Tower Hotel

Sunset Marquis Hotel & Villas

Palihouse

**WES**

West Hollywood

GREYSTONE MANSION

Coldwater Canyon Dr.

Doheny Rd.

SUNSET PLAZA

MILK

The London West Hollywood at Beverly Hills

SWEET LADY JANE

N. Croft Ave.

N. Sweetzer Ave.

N. Kings Rd.

N. La Jolla Ave.

Willoughby Ave.

Chamberlain

Pali

VIRGINIA ROBINSON GARDENS

Lexington Rd.

Melrose Ave

Le Parc Suite Hotel

Benedict Canyon Dr.

Beverly Hills Hotel

Sunset Blvd.

N. Hillcrest Rd.

Doheny Dr.

PACIFIC DESIGN CENTER

**BEVERLY HILLS**

Foothill Rd.

Carmelita Ave.

AVENUES OF ART AND DESIGN

TAIL O' THE PUP

LOS ANGELE FARMER MARKE

Rode Dr.

Roxbury Dr.

Elevado Dr.

Santa Monica Blvd.

Beverly Blvd.

San Vicente Blvd.

NEWSROOM

Farmer's Daughter Hotel

S. Fairfax Ave.

Los Angeles Country Club

W. 3rd St.

Viceroy L'Ermitage Beverly Hills

Four Seasons Hotel, Los Angeles at Beverly Hills

Colgate Ave.

The Crescent Beverly Hills

Burton Wy.

Dayton Wy.

PALEY CENTER FOR MEDIA

Montage Beverly Hills

Clifton Wy.

RODEO DRIVE

SLS Hotel at Beverly Hills

LOS ANGELES MUSEUM OF THE HOLOCAUST

The Garden Cottage Bed and Breakfast

W. 6th St.

LACMA

Beverly Glen Blvd.

Wilshire Blvd.

Waldorf Astoria Beverly Hills

Mosaic Hotel

Wilshire Blvd.

PETERSEN AUTOMOTIVE MUSEUM

Beverly Hilton

Charleville Blvd.

Sirtaj

La Cienega Park

Beverly Hills Plaza Hotel

Peninsula Beverly Hills

Maison 140

Beverly Wilshire, a Four Seasons Hotel

S. La Cienega Blvd.

Century Park E.

Roxbury Dr.

Beverly Dr.

Olympic Blvd.

Avalon

Avenue of the Stars

W. Pico Blvd.

MUSEUM OF TOLERANCE

Monte Mar Dr.

W. Olympic Blvd.

**CENTURY CITY**

Hillcrest Country Club

S. Robertson Blvd.

W. 18th St.

S. Fairfax Ave.

Venice Blvd.

Tennessee Ave.

Ranch Park Golf Club

Cadillac Ave.

S. Washington Blvd.

Westwood Blvd.

Overland Ave.

Manning Ave.

Motor Ave.

Castle Heights Ave.

Cattaraugus Ave.

Palms Blvd.

National Blvd.

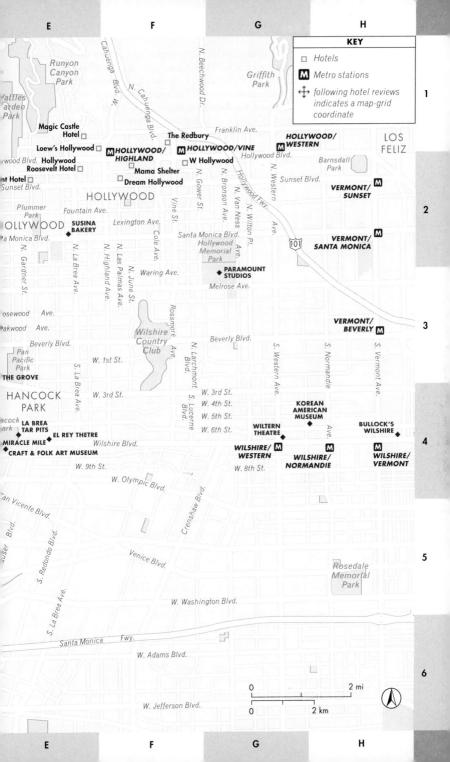

indoor/outdoor fireplace; lively on-site restaurant Crescent Bar and Terrace; economic room available for $148. **Cons:** gym an additional fee; no elevator. [$] *Rooms from: $149* ✉ *403 N. Crescent Dr., Beverly Hills* ☎ *310/247–0505* 🌐 *www.crescentbh.com* 🛏 *35 rooms* 🍴 *No meals* ✣ *2:B3.*

$$$$ HOTEL 🏨 **Four Seasons Hotel, Los Angeles at Beverly Hills.** High hedges and patio gardens make this hotel a secluded retreat that even the hum of traffic can't permeate—one reason it's a favorite of Hollywood's elite, whom you might spot at the pool and espresso bar. **Pros:** tropical terrace with pool; high-end Italian eatery Culina on-site; great massages and nail salon. **Cons:** Hollywood scene in bar and restaurant means rarefied prices. [$] *Rooms from: $625* ✉ *300 S. Doheny Dr., Beverly Hills* ☎ *310/273–2222, 800/332–3442* 🌐 *www.fourseasons.com/losangeles* 🛏 *285 rooms* 🍴 *No meals* ✣ *2:C3.*

$$ HOTEL 🏨 **Maison 140.** Colonial chic reigns in this three-story, 1930s grand boutique hotel, within walking distance to Beverly Hills' golden triangle of shopping. **Pros:** adjacent to pool and restaurant at sister property Mosaic Hotel; French–meets–Far East design; cozy Bar Noir perfect for a nightcap. **Cons:** few amenities; room service comes from adjacent property; compact rooms and bathrooms. [$] *Rooms from: $225* ✉ *140 S. Lasky Dr., Beverly Hills* ☎ *310/281–4000, 800/670–6182* 🌐 *www.maison140.com* 🛏 *43 rooms* 🍴 *No meals* ✣ *2:B4.*

$$$$ HOTEL FAMILY Fodor's Choice ★ 🏨 **Montage Beverly Hills.** The nine-story, Mediterranean-style palazzo is dedicated to welcoming those who relish luxury, providing classic style and exemplary service. **Pros:** secret whiskey bar tucked upstairs; Gornick & Drucker Barber Shop on-site; obliging, highly trained staff; families love the kids' club Paintbox. **Cons:** the hefty tab for all this finery. [$] *Rooms from: $695* ✉ *225 N. Cañon Dr., Beverly Hills* ☎ *310/860–7800, 888/860–0788* 🌐 *www.montagebeverlyhills.com/beverlyhills* 🛏 *201 rooms* 🍴 *No meals* ✣ *2:B4.*

$$$ HOTEL 🏨 **Mosaic Hotel.** Stylish, comfortable, and decked out with the latest tech, the Mosaic is on a quiet side street that's central to the Beverly Hills business district. **Pros:** intimate lobby bar Hush; simulated moonlight at poolside lounge; free Wi-Fi and local shuttle service. **Cons:** small and shaded pool; tiny lobby. [$] *Rooms from: $395* ✉ *125 S. Spalding Dr., Beverly Hills* ☎ *310/278–0303, 800/463–4466* 🌐 *www.mosaichotel.com* 🛏 *49 rooms* 🍴 *No meals* ✣ *2:B4.*

$$$$ HOTEL Fodor's Choice ★ 🏨 **Peninsula Beverly Hills.** This French Rivera–style palace overflowing with antiques and art is a favorite of boldface names, but visitors consistently describe a stay here as near perfect. **Pros:** Belvedere restaurant on-site is a lunchtime favorite; sunny pool area with cabanas; complimentary Rolls-Royce takes you to nearby Beverly Hills. **Cons:** very expensive; room decor might feel too ornate for some. [$] *Rooms from: $595* ✉ *9882 S. Santa Monica Blvd., Beverly Hills* ☎ *310/551–2888, 800/462–7899* 🌐 *beverlyhills.peninsula.com* 🛏 *195 rooms* 🍴 *No meals* ✣ *2:B4.*

$$ HOTEL 🏨 **Sirtaj.** Hidden on a residential street a block from Rodeo Drive, the new Sirtaj Hotel with an East Indian design caters to travelers wanting to be in Beverly Hills' Golden Triangle without the steep price tag. **Pros:** award-winning restaurant p.s. beverly hills on-site; freshly squeezed OJ at check-in; guests receive discounted day passes to Equinox gym. **Cons:** no pool or on-site gym; only nearby parking is valet ($30). [$] *Rooms*

from: *$239* ✉ *120 S. Reeves Dr., Beverly Hills* ☎ *310/248–2402* ⊕ *www.sirtajhotel.com* ⌲ *32 rooms* ⦿ *No meals* ✚ *2:C4.*

**$$$$** 🏨 **SLS Hotel at Beverly Hills.** From the sleek, Philippe Starck–designed lobby
HOTEL and lounge with fireplaces, hidden nooks, and a communal table, to poolside cabanas with DVD players, this hotel offers a cushy, dreamlike stay. **Pros:** on-property cuisine masterminded by Jose Andres; fully stocked bar in each room; dreamy Ciel spa. **Cons:** standard rooms are compact; pricey dining and parking; design might seem cold to some. $ *Rooms from: $639* ✉ *465 S. La Cienega Blvd., Beverly Hills* ☎ *310/247–0400* ⊕ *www.slshotels.com* ⌲ *297 rooms* ⦿ *No meals* ✚ *2:C4.*

**$$$$** 🏨 **Viceroy L'Ermitage Beverly Hills.** This hotel is the picture of luxury:
HOTEL French doors open to a mini balcony with views of the Hollywood sign; inside rooms you'll find soaking tubs and oversize bath towels, and they even offer spa treatment for your pet. **Pros:** handcrafted cocktails at Avec Nous on-site; enormous guest rooms; rooftop pool with gorgeous views. **Cons:** small spa and pool. $ *Rooms from: $495* ✉ *9291 Burton Way, Beverly Hills* ☎ *310/278–3344, 800/768–9009* ⊕ *www.viceroyhotelsandresorts.com/en/beverlyhills* ⌲ *119 rooms* ⦿ *No meals* ✚ *2:C3.*

**$$$$** 🏨 **Waldorf Astoria Beverly Hills.** The new belle of Beverly Hills, this Pierre-
HOTEL Yves Rochon–designed five-star property impresses with a top-notch spa, rooftop pool with VIP cabanas, a restaurant program created by Jean-Georges Vongerichten, and state-of-the-art amenities. **Pros:** impeccable service; Netflix, Hulu, and bluetooth speakers in room; chic rooftop pool. **Cons:** one of L.A.'s priciest rooms; on the busy corner of Wilshire and Santa Monica. $ *Rooms from: $815* ✉ *9850 Wilshire Blvd., Beverly Hills* ☎ *310/860–6666* ⊕ *www.waldorfastoriabeverly-hills.com* ⌲ *170 rooms* ⦿ *No meals* ✚ *2:B4.*

## BEL AIR

**$$$$** 🏨 **Hotel Bel-Air.** This Spanish Mission–style icon has been a discreet hill-
HOTEL side retreat for celebrities and society types since 1946, and was given a
Fodor'sChoice face-lift by star designers Alexandra Champalimaud and David Rock-
★ well. **Pros:** Bang & Olfusen TVs; fireplace and private patio in many rooms; alfresco dining at Wolfgang Puck restaurant. **Cons:** attracts society crowd; hefty price tag; a car is essential. $ *Rooms from: $525* ✉ *701 Stone Canyon Rd., Bel Air* ☎ *310/472–1211, 800/648–4097* ⊕ *www.hotelbelair.com* ⌲ *91 rooms* ⦿ *No meals* ✚ *3:C1.*

**$$** 🏨 **Luxe Sunset Boulevard Hotel.** On 7 landscaped acres near the Getty
HOTEL Center, the cozy residential Luxe feels like a secluded country club—
FAMILY but it's also next to the I–405 for easy freeway access. **Pros:** in-room massage treatments; On Sunset restaurant on property; fun perks like bubble baths. **Cons:** some freeway noise; off a busy intersection; a car is essential. $ *Rooms from: $299* ✉ *11461 Sunset Blvd., Bel Air* ☎ *310/476–6571, 800/468–3541* ⊕ *www.luxehotels.com* ⌲ *161 rooms* ⦿ *No meals* ✚ *3:C1.*

## WEST HOLLYWOOD

**$$** 🏨 **ANdAZ West Hollywood.** On the north side of the Sunset Strip, the
HOTEL ANdAZ is Hyatt's fun younger sister, catering to hipsters, techies, and rock stars lounging in the lobby as "hosts" check them in via tablets (there's no front desk). **Pros:** fridge stocked with healthy drinks and

snacks; ambitious hotel dining and bar concepts; gym overlooks Sunset Boulevard. **Cons:** traffic congestion impedes access; Sunset Strip is wildly popular on weekends and holidays; expensive parking ($44). [$] *Rooms from: $299* ✉ *8401 Sunset Blvd., West Hollywood* ☎ *323/656–1234, 800/233–1234* 🌐 *www.andaz.com* 🛏 *238 rooms* 🍴 *No meals* ✣ *2:D2.*

$$ HOTEL 🏨 **Chamberlain.** On a leafy residential side street, the Chamberlain is steps from Santa Monica Boulevard and close to the Sunset Strip, bringing in fashionable young professionals and 24-hour party people looking to roam West Hollywood. **Pros:** excellent guests-only dining room and bar; suites come with fireplace and balcony; 24-hour fitness center. **Cons:** compact bathrooms. [$] *Rooms from: $249* ✉ *1000 Westmount Dr., West Hollywood* ☎ *310/657–7400, 800/201–9652* 🌐 *www.chamberlainwesthollywood.com* 🛏 *114 suites* 🍴 *No meals* ✣ *2:C2.*

$$ HOTEL Fodor's Choice ★ 🏨 **Farmer's Daughter Hotel.** A favorite of *The Price Is Right* and *Dancing with the Stars* hopefuls (both TV shows tape at the CBS studios nearby), this hotel has a tongue-in-cheek country style with a hopping Sunday brunch, and a little pool accented by giant rubber duckies. **Pros:** bikes for rent; daily yoga; book lending library. **Cons:** shaded pool; no bathtubs; staff can be stiff. [$] *Rooms from: $260* ✉ *115 S. Fairfax Ave., West Hollywood* ☎ *323/937–3930, 800/334–1658* 🌐 *www.farmersdaughterhotel.com* 🛏 *65 rooms* 🍴 *No meals* ✣ *2:D3.*

$ B&B/INN 🏨 **The Garden Cottage Bed and Breakfast.** Located in one of Los Angeles's most walkable and picturesque neighborhoods, this Spanish/Mediterranean-style duplex surrounded by fountains and foliage invites travelers to make themselves at home, an easily accomplished mission with the help of the effusive hosts, Ahuva and Bob. **Cons:** cottage has no bathtub; the cozy environment doesn't allow for anonymity; no credit cards accepted. [$] *Rooms from: $185* ✉ *8318 W. 4th St., Beverly–La Brea* ☎ *323/653–5616* 🌐 *www.gardencottagela.com* 💳 *No credit cards* 🛏 *4 rooms* 🍴 *Breakfast* ✣ *2:D4.*

$$$ HOTEL 🏨 **The Grafton on Sunset.** It's easy to tap into the Sunset Strip energy at The Grafton, especially at the hotel's jazzed-up Oliver's Prime steak house and rock and roll–styled lounge, Bar 20, or at the mosaic-tiled waterfall pool area. **Pros:** heated saline pool; interior courtyard; free transportation within 3 miles. **Cons:** higher-priced weekend stays; Strip traffic; small standard rooms. [$] *Rooms from: $349* ✉ *8462 W. Sunset Blvd., West Hollywood* ☎ *323/654–4600, 800/821–3660* 🌐 *www.graftononsunset.com* 🛏 *108 rooms* 🍴 *No meals* ✣ *2:C2.*

$$$$ HOTEL FAMILY 🏨 **The James West Hollywood.** West Hollywood's most exciting new property in three decades, this luxe retreat proves its worth with perks like in-room mixology programs, treats for your pet, and a food program manned by award-winning chefs. **Pros:** in the heart of WeHo; huge penthouse lofts and poolside bungalow suites; 24-hour gym. **Cons:** crowded neighborhood; expensive parking ($46). [$] *Rooms from: $450* ✉ *8490 Sunset Blvd., West Hollywood* ☎ *877/578–3215* 🌐 *www.jameshotels.com/west-hollywood* 🛏 *286 rooms* 🍴 *No meals* ✣ *2:D2.*

$$ HOTEL 🏨 **Le Parc Suite Hotel.** On a tree-lined residential street close to CBS Television City and the Pacific Design Center, this congenial low-rise hotel aims to make guests feel coddled, with extremely personalized service and a strong commitment to privacy. **Pros:** great views from rooftop

pool deck; lighted tennis court; rooms have sunken living rooms with fireplaces. **Cons:** small lobby. [$] *Rooms from: $299* ✉ *733 W. Knoll Dr., West Hollywood* ☎ *310/855–8888, 800/578–4837* 🌐 *www.leparcsuites.com* 🛏 *154 suites* 🍴 *No meals* ✥ *2:C3.*

$$$ HOTEL 🏨 **The London West Hollywood at Beverly Hills.** Just off the Sunset Strip, cosmopolitan and chic in design, especially after the $27-million renovation in 2015, the London West Hollywood is known for its large suites, rooftop pool with citywide views, and luxury touches throughout. **Pros:** state-of-the-art fitness center; Chef Anthony Keen oversees dining program; 110-seat screening room. **Cons:** too refined for kids to be comfortable; lower floors have mundane views. [$] *Rooms from: $395* ✉ *1020 N. San Vicente Blvd., West Hollywood* ☎ *310/854–1111, 866/282–4560* 🌐 *www.thelondonwesthollywood.com* 🛏 *225 suites* 🍴 *No meals* ✥ *2:C2.*

$$$ HOTEL 🏨 **Mondrian Los Angeles.** The Mondrian has a city club feel; socializing begins in the lobby bar and lounge, and extends from the Ivory on Sunset restaurant to the scenic patio and pool, where you can listen to music underwater, to the lively Sky Bar. **Pros:** acclaimed Sky Bar on property; Benjamin Noriega-Ortiz guest room design; double-paned windows keep out noise. **Cons:** pricy valet parking only ($44); late-night party scene; majority of rooms are suites, upping the rate. [$] *Rooms from: $379* ✉ *8440 Sunset Blvd., West Hollywood* ☎ *323/650–8999, 800/606–6090* 🌐 *www.mondrianhotel.com* 🛏 *236 rooms* 🍴 *No meals* ✥ *2:D2.*

$$ RENTAL 🏨 **Palihouse West Hollywood.** Inside an unassuming condo complex just off West Hollywood's main drag, you'll find DJs spinning tunes on the ground floor and a gorgeous collection of assorted suites with fully equipped kitchens upstairs. **Pros:** fun scene at lobby bar; eclectic design; balconies with Ping-Pong tables in certain suites. **Cons:** lobby can be loud in the evenings; no pool. [$] *Rooms from: $280* ✉ *8465 Holloway Dr., West Hollywood* ☎ *323/656–4100* 🌐 *www.palihousewesthollywood.com* 🛏 *37 suites* 🍴 *No meals* ✥ *2:D2.*

$$ HOTEL 🏨 **The Standard.** Hotelier André Balazs created this kitschy Sunset Strip hotel out of a former retirement home, and a '70s aesthetic abounds with pop art, shag carpets, and suede sectionals in the lobby, and beanbag chairs, surfboard tables, and Warhol poppy-print curtains in the rooms. **Pros:** late-night dining on-site; choose your own checkout time; secret nightclub mmhmmm. **Cons:** for partying more than for resting; staff big on attitude rather than service. [$] *Rooms from: $279* ✉ *8300 Sunset Blvd., West Hollywood* ☎ *323/650–9090* 🌐 *www.standardhotel.com* 🛏 *139 rooms* 🍴 *No meals* ✥ *2:D2.*

$$$ HOTEL Fodor's Choice ★ 🏨 **Sunset Marquis Hotel & Villas.** If you're in town to cut your new hit single, you'll appreciate this near-the-Strip hidden retreat in the heart of WeHo, with two on-site recording studios. **Pros:** favorite among rock stars; 53 villas with lavish extras; exclusive Bar 1200; free passes to Equinox nearby. **Cons:** rooms can feel dark; small balconies. [$] *Rooms from: $365* ✉ *1200 N. Alta Loma Rd., West Hollywood* ☎ *310/657–1333, 800/858–9758* 🌐 *www.sunsetmarquis.com* 🛏 *154 rooms* 🍴 *No meals* ✥ *2:C2.*

$$$$ HOTEL 🏨 **Sunset Tower Hotel.** A 1929 art deco landmark once known as the Argyle, this boutique hotel on the Sunset Strip brings out as many locals as it does tourists. **Pros:** incredible city views; Tower Bar a favorite of Hollywood's elite; exclusive spa favored by locals. **Cons:** wedged into the Strip, so the driveway is a challenge; small standard

rooms. $\boxed{\$}$ *Rooms from: $495* ✉ *8358 Sunset Blvd., West Hollywood* ☎ *323/654–7100, 800/225–2637* ⊕ *www.sunsettowerhotel.com* ⤵ *64 rooms* ⦿ *No meals* ✛ *2:D2.*

### CULVER CITY

**$$**  🍴 **Culver Hotel.** This 1924 flatiron building smack in the center of
HOTEL   Downtown contains a slice of Culver City's history—it was at one
time owned by John Wayne, and also housed all 124 "munchkins"
during the filming of *The Wizard of Oz.* **Pros:** Grand Lobby restaurant
doubles as jazz venue; close to studios and restaurants. **Cons:** small
standard rooms; antique decor might not appeal to everyone. $\boxed{\$}$ *Rooms
from: $300* ✉ *9400 Culver Blvd., Culver City* ☎ *310/558–9400* ⊕ *www.
culverhotel.com* ⤵ *46 rooms* ⦿ *No meals* ✛ *3:E3.*

### WESTWOOD

**$$$**  🍴 **Hotel Palomar Los Angeles–Westwood.** A convivial lobby and smartly
HOTEL   designed rooms set this Kimpton-managed hotel apart from other chains;
because of its proximity to UCLA, the Palomar is perfect for friends and
families of students. **Pros:** luxe touches like Frette linens; rooms come
with a yoga mat; free coffee in the morning; nightly wine hour. **Cons:**
isolated on a busy thoroughfare. $\boxed{\$}$ *Rooms from: $350* ✉ *10740 Wilshire
Blvd., Westwood* ☎ *310/475–8711, 800/472–8556* ⊕ *www.hotelpalo-
mar-lawestwood.com* ⤵ *264 rooms* ⦿ *No meals* ✛ *3:D2.*

**$$$$**  🍴 **W Los Angeles–West Beverly Hills.** Retreat to this quiet and artful oasis
HOTEL   steps from UCLA, where you can find a cabana-lined pool and sleek
FAMILY  lounge, two on-site restaurants with regional cuisine, and a spa that
serves brownies and champagne post-massage. **Pros:** free yoga; all
rooms are suites; live DJs on weekend. **Cons:** not as lively as other
W properties; subdued decor; expensive valet parking ($46, plus tax).
$\boxed{\$}$ *Rooms from: $750* ✉ *930 Hilgard Ave., Westwood* ☎ *310/208–8765*
⊕ *www.wlosangeles.com* ⤵ *297 suites* ⦿ *No meals* ✛ *3:D1.*

## SANTA MONICA AND THE BEACHES

L.A.'s laid-back beach towns are the ideal place for enjoying the trifecta
of coastal living: sun, sand, and surf. From moneyed Malibu to the
original surf city, Huntington Beach, each city retains a character and
feel of its own, but collectively, these beach towns are family-friendly,
scenic, and dotted with waterfront hotels (try the Fairmont Miramar's
Bungalow bar or Viceroy in Santa Monica for nighttime drinks, even
if you're not staying in the area).

### SANTA MONICA

**$$$**  🍴 **The Ambrose.** An air of tranquillity pervades the beach-chic four-story
HOTEL   Ambrose, which blends right into its mostly residential Santa Monica
neighborhood. **Pros:**"green" practices: nontoxic cleaners, recycling
bins; partial ocean view. **Cons:** quiet, residential area of Santa Monica;
parking fee ($27). $\boxed{\$}$ *Rooms from: $345* ✉ *1255 20th St., Santa Mon-
ica* ☎ *310/315–1555, 877/262–7673* ⊕ *www.ambrosehotel.com* ⤵ *77
rooms* ⦿ *Breakfast* ✛ *3:G1.*

**$$**  🍴 **Bayside Hotel.** Tucked snugly into a narrow corner lot, the supremely
HOTEL   casual Bayside's greatest asset is its prime spot directly across from the
beach, within walkable blocks from the Third Street Promenade and Santa

Monica Pier. **Pros:** cheaper weeknight stays; beach access and views. **Cons:** homeless encampments nearby; basic bedding; thin walls. [$] *Rooms from: $249* ✉ *2001 Ocean Ave., Santa Monica* ☎ *310/396–6000, 800/525–4447* 🌐 *baysidehotel.com* 🛏 *45 rooms* 🍴 *No meals* ✣ *3:G2.*

$$ B&B/INN Fodor's Choice ★ **Channel Road Inn.** A quaint surprise in Southern California, the Channel Road Inn is every bit the country retreat bed-and-breakfast lovers adore, with four-poster beds, fluffy duvets, and a cozy living room with a fireplace. **Pros:** free wine and hors d'oeuvres every evening; home-cooked breakfast included; meditative rose garden on-site. **Cons:** no pool; need a car to get around. [$] *Rooms from: $225* ✉ *219 W. Channel Rd., Santa Monica* ☎ *310/459–1920* 🌐 *www.channelroadinn.com* 🛏 *15 rooms* 🍴 *Breakfast* ✣ *3:A3.*

$$$$ HOTEL **Fairmont Miramar Hotel & Bungalows Santa Monica.** A mammoth Moreton Bay fig tree dwarfs the main entrance of the 5-acre beach-adjacent Santa Monica wellness retreat, and lends its name to the inviting on-site Mediterranean-inspired restaurant, FIG, which focuses on local ingredients. **Pros:** guests can play games on the heated patio; swanky open-air cocktail spot The Bungalow on-site; stay in retrofitted '20s and '40s bungalows. **Cons:** all this luxury comes at a big price. [$] *Rooms from: $439* ✉ *101 Wilshire Blvd., Santa Monica* ☎ *310/576–7777, 866/540–4470* 🌐 *www.fairmont.com/santamonica* 🛏 *334 rooms* 🍴 *No meals* ✣ *3:F2.*

$$$$ HOTEL **The Georgian Hotel.** Driving by, you can't miss The Georgian: the art deco exterior is aqua, with ornate bronze grillwork and a charming oceanfront veranda. **Pros:** many ocean-view rooms; front terrace is a great people-watching spot; free Wi-Fi. **Cons:**"vintage" bathrooms; some rooms have unremarkable views. [$] *Rooms from: $429* ✉ *1415 Ocean Ave., Santa Monica* ☎ *310/395–9945, 800/538–8147* 🌐 *www.georgianhotel.com* 🛏 *84 rooms* 🍴 *No meals* ✣ *3:F2.*

$$$$ HOTEL **Hotel Casa del Mar.** In the 1920s it was a posh beach club catering to the city's elite; now the Casa del Mar is one of SoCal's most luxurious and pricey beachfront hotels with three extravagant two-story penthouses, a raised deck and pool, a newly reimagined spa, and an elegant ballroom facing the sand. **Pros:** excellent dining at Catch; modern amenities; lobby socializing; gorgeous beachfront rooms. **Cons:** no room balconies; without a doubt, one of L.A.'s most pricey beach stays. [$] *Rooms from: $700* ✉ *1910 Ocean Way, Santa Monica* ☎ *310/581–5533, 800/898–6999* 🌐 *www.hotelcasadelmar.com* 🛏 *129 rooms* 🍴 *No meals* ✣ *3:G2.*

$$$$ HOTEL **Hotel Shangri-La.** Across from Santa Monica's oceanfront Palisades Park, the 1939-built art deco Hotel Shangri-La is now in tune with the 21st century, after its two-year-long gleaming update has preserved the original brilliantly white curved facade. **Pros:** sunken Jacuzzis in bathrooms; ONYX rooftop bar is the place to be; vintage and custom deco accents throughout. **Cons:** some rooms are tight like cruise-ship quarters; pricey parking rates ($42). [$] *Rooms from: $550* ✉ *301 Ocean Ave., Santa Monica* ☎ *310/394–2791* 🌐 *www.shangrila-hotel.com* 🛏 *71 rooms* 🍴 *No meals* ✣ *3:F2.*

$$$$ HOTEL FAMILY **Le Meridien Delfina Santa Monica.** Not far from the I–10 and four blocks from the new Expo Line, this hotel appeals to business travelers and jet-setting leisure travelers who fancy the sleek interiors, free self-parking, and close proximity to beaches and restaurants. **Pros:** casual and

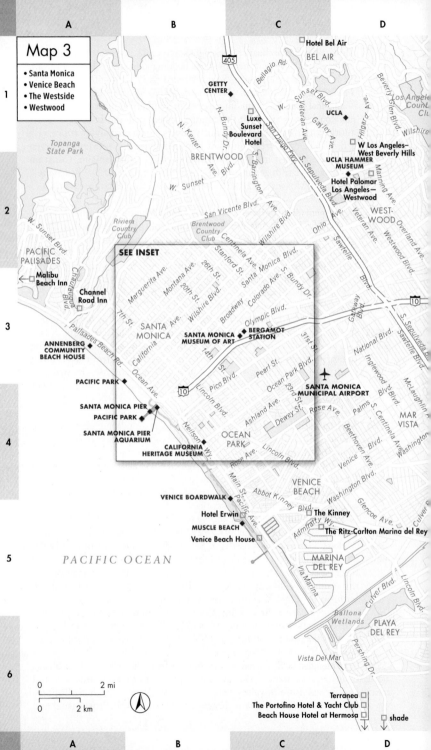

# Map 3

- Santa Monica
- Venice Beach
- The Westside
- Westwood

**405**

Hotel Bel Air

BEL AIR

Bellagio Rd.

GETTY CENTER ◆

Luxe Sunset Boulevard Hotel □

UCLA ◆

W. Sunset Blvd.

Veteran Ave.

Galley Ave.

Beverly Glen Blvd.

Los Angeles County Clu

Wilshire

W Los Angeles–West Beverly Hills □

UCLA HAMMER MUSEUM ◆

Hotel Palomar Los Angeles–Westwood □

Manning Ave.

BRENTWOOD

N. Kenter Ave.

N. Bundy Dr.

S. Barrington Ave.

San Diego Fwy.

WEST-WOOD

Westwood Ave.

Overland Ave.

Topanga State Park

W. Sunset

San Vicente Blvd.

Brentwood Country Club

Wilshire Blvd.

Ohio Ave.

Sawtelle Blvd.

Veteran Ave.

Riviera Country Club

Centinela Ave.

**10**

Sawtelle Blvd.

S. Sepulveda Blvd.

W. Sunset Blvd.

PACIFIC PALISADES

Chautauqua Blvd.

Malibu Beach Inn ←

Channel Road Inn □

**SEE INSET**

Marguerita Ave.

Montana Ave.

26th St.

20th St.

Wilshire Blvd.

Stanford St.

Santa Monica Blvd.

Colorado Ave.

S. Bundy Dr.

7th St.

Broadway

Olympic Blvd.

National Blvd.

Inglewood Blvd.

Sawtelle Bl

McLaughlin A

SANTA MONICA

SANTA MONICA MUSEUM OF ART ◆

BERGAMOT STATION ◆

31st St.

14th St.

S. Sepulveda Blvd.

Palisades Beach Rd.

California Ave.

Pico Blvd.

Pearl St.

Ocean Park Blvd.

23rd St.

✈ SANTA MONICA MUNICIPAL AIRPORT

MAR VISTA

ANNENBERG COMMUNITY BEACH HOUSE ◆

PACIFIC PARK ◆

Ocean Ave.

Lincoln Blvd.

**10**

Ashland Ave.

Dewey St.

Rose Ave.

Palms

S. Centinela Ave

Washington

SANTA MONICA PIER ◆
PACIFIC PARK ◆

SANTA MONICA PIER AQUARIUM ◆

CALIFORNIA HERITAGE MUSEUM ◆

Neilson Wy.

OCEAN PARK

Rose Ave.

Lincoln Blvd.

Beethoven Blvd.

Venice Blvd.

VENICE BEACH

Washington Blvd.

Glencoe Ave.

Culver Ave.

VENICE BOARDWALK ◆

Hotel Erwin □

MUSCLE BEACH ◆

Venice Beach House □

Main St.

Pacific Ave.

Abbot Kinney Blvd.

The Kinney □

Admiralty Wy.

The Ritz-Carlton Marina del Rey □

MARINA DEL REY

## PACIFIC OCEAN

Via Marina

Culver Blvd.

Lincoln Blvd.

Ballona Wetlands

PLAYA DEL REY

Pershing Dr.

Vista Del Mar

0     2 mi
0     2 km

Terranea □
The Portofino Hotel & Yacht Club □
Beach House Hotel at Hermosa □

□ shade

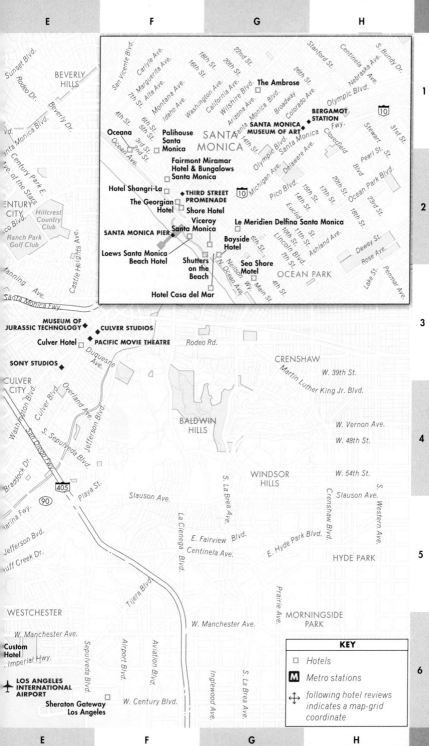

upscale eateries on property; retro designer touches; cabanas and pool on ground floor. **Cons:** not as centrally located as some Santa Monica hotels; fee for Wi-Fi. [$] *Rooms from: $550* ✉ *530 Pico Blvd., Santa Monica* ☎ *310/399–9344, 888/627–8532* 🌐 *www.lemeridiendelfina.com* 🛏 *310 rooms* 🍴 *No meals* ✥ *3:G2.*

$$$$ HOTEL FAMILY 🏨 **Loews Santa Monica Beach Hotel.** Walk to the ocean side of the soaring atrium at this family- and pet-friendly hotel, and you feel like you're on a cruise ship: massive windows give way to the expansive sea below, sunny staff seems content to assist with your needs, and a massive photo screen behind reception intuits a sense of place. **Pros:** resort vibe with three restaurants; walk to beach; upgraded spa and fitness center. **Cons:** small pool; parking is pricey ($50). [$] *Rooms from: $459* ✉ *1700 Ocean Ave., Santa Monica* ☎ *310/458–6700, 800/235–6397* 🌐 *www.loewshotels.com* 🛏 *347 rooms* 🍴 *No meals* ✥ *3:F2.*

$$$$ HOTEL FAMILY 🏨 **Oceana.** Generous-size suites, soundproofed windows, an open-air courtyard and pool, and ocean proximity give this hotel a distinctly SoCal beach vibe. **Pros:** walk to prime shopping districts; Tower 8 restaurant has stunning ocean views; champagne at check-in. **Cons:** small pool. [$] *Rooms from: $495* ✉ *849 Ocean Ave., Santa Monica* ☎ *310/393–0486, 800/777–0758* 🌐 *www.hoteloceanasantamonica.com* 🛏 *70 suites* 🍴 *No meals* ✥ *3:F2.*

$$ HOTEL 🏨 **Palihouse Santa Monica.** Tucked in a posh residential area three blocks from the sea and lively Third Street Promenade, Palihouse Santa Monica caters to design-minded world travelers, with spacious rooms and suites decked out in whimsical antiques. **Pros:** Apple TV in rooms; walking distance to Santa Monica attractions; fully equipped kitchens. **Cons:** no pool; decor might not appeal to more traditional travelers. [$] *Rooms from: $300* ✉ *1001 3rd St., Santa Monica* ☎ *310/394–1279* 🌐 *www.palihousesantamonica.com* 🛏 *38 rooms* 🍴 *No meals* ✥ *3:F2.*

$ HOTEL 🏨 **Sea Shore Motel.** On Santa Monica's busy Main Street, the Sea Shore is a throwback to Route 66 and to '60s-style, family-run roadside motels, and is surrounded by an ultra-trendy neighborhood. **Pros:** close to beach and restaurants; free Wi-Fi and parking; popular rooftop deck and on-site restaurant, Amelia's. **Cons:** street noise; motel-style decor and beds. [$] *Rooms from: $155* ✉ *2637 Main St., Santa Monica* ☎ *310/392–2787* 🌐 *www.seashoremotel.com* 🛏 *24 rooms* 🍴 *No meals* ✥ *3:G3.*

$$$$ HOTEL Fodor's Choice ★ 🏨 **Shore Hotel.** With views of the Santa Monica Pier, this hotel with a friendly staff offers eco-minded travelers stylish rooms with a modern design, just steps from the sand and sea. **Pros:** near beach and Third Street Promenade; rainfall showerheads; solar-heated pool and hot tub. **Cons:** expensive rooms and parking fees; fronting busy Ocean Avenue. [$] *Rooms from: $539* ✉ *1515 Ocean Ave., Santa Monica* ☎ *310/458–1515* 🌐 *shorehotel.com* 🛏 *164 rooms* 🍴 *No meals* ✥ *3:F2.*

$$$$ HOTEL FAMILY Fodor's Choice ★ 🏨 **Shutters on the Beach.** Set right on the sand, this inn has become synonymous with staycations, and while the hotel's service gets mixed reviews from some readers, the beachfront location and show-house decor make this one of SoCal's most popular luxury hotels. **Pros:**

built-in cabinets filled with art books and curios; rooms designed by Michael Smith; rooms come with whirlpool tub. **Cons:** service could improve; very expensive. ⓢ *Rooms from: $800* ✉ *1 Pico Blvd., Santa Monica* ☎ *310/458–0030, 800/334–9000* ⊕ *www.shuttersonthebeach. com* ⇱ *198 rooms* ❑ *No meals* ✛ *3:G2.*

**$$$** ⊓ **Viceroy Santa Monica.** Whimsy abounds at this stylized seaside
HOTEL escape—just look at the porcelain dogs as lamp bases and Spode china plates mounted on the walls—yet the compact rooms, which all have French balconies, and sexy mirrored walls, draw quite the upscale clientele. **Pros:** in-room aromatherapy products; lobby and poolside socializing; pedestrian-friendly area. **Cons:** super-pricey bar and dining; pool for dipping, not laps. ⓢ *Rooms from: $399* ✉ *1819 Ocean Ave., Santa Monica* ☎ *310/260–7500, 800/622–8711* ⊕ *www.viceroysantamonica. com* ⇱ *162 rooms* ❑ *No meals* ✛ *3:G2.*

## LOS ANGELES INTERNATIONAL AIRPORT

**$** ⊓ **Custom Hotel.** Close enough to LAX to see the runways, the Cus-
HOTEL tom Hotel is a playful and practical redo of a 12-story, mid-century modern tower by famed L.A. architect Welton Becket (of Hollywood's Capitol Records' building and the Dorothy Chandler Pavilion). **Pros:** shuttle to LAX; close to beach and airport; socializing at poolside restaurant/lounge Deck 33. **Cons:** at the desolate end of Lincoln Boulevard. ⓢ *Rooms from: $179* ✉ *8639 Lincoln Blvd., Los Angeles International Airport* ☎ *310/645–0400, 877/287–8601* ⊕ *www.jdvhotels. com/hotels/california/los-angeles-hotels/custom-hotel* ⇱ *250 rooms* ❑ *No meals* ✛ *3:E6.*

**$** ⊓ **Sheraton Gateway Los Angeles.** LAX's swanky hotel just had some
HOTEL serious work done to its already sleek look, yet the appeal is in more than just the style; in-transit visitors love the 24-hour room service, fitness center, and airport shuttle. **Pros:** significantly lower weekend rates; free LAX shuttle; on-site restaurant, Costero California Bar and Bistro, slings craft beer. **Cons:** convenient to airport but not much else. ⓢ *Rooms from: $149* ✉ *6101 W. Century Blvd., Los Angeles International Airport* ☎ *310/642–1111, 800/325–3535* ⊕ *www.sheratonlosangeles.com* ⇱ *802 rooms* ❑ *No meals* ✛ *3:F6.*

## VENICE

**$$$** ⊓ **Hotel Erwin.** A boutique hotel a block off the Venice Beach Boardwalk,
HOTEL the Erwin has spacious, airy rooms and a local-favorite rooftop bar and lounge (appropriately named High). **Pros:** dining emphasizes fresh ingredients; playful design in guest rooms. **Cons:** some rooms face a noisy alley; no pool. ⓢ *Rooms from: $319* ✉ *1697 Pacific Ave., Venice* ☎ *310/452–1111, 800/786–7789* ⊕ *www.hotelerwin.com* ⇱ *119 rooms* ❑ *No meals* ✛ *3:C5.*

**$$** ⊓ **The Kinney.** Walking distance to Venice Beach and Abbot Kinney's
HOTEL artsy commercial strip, this playful new hotel caters to younger budget
Fodor'sChoice travelers; enjoy the cozy outdoor space, or curl up in the lobby with
★ a book and listen to the tunes spun on the house record player. **Pros:** affordable, artistic rooms; Ping-Pong area; Jacuzzi bar. **Cons:** valet parking is a must ($15). ⓢ *Rooms from: $239* ✉ *737 Washington Blvd.,*

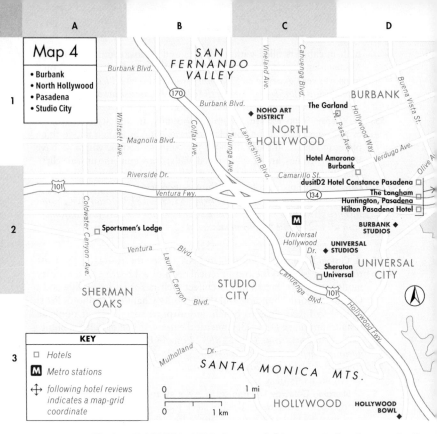

## Map 4

- Burbank
- North Hollywood
- Pasadena
- Studio City

**A** **B** **C** **D**

**1**

Burbank Blvd.

*SAN FERNANDO VALLEY*

170

Burbank Blvd.

BURBANK

NOHO ART DISTRICT ◆

The Garland

NORTH HOLLYWOOD

Magnolia Blvd.

Hollywood Way

Verdugo Ave.

Buena Vista St.

Olive A

Hotel Amarano Burbank

Riverside Dr.

Camarillo St.

dusitD2 Hotel Constance Pasadena □

101

Ventura Fwy.

134

The Langham Huntington, Pasadena

Hilton Pasadena Hotel □

**2**

Sportsmen's Lodge □

M

Universal Hollywood Dr.

BURBANK STUDIOS ◆

UNIVERSAL ◆ STUDIOS

UNIVERSAL CITY

Ventura

Laurel Canyon

Blvd.

Canoga

Sheraton Universal □

SHERMAN OAKS

STUDIO CITY

Blvd.

101

Hollywood Fwy.

**3**

### KEY

□ *Hotels*

M *Metro stations*

✛ *following hotel reviews indicates a map-grid coordinate*

Mulholland Dr.

*SANTA MONICA MTS.*

0 ——— 1 mi
0 ——— 1 km

HOLLYWOOD

HOLLYWOOD BOWL ◆

---

Venice ☎ 310/821–4455 ⊕ www.thekinneyvenicebeach.com 🛏 68 rooms ⚬|⚬ Breakfast ✛ 3:C5.

**$**
**HOTEL**
Ⅲ **Venice Beach House.** A vestige of Venice's founding days, the Venice Beach House was one of the seaside enclave's first mansions, and many Craftsman-era details remain—dark woods, a glass-enclosed breakfast nook, a lattice-framed portico, and a fleet of stairs. **Pros:** historic home with many charms; steps from beach and bike bath; some budget rooms without baths are cheapest in the area. **Cons:** privacy and noise issues; parking $15; full prepayment required with cancellation penalties. $ *Rooms from: $190* ⊠ *15 30th Ave., Venice* ☎ 310/823–1966 ⊕ www.venicebeachhouse.com 🛏 9 rooms ⚬|⚬ Breakfast ✛ 3:C5.

### MARINA DEL REY

**$$$$**
**HOTEL**
**FAMILY**
**Fodor's Choice**
★
Ⅲ **The Ritz-Carlton Marina del Rey.** You might have a sense of déjà vu here—this resort, overlooking L.A.'s largest marina's boats, is a favorite location of dozens of TV and film productions. **Pros:** sparkling gym and large kid-friendly chlorine-free pool; chic restaurant Cast & Plow on-site; feather beds and marble baths in rooms. **Cons:** formal dining only (poolside eatery open in summer only); $40 valet parking. $ *Rooms from: $449* ⊠ *4375 Admiralty Way, Marina del Ray* ☎ 310/823–1700, 800/241–3333 ⊕ www.ritzcarlton.com 🛏 304 rooms ⚬|⚬ No meals ✛ 3:C5.

### MALIBU

$$$$
B&B/INN

**Malibu Beach Inn.** Set right on exclusive Carbon Beach, Malibu's hideaway for the super-rich remains the room to nab along the coast, with an ultrachic new look thanks to designer Waldo Fernandez, and an upscale restaurant and wine bar overlooking the Pacific. **Pros:** see the ocean from your private balcony; wine list curated by sommelier Laurie Sutton. **Cons:** billionaire's travel budget required; noise of PCH; no pool, gym, or hot tub. $ *Rooms from: $575* ⊠ *22878 Pacific Coast Hwy., Malibu* ☎ *310/456–6444* ⊕ *www.malibubeachinn.com* ↘ *47 rooms* ⦾ *No meals* ✛ *3:A3.*

### MANHATTAN BEACH

$$$
HOTEL

**shade.** Super-contemporary design makes this hotel, rooftop pool, and sundeck feel like an adults-only playground, and it's just a short walk to the shoreline, the local pier, and Manhattan Beach's lively downtown. **Pros:** fun freebies like cake-pops; passes to Equinox gym; cool amenities like "chromatherapy" lighting and in-room martini shaker. **Cons:** sharp-edged furniture; recommended for adults or older kids only; small dipping pool. $ *Rooms from: $395* ⊠ *1221 N. Valley Dr., Manhattan Beach* ☎ *310/546–4995, 866/742–3377* ⊕ *www. shadehotel.com* ↘ *38 rooms* ⦾ *Breakfast* ✛ *3:D6.*

### HERMOSA BEACH

$$
HOTEL
Fodor's Choice
★

**Beach House Hotel at Hermosa.** Bordering The Strand (SoCal's famous bike path on the beach), Beach House looks like a New England sea cottage from a century ago, but has contemporary amenities in its studio suites. **Pros:** in-room massages available; enjoy delicious muffins and coffee (and more) in the breakfast room; oceanfront rooms and sunset views. **Cons:** noise from the busy Strand; no pool; Continental breakfast only. $ *Rooms from: $299* ⊠ *1300 The Strand, Hermosa Beach* ☎ *310/374–3001, 888/895–4559* ⊕ *www.beach-house.com* ↘ *96 suites* ⦾ *Breakfast* ✛ *3:D6.*

### REDONDO BEACH

$$
HOTEL
FAMILY

**The Portofino Hotel & Yacht Club.** Open your balcony door and listen to calls of seabirds and sea lions from ocean- and channel-side rooms; marina-side rooms look over sailboats and docks. **Pros:** bike or walk to beach from the hotel's private peninsula; excellent Baleen restaurant overlooking the harbor; sophisticated interior. **Cons:** higher rates in summer and for ocean-view rooms. $ *Rooms from: $299* ⊠ *260 Portofino Way, Redondo Beach* ☎ *310/379–8481, 800/468–4292* ⊕ *www. hotelportofino.com* ↘ *166 rooms* ⦾ *No meals* ✛ *3:D6.*

### RANCHO PALOS VERDES

$$$
RESORT
FAMILY
Fodor's Choice
★

**Terranea.** The Pacific Ocean and Catalina Island are within view at Terranea, L.A.'s only full-service oceanfront resort straddling 102 terraced acres at land's end on the scenic Palos Verdes Peninsula. **Pros:** pool slide and children's center; blissful oceanfront spa; four saline pools and hot tubs. **Cons:** pricey on-site dining; with resort fee and parking this luxury becomes very expensive. $ *Rooms from: $395* ⊠ *100 Terranea Way, Rancho Palos Verdes* ☎ *310/265–2800* ⊕ *www. terranea.com* ↘ *582 rooms* ⦾ *No meals* ✛ *3:D6.*

## PASADENA

Pasadena is not only an easy detour from Los Angeles, it's also a charming, historic, and residential city that can serve as your base while visiting the area. This small-town feel means a relaxing, slow pace, with the attractions of L.A. still within your reach. Nearby towns of Eagle Rock and Highland Park are some of the area's up-and-coming destinations populated with hip boutiques and fun restaurants.

$$ HOTEL **dusitD2 Hotel Constance Pasadena.** Set in one of L.A.'s most historic properties and along the Rose Bowl parade route, the first California outpost of the Thai hotel group Dusit boasts affordable technologically advanced rooms, and a cabana-lined pool deck constructed in 2017. The spacious lobby, manned by a friendly staff, houses Perry's restaurant and lounge. **Pros:** walking distance to great restaurants; hospitable staff; courtyard lit with string lights. **Cons:** small rooms. [$] *Rooms from: $249 ✉ 928 E. Colorado Blvd., Pasadena ☎ 626/898–7900 🌐 www.dusit.com/dusitd2/pasadena 🛏 129 rooms 🍴 No meals ⊕ 4:D2.*

$$ HOTEL **Hilton Pasadena Hotel.** Two blocks south of busy Colorado Boulevard, the Hilton Pasadena is still within walking distance of the city's vast convention center and close to Old Town's boundless options for shopping and dining. **Pros:** amiable and helpful staff; central downtown Pasadena location. **Cons:** compact bathrooms; so-so dining options; small pool. [$] *Rooms from: $239 ✉ 168 S. Los Robles Ave., Pasadena ☎ 626/577–1000, 800/445–8667 🌐 www.hilton.com 🛏 296 rooms 🍴 No meals ⊕ 4:D2.*

$$$$ HOTEL FAMILY Fodor's Choice ★ **The Langham Huntington, Pasadena.** Fronted by the historic Horseshoe Garden, this 1907 grande dame spans 23 acres and includes an Italianate-style main building, Spanish Revival cottages, a lanai, an azalea-filled Japanese garden, and several dining options. **Pros:** great for a romantic escape; delicious Cal-French restaurant Royce; top-notch Chuan Spa. **Cons:** in a suburban neighborhood far from local shopping and dining. [$] *Rooms from: $429 ✉ 1401 S. Oak Knoll Ave., Pasadena ☎ 626/568–3900 🌐 www.pasadena.langhamhotels.com 🛏 380 rooms 🍴 No meals ⊕ 4:D2.*

# ORANGE COUNTY AND CATALINA ISLAND

With Disneyland and Knott's Berry Farm

# WELCOME TO ORANGE COUNTY AND CATALINA ISLAND

## TOP REASONS TO GO

★ **Disney Magic:** Walking down Main Street, U.S.A., with Sleeping Beauty Castle straight ahead, you really will feel like you're in one of the happiest places on Earth.

★ **Beautiful Beaches:** Surf, swim, paddleboard, or just relax on one of the state's most breathtaking stretches of coastline. Keep in mind the water may be colder and rougher than you expect.

★ **Island Getaways:** Just a short high-speed catamaran ride from the shore, Catalina Island feels 1,000 miles away from the mainland. Wander around charming Avalon, or explore the unspoiled beauty of the island's wild interior.

★ **The Fine Life:** Some of the state's wealthiest communities are in coastal Orange County, so spend at least part of your stay here experiencing how the other half lives.

★ **Family Fun:** Ride roller coasters, eat ice cream, bike on oceanfront paths, fish off ocean piers, or try bodysurfing.

**1 Disneyland Resort.** Once a humble vision of Walt Disney's, Southern California's top family and tourist destination has grown to become a megaresort, with more attractions spilling over into Disney's California Adventure. There's plenty here to entertain kids and adults alike.

**2 Knott's Berry Farm.** Amusement park lovers should check out this Buena Park attraction, with thrill rides, the *Peanuts* gang, and lots of fried chicken and boysenberry pie.

**3 Coastal Orange County.** The OC's beach communities may not be quite as glamorous as they appear on TV, but coastal spots like Huntington Beach, Newport Harbor, and Laguna Beach are perfect for chilling out in a oceanfront hotel.

**12**

## GETTING ORIENTED

Like Los Angeles, Orange County stretches over a large area, lacks a singular focal point, and has limited public transportation. You'll need a car and a sensible game plan to make the most of your visit. Anaheim, home of Disneyland, has every style of hotel imaginable, from family-friendly motels to luxurious high-rises. The coastal cities are more expensive but have cooler weather in the summer, and marvelous beaches that you can enjoy throughout the year.

**4 Catalina Island.** This unspoiled island paradise—with its pocket-size town, Avalon, and large nature preserve—is just off the Orange County coast.

Updated
by Kathy A.
McDonald

With its tropical flowers and palm trees, the stretch of coast between Seal Beach and San Clemente is often called the California Riviera. Exclusive Newport Beach, artsy Laguna, and the surf town of Huntington Beach are the stars, but lesser-known gems on the glistening coast—such as Corona del Mar—are also worth visiting. Offshore, meanwhile, lies gorgeous Catalina Island, a terrific spot for diving, snorkeling, and hiking.

Few of the citrus groves that gave Orange County its name remain. This region south and east of Los Angeles is now ruled by tourism and high-tech business rather than agriculture. Despite a building boom that began in the 1990s, the area is still a place to find wilderness trails, canyons, greenbelts, and natural environs. Just offshore is a deep-water wilderness that's possible to explore via daily whale-watching excursions.

# PLANNING

### GETTING HERE AND AROUND
#### AIR TRAVEL
Orange County's main facility is John Wayne Airport Orange County (SNA), which is served by six major domestic airlines and one commuter line. Long Beach Airport (LGB) is served by four airlines, including its major player, JetBlue. It's roughly 20 to 30 minutes by car from Anaheim.

Super Shuttle and Prime Time Airport Shuttle provide transportation from John Wayne and LAX to the Disneyland area of Anaheim. Round-trip fares average about $25 per person from John Wayne and $16 to $42 from LAX.

12

## BUS TRAVEL

The Orange County Transportation Authority will take you virtually anywhere in the county, but it will take time; OCTA buses go from Knott's Berry Farm and Disneyland to Huntington Beach and Newport Beach. Bus 1 travels along the coast; buses 701 and 721 provide express service to Los Angeles.

Information **Orange County Transportation Authority.** ☎ *714/636-7433* ⊕ *www.octa.net.*

## CAR TRAVEL

The San Diego Freeway (I–405), the coastal route, and the Santa Ana Freeway (I–5), the inland route, run north–south through Orange County. South of Laguna, I–405 merges into I–5 (called the San Diego Freeway south from this point). A toll road, Highway 73, runs 15 miles from Newport Beach to San Juan Capistrano; it costs $5.10–$7.61 (lower rates are for weekends and off-peak hours) and is usually less jammed than the regular freeways. Do your best to avoid all Orange County freeways during rush hours (6–9 am and 3:30–6:30 pm). Highway 55 leads to Newport Beach. The Pacific Coast Highway (Highway 1) allows easy access to beach communities and is the most scenic route but expect it to be crowded, especially on summer weekends and holidays.

## FERRY TRAVEL

There are two ferries that service Catalina Island; Catalina Express runs from Long Beach (about 90 minutes) and from Newport Beach (about 75 minutes). Reservations are strongly advised for summers and weekends. During the winter months, ferry crossings are not as frequent as in the summer high season.

## TRAIN TRAVEL

Amtrak makes daily stops in Orange County at all major towns. Metrolink is a weekday commuter train that runs to and from Los Angeles and Orange County.

Information **Amtrak.** ☎ *800/872-7245* ⊕ *www.amtrak.com.* **Metrolink.** ☎ *800/371-5465* ⊕ *www.metrolinktrains.com.*

⇨ *For more information on Getting Here and Around, see Travel Smart Los Angeles.*

## RESTAURANTS

Much like L.A., restaurants in Orange County are generally casual, and you'll rarely see suits and ties. However, at top resort hotel dining rooms, many guests choose to dress up.

Of course, there's also a swath of casual places along the beachfronts—seafood takeout, taquerias, burger joints—that won't mind if you wear flip-flops. Reservations are recommended for the nicest restaurants.

Many places don't serve past 11 pm, and locals tend to eat early. Remember that according to California law, smoking is prohibited in all enclosed areas.

### HOTELS

Along the coast there are remarkable luxury resorts; if you can't afford a stay, pop in for the view at Laguna Beach's Montage or the always welcoming Ritz-Carlton at Dana Point. For a taste of the OC glam life, have lunch overlooking the yachts of Newport Bay at the Balboa Bay Resort.

As a rule, lodging prices tend to rise the closer the hotels are to the beach. If you're looking for value, consider a hotel that's inland along the I–405 freeway corridor.

In most cases, you can take advantage of some of the facilities of the high-end resorts, such as restaurants and spas, even if you aren't an overnight guest.

*Restaurant and hotel reviews have been shortened. For full information, visit Fodors.com.*

| WHAT IT COSTS | | | |
| --- | --- | --- | --- |
| $ | $$ | $$$ | $$$$ |
| Restaurants | under $16 | $16–$22 | $23–$30 | over $30 |
| Hotels | under $120 | $120–$175 | $176–$250 | over $250 |

Prices in the restaurant reviews are the average cost of a main course at dinner or, if dinner is not served, at lunch. Prices in the hotel reviews are the lowest cost of a standard double room in high season.

### VISITOR INFORMATION

Visit Anaheim is an excellent resource for both leisure and business travelers and can provide materials on many area attractions. Kiosks at the Anaheim Convention Center act as a digital concierge and allow visitors to plan itineraries and buy tickets to area attractions.

The Orange County Visitor Association's website is also a useful source of information.

**Information Orange County Visitors Association.** ⊕ *www.visittheoc.com.* **Visit Anaheim.** ⊠ *Anaheim Convention Center, 800 W. Katella Ave., Anaheim* ☎ *714/765–8888* ⊕ *www.visitanaheim.org.*

# DISNEYLAND RESORT

*26 miles southeast of Los Angeles, via I–5.*

The snowcapped Matterhorn, the centerpiece of the Magic Kingdom, punctuates the skyline of Anaheim. Since 1955, when Walt Disney chose this once-quiet farming community for the site of his first amusement park, Disneyland has attracted more than 635 million visitors and tens of thousands of workers, and Anaheim has been their host.

To understand the symbiotic relationship between Disneyland and Anaheim, you need only look at the $4.2 billion spent in a combined effort to revitalize Anaheim's tourist center and run-down areas, and to expand and renovate the Disney properties into what is known now as Disneyland Resort.

The resort is a sprawling complex that includes Disney's two amusement parks; three hotels; and Downtown Disney, a shopping, dining, and entertainment promenade. Anaheim's tourist center includes Angel Stadium of Anaheim, home of baseball's 2002 World Series Champion, Los Angeles Angels of Anaheim; the Honda Center (formerly the Arrowhead Pond), which hosts concerts and the Anaheim Ducks hockey team; and the enormous Anaheim Convention Center.

## GETTING THERE

Disney is about a 30-mile drive from either LAX or Downtown. From LAX, follow Sepulveda Boulevard south to the I–105 freeway and drive east 16 miles to the I–605 north exit. Exit at the Santa Ana Freeway (I–5) and continue south for 12 miles to the Disneyland Drive exit. Follow signs to the resort. From Downtown, follow I–5 south 28 miles and exit at Disneyland Drive. **Disneyland Resort Express** (☎ 800/828–6699 ⊕ graylineanaheim.com) offers daily nonstop bus service between LAX, John Wayne Airport, and Anaheim. Reservations are not required. The cost is $30 one-way from LAX; and $20 from John Wayne Airport.

## SAVING TIME AND MONEY

If you plan to visit for more than a day, you can save money by buying two- three-, four-, and five-day Park Hopper tickets that grant same-day "hopping" privileges between Disneyland and Disney's California Adventure. You get a discount on the multiple-day passes if you buy online through the Disneyland website.

Single-day admission prices vary by date. A one-day Park Hopper pass costs $155–$169 for anyone 10 or older, $149–$163 for kids ages 3–9 depending on what day you go. Admission to either park (but not both) is $97–$124 or $89–$119 for kids 3–9; kids 2 and under are free.

In addition to tickets, parking is $18–$35 (unless your hotel has a shuttle or is within walking distance), and meals in the parks and at Downtown Disney range from $10 to $50 per person.

---

## ƆISNEYLAND

FAMILY **Disneyland.** One of the biggest misconceptions people have about
FodorśChoice Disneyland is that it's the same as Florida's mammoth Walt Disney
★ World, or one of the Disney parks overseas. But Disneyland, which opened in 1955 and is the only one of the parks to have been overseen by Walt himself, has a genuine historic feel and occupies a unique place in the Disney legend. Expertly run, perfectly maintained, with polite and helpful staff ("cast members" in the Disney lexicon), the park has plenty that you won't find anywhere else—such as the Indiana Jones Adventure ride and Storybook Land, with its miniature replicas of animated Disney scenes from classics such as *Pinocchio* and *Alice in Wonderland*. Characters appear for autographs and photos throughout the day; times and places are posted at the entrances. Live shows, parades, strolling musicians, fireworks on weekends, and endless snack choices add to the carnival atmosphere. You can also meet some of the animated icons at one of the character meals

served at the three Disney hotels (open to the public). Belongings can be stored in lockers just off Main Street; stroller rentals at the entrance gate are a convenient option for families with small tykes. ✉ *1313 S. Disneyland Dr., between Ball Rd. and Katella Ave., Anaheim* ☎ *714/781–4636 guest information* ⊕ *www.disneyland.com* ☞ *$95–$119; parking $18.*

## PARK NEIGHBORHOODS
*Neighborhoods for Disneyland are arranged in geographic order.*

### MAIN STREET, U.S.A.
Walt's hometown of Marceline, Missouri, was the inspiration behind this romanticized image of small-town America, circa 1900. The sidewalks are lined with a penny arcade and shops that sell everything from tradable pins to Disney-themed clothing, an endless supply of sugar confections, and a photo shop that offers souvenirs created via Disney's PhotoPass (on-site photographers capture memorable moments digitally—you can access in person or online). Main Street opens half an hour before the rest of the park, so it's a good place to explore if you're getting an early start to beat the crowds (it's also open an hour after the other attractions close, so you may want to save your shopping for the end of the day). **Main Street Cinema** offers a cool respite from the crowds and six classic Disney animated shorts, including *Steamboat Willie*. There's rarely a wait to enter. Grab a cappuccino and fresh-made pastry at the Jolly Holiday bakery to jump-start your visit. Board the **Disneyland Railroad** here to save on walking; it tours all the lands and offers unique views of Splash Mountain, the Grand Canyon, and Primeval World dioramas.

### NEW ORLEANS SQUARE
This mini–French Quarter, with narrow streets, hidden courtyards, and live street performances, is home to two iconic attractions and the Cajun-inspired Blue Bayou restaurant. **Pirates of the Caribbean** now features Jack Sparrow and the cursed Captain Barbossa of the blockbuster series, plus enhanced special effects and battle scenes (complete with cannonball explosions). Nearby **Haunted Mansion** continues to spook guests with its stretching room and "doombuggy" rides (there's now an expanded storyline for the beating-heart bride). The *Nightmare Before Christmas* holiday overlay is an annual tradition. This is a good area to get a casual bite to eat; the clam chowder in sourdough bread bowls, sold at the French Market Restaurant and Royal Street Veranda, is a popular choice. Food carts offer everything from just-popped popcorn, to churros, and even fresh fruit.

### FRONTIERLAND
Between Adventureland and Fantasyland, Frontierland transports you to the wild, wild West with its rustic buildings, shooting gallery, mountain range, and foot-stompin' dance hall. The marquee attraction, **Big Thunder Mountain Railroad,** is a relatively tame roller coaster ride (no steep descents) that takes the form of a runaway mine car as it rumbles past desert canyons and an old mining town. Tour the Rivers of America on the **Mark Twain Riverboat** in the company of a grizzled old river pilot or circumnavigate the globe on the **Sailing Ship Columbia,** though

# Disneyland

**MICKEY'S TOONTOWN**

Minnie's House
Mickey's House
Chip 'n Dale Treehouse
Gadget's Go Coaster
Donald's Boat
Goofy's Playhouse
Roger Rabbit's Car Toon Spin

Fantasyland Theatre

It's A Small World

San Diego Freeway
5

**DISNEYLAND PARK**

**FANTASYLAND**

Casey Jr. Circus Train
Dumbo the Flying Elephant
Storybook Land Canal Boats
King Arthur Carousel
Peter Pan's Flight
Mad Tea Party
Mr. Toad's Wild Ride
Alice in Wonderland

Rivers of America

**FRONTIERLAND**

Big Thunder Mountain RR
Pinocchio's Daring Journey
Snow White's Scary Adventures
Fantasy Faire
Matterhorn Bobsleds
Finding Nemo's Submarine Voyage

Autopia

The Many Adventures of Winnie the Pooh

**CRITTER COUNTRY**

Canoes
Tom Sawyer Island
Mark Twain Riverboat
Sailing Ship Columbia
Splash Mountain

Plaza Garden Stage
Central Plaza

Buzz Lightyear Astro Blasters

Star Wars Launch Bay

Shootin' Exposition
Golden Horseshoe Stage
Astro Orbiter
Star Tours- The Adventure Continues

Haunted Mansion
Rafts
Enchanted Tiki Room
Star Wars Path of the Jedi

**TOMORROWLAND**

Pirates of the Caribbean

**NEW ORLEANS SQUARE**

Tarzan's Treehouse

Jungle Cruise

**ADVENTURE-LAND**

Parade Route

Space Mountain

Indiana Jones Adventure

Main Street Cinema

**MAIN STREET, U.S.A.**

Disneyland Railroad

House of Blues Stage

**DOWNTOWN DISNEY**

AMC Theaters

LEGO Imagination Center

Soarin' Around the World

Monsters Inc. Mike & Sulley to the Rescue

Grand Californian Hotel

Sunset Showcase Theatre

Hollywood Backlot Stage

**HOLLYWOOD LAND**

Turtle Talk with Crush

**SUNSHINE PLAZA**

Disney's Frozen

Paradise Pier Hotel

Grizzly River Run

**GRIZZLY PEAK**

Redwood Creek Challenge Trail

Wine Country Trattoria

**BUENA VISTA STREET**

Disney Junior

Disney Animation

It's Tough To Be a Bug

**"A BUG'S LAND"**

Flik's Flyers

Guardians of the Galaxy- Mission: BREAKOUT!

Little Mermaid- Ariel's Undersea Adventure

Goofy's Sky School

Jumpin' Jellyfish

Golden Zephyr

The Bakery Tour

Tuck and Roll's Drive 'Em Buggies

**DISNEY CALIFORNIA ADVENTURE**

**PACIFIC WHARF**

**PARADISE PIER**

Mickey's Fun Wheel

Luigi's Rollickin' Roadsters

**CARS LAND**

Radiator Springs Racers

Toy Story Midway Mania

California Screamin'

Games of the Boardwalk

King Triton's Carousel

Disneyland Drive

Harbor Boulevard

Katella Avenue

**KEY**

Restrooms
Rail Line
Monorail

its operating hours are usually limited to weekends. From here, you can raft over to Pirate's Lair on **Tom Sawyer Island,** which now features pirate-themed caves, treasure hunts, and music, along with plenty of caves and hills to climb and explore. If you don't mind tight seating, have a snack at The Golden Horseshoe saloon, where Walt himself used to hang out.

## CRITTER COUNTRY
Down-home country is the theme in this shaded corner of the park, where Winnie the Pooh and Davy Crockett make their homes. Here you can find **Splash Mountain,** a classic flume ride with music, and appearances by Brer Rabbit and other *Song of the South* characters. Don't forget to check out your photo (the camera snaps close-ups of each car just before it plunges into the water) on the way out. The patio of the popular Hungry Bear Restaurant has great views of Tom Sawyer's Island and Davy Crockett's Explorer Canoes.

## ADVENTURELAND
Modeled after the lands of Africa, Polynesia, and Arabia, this tiny tropical paradise is worth braving the crowds that flock here for the ambience and better-than-average food. Sing along with the animatronic birds and tiki gods in the **Enchanted Tiki Room,** sail the rivers of the world with joke-cracking skippers on **Jungle Cruise,** and climb the *Disneyodendron semperflorens* (the always-blooming Disney tree) to **Tarzan's Treehouse,** where you can walk through scenes, some interactive, from the 1999 animated film. Cap off the visit with a wild Jeep ride at **Indiana Jones Adventure,** where the special effects and decipherable hieroglyphics distract you while you're waiting in line. The skewers (some vegetarian options available) at Bengal Barbecue, and pineapple whip at Tiki Juice Bar are some of the best fast-food options in the park.

## FANTASYLAND
Sleeping Beauty Castle marks the entrance to Fantasyland, a visual wonderland of princesses, spinning teacups, flying elephants, and other classic storybook characters. Rides, and shops such as the princess-themed Bibbidi Bobbidi Boutique, take precedence over restaurants in this area of the park, but outdoor carts sell everything from churros to turkey legs. Tots love the **King Arthur Carousel, Casey Jr. Circus Train,** and **Storybook Land Canal Boats.** This is also home to **Mr. Toad's Wild Ride, Peter Pan's Flight,** and **Pinocchio's Daring Journey,** all classic movie-theater-dark rides that immerse riders in Disney fairy tales. The Abominable Snowman pops up on the **Matterhorn Bobsleds,** a roller coaster that twists and turns up and around on a made-to-scale model of the real Swiss mountain. Anchoring the east end of Fantasyland is **it's a small world,** a smorgasbord of dancing animatronic dolls, cuckoo clock–covered walls, and variations of the song everyone knows, or soon *will* know, by heart. Beloved Disney characters like Ariel from *The Little Mermaid* are also part of the mix. Fantasy Faire is a fairy tale–style village that collects all the Disney princesses together. Each has her own reception nook in the Royal Hall. Condensed retellings of *Tangled* and *Beauty and the Beast* take place at the Royal Theatre.

## BEST TIPS FOR DISNEYLAND

■TIP➔ As of 2017, all visitors must pass through metal detectors, and bags are searched before entering the Disneyland Resort. Allot 10–15 extra minutes for passing through the security line.

**Buy entry tickets in advance.** Nearby hotels sell park admission tickets; you can also buy them through Disney's website. With package deals, like those offered through AAA, tickets are included.

Lines at ticket booths can take over an hour on busy days. Save time by buying in advance.

**Come midweek.** Weekends, especially in summer, are a mob scene. Holidays are crowded, too. A rainy winter weekday is often the least crowded time to visit.

**Plan your times to hit the most popular rides.** Get to the park as early as possible, even before the gates open, and make a beeline for the top rides before the crowds reach a critical mass. Late evening is when the hordes thin out, and you can catch a special show or parade. Save the quieter attractions for mid afternoon.

**Use FASTPASS.** These passes allow you to reserve your place in line at some of the most crowded attractions (only one at a time). Distribution machines are posted near the entrances of each attraction. Feed in your park admission ticket, and you'll receive a pass with a printed time frame (generally up to 1–1½ hours later) during which you can return to wait in a much shorter line.

**Avoid peak mealtime crowds.** Start the day with a big breakfast so you won't be too hungry at noon, when restaurants and vendors get slammed. Wait to have lunch until after 1 pm.

If you want to eat at the **Blue Bayou** in New Orleans Square, you can make a reservation up to six months in advance online. Another (cheaper) option is to bring your own snacks. It's always a good idea to bring water.

**Check the daily events schedule online or at the park entrance.** During parades, fireworks, and other special events, sections of the parks are filled with crowds. This can work in your favor or against you: an event could make it difficult to get around a park—but if you plan ahead, you can take advantage of the distraction to hit popular rides.

**Send the teens next door.** Disneyland's newer sister park, California Adventure, features more intense rides suitable for older kids (Park Hopper passes include admission to both parks).

### MICKEY'S TOONTOWN

Geared toward small fries, this lopsided cartoonlike downtown, complete with cars and trolleys that invite exploring, is where Mickey, Donald, Goofy, and other classic Disney characters hang their hats. One of the most popular attractions is **Roger Rabbit's Car Toon Spin,** a twisting, turning cab ride through the Toontown of *Who Framed Roger Rabbit?* You can also walk through **Mickey's House** to meet and be photographed with the famous mouse, take a low-key ride on **Gadget's Go Coaster,** or bounce around the fenced-in playground in front of **Goofy's Playhouse.**

## TOMORROWLAND

This popular section of the park continues to tinker with its future, adding and enhancing rides regularly. *Star Wars* themed attractions can't be missed, like the immersive, 3-D **Star Tours – The Adventures Continue,** where you can join the Rebellion in a galaxy far, far away. **Finding Nemo's Submarine Voyage** updates the old Submarine Voyage ride with the exploits of Nemo, Dory, Marlin, and other characters from the Disney-Pixar film. Try to visit this popular ride early in the day if you can, and be prepared for a wait. The interactive **Buzz Lightyear Astro Blasters** lets you zap your neighbors with laser beams and compete for the highest score. Hurtle through the cosmos on **Space Mountain** or check out mainstays like the futuristic **Astro Orbiter** rockets, **Star Wars Launch Bay,** which showcases costumes, models, and props from the franchise, and **Star Wars, Path of the Jedi,** which catches viewers up on all the movies with a quick 12-minute film. Disneyland Monorail and Disneyland Railroad both have stations here. There's also a video arcade and dancing water fountain that makes a perfect playground for kids on hot summer days. The Jedi Training Academy spotlights future Luke Skywalkers in the crowd.

> ### DISNEY'S TOP ATTRACTIONS
>
> **Indiana Jones:** You're at the wheel for this thrilling ride through a cursed temple. Watch out for boulders!
>
> **Haunted Mansion:** A "doombuggy" takes you through a spooky old plantation mansion.
>
> **Matterhorn Bobsleds:** At the center of the Magic Kingdom, this roller coaster simulates bobsleds.
>
> **Pirates of the Caribbean:** Watch buccaneers wreak havoc as you float along in a rowboat.
>
> **Space Mountain:** This scary-but-thrilling roller coaster is indoors—and mostly in the dark.

Besides the eight lands, the daily live-action shows and parades are always crowd-pleasers. Among these is **Fantasmic!** a musical, fireworks, and laser show in which Mickey and friends wage a spellbinding battle against Disneyland's darker characters. ■TIP→ Arrive early to secure a good view; if there are two shows scheduled for the day, the second one tends to be less crowded. A fireworks display lights up weekends and most summer evenings. Brochures with maps, available at the entrance, list show and parade times.

## DISNEY CALIFORNIA ADVENTURE

FAMILY

Fodor's Choice
★

**Disney California Adventure.** The sprawling Disney California Adventure, adjacent to Disneyland (their entrances face each other), pays tribute to the Golden State with eight theme areas that re-create vintage architectural styles and embrace several hit Pixar films via engaging attractions. Visitors enter through the art deco–style Buena Vista Street, past shops and a helpful information booth that advises wait times on attractions. The 12-acre Cars Land features Radiator Springs Racers, a speedy trip in six-passenger speedsters through scenes featured in the blockbuster hit. (FASTPASS tickets for the ride run out early most days.) Other popular attractions include World of Color, a nighttime water-effects show, and Toy Story Mania!, an

## DID YOU KNOW?

The plain purple teacup in Disneyland's Mad Tea Party ride spins the fastest—though no one knows why.

interactive adventure ride hosted by Woody and Buzz Lightyear. At night the park takes on neon hues as glowing signs light up Route 66 in Cars Land and Mickey's Fun Wheel, a giant Ferris wheel on the Paradise Pier. Unlike at Disneyland, cocktails, beer, and wine are available; craft beers and premium wines from California are poured. Live nightly entertainment also features a 1930s jazz troupe that arrives in a vintage jalopy. ⊠ *1313 S. Disneyland Dr., between Ball Rd. and Katella Ave., Anaheim* ☎ *714/781–4636* ⊕ *www.disneyland.com* ✎ *$95–$119; parking $18.*

## PARK NEIGHBORHOODS

### BUENA VISTA STREET

California Adventure's grand entryway re-creates the lost 1920s Los Angeles that Walt Disney encountered when he moved to the Golden State. There's a **Red Car trolley** (modeled after Los Angeles's bygone streetcar line); hop on for the brief ride to Hollywood Land. Buena Vista Street is also home to a Starbucks outlet—within the Fiddler, Fifer & Practical Café—and the upscale Carthay Circle Restaurant and Lounge, which serves modern craft cocktails and beer.

### GRIZZLY PEAK

This woodsy land celebrates the great outdoors. Test your skills on the **Redwood Creek Challenge Trail,** a challenging trek across net ladders and suspension bridges. **Grizzly River Run** mimics the river rapids of the Sierra Nevadas; be prepared to get soaked.

**Soarin' Around the world** is a spectacular simulated hang-gliding ride over internationally known landmarks like Switzerland's Matterhorn and India's Taj Mahal.

### HOLLYWOOD LAND

With a main street modeled after Hollywood Boulevard, a fake sky backdrop, and real soundstages, this area celebrates California's film industry. **Disney Animation** gives you an insider's look at how animators create characters. **Turtle Talk with Crush** lets kids have an unscripted chat with a computer-animated Crush, the sea turtle from *Finding Nemo*. The Hyperion Theater hosts **Frozen,** a 45-minute live performance from a Broadway-sized cast with terrific visual effects. ■ TIP➔ Plan on getting in line about half an hour in advance; the show is worth the wait. On the film-inspired ride, **Monsters, Inc. Mike & Sulley to the Rescue,** visitors climb into taxis and travel the streets of Monstropolis on a mission to safely return Boo to her bedroom. **Guardians of the Galaxy – Mission: BREAKOUT!** which opened in summer 2017, replaced the now-closed Twilight Zone Tower of Terror.

### A BUG'S LAND

Inspired by the 1998 film *A Bug's Life,* this section skews its attractions to an insect's point of view. Kids can spin around in giant takeout Chinese food boxes on **Flik's Flyers,** and hit the bug-shaped bumper cars on **Tuck and Roll's Drive 'Em Buggies.** The short show *It's Tough to Be a Bug!* gives a 3-D look at insect life.

### CARS LAND

Amble down Route 66, the main thoroughfare of Cars Land, and discover a pitch-perfect re-creation of the vintage highway. Quick eats are found at the Cozy Cone Motel (in a teepee-shaped motor court) while

**12**

Flo's V8 café serves hearty comfort food. Start your day at Radiator Springs Racers, the park's most popular attraction, where waits can be two hours or longer. Strap into a nifty sports car and meet the characters of Pixar's *Cars*; the ride ends in a speedy auto race through the red rocks and desert of Radiator Springs.

### PACIFIC WHARF
In the midst of the California Adventure you'll find 10 different dining options, from light snacks to full-service restaurants. The Wine Country Trattoria is a great place for Italian specialties; relax outside on the restaurant's terrace for a casual bite while sipping a Califorona-made craft beer or wine. Mexican cuisine and potent margaritas are available at the Cocina Cucamonga Mexican Grill and Rita's Baja Blenders, and Lucky Fortune Cookery serves Chinese stir-fry dishes.

### PARADISE PIER
This section re-creates the glory days of California's seaside piers. If you're looking for thrills, the **California Screamin'** roller coaster takes its riders from 0 to 55 mph in about four seconds and proceeds through scream tunnels, steeply angled drops, and a 360-degree loop. **Goofy's Sky School** is a rollicking roller coaster ride that goes up three stories and covers more than 1,200 feet of track. **Mickey's Fun Wheel,** a giant Ferris wheel, provides a good view of the grounds, though some cars spin and sway for more kicks. There are also carnival games, an aquatic-themed carousel, and Ariel's Grotto, where future princesses can dine with the mermaid and her friends (reservations are a must). Get a close-up look at Ariel's world on **Little Mermaid—Ariel's Undersea Adventure.** The best views of the nighttime music, water, and light show, **World of Color,** are from the paths along Paradise Bay. FASTPASS tickets are available. Or for a guaranteed spot, book dinner at the Wine Country Trattoria that includes a ticket to a viewing area to catch all the show's stunning visuals.

### OTHER ATTRACTIONS
FAMILY **Downtown Disney District.** The Downtown Disney District is a 20-acre promenade of dining, shopping, and entertainment that connects the resort's hotels and theme parks. At **Ralph Brennan's Jazz Kitchen** you can dig into New Orleans–style food and music. Sports fans gravitate to **ESPN Zone,** which serves American food from the grill, and lets visitors play video games or watch worldwide sports events telecast through 120 HDTVs. An **AMC** multiplex movie theater with stadium-style seating plays the latest blockbusters and, naturally, a couple of kid flicks. Shops sell everything from Disney goods to antique jewelry—don't miss **Disney Vault 28,** a hip boutique that sells designer-made Disney wear and couture clothing and accessories. At the mega-sized **Lego Store** there are hands-on demonstrations and space to play with the latest Lego creations. Anna & Elsa's Store speedily makes over kids into their favorite character from the hit film *Frozen.* Parking is a deal: the first two hours are free, our four hours with validation. All visitors must pass through a security checkpoint and metal detectors before entering. ⊠ *1580 Disneyland Dr., Anaheim* ☎ *714/300–7800* ⊕ *disneyland. disney.go.com/downtown-disney* ✉ *Free.*

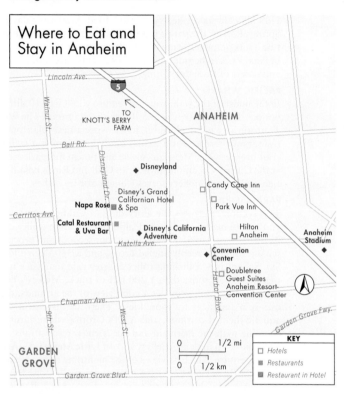

Where to Eat and Stay in Anaheim

## WHERE TO EAT

**$$$**

MEDITERRANEAN

✕ **Catal Restaurant & Uva Bar.** Famed chef Joachim Splichal and his staff take a relaxed approach at this bi-level Mediterranean spot where 40 wines by the glass, craft beers, and craft cocktails pair well with his Spanish-influenced dishes. Upstairs, Catal's menu has tapas, a variety of flavorful paellas (lobster is worth the splurge), and charcuterie. ■ TIP→ **Reserve a table on the outdoor terrace for an awesome view of the Disneyland fireworks. Known for:** people-watching; gourmet burgers; paella. ⑤ *Average main: $30 ⊠ Downtown Disney District, 1580 S. Disneyland Dr., Suite 103, Anaheim* ☎ *714/774–4442* ⊕ *www.patinagroup.com.*

**$$$$**

AMERICAN

✕ **Napa Rose.** Done up in a handsome Craftsman style, Napa Rose's rich seasonal cuisine is matched with an extensive wine list, with 1,000 labels and 80 available by the glass. For a look into the open kitchen, sit at the counter and watch the chefs as they whip up such signature dishes as grilled diver scallops and chanterelles, and roasted lamp chops topped with pomegranate. **Known for:** excellent wine list; kid-friendly options; grilled diver scallops. ⑤ *Average main: $45 ⊠ Disney's Grand Californian Hotel, 1600 S. Disneyland Dr., Anaheim* ☎ *714/300–7170, 714/781–3463 reservations* ⊕ *disneyland.disney. go.com/grand-californian-hotel/napa-rose.*

**12**

## WHERE TO STAY

$$ ⛉ **Candy Cane Inn.** One of the Disneyland area's first hotels, the Candy
HOTEL  Cane is one of Anaheim's most relaxing properties, with spacious and
FAMILY  understated rooms and an inviting palm-fringed pool. **Pros:** proximity to
everything Disney; friendly service; well-lighted property. **Cons:** rooms
and lobby are on the small side; all rooms face parking lot. $ *Rooms
from: $158 ⊠ 1747 S. Harbor Blvd., Anaheim ☎ 714/774–5284,
800/345–7057 ⊕ www.candycaneinn.net ⤳ 171 rooms* ⊚*l Breakfast.*

$$$$ ⛉ **Disney's Grand Californian Hotel & Spa.** The most opulent of Disney-
RESORT  land's three hotels, the Craftsman-style Grand Californian offers views
FAMILY  of Disney California Adventure and Downtown Disney. **Pros:** gorgeous
Fodor's Choice  lobby; family friendly; direct access to California Adventure. **Cons:**
★  the self-parking lot is across the street; standard rooms are on the
small side. $ *Rooms from: $461 ⊠ 1600 S. Disneyland Dr., Anaheim
☎ 714/635–2300 ⊕ disneyland.disney.go.com/grand-californian-hotel
⤳ 998 rooms* ⊚*l No meals.*

$$ ⛉ **Doubletree Guest Suites Anaheim Resort-Convention Center.** This busy
HOTEL  hotel near the Anaheim Convention Center and a 20-minute walk from
Disneyland caters to business travelers and vacationers alike. **Pros:** huge
suites; walking distance to a variety of restaurants. **Cons:** a bit far
from Disneyland; pool area is small. $ *Rooms from: $129 ⊠ 2085 S.
Harbor Blvd., Anaheim ☎ 714/750–3000, 800/215–7316 ⊕ double-
treeanaheim.com ⤳ 252 rooms* ⊚*l No meals.*

$$ ⛉ **Hilton Anaheim.** Next to the Anaheim Convention Center, this busy
HOTEL  Hilton is one of the largest hotels in Southern California, with a restau-
FAMILY  rant and food court, cocktail lounges, a full-service gym, and its own
Starbucks. **Pros:** efficient service; great children's programs; some rooms
have views of the park fireworks. **Cons:** huge size can be daunting;
fee to use health club. $ *Rooms from: $159 ⊠ 777 Convention Way,
Anaheim ☎ 714/750–4321, 800/445–8667 ⊕ www.anaheim.hilton.com
⤳ 1,572 rooms* ⊚*l No meals.*

$$ ⛉ **Park Vue Inn.** Watch the frequent fireworks from the rooftop sundeck
HOTEL  at this bougainvillea-covered Spanish-style inn, one of the closest lodgings
FAMILY  to Disneyland's main gate. **Pros:** easy walk to Disneyland, Downtown
Disney, and Disney California Adventure; free parking until midnight
on checkout day; some rooms have bunk beds. **Cons:** all rooms face the
parking lot; rooms near the breakfast room can be noisy. $ *Rooms from:
$159 ⊠ 1570 S. Harbor Blvd., Anaheim ☎ 714/772–3691, 800/334–
7021 ⊕ www.parkvueinn.com ⤳ 86 rooms* ⊚*l Breakfast.*

# KNOTT'S BERRY FARM

*25 miles south of Los Angeles, via I–5, in Buena Park.*

FAMILY  **Knott's Berry Farm.** The land where the boysenberry was invented (by
crossing raspberry, blackberry, and loganberry bushes) is now occupied
by Knott's Berry Farm. In 1934 Cordelia Knott began serving chicken
dinners on her wedding china to supplement her family's income. The
dinners and her boysenberry pies proved more profitable than hus-
band Walter's farm, so the two moved first into the restaurant business
and then into the entertainment business. The park is now a 160-acre

242 <     **Orange County and Catalina Island**

complex with 40 rides, dozens of restaurants and shops, arcade games, live shows, a brick-by-brick replica of Philadelphia's Independence Hall, and loads of Americana. Although it has plenty to keep small children occupied, the park is best known for its awesome rides. The Boardwalk area is home to several coasters, including the stomach-churning Rip Tide that turns thrill-seekers upside down and around several times, plus water features to cool things off on hot days, and a lighted promenade. And, yes, you can still get that boysenberry pie (and jam, juice— you name it). ⊠ *8039 Beach Blvd., Buena Park ✛ Between La Palma Ave. and Crescent St., 2 blocks south of Hwy. 91* ☎ *714/220–5200* ⊕ *www.knotts.com* ⊠ *$75.*

## PARK NEIGHBORHOODS

### THE BOARDWALK

Not-for-the-squeamish thrill rides and skill-based games dominate the scene at the **boardwalk.** Roller coasters—Coast Rider, Surfside Glider, and Pacific Scrambler—surround a pond that keeps things cooler on hot days. Go head over heels on the **Boomerang** roller coaster, then do it again—in reverse. The boardwalk is also home to a string of test-your-skill games that are fun to watch whether you're playing or not, and Johnny Rockets, the park's all-American diner.

### CAMP SNOOPY

It can be gridlock on weekends, but kids love this miniature High Sierra wonderland where the *Peanuts* gang hangs out. Tykes can push and pump their own mini-mining cars on **Huff and Puff,** soar around via **Charlie Brown's Kite Flyer,** and hop aboard **Woodstock's Airmail,** a kids' version of the park's Supreme Scream ride. Most of the rides here are geared toward kids only, leaving parents to cheer them on from the sidelines. **Sierra Sidewinder,** a roller coaster near the entrance of Camp Snoopy, is aimed at older children, with spinning saucer-type vehicles that go a maximum speed of 37 mph.

### FIESTA VILLAGE

Over in **Fiesta Village** are two more musts for adrenaline junkies: **Montezooma's Revenge,** a roller coaster that goes from 0 to 55 mph in less than five seconds, and **Jaguar!,** which simulates the motions of a cat stalking its prey, twisting, spiraling, and speeding up and slowing down as it takes you on its stomach-dropping course. There's also **Hat Dance,** a version of the spinning teacups but with sombreros, and a 100-year-old **Dentzel carousel,** complete with an antique organ and menagerie of hand-carved animals. In a nod to history, there are restored scale models of the California Missions at Fiesta Village's southern entrance.

### GHOST TOWN

Clusters of authentic old buildings relocated from their original mining-town sites mark this section of the park. You can stroll down the street, stop and chat with a blacksmith, pan for gold (for a fee), crack open a geode, check out the chalkboard of a circa-1875 schoolhouse, and ride an original Butterfield stagecoach. Looming over it all is **GhostRider,** Orange County's first wooden roller coaster. Traveling up to 56 mph and reaching 118 feet at its highest point, the park's biggest attraction is riddled with sudden dips and curves, subjecting riders to forces up to three times that of gravity. On the Western-theme **Silver Bullet,** riders are sent to a height of 146 feet and then back down 109 feet. Riders spiral, corkscrew, fly into a cobra roll, and experience overbanked curves. The **Calico Mine** ride descends into a replica of a working gold mine complete with 50 animatronic figures. The **Timber Mountain Log Ride** is a visitor favorite: the flume ride tours through pioneer scenes before splashing down. Also found here is the **Pony Express,** a roller coaster that lets riders saddle up on packs of "horses" tethered to platforms that take off on a series of hairpin turns and travel up to 38 mph. Don't miss the **Western Trails Museum,** a dusty old gem full of Old West memorabilia and rural Americana, plus menus from the original chicken restaurant, and an impressive antique button collection. **Calico Railroad** departs regularly from Ghost Town station for a round-trip tour of the park (bandit holdups notwithstanding).

This section is also home to **Big Foot Rapids,** a splash-fest of whitewater river rafting over towering cliffs, cascading waterfalls, and wild rapids. Don't miss the visually stunning show at **Mystery Lodge,** which tells the story of Native Americans in the Pacific Northwest with lights, music, and special effects.

### INDIAN TRAILS
Celebrate Native American traditions through interactive exhibits like tepees and daily dance and storytelling performances.

**Knott's Soak City Waterpark** is directly across from the main park on 13 acres next to Independence Hall. It has a dozen major water rides; **Pacific Spin** is an oversize waterslide that drops riders 75 feet into a catch pool. There's also a children's pool, a 750,000-gallon wave pool, and a funhouse. Soak City's season runs mid-May to mid-September. It's open daily after Memorial Day, weekends only after Labor Day, and then closes for the season.

---

## WHERE TO EAT AND STAY

$$
AMERICAN
FAMILY
✕ **Mrs. Knott's Chicken Dinner Restaurant.** Cordelia Knott's fried chicken and boysenberry pies drew crowds so big that Knott's Berry Farm was built to keep the hungry customers occupied while they waited. The restaurant's current incarnation (outside the park's entrance) still serves crispy fried chicken, along with fluffy handmade biscuits, mashed potatoes, and Mrs. Knott's signature chilled cherry-rhubarb compote. **Known for:** fried chicken; family friendly; outdoor dining. $ *Average main: $22* ⊠ *Knott's Berry Farm Marketplace, 8039 Beach Blvd., Buena Park* ☎ *714/220–5055* ⊕ *www.knotts.com/california-marketplace/ mrs-knott-s-chicken-dinner-restaurant.*

$
RESORT
FAMILY
**Knott's Berry Farm Hotel.** This convenient high-rise hotel is run by the park and sits right on park grounds surrounded by graceful palm trees. **Pros:** easy access to Knott's Berry Farm; plenty of family activities; basketball court. **Cons:** lobby and hallways can be noisy; public areas show significant wear and tear. $ *Rooms from: $99* ⊠ *7675 Crescent Ave., Buena Park* ☎ *714/995–1111, 866/752–2444* ⊕ *www.knottshotel.com* ⮑ *320 rooms* ⦿ *No meals.*

A mural at Huntington Beach

# THE COAST

Running along the Orange County coastline is scenic Pacific Coast Highway (Highway 1, known locally as the PCH). Older beachfront settlements, with their modest bungalow-style homes, are joined by posh gated communities. The pricey land between Newport Beach and Laguna Beach is where ex-Laker Kobe Bryant, novelist Dean Koontz, those infamous Real Housewives of Bravo, and a slew of finance moguls live.

Though the coastline is rapidly being filled in, there are still a few stretches of beautiful, protected open land. And at many places along the way you can catch an idealized glimpse of the Southern California lifestyle: surfers hitting the beach, boards under their arms.

## LONG BEACH

*About 25 miles southeast of Los Angeles, via I–110 south.*

### EXPLORING

FAMILY **Aquarium of the Pacific.** Sea lions, nurse sharks, and penguins, oh my!—this aquarium focuses on creatures of the Pacific Ocean. The main exhibits include large tanks of sharks, sting rays, and ethereal sea dragons, which the aquarium has successfully bred in captivity. The Great Hall features the multimedia attraction *Penguins*, a panoramic film that captures the world of this endangered species. Be sure to say hello to Betty, a rescue at the engaging sea otter exhibit. For a non-aquatic experience, head to Lorikeet Forest, a walk-in aviary full of the friendliest parrots from Australia. Buy a cup of nectar and smile as you become a human bird perch. If you're a true animal lover, book an up-close-and-personal Animal Encounters Tour ($109) to learn about and assist in the care and feeding of the animals; or find out how the aquarium functions with the extensive Behind the Scenes Tour ($42.95 for adults, including admission). Certified divers can book a supervised dive in the aquarium's Tropical Reef Habitat ($299). Twice daily whale-watching trips on the *Harbor Breeze* depart from the dock adjacent to the aquarium; summer sightings of blue whales are an unforgettable thrill. ✉ *100 Aquarium Way, Long Beach* ☎ *562/590–3100* 🌐 *www.aquariumofpacific.org* 🎟 *$29.95.*

FAMILY ***Queen Mary.*** The *Queen Mary*, though berthed, is an impressive example of 20th-century cruise ship opulence and sadly the last of its kind. The beautifully preserved art deco–style ocean liner was launched in 1936 and made 1,001 transatlantic crossings before finally berthing in Long Beach in 1967. Today there's a popular Princess Diana exhibit, a wine tasting room, and a daily British-style high tea.

On board you can take one of three daily or five weekend tours, such as the informative Glory Days Historical walk or the downright spooky Haunted Encounters tour. (Spirits have reportedly been spotted in the pool and engine room.) You could stay for dinner at one of the ship's restaurants, listen to live jazz in the original first-class lounge, or even spend the night in one of the 346 wood-panel cabins. The ship's neighbor, a geodesic dome originally built to house Howard Hughes's *Spruce Goose* aircraft, now serves as a terminal for Carnival Cruise Lines, making the *Queen Mary* the perfect pit stop before or after a cruise. Anchored next to the *Queen* is the *Scorpion,* a Russian submarine you can tour for a look at Cold War history. ✉ *1126 Queens Hwy., Long Beach* ☎ *877/342–0738* 🌐 *www.queenmary.com* 🎟 *Tours $16–$80, including a self-guided audio tour.*

## WHERE TO STAY

$$ HOTEL FAMILY 🏨 **Queen Mary Hotel.** Experience the golden age of transatlantic travel without the seasickness: a 1936–art deco style reigns on the *Queen Mary,* from the ship's mahogany paneling to its nickel-plated doors to the majestic Grand Salon. **Pros:** a walkable historic Promenade deck; views from Long Beach out to the Pacific; art deco details. **Cons:** spotty service; vintage soundproofing makes for a challenging night's sleep; mandatory Wi-Fi fee. [$] *Rooms from: $149* ✉ *1126 Queens Hwy., Long Beach* ☎ *562/435–3511, 877/342–0742* 🌐 *www.queenmary.com* 🛏 *346 staterooms* 🍴 *No meals.*

$$ B&B/INN 🏨 **The Varden.** Constructed in 1929 to house Bixby Knolls Sr.'s mistress, Dolly Varden, this small, historic, European-style hotel, on the metro line in downtown Long Beach, now caters to worldly budget travelers. Compact rooms are mostly white and blend modern touches like flat-screen TVs and geometric silver fixtures with period details like exposed beams, Dakota Jackson periwinkle chairs, and round penny-tile baths. **Pros:** great value for downtown location; discount passes to Gold's Gym across the street; complimentary Continental breakfast. **Cons:** no resort services; small rooms. [$] *Rooms from: $159* ✉ *335 Pacific Ave., Long Beach* ☎ *562/432–8950* 🌐 *www.thevardenhotel.com* 🛏 *35 rooms.*

## NEWPORT BEACH

*6 miles south of Huntington Beach via the Pacific Coast Highway.*

Newport Beach has evolved from a simple seaside village to an icon of chic coastal living. Its ritzy reputation comes from mega-yachts bobbing in the harbor, boutiques that rival those in Beverly Hills, and spectacular homes overlooking the ocean.

The city boasts some of the cleanest beaches in Southern California; inland Newport Beach's concentration of high-rise office buildings, shopping centers, and luxury hotels drive the economy. But on the city's Balboa Peninsula, you can still catch a glimpse of a more humble, down-to-earth town scattered with taco spots, tackle shops, and sailor bars.

### ESSENTIALS

**Visitor and Tour Information Visit Newport Beach.** ⊠ *Atrium Court at Fashion Island, 401 Newport Center Dr.* ☎ *855/563–9767* ⊕ *www.visitnewportbeach.com.*

### EXPLORING

**Balboa Island.** This sliver of terra firma in Newport Harbor boasts quaint streets tightly packed with impossibly charming multimillion-dollar cottages. The island's main drag, Marine Avenue, is lined with equally picturesque cafés and shops.

**NEED A BREAK**

**Sugar 'N Spice.** Stop by ice cream parlor Sugar 'N Spice for a Balboa Bar—a slab of vanilla ice cream dipped first in chocolate and then in a topping of your choice such as hard candy or Oreo crumbs. Other parlors serve the concoction, but Sugar 'N Spice claims to have invented it back in 1945. ⊠ *310 Marine Ave., Balboa Island* ☎ *949/673–8907.*

FAMILY **Balboa Peninsula.** Newport's best beaches are on Balboa Peninsula, where many jetties pave the way to ideal swimming areas. The most intense spot for bodysurfing in Orange County, and arguably on the West Coast, known as the **Wedge,** is at the south end of the peninsula. It was created by accident in the 1930s when the Federal Works Progress Administration built a jetty to protect Newport Harbor. ■TIP➜ Rip currents mean it's strictly for the pros—but it sure is fun to watch an experienced local ride it. ⊕ *www.visitnewportbeach.com/vacations/balboa-peninsula.*

FAMILY **Discovery Cube's Ocean Quest.** This family-friendly destination has exhibits on the history of the harbor, ocean explorers, and scientific aspects of the Pacific Ocean. There's a fleet of ship models: some date to 1798, and one is made entirely of gold and silver. Other fun features include a touch tank holding local sea creatures and a lab for kids that encourages innovation. ⊠ *600 E. Bay Ave.* ☎ *949/675–8915* ⊕ *www.oceanquestoc.org* ☞ *$3* ⊗ *Closed Mon.–Thurs.*

**Newport Harbor.** Sheltering nearly 16,000 small boats, Newport Harbor may seduce even those who don't own a yacht. Spend an afternoon exploring the charming avenues and surrounding alleys; take California's longest running auto ferry across to Balboa Island. The fare is $2 for car and driver for the scenic crossing. Several grassy areas on the primarily residential Lido Isle have views of the water. ⊠ *Pacific Coast Hwy.* ⊕ *www.balboaislandferry.com.*

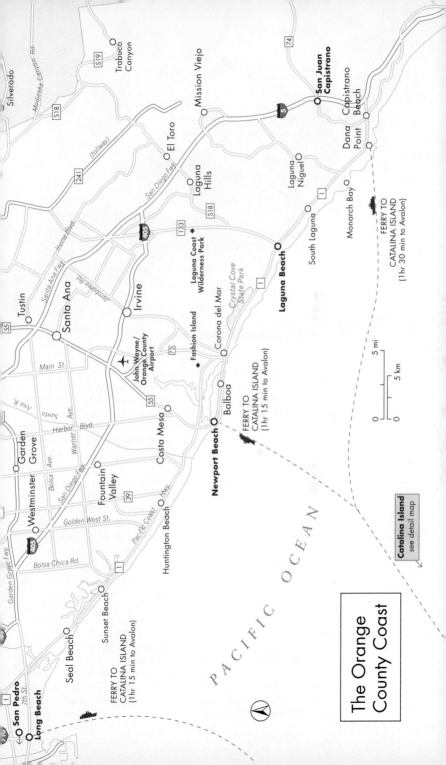

# The Orange County Coast

Catalina Island
see detail map

FERRY TO
CATALINA ISLAND
(1hr 30 min to Avalon)

FERRY TO CATALINA ISLAND
(1hr 15 min to Avalon)

FERRY TO
CATALINA ISLAND
(1hr 15 min to Avalon)

PACIFIC OCEAN

5 mi

5 km

San Juan
Capistrano

Capistrano Beach

Dana Point

Laguna Niguel

Monarch Bay

South Laguna

Laguna Beach

Crystal Cove
State Park

Corona del Mar

Fashion Island

Balboa

Newport Beach

Laguna Coast
Wilderness Park

Laguna Hills

Mission Viejo

El Toro

Irvine

Santa Ana

Tustin

Costa Mesa

Fountain
Valley

Huntington Beach

Sunset Beach

Seal Beach

Long Beach

San Pedro

Garden
Grove

Westminster

Trabuco
Canyon

Silverado

Main St.

Harbor   Blvd.

Warner   Ave.

Bolsa   Ave.

Golden West St.

Bolsa Chica Rd.

Pacific Coast   Hwy.

Garden Grove Fwy.

7th St.

San Diego Fwy.

Santa Ana Fwy.

Irvine Blvd.

Jamboree Rd.

Santa Ana R.

Modjeska Canyon Rd.

John Wayne/
Orange County
Airport

(tollway)

San Diego Fwy.

55

55

39

405

405

241

133

S18

S18

S19

S18

73

74

5

1

1

Riding the waves at Newport Beach

FAMILY **Newport Pier.** Jutting out into the ocean near 20th Street, Newport Pier is a popular fishing spot. Street parking is difficult, so grab the first space you find and be prepared to walk. Early on Wednesday–Sunday mornings you're likely to encounter dory fishermen hawking their predawn catches, as they've done for generations. On weekends the area is alive with kids of all ages on in-line skates, skateboards, and bikes dodging pedestrians and whizzing past fast-food joints and classic dive bars. ⊠ *72 McFadden Pl.*

**Orange County Museum of Art.** This museum features a collection of modernist paintings and sculpture by California artists like Richard Diebenkorn, Ed Ruscha, Robert Irwin, and Chris Burden. There are also cutting-edge international works and changing contemporary art exhibitions. ⊠ *850 San Clemente Dr.* ☎ *949/759–1122* ⊕ *www.ocma. net* ⊠ *$10; free on Fri.* ☽ *Closed Mon. and Tues.*

## WHERE TO EAT

$$$$ ✕ **Basilic.** This intimate French-Swiss bistro adds a touch of old-world
BRASSERIE elegance to the island with its white linen and flower-topped tables. Chef Bernard Althaus grows the herbs used in his classic French dishes. **Known for:** French classics; fine wine; old-school ambience. $ *Average main: $32* ⊠ *217 Marine Ave., Balboa Island* ☎ *949/673–0570* ⊕ *www. basilicrestaurant.com* ☽ *Closed Sun. No lunch Mon.*

$ ✕ **Bear Flag Fish Co.** Expect long lines in summer at this indoor/out-
SEAFOOD door dining spot serving up the freshest local fish (swordfish, sea bass,
FAMILY halibut, and tuna) and a wide range of creative seafood dishes (the Hawaiian-style *poke* salad with ahi tuna is a local favorite). Order at the counter, which doubles as a seafood market, and sit inside the airy

dining room or outside on a grand patio. **Known for:** freshest seafood; fish tacos; craft beers. $ *Average main: $12* ✉ *Newport Peninsula, 3421 Via Lido* ☎ *949/673–3474* ⊕ *www.bearflagfishco.com.*

$$$$
SEAFOOD
✕ **The Cannery.** This 1920s cannery building still teems with fish, but now they go into dishes on the eclectic Pacific Rim menu rather than being packed into crates. Settle in at the sushi bar, in the dining room, or on the patio before choosing between sashimi, seafood platters, or the upscale surf-and-turf with filet mignon and grilled Maine lobsters. **Known for:** waterfront views; seafood specialties; craft cocktails. $ *Average main: $35* ✉ *3010 Lafayette Rd.* ☎ *949/566–0060* ⊕ *www.canderynewport.com.*

$$$
AMERICAN
✕ **3-Thirty-3.** This stylish eatery attracts a convivial crowd—both young and old—for midday, sunset, and late-night dining. A long list of small, shareable plates heightens the camaraderie. **Known for:** happy hour; brunch burritos; generous portions. $ *Average main: $26* ✉ *333 Bayside Dr.* ☎ *949/673–8464* ⊕ *www.3thirty3nb.com.*

## WHERE TO STAY

$$$$
RESORT
FAMILY
🏨 **Balboa Bay Resort.** Sharing the same frontage as the private Balboa Bay Club that long ago hosted Humphrey Bogart, Lauren Bacall, and the Reagans, this waterfront resort has one of the best bay views around. **Pros:** exquisite bay-front views; comfortable beds; a raked beach for guests. **Cons:** not much within walking distance; $25 nightly hospitality fee. $ *Rooms from: $309* ✉ *1221 W. Coast Hwy.* ☎ *949/645–5000* ⊕ *www.balboabayresort.com* ⤴ *159 rooms* ❄ *No meals.*

$$$$
HOTEL
🏨 **The Island Hotel.** Across a palm tree-lined boulevard from stylish Fashion Island, this 20-story tower caters to business types during the week and luxury seekers on weekends. **Pros:** lively lounge scene; first-class spa; great location. **Cons:** steep valet parking prices; some rooms have views of mall parking. $ *Rooms from: $259* ✉ *690 Newport Center Dr.* ☎ *949/759–0808, 877/591–9145* ⊕ *www.islandhotel.com* ⤴ *378 rooms* ❄ *No meals.*

## SPORTS AND THE OUTDOORS
### BOAT RENTALS

FAMILY
**Balboa Boat Rentals.** You can tour Lido and Balboa isles with kayaks ($18 an hour), stand-up paddleboards ($25 an hour), small motorboats ($75 an hour), and electric boats ($80 to $95 an hour) at Balboa Boat Rentals. ✉ *510 E. Edgewater Ave.* ☎ *949/673–7200* ⊕ *www.boats4rent.com.*

### BOAT TOURS

FAMILY
**Catalina Flyer.** At Balboa Pavilion, the Catalina Flyer operates a 90-minute daily round-trip passage to Catalina Island for $70. Reservations are required; check the schedule in January and February, as crossings may be canceled due to annual maintenance. ✉ *400 Main St.* ☎ *949/673–5245* ⊕ *www.catalinainfo.com.*

**Hornblower Cruises & Events.** This operator books three-hour weekend dinner cruises with dancing for $87. The two-hour Sunday brunch cruise starts at $68. Cruises traverse the mostly placid and scenic waters of Newport Harbor. ✉ *2431 W. Coast Hwy.* ☎ *888/467–6256* ⊕ *www.hornblower.com.*

A whimbrel hunts for mussels at Crystal Cove State Park.

### FISHING

FAMILY **Davey's Locker.** In addition to a complete tackle shop, Davey's Locker offers half-day sportfishing trips starting at $41.50. Whale-watching excursions begin at $26 for weekdays. ✉ *Balboa Pavilion, 400 Main St.* ☎ *949/673–1434* ⊕ *www.daveyslocker.com.*

### SHOPPING

Fodor'sChoice **Fashion Island.** Shake the sand out of your shoes to head inland to the
★ ritzy Fashion Island outdoor mall, a cluster of arcades and courtyards complete with koi pond, fountains, and a family-friendly trolley—plus some awesome ocean views. It has the luxe department stores Neiman Marcus and Bloomingdale's, plus expensive spots like Jonathan Adler, Kate Spade, and Michael Stars. ✉ *401 Newport Center Dr., between Jamboree and MacArthur Blvds., off PCH* ☎ *949/721–2000, 855/658–8527* ⊕ *www.shopfashionisland.com.*

## LAGUNA BEACH

*10 miles south of Newport Beach on PCH, 60 miles south of Los Angeles, I–5 south to Hwy. 133, which turns into Laguna Canyon Rd.*

Fodor'sChoice Driving in along Laguna Canyon Road from the I–405 freeway gives
★ you the chance to cruise through a gorgeous coastal canyon, large stretches of which remain undeveloped, before arriving at a glistening wedge of ocean.

Laguna's welcome mat is legendary. On the corner of Forest and Park avenues is a gate proclaiming, "This gate hangs well and hinders none, refresh and rest, then travel on." A gay community has long been established here; art galleries dot the village streets, and there's usually someone daubing up in Heisler Park. Along the Pacific Coast Highway you'll find dozens of clothing boutiques, jewelry stores, and cafés.

### ESSENTIALS

**Visitor and Tour Information Visit Laguna Beach Visitors Center.** ✉ *381 Forest Ave.* ☎ *949/497–9229, 800/877–1115* 🌐 *www.visitlagunabeach.com.*

## EXPLORING

**Laguna Art Museum.** This museum displays American art, with an emphasis on California artists from all periods. Special exhibits change quarterly. ✉ *307 Cliff Dr.* ☎ *949/494–8971* 🌐 *www.lagunaartmuseum.org* 🎫 *$7* 🕒 *Closed Wed.*

FAMILY **Laguna Coast Wilderness Park.** The Laguna Coast Wilderness Park is spread over 7,000 acres of fragile coastal territory, including the canyon. The 40 miles of trails are great for hiking and mountain biking, and are open daily, weather permitting. Docent-led hikes are given most weekends. No dogs are allowed in the park. ✉ *18751 Laguna Canyon Rd.* ☎ *949/923–2235* 🌐 *www.ocparks.com/parks/lagunac* 🎫 *$3 parking.*

FAMILY Fodor's Choice ★ **Main Beach Park.** A stocky 1920s lifeguard tower marks Main Beach Park, where a wooden boardwalk separates the sand from a strip of lawn. Walk along this soft-sand beach, or grab a bench and watch people bodysurfing, playing volleyball, or scrambling around two half-basketball courts. The beach also has children's play equipment. Most of Laguna's hotels are within a short (but hilly) walk. **Amenities:** lifeguards; showers; toilets. **Best for:** sunset; swimming; walking. ✉ *Broadway at S. Coast Hwy.* 🌐 *www.visitlagunabeach.com.*

FAMILY **1,000 Steps Beach.** Off South Coast Highway at 9th Street, 1,000 Steps Beach is a hard-to-find spot tucked away in a neighborhood with great waves and hard-packed, white sand. There aren't really 1,000 steps down (but when you hike back up, it'll certainly feel like it). Sea caves and tide pools enhance this already beautiful natural spot. **Amenities:** parking. **Best for:** sunset; surfing; swimming. ✉ *S. Coast Hwy., at 9th St.*

FAMILY **Wood's Cove.** Off South Coast Highway, Wood's Cove is especially quiet during the week. Big rock formations hide lurking crabs. This is a prime scuba-diving spot, and at high tide much of the beach is underwater. Climbing the steps to leave, you can see a Tudor-style mansion that was once home to Bette Davis. Street parking is limited. **Amenities:** none. **Best for:** snorkeling; scuba diving; sunset. ✉ *Diamond St. and Ocean Way* 🌐 *www.visitlagunabeach.com.*

## WHERE TO EAT

$$$ INTERNATIONAL 🍴 **Sapphire Laguna.** This Laguna Beach establishment set in a historic Craftsman is part gourmet pantry (a must-stop for your every picnic need) and part global dining adventure. Iranian-born chef Azmin Ghahreman takes you on a journey through Europe and Asia with dishes ranging from a summer vegetable gazpacho to banana-curried black cod. **Known for:** cheese selection; weekend brunch; pet-friendly patio. [$] *Average main: $27* ✉ *The Old Pottery Place, 1200 S. Coast Hwy.* ☎ *949/715–9888* 🌐 *www.sapphirelaguna.com.*

**$$$$** ✕ **Studio.** In a nod to Laguna's art history, Studio has house-made
MODERN specialties that entice the eye as well as the palate. The restaurant
AMERICAN occupies its own Craftsman-style bungalow, atop a 50-foot bluff over-
Fodor's Choice looking the Pacific. **Known for:** attentive service; chef's tasting menu;
★ great for special occasions. $ *Average main: $55* ⊠ *Montage Laguna
Beach, 30801 S. Coast Hwy.* ☎ *949/715–6420* ⊕ *www.studiolaguna-
beach.com* ⊗ *Closed Mon. No lunch.*

**$** ✕ **Zinc Café & Market.** Families flock to this small Laguna Beach institu-
VEGETARIAN tion for reasonably priced breakfast and lunch options. Try the signa-
FAMILY ture quiches or poached egg dishes in the morning, or swing by later in
the day for healthy salads, house-made soups, quesadillas, or pizzettes.
**Known for:** gourmet goodies; avocado toast; busy outdoor patio. $ *Av-
erage main: $15* ⊠ *350 Ocean Ave.* ☎ *949/494–6302* ⊕ *www.zinccafe.
com* ⊗ *No dinner Nov.–Apr.*

## WHERE TO STAY

**$$$** 🏨 **La Casa del Camino.** The look is Old California at the 1929-built La
HOTEL Casa del Camino, with dark woods, arched doors, and wrought iron
in the lobby. **Pros:** breathtaking views from rooftop lounge; personable
service; close to beach. **Cons:** some rooms face the highway; frequent
events can make hotel noisy; some rooms are very small. $ *Rooms
from: $229* ⊠ *1289 S. Coast Hwy.* ☎ *949/497–2446, 855/634–5736*
⊕ *www.lacasadelcamino.com* ⤳ *36 rooms* ⊙| *No meals.*

**$$$$** 🏨 **Montage Laguna Beach.** Laguna's connection to the Californian
RESORT plein-air artists is mined for inspiration at this head-turning, lavish
FAMILY hotel. **Pros:** top-notch, enthusiastic service; idyllic coastal location;
Fodor's Choice numerous sporty pursuits available offshore. **Cons:** multi-night stays
★ required on weekends and holidays; $40 valet parking; $38 daily
resort fee. $ *Rooms from: $695* ⊠ *30801 S. Coast Hwy.* ☎ *949/715–
6000, 866/271–6953* ⊕ *www.montagehotels.com/lagunabeach* ⤳ *248
rooms* ⊙| *No meals.*

**$$$$** 🏨 **Surf & Sand Resort.** One mile south of downtown, on an exquisite
RESORT stretch of beach with thundering waves and gorgeous rocks, this is
a getaway for those who want a boutique hotel experience with-
out all the formalities. **Pros:** easy beach access; intimate property;
slightly removed from Main Street crowds. **Cons:** pricey valet park-
ing; surf can be quite loud. $ *Rooms from: $575* ⊠ *1555 S. Coast
Hwy.* ☎ *949/497–4477, 877/741–5908* ⊕ *www.surfandsandresort.
com* ⤳ *167 rooms* ⊙| *No meals.*

## SHOPPING

Coast Highway, Forest and Ocean avenues, and Glenneyre Street are
full of art galleries, fine jewelry stores, and clothing boutiques.

FAMILY **Candy Baron.** Get your sugar fix at the time-warped Candy Baron,
filled with old-fashioned goodies like gumdrops, bull's-eyes, and more
than 50 flavors of saltwater taffy. ⊠ *231 Forest Ave.* ☎ *949/497–7508*
⊕ *www.thecandybaron.com.*

Looking for shells on Laguna Beach, one of the nicest stretches of sand in Southern California

## SAN JUAN CAPISTRANO

*5 miles north of Dana Point, Hwy. 74, 60 miles north of San Diego, I–5.*

San Juan Capistrano is best known for its historic mission, where the swallows traditionally return each year, migrating from their winter haven in Argentina, but these days they are more likely to choose other local sites for nesting. St. Joseph's Day, March 19, launches a week of fowl festivities. Charming antiques stores, which range from pricey to cheap, line Camino Capistrano.

### GETTING HERE AND AROUND

If you arrive by train, which is far more romantic and restful than battling freeway traffic, you'll be dropped off across from the mission at the San Juan Capistrano depot. With its appealing brick café and preserved Santa Fe cars, the depot retains much of the magic of early American railroads. If driving, park near Ortega and Camino Capistrano, the city's main streets.

### EXPLORING

FAMILY **Mission San Juan Capistrano.** Founded in 1776 by Father Junípero Serra,
Fodor'sChoice Mission San Juan Capistrano was one of two Roman Catholic out-
★ posts between Los Angeles and San Diego. The Great Stone Church, begun in 1797, is the largest structure created by the Spanish in California. Many of the mission's adobe buildings have been preserved to illustrate mission life, with exhibits of an olive millstone, tallow ovens, tanning vats, metalworking furnaces, and the padres' living quarters. The gardens, with their fountains, are a lovely spot in which to wander. The bougainvillea-covered Serra Chapel is believed to be

Mission San Juan Capistrano

the oldest church still standing in California, and is the only building remaining in which Fr. Serra actually led Mass. Mass takes place weekdays at 7 am in the chapel. Enter via a small gift shop in the gatehouse. ✉ *Camino Capistrano and Ortega Hwy.* ☎ *949/234–1300* 🌐 *www.missionsjc.com* 🎟 *$9.*

## WHERE TO EAT

$$ AMERICAN

🍴 **The Ramos House Cafe.** It may be worth hopping the Amtrak to San Juan Capistrano just for the chance to have breakfast or lunch at one of Orange County's most beloved restaurants located in an historic board-and-batten home dating back to 1881. This café sits practically on the railroad tracks across from the depot—nab a table on the patio and dig into a hearty breakfast, such as the smoked bacon scramble. **Known for:** Southern specialties; weekend brunch; historic setting. [$] *Average main: $20* ✉ *31752 Los Rios St.* ☎ *949/443–1342* 🌐 *www.ramoshouse.com* 🕒 *Closed Mon. No dinner.*

## NIGHTLIFE

**Swallow's Inn.** Across the way from Mission San Juan Capistrano you'll spot a line of Harleys in front of the Swallow's Inn. Despite a somewhat tough look, it attracts all kinds—bikers, surfers, modern-day cowboys, grandparents—for a drink, a casual bite, karaoke nights, and some rowdy live country music. ✉ *31786 Camino Capistrano* ☎ *949/493–3188* 🌐 *www.swallowsinn.com.*

# CATALINA ISLAND

Fodor'sChoice ★ Just 22 miles out from the L.A. coastline, across from Newport Beach and Long Beach, Catalina has virtually unspoiled mountains, canyons, coves, and beaches; best of all, it gives you a glimpse of what undeveloped Southern California once looked like.

Water sports are a big draw, as divers and snorkelers come for the exceptionally clear water surrounding the island. Kayakers are attracted to the calm cove waters and thrill seekers have made the eco-themed zip line so popular, there are nighttime tours via flashlight in summer. The main town, Avalon, is a charming, old-fashioned beach community, where yachts and pleasure boats bob in the crescent bay. Wander beyond the main drag and find brightly painted little bungalows fronting the sidewalks; golf carts are the preferred mode of transport.

In 1919, William Wrigley Jr., the chewing-gum magnate, purchased a controlling interest in the company developing Catalina Island, whose most famous landmark, the Casino, was built in 1929 under his orders. Because he owned the Chicago Cubs baseball team, Wrigley made Catalina the team's spring training site, an arrangement that lasted until 1951.

In 1975, the Catalina Island Conservancy, a nonprofit foundation, acquired about 88% of the island to help preserve the area's natural flora and fauna, including the bald eagle and the Catalina Island fox. These days the conservancy is restoring the rugged interior country with plantings of native grasses and trees. Along the coast you might spot oddities like electric perch, saltwater goldfish, and flying fish.

## GETTING HERE AND AROUND

### FERRY TRAVEL

Two companies offer ferry service to Catalina Island. The boats have both indoor and outdoor seating and snack bars. Excessive baggage is not allowed, and there are extra fees for bicycles and surfboards. The waters around Santa Catalina can get rough, so if you're prone to seasickness, come prepared. Winter, holiday, and weekend schedules vary, so reservations are recommended.

Catalina Express makes an hour-long run from Long Beach or San Pedro to Avalon and a 90-minute run from Dana Point to Avalon with some stops at Two Harbors. Round-trip fares begin at $73.50, with discounts for seniors and kids. On busy days, a $15 upgrade to the Commodore Lounge, when available, is worth it. Service from Newport Beach to Avalon is available through the Catalina Flyer. Boats leave from Balboa Pavilion at 9 am (in season), take 75 minutes to reach the island, and cost $70 round-trip. Return boats leave Catalina at 4:30 pm. Reservations are required for the Catalina Flyer and recommended for all weekend and summer trips. ■ TIP➜ Keep an eye out for dolphins, which sometimes swim alongside the ferries.

Ferry Contacts **Catalina Express.** ☎ *800/481–3470, 562/485–3300* ⊕ *www. catalinaexpress.com.* **Catalina Flyer.** ☎ *949/673–5245* ⊕ *www.catalinainfo.com.*

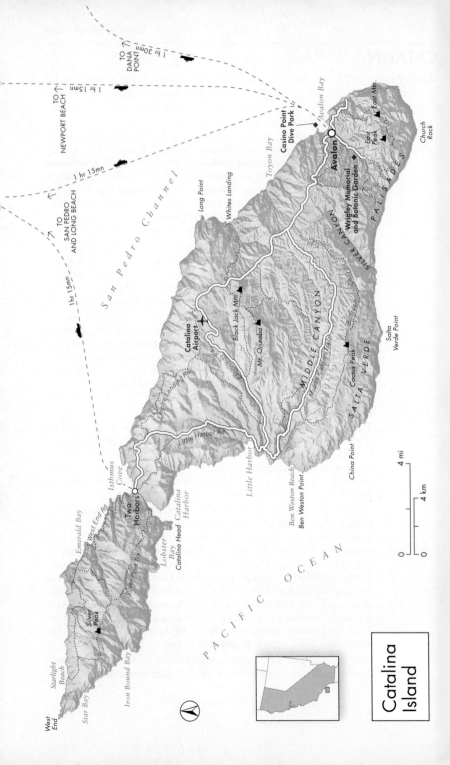

TO
DANA
POINT

1 hr 30mn

TO
NEWPORT BEACH

1 hr 15mn

1 hr 15mn

TO
SAN PEDRO
AND LONG BEACH

1 hr 15mn

San Pedro Channel

Avalon Bay

Casino Point
Dive Park

Avalon

East Mtn.

Church
Rock

East
Peak

PALISADES

Wrigley Memorial
and Botanic Garden

Toyon Bay

Long Point

Whites Landing

SILVER CANYON

Salta
Verde Point

Black Jack Mtn.

MIDDLE CANYON

Catalina
Airport

Bullrush Canyon Trail

Mt. Orizaba

SALTA VERDE

Empire Landing Rd.

Soapstone Rd.

Cactus Peak

Middle Canyon Trail

Little Harbor Rd.

China Point

Little Harbor

Ben Weston Beach
Ben Weston Point

4 mi

Isthmus Cove

4 km

Two Harbors

Emerald Bay

West End Rd.

Lobster
Bay

Catalina Harbor

Catalina Head

Silver Peak Trail

Starlight Beach

West
End

Silver
Peak

Star Bay

Iron Bound Bay

PACIFIC OCEAN

PACIFIC OCEAN

Catalina
Island

**12**

## GOLF CARTS

Golf carts constitute the island's main form of transportation for sightseeing in the area; however, some parts of town are off-limits, as is the island's interior. You can rent them along Avalon's Crescent Avenue and Pebbly Beach Road for about $40 per hour with a $40 deposit, payable via cash or traveler's check only.

**Golf Cart Rentals Island Rentals.**
✉ *125 Pebbly Beach Rd., Avalon*
☎ *310/510–1456* ⊕ *www.catalinagolfcartrentals.com.*

## HELICOPTER TRAVEL

Island Express helicopters depart from San Pedro (Friday, Saturday, and Sunday only), Santa Ana, Burbank, and Long Beach next to the *Queen Mary* (8 am–dusk). The trip from Long Beach takes about 15 minutes and costs $125 one-way, $250 round-trip. Reservations a week in advance are recommended; some flights require a minimum passenger load.

**Helicopter Contacts Island Express.** ☎ *800/228–2566* ⊕ *www.islandexpress.com.*

### WHERE THE BUFFALO ROAM

Zane Grey, the writer who put the Western novel on the map, spent a lot of time on Catalina, and his influence is still evident in a peculiar way. When the movie version of Grey's book *The Vanishing American* was filmed here in 1924, American bison were ferried across from the mainland to give the land that Western plains look. After the moviemakers packed up and left, the buffalo stayed, and a small herd of about 150 of these majestic creatures still remains, grazing the interior and reinforcing the island's image as the last refuge from SoCal's urban sprawl.

## TIMING

Although Catalina can be seen in one very hectic day, several inviting hotels make it worth extending your stay for one or more nights. A short itinerary might include breakfast on the pier, a tour of the interior, a snorkeling excursion at Casino Point, or beach day at the Descanso Beach Club and a romantic waterfront dinner in Avalon.

After late October, rooms are much easier to find on short notice, rates drop dramatically, and many hotels offer packages that include transportation from the mainland and/or sightseeing tours. January to March you have a good chance of spotting migrating gray whales on the ferry crossing.

## TOURS

Santa Catalina Island Company runs nine land tours and six ocean tours, including the *Flying Fish* boat trip (summer evenings only); a comprehensive inland motor tour; a tour of Skyline Drive; several Casino tours; a scenic tour of Avalon; a glass-bottom-boat tour; an undersea tour on a semisubmersible vessel; an eco-themed zip-line tour that traverses a scenic canyon; a speedy Ocean Runner expedition that searches for all manner of sea creatures. Reservations are highly recommended for the inland tours. Tours cost $13 to $129. There are ticket booths on the Green Pleasure Pier, at the Casino, in the plaza, and at the boat landing. Catalina Adventure Tours, which has booths at the boat landing and on the pier, also arranges excursions at comparable prices.

The Catalina Island Conservancy organizes custom ecotours and hikes of the interior. Naturalist guides drive open Jeeps through some gorgeously untrammeled parts of the island. Tours start at $70 per person for a two-hour trip (two-person minimum); you can also book half- and full-day tours. The tours run year-round.

### ESSENTIALS

**Visitor and Tour Information Catalina Adventure Tours.** ☎ 877/510–2888 ⊕ *www.catalinaadventuretours.com.* **Catalina Island Chamber of Commerce & Visitors Bureau.** ✉ *1 Green Pleasure Pier, Avalon* ☎ *310/510–1520* ⊕ *www. catalinachamber.com.* **Catalina Island Conservancy.** ✉ *125 Claressa Ave., Avalon* ☎ *310/510–2595* ⊕ *www.catalinaconservancy.org.* **Santa Catalina Island Company.** ☎ *877/778–8322* ⊕ *www.visitcatalinaisland.com.*

## AVALON

*A 1- to 2-hour ferry ride from Long Beach, Newport Beach, or San Pedro; a 15-minute helicopter ride from Long Beach or San Pedro, slightly longer from Santa Ana.*

Avalon, Catalina's only real town, extends from the shore of its natural harbor to the surrounding hillsides. Its resident population is about 3,800, but it swells with tourists on summer weekends. Most of the city's activity, however, is centered on the pedestrian mall on Crescent Avenue, and most sights are easily reached on foot. Private cars are restricted and rental cars aren't allowed, but taxis, trams, and shuttles can take you anywhere you need to go. Bicycles, electric bikes, and golf carts can be rented from shops along Crescent Avenue.

### EXPLORING

Fodor'sChoice  **Casino.** This circular white structure is one of the finest examples of
★    art deco architecture anywhere. Its Spanish-inspired floors and murals gleam with brilliant blue and green Catalina tiles. In this case, *casino,* the Italian word for "gathering place," has nothing to do with gambling. First-run movies are screened nightly at the Avalon Theatre, noteworthy for its classic 1929 theater pipe organ and art deco wall murals.

The Santa Catalina Island Company leads two tours of the Casino—the 30-minute basic tour ($13) and the 90-minute behind-the-scenes tour ($27), which leads visitors through the green room and into the Wrigleys' private lounge. ✉ *1 Casino Way* ☎ *310/510–0179 theater* ⊕ *www. visitcatalinaisland.com.*

**Casino Point Dive Park.** In front of the Casino are the crystal-clear waters of the Casino Point Dive Park, a protected marine preserve where moray eels, bat rays, spiny lobsters, harbor seals, and other sea creatures cruise around kelp forests and along the sandy bottom. It's a terrific site for scuba diving, with some shallow areas suitable for snorkeling. Equipment can be rented on and near the pier. The shallow waters of Lover's Cove, east of the boat landing, are also good for snorkeling. ✉ *Avalon.*

FAMILY  **Catalina Island Museum.** The exterior of the Catalina Island Museum is a nod to Catalina Island's developer William Wrigley Jr.—it's modeled after Wrigley Field in Chicago. Inside, the museum traces the island's history from it's pre-contact days and native Chumash to its role in Hollywood history and beyond. Two galleries host travelling exhibitions. The view from the outside terrace takes in lovely Avalon and its picturesque harbor. A small gift shop offers reproductions of the island's signature colorful Catalina pottery tiles. ⊠ *217 Metropole Ave.* ☎ *310/510–2414* ⊕ *www.catalinamuseum.org* ⊠ *$12.*

FAMILY **Green Pleasure Pier.** Head to the Green Pleasure Pier for a good vantage point of Avalon. On the pier you can find the visitor information, snack stands, and scads of squawking seagulls. It's also the landing where visiting cruise-ship passengers catch tenders back out to their ship. ⊠ *End of Catalina Ave.*

**Wrigley Memorial and Botanic Garden.** Two miles south of the bay is Wrigley Memorial and Botanic Garden, home to plants native to Southern California. Several grow only on Catalina Island—Catalina ironwood, wild tomato, and rare Catalina mahogany. The Wrigley family commissioned the garden as well as the monument, which has a grand staircase and a Spanish-style mausoleum inlaid with colorful Catalina tile. Wrigley Jr. was once buried here but his remains were moved to Pasadena during the Second World War. ⊠ *Avalon Canyon Rd.* ☎ *310/510–2897* ⊕ *www.catalinaconservancy.org* ⊠ *$7.*

## WHERE TO EAT

$$$ ✕ **Bluewater Grill.** Overlooking the ferry landing and the entire harbor,
SEAFOOD the open-to-the-salt-air Bluewater Grill offers freshly caught fish, savory
FAMILY chowders, and all manner of shellfish. If they're on the menu, don't miss the swordfish steak or the sand dabs. **Known for:** fresh local fish; happy hour; harbor views. Ⓢ *Average main: $25* ⊠ *306 Crescent Ave.* ☎ *310/510–3474* ⊕ *www.bluewatergrill.com.*

$ ✕ **Descanso Beach Club.** Set on an expansive deck overlooking the water,
AMERICAN Descanso Beach Club serves a wide range of favorites: peel-and-eat
FAMILY shrimp, hamburgers, salads, nachos, and wraps are all part of the selection. Watch the harbor seals frolic just offshore while sipping the island's super-sweet signature cocktail, the Buffalo Milk, a mix of fruit liqueurs, vodka, and whipped cream. **Known for:** tropical beach vibe; scenic views; chic cabana rentals. Ⓢ *Average main: $15* ⊠ *Descanso Beach, 1 Descanso Ave.* ☎ *310/510–7410.*

$$$ ✕ **The Lobster Trap.** Seafood rules at the Lobster Trap—the restaurant's
SEAFOOD owner has his own boat and fishes for the catch of the day and, in season, spiny lobster. Ceviche is a great starter, always fresh and brightly flavored. **Known for:** locally caught seafood; convivial atmosphere; locals' hangout. Ⓢ *Average main: $24* ⊠ *128 Catalina St.* ☎ *310/510–8585* ⊕ *catalinalobstertrap.com.*

## WHERE TO STAY

$$$ 🛏 **Aurora Hotel & Spa.** In a town dominated by historic properties, the
HOTEL Aurora is refreshingly contemporary, with a hip attitude and sleek furnishings. **Pros:** trendy design; quiet location off main drag; close to restaurants. **Cons:** standard rooms are small, even by Catalina standards; no elevator. Ⓢ *Rooms from: $249* ⊠ *137 Marilla Ave.* ☎ *310/510–0454* ⊕ *www.auroracatalina.com* ⮐ *18 rooms* ⊠ *Breakfast.*

$$$ HOTEL FAMILY **Hotel Villa Portofino.** Steps from the Green Pleasure Pier, this European-style hotel creates an intimate feel with brick courtyards and walkways and suites named after Italian cities. **Pros:** romantic; close to beach; incredible sundeck. **Cons:** ground-floor rooms can be noisy; some rooms are on small side; no elevator. [$] *Rooms from: $179* ✉ *111 Crescent Ave.* ☎ *310/510–0555, 888/510–0555* 🌐 *www.hotelvillaportofino.com* 🛏 *35 rooms* 🍴 *Breakfast.*

$$$$ HOTEL FAMILY **Hotel Vista del Mar.** On the bay-facing Crescent Avenue, this third-floor property is steps from the beach, where complimentary towels, chairs, and umbrellas await guests. **Pros:** comfortable beds; central location; modern decor. **Cons:** no restaurant or spa facilities; few rooms with ocean views; no elevator. [$] *Rooms from: $295* ✉ *417 Crescent Ave.* ☎ *310/510–1452, 800/601–3836* 🌐 *www.hotel-vistadelmar.com* 🛏 *14 rooms* 🍴 *Breakfast.*

$$$$ B&B/INN **Mt. Ada.** If you stay in the mansion where Wrigley Jr. once lived, you can enjoy all the comforts of a millionaire's home—at a millionaire's prices. **Pros:** timeless charm; shuttle from heliport and dock; incredible views. **Cons:** smallish rooms and bathrooms; expensive. [$] *Rooms from: $480* ✉ *398 Wrigley Rd.* ☎ *310/510–2030, 877/778–8322* 🌐 *www.visitcatalinaisland.com* 🕒 *Closed mid-Jan.–early Feb.* 🛏 *6 rooms* 🍴 *Some meals.*

$$$$ HOTEL FAMILY **Pavilion Hotel.** This mid-century-modern-style hotel is Avalon's most citified spot, though just a few steps from the sand. **Pros:** centrally located, steps from the beach and harbor; friendly staff; plush bedding. **Cons:** no pool. [$] *Rooms from: $265* ✉ *513 Crescent Ave.* ☎ *310/510–1788, 877/778–8322* 🌐 *www.visitcatalinaisland.com* 🛏 *71 rooms* 🍴 *Breakfast.*

## SPORTS AND THE OUTDOORS

### BICYCLING

FAMILY **Brown's Bikes.** Look for rentals on Crescent Avenue and Pebbly Beach Road, where Brown's Bikes is located. Beach cruisers and mountain bikes start at at $20 per day. Electric bikes are also on offer. ✉ *107 Pebbly Beach Rd.* ☎ *310/510–0986* 🌐 *www.catalinabiking.com.*

### DIVING AND SNORKELING

The Casino Point Underwater Park, with its handful of wrecks, is best suited for diving. Lover's Cove is better for snorkeling (but you'll share the area with glass-bottom boats). Both are protected marine preserves.

**Catalina Divers Supply.** Head to Catalina Divers Supply to rent equipment, sign up for guided scuba and snorkel tours, and attend certification classes. It also has an outpost at the Dive Park at Casino Point. ✉ *7 Green Pleasure Pier* ☎ *310/510–0330* 🌐 *www.catalinadiverssupply.com.*

# TRAVEL SMART
# LOS ANGELES

# GETTING HERE AND AROUND

The Los Angeles metro area has more than 13 million residents, so be prepared to rent a car and fight for space on the freeway (especially at rush hour) to make your way along the array of destinations that span from the carefree beaches of the coastline to the glitz and glamour of Beverly Hills shops, the nightlife of Hollywood, and the film studio action of the Valley. It's worth it. Nowhere else in the country can you spot celebrities over breakfast, or sunbathe on the beach and head to the slopes for skiing on the same day.

## ▌ AIR TRAVEL

Nonstop flights from New York to Los Angeles take about six hours; with the three-hour time change, you can leave JFK by 8 am and be in L.A. by 11 am. Some flights may require a midway stop, making the total excursion between 7½ and 8½ hours. Flight times are 3 hours from Dallas, 4 hours from Chicago, and 11½ hours from London.

### AIRPORTS

The seventh-largest airport in the world in terms of passenger traffic, Los Angeles International Airport (LAX) is served by more than 65 major airlines. Because of heavy traffic around the airport (not to mention the city's extended rush hours), you should allow yourself plenty of extra time. All departures are from the upper level, while arrivals are on the lower level.

Several secondary airports serve the city. Hollywood Burbank Airport in Burbank is close to Downtown L.A., so it's definitely worth checking out. Long Beach Airport is equally convenient. Flights to Orange County's John Wayne Airport are often more expensive than those to the other secondary airports. Also check out Long Beach Airport and L.A./Ontario International Airport.

Driving times from LAX to different parts of the city vary considerably: it will take you 20 minutes to get to Santa Monica, 30 minutes to Beverly Hills, and at least 45 minutes to get to Downtown L.A. In heavy traffic it can take much longer. From Hollywood Burbank Airport, it's 30 minutes to Downtown. Plan on at least 45 minutes for the drive to Long Beach Airport, and an hour from John Wayne Airport or L.A./Ontario International Airport.

**Airport Information Hollywood Burbank Airport** (*BUR*). ⊠ *2627 N. Hollywood Way, near I–5 and U.S. 101, Burbank* ☎ *818/840–8840* ⊕ *www.bobhopeairport.com.* **John Wayne Airport** (*SNA*). ⊠ *18601 Airport Way, Santa Ana* ☎ *949/252–5200* ⊕ *www.ocair.com.* **Long Beach Airport** (*LGB*). ⊠ *4100 Donald Douglas Dr., Long Beach* ☎ *562/570–2600* ⊕ *www.lgb. org.* **Los Angeles International Airport** (*LAX*). ⊠ *1 World Way, off Hwy. 1* ☎ *855/463–5252* ⊕ *www.lawa.org.* **L.A./Ontario International Airport** (*ONT*). ⊠ *E. Airport Dr., off I–10, Ontario* ☎ *909/937–2700* ⊕ *www.flyontario.com.*

### GROUND TRANSPORTATION

If you're not renting a car, a taxi is the most convenient way to get to and from the airport. The rates between Downtown and LAX start at $50.50, but can increase significantly if there's a backup on the freeway. Getting Downtown from Hollywood Burbank Airport costs $40 to $50. Taxis to and from L.A./Ontario International Airport run on a meter and cost $60 and $70, depending on traffic. From Long Beach Airport, trips to Downtown L.A. are metered and cost roughly $72.

For two or three passengers, shuttles can be an economical option at $17 to $35. These big vans typically circle the airport, departing when they're full. Your travel time depends on how many other travelers are dropped off before you. At LAX, SuperShuttle allows walk-on shuttle passengers without prior reservations; if you're headed to the airport, call at least 24 hours in advance.

Operated by Los Angeles World Airports, FlyAway buses travel between LAX and Van Nuys, Westwood, La Brea, and Union Station in Downtown L.A. The cost is $8 to $10, and is payable only by credit or debit card. With departure at least every hour, buses run 24 hours a day.

Most Angelenos use ride-share apps like Lyft, which you can download to your smartphone. The app will estimate the cost before you accept the ride. A ride from the airport (drivers are permitted to pick you up at the departure terminals) to the Eastside could cost as much as $40-plus, or less if you pick up another passenger along the way.

**Airport Transportation FlyAway.**
☎ 866/435-9529 ⊕ www.lawa.org/flyaway.
**SuperShuttle.** ☎ 323/775-6600, 800/258-3826 ⊕ www.supershuttle.com.

### FLIGHTS

Delta, United, Southwest, and American have the most nonstop flights to Los Angeles International Airport. Jet-Blue and Southwest also have numerous daily flights to airports in and around Los Angeles.

## ■ BUS TRAVEL

Inadequate public transportation has plagued L.A. for decades. That said, many local trips can be made, with time and patience, by buses run by the Los Angeles County Metropolitan Transit Authority. In certain cases—visiting the Getty Center, for instance, or Universal Studios—buses may be your best option. There's a special Dodger Stadium Express that shuttles passengers between Union Station and the world-famous ballpark for home games. It's free if you have a ticket in hand, and saves you parking-related stress.

Metro Buses cost $1.75, plus 50¢ for each transfer to another bus or to the subway. A one-day pass costs $7, and a weekly pass is $25 for unlimited travel on all buses and trains. Passes are valid

from Sunday through Saturday. For the fastest service, look for the red-and-white Metro Rapid buses; these stop less frequently and are able to extend green lights. There are 25 Metro Rapid routes, including along Wilshire and Vermont boulevards.

Other bus services make it possible to explore the entire metropolitan area. DASH minibuses cover six different circular routes in Hollywood, Mid-Wilshire, and Downtown. You pay 50¢ every time you get on. The Santa Monica Municipal Bus Line, also known as the Big Blue Bus, is a pleasant and inexpensive way to move around the Westside. Trips cost $1.25. An express bus to and from Downtown L.A., run by Culver CityBus, costs $2.50. Transfers to Metro or Metro Rail are 50¢.

You can pay your fare in cash on MTA, Santa Monica, and Culver City buses, but you must have exact change. You can buy MTA TAP cards at Metro Rail stations, customer centers throughout the city, and at some convenience and grocery stores.

**Bus Information Culver CityBus.**
☎ 310/253-6510 ⊕ www.culvercity.org. **DASH.**
☎ 310/808-2273 ⊕ www.ladottransit.com.
**Los Angeles County Metropolitan Transit Authority.** ☎ 323/466-3876 ⊕ www.metro.
net. **Santa Monica Municipal Bus Line.**
☎ 310/451-5444 ⊕ www.bigbluebus.com.

## ■ CAR TRAVEL

If you're used to urban driving, you shouldn't have too much trouble navigating the streets of Los Angeles. If not, L.A. can be unnerving. However, the city has evolved with drivers in mind. Streets are wide and parking garages abound, so it's more car-friendly than many older big cities.

If you get discombobulated while on the freeway, remember this rule of thumb: even-numbered freeways run east and west, odd-numbered freeways run north and south.

## GASOLINE

As of this writing, gasoline costs around $2.50 a gallon. Most stations are self-service; the few remaining full-service stations are mostly in and around the Westside. There are plenty of stations everywhere. Most stay open late, and many are open 24 hours.

## GETTING AROUND

There are plenty of identical or similarly named streets in L.A. (Beverly Boulevard and Beverly Drive, for example), so be as specific as you can when asking directions or inputting into a map app. Expect sudden changes in addresses as streets pass through neighborhoods, then incorporated cities, then back into neighborhoods. This can be most bewildering on Robertson Boulevard, an otherwise useful north–south artery that, by crossing through L.A., West Hollywood, and Beverly Hills, dips in and out of several such numbering shifts in a matter of miles.

## PARKING

Parking rules are strictly enforced in Los Angeles, so make sure you check for signs and read them carefully. Illegally parked cars are ticketed or towed quickly. Parking prices vary from 25¢ (in public lots and at meters) to $2 per half hour (in private lots). Downtown and Century City rates may be as high as $25 an hour, though prices tend to drop on weekends.

Parking in Downtown L.A. can be tough, especially on weekdays. Try the garage at the FIG at 7th retail complex (⊠ 725 S. Figueroa St. which is spacious, reasonably priced, and visitor-friendly. It's $13 before 9 am and $8 after 4 pm and on weekends.

In Hollywood, the underground facility at the Hollywood & Highland shopping complex (⊠ 6801 Hollywood Blvd.) charges $2 for the first two hours. In Beverly Hills, the first two hours are free at several lots on or around Rodeo Drive. The Westside Pavilion (⊠ 10800 Pico Blvd.) offers three hours of free parking at its garage.

At some shops, most restaurants, and hotels in Los Angeles, valet parking is virtually assumed. The cost is usually $6 to $16. Keep small bills on hand to tip the valets.

## ROAD CONDITIONS

Beware of weekday rush-hour traffic, which is heaviest from 7 am to 10 am, and 3 pm to 7 pm. Go511.com and the Waze app offer real-time traffic information, and the California Highway Patrol has a road-conditions hotline. To encourage carpooling, some crowded freeways reserve an express lane for cars carrying more than one passenger.

Parallel streets can often provide viable alternatives to jam-packed freeways, notably Sepulveda Boulevard for I–405; Venice and Washington boulevards for I–10 from Mid-Wilshire west to the beach; and Ventura Boulevard, Moorpark Street, or Riverside Drive for U.S. 101 through the San Fernando Valley.

**Information Caltrans Current Highway Conditions.** ☎ 800/427–7623 for road conditions ⊕ www.dot.ca.gov. **Go511.** ☎ 511 ⊕ www.go511.com.

## ROADSIDE EMERGENCIES

For minor problems faced by motorists (running out of gas, blowing a tire, needing a tow to the nearest phone), California's Department of Transportation has a Metro Freeway Service Patrol. More than 145 tow trucks patrol the freeways offering free aid to stranded drivers. Reach them on your cell phone by calling 511.

If your car breaks down on an interstate, pull over onto the shoulder and call the state police from your cell phone or walk to the nearest emergency roadside phone. When calling for help, note your location according to the small green mileage markers posted along the highway.

**Emergency Services Metro Freeway Service Patrol.** ☎ 511 for breakdowns ⊕ www.go511.com.

## RULES OF THE ROAD

Seat belts are required for all passengers in California, as is the use of federally approved car seats for children under nine or less than 4 feet 9 inches tall. California law requires that drivers use hands-free devices when talking on cell phones. Texting and driving is illegal and results in a hefty fine.

The speed limit is 25 to 35 mph on city streets and 65 mph on freeways unless otherwise posted. Some towns, including Beverly Hills and Culver City, use cameras at traffic lights to reduce speeding. Speeding can earn you fines starting at $266. It is illegal to drive in California with a blood alcohol content of 0.08% or above (0.01% if you're under 21). There are strict penalties for first offenders. Checkpoints are set up on weekends and holidays across the county.

Parking infractions can result in penalties starting at $68. Having your vehicle towed and impounded will cost nearly $300 even if you pay up immediately, and more if you don't. LAX is notorious for handing out tickets to drivers circling its busy terminals; avoid the no-parking zones and keep loading or unloading to a minimum.

Turning right on red after a complete stop is legal unless otherwise posted. Many streets in Downtown L.A. are one-way, and a left turn from one one-way street onto another is allowed. On some major arteries, left turns are illegal during rush hour. Certain carpool lanes, designated by signage and a white diamond, are reserved for cars with more than one passenger. Freeway on-ramps often have stop-and-go signals to regulate the flow of traffic, but cars in high-occupancy-vehicle (HOV) lanes can pass the signal without stopping.

Keep in mind that pedestrians always have the right of way in California; not yielding to them, even if they're jaywalkers, may result in a $211 ticket.

## CAR RENTAL

In Los Angeles, a car is a necessity. Keep in mind that you'll likely be spending a lot of time in it, and options like a plug for your cell phone could make a significant difference in your day-to-day comfort.

Major-chain rates in L.A. begin at $38 a day and $300 a week, plus sales tax and concession fees. Luxury vehicles start at $75 a day. Open-top convertibles are a popular choice for visitors wanting to make the most of the sun. Note that the major agencies offer services for travelers with disabilities, such as hand-controls, for little or no extra cost.

In California you must be 21 and have a valid credit card to rent a car. Some agencies won't rent to those under 25, and those that do may charge extra.

**Automobile Associations American Automobile Association** (*AAA*). ☎ *315/797–5000* ⊕ *www.aaa.com.* **National Automobile Club.** ☎ *650/294–7000* ⊕ *www.thenac.com.*

# ▌ METRO TRAVEL

Metro Rail covers only a small part of L.A.'s vast expanse, but it's convenient, frequent, and inexpensive. Most popular with visitors is the underground Red Line, which runs from Downtown's Union Station through Mid-Wilshire, Hollywood, and Universal City on its way to North Hollywood, stopping at the most popular tourist destinations along the way.

The light-rail Green Line stretches from Redondo Beach to Norwalk, while the partially underground Blue Line travels from Downtown to the South Bay. The monorail-like Gold Line extends from Union Station to Pasadena and out to the deep San Gabriel Valley and Azusa. The Orange Line, a 14-mile bus corridor, connects the North Hollywood subway station with the western San Fernando Valley.

Most recently extended was the Expo Line, which connects Downtown to the Westside, and terminates in Santa Monica, two blocks from the Pacific Ocean.

Daily service is offered from about 4:30 am to 12:30 am, with departures every 5 to 15 minutes. On weekends trains run until 2 am. Buy tickets from station vending machines; fares are $1.75, or $7 for an all-day pass. Bicycles are allowed on Metro Rail trains at all times.

**Rail Information** Los Angeles County Metropolitan Transit Authority. ☎ 323/466–3876 ⊕ www.metro.net.

## ∎ TAXI, LIMO, AND RIDESHARE TRAVEL

Instead of trying to hail a taxi on the street, phone one of the many taxi companies. The Curb Taxi app allows for online hailing of L.A. taxis. The metered rate is $2.70 per mile, plus a $2.85 per-fare charge. Taxi rides from LAX have an additional $4 surcharge. Be aware that distances are greater than they might appear on the map so fares add up quickly.

On the other end of the price spectrum, limousines come equipped with everything from full bars to nightclub-style sound-and-light systems. Most charge by the hour, minimum hours sometimes required.

Request a ride using apps like Lyft, and a driver will usually arrive within minutes. Fares increase during busy times, but it's often the most affordable option, especially for the convenience.

**Limo Companies** Apex Limo. ☎ 818/637–2277, 877/427–1777 for 24-hr pickup ⊕ www.apexlimola.com. **Dav El Chauffeured Transportation Network.** ☎ 800/922–0343 ⊕ www.davel.com. **First Class Limousine Service.** ☎ 800/400–9771 ⊕ www.first-classlimo.com. **Wilshire Limousine Services.** ☎ 888/813–8420 ⊕ www.wilshirelimousine.com.

**Taxi Companies** Beverly Hills Cab Co. ☎ 800/273–6611 ⊕ www.beverlyhillscabco.com. **Independent Cab Co.** ☎ 800/521–8294 ⊕ www.taxi4u.com. **LA Checker Cab.** ☎ 800/300–5007 ⊕ www.ineedtaxi.com. **United Independent Taxi.** ☎ 800/822–8294, 323/207–8294 text to order taxi ⊕ www.unitedtaxi.com. **Yellow Cab Los Angeles.** ☎ 424/222–2222 ⊕ www.layellowcab.com.

## ∎ TRAIN TRAVEL

Downtown's Union Station is one of the great American railroad terminals. The interior includes comfortable seating, a restaurant, and several snack bars. As the city's rail hub, it's the place to catch an Amtrak, Metrolink commuter train or the Red, Gold, or Purple lines. Among Amtrak's Southern California routes are 11 daily trips to San Diego and 6 to Santa Barbara. Amtrak's luxury *Coast Starlight* travels along the spectacular coastline from Seattle to Los Angeles in just a day and a half (though it's often a little late). The *Sunset Limited* arrives from New Orleans, and the *Southwest Chief* comes from Chicago.

**Information** Amtrak. ☎ 800/872–7245 ⊕ www.amtrak.com. **Metrolink.** ☎ 800/371–5465 ⊕ www.metrolinktrains.com. **Union Station.** ✉ 800 N. Alameda St. ☎ 213/683–6979 ⊕ www.unionstationla.com.

# ESSENTIALS

## ▌HEALTH

The air pollution in L.A. may affect sensitive people in different ways. When pollution levels are high, it's a good idea to plan a day indoors or on a windy beach. The sun can burn even on overcast days, and the dry heat can dehydrate, so wear hats, sunglasses, and sunblock, and carry water with you.

## ▌HOURS OF OPERATION

Los Angeles is not a 24-hour city like New York, but in many places business hours extend well into the evening, especially for bigger stores and shopping centers. On Monday, many bars, restaurants, and shops (including outdoor sports outlets) remain closed.

Many L.A. museums are closed on Monday and major holidays. A few of the preeminent art museums, including the Norton Simon and Los Angeles County Museum of Art, stay open on Monday. Instead, the Norton Simon is closed Tuesday, the Los Angeles County museum on Wednesday. Most museums close around 5 or 6 pm, staying open late at least one night a week. Many museums, large and small, have weekly or monthly free days or hours when no admission is charged.

Most stores in Los Angeles are open 10 to 6, although many stay open until 9 pm or later, particularly those in shopping malls, trendy areas such as Melrose Avenue, and in Santa Monica. Most shops are open on Sunday, though they may have earlier hours.

## ▌MONEY

Although not inexpensive, costs in Los Angeles tend to be a bit lower than in other major cities such as New York and San Francisco. For instance, in a low-key local diner, a cup of coffee might cost around $2. In high-profile establishments, costs escalate; a cup of coffee in a trendy eatery can cost as much as $7.

| ITEM | AVERAGE COST |
|---|---|
| Cup of Coffee | $2 |
| Glass of Wine | $9 |
| Beer | $8 |
| Sandwich | $12 |
| 15-Minute Taxi Ride | $30 |
| Museum Admission | $15 |

Prices throughout this guide are given for adults. Reduced fees are almost always available for children, students, and senior citizens.

## ▌RESTROOMS

You can assume that gas stations along the highways outside of town will have a bathroom available, but this isn't true of every station in L.A. itself. Restrooms in parks can be subpar. Restaurants and bars may have signs that read "For Patrons Only" so that you're obliged to buy something to use the facilities. Better bets for relatively clean, obligation-free restrooms are those in department stores, fast-food outlets, and coffee shops.

## ▌SAFETY

Very minor earthquakes occur frequently in Southern California; most of the time they're so slight that you won't notice them. If you feel a stronger tremor, follow basic safety precautions. If you're indoors, take cover in a doorway or under a table or desk—whichever is closest. Protect your head with your arms. Stay clear of windows, mirrors, or anything that might fall from the walls. Do not use elevators. If you're in an open space, move away from buildings, trees, and power lines. If you're outdoors near buildings, duck into a doorway. If you're driving, pull over to the side of the road, avoiding overpasses, bridges, and power lines, and stay inside the car. Expect aftershocks, and take cover again if they are strong.

Of the Metro lines, the Red, Green, and Expo lines are the safest and are more regularly patrolled. The Blue Line can be sketchy after dark. Avoid riding in empty cars, and move with the crowd when going from the station to the street.

# ▌TAXES

The sales tax in Los Angeles is 9.75%, one of the highest in California. There's none on most groceries, but there is on newspapers and magazines. The tax on hotel rooms ranges from 13% to 15.5%. Food tax varies, but expect to pay around 9.5%.

# ▌TIME

Los Angeles is in the Pacific time zone, two hours behind Chicago, three hours behind New York, and eight hours behind London.

# ▌TIPPING

The customary tip rate is 15%–20% for waiters and taxi drivers and 15% –20% for hairdressers and barbers. Bellhops and baggage handlers receive $1–$2 per bag; parking valets and hotel housekeepers are usually tipped $2–$3. Bartenders get about $1 per drink.

# ▌TOURS

You can explore L.A. from many vantage points and even more topical angles. Not surprisingly, lots of guides include dollops of celebrity history and gossip. Most tours run year-round, and most require advance reservations.

### BUS AND VAN TOURS
Guideline Tours offers sightseeing trips all around L.A., including Downtown, Universal Studios, and Hollywood. Starline Tours picks up passengers from the TCL Chinese Theatre and in Santa Monica. The company offers double-decker hop on/off tours around town and operates tours to Disneyland, Universal Studios, and Six Flags Magic Mountain. The slightly tawdry TMZ Celebrity Tour of reputed celebrity hot spots leaves from two locations: in front of the Hard Rock in Hollywood, or the Grove.

**Fees and Schedules Guideline Tours.** ☎ 323/465–3004, 800/604–8433 ⊕ www.tourslosangeles.com. **Starline Tours.** ☎ 800/959–3131 ⊕ www.starlinetours. com. **TMZ Celebrity Tour.** ☎ 844/869–8687 ⊕ www.tmz.com/tour.

### HELICOPTER TOURS
If you want an aerial tour, lift off with Orbic Air. Based at Hollywood Burbank Airport, the company has been flying its four-passenger helicopters for more than 25 years, and the pilots have years of experience. It's $99 per person for the basic 15-minute Hollywood Sign tour.

**Fees and Schedules Orbic Air.** ☎ 818/561–4838 ⊕ www.orbicair.com.

### SCOOTER TOURS
For an unusual perspective on L.A.'s attractions, you can take a tour of the city on a Segway electric scooter. The $89 Segwow tours might include the UCLA campus, Santa Monica, or Downtown. The guided rides last just over two hours.

**Fees and Schedules Segwow.** ☎ 310/358–5900 ⊕ www.segwow.com.

### SPECIAL-INTEREST TOURS
With Architecture Tours L.A., you can zip all over the city in a comfortable minivan on a private tour with a historian. Rates start at $75 per person. Esotouric has an innovative take on the city; its varied weekend bus tours ($58 and up) explore historic architecture along Route 66, and the darker side of L.A. that Raymond Chandler revealed in books like *The Big Sleep* and *The Long Goodbye*.

Beverly Hills operates year-round trolley tours focused on art and architecture. They last 40 minutes and depart from 11 am to 4 pm every weekend throughout the year, as well as Tuesday to Friday in the summer. Tickets cost $5. Soak up the glow of classic neon signs from an open double-decker bus on tours offered by the Museum of Neon Art. They cost $55 and are offered May through September.

Take My Mother Please will arrange lively, thematic combination walking and driving tours; for instance, you could explore sights associated with the film *L.A. Confidential*. Rates start at $450 for up to three people for a half day.

**Fees and Schedules Architecture Tours L.A.** ☎ 323/464–7868 ⊕ www.architecturetoursla. com. **Beverly Hills Trolley Tours.** ✉ Dayton Way and Rodeo Dr., Beverly Hills ☎ 310/285–1128 ⊕ www.beverlyhills.org/exploring/trolley-tours. **Esotouric.** ☎ 213/373–1947 ⊕ www. esotouric.com. **Neon Cruise.** ☎ 818/696–2149 ⊕ www.neonmona.org/neon-cruise. **Take My Mother Please.** ☎ 323/737–2200 ⊕ www. takemymotherplease.com.

## WALKING TOURS

Red Line Tours offers daily one- and two-hour walking tours of behind-the-scenes Hollywood. Tours, which cost $25, are led by docents and include headsets to block out street noise. The Los Angeles Conservancy's 2½-hour-long walking tours ($10) cover the Downtown area.

**Fees and Schedules Los Angeles Conservancy.** ☎ 213/623–2489 ⊕ www.laconservancy.org. **Red Line Tours.** ✉ 6708 Hollywood Blvd. ☎ 323/402–1074 ⊕ www.redlinetours.com.

## ▌VISITOR INFORMATION

Discover Los Angeles, the city's official tourism site, is fun and informative, with an annually updated general information packet that includes suggestions for entertainment, lodging, and dining, and a list of special events. There are two visitor information centers, both accessible to Metro stops: the Hollywood & Highland entertainment complex and Union Station.

The Santa Monica Convention and Visitors Bureau runs a drop-in visitor information center on Main Street that is open daily 9 to 5, as well as three kiosks at Palisades Park, the Santa Monica Pier, and the Third Street Promenade.

**Contacts Beverly Hills Conference and Visitors Bureau.** ☎ 310/248–1015, 800/345–2210 ⊕ www.lovebeverlyhills.com. **Discover Los Angeles.** ☎ 213/624–7300, 800/228–2452 ⊕ www.discoverlosangeles. com. **Hollywood Chamber of Commerce.** ☎ 323/469–8311 ⊕ www.hollywoodchamber. net. **Long Beach Area Convention and Visitors Bureau.** ☎ 562/436–3645 ⊕ www. visitlongbeach.com. **Pasadena Convention & Visitor Bureau.** ☎ 800/307–7977 ⊕ www. visitpasadena.com. **Santa Monica Travel & Tourism.** ☎ 310/393-7593, 800/544–5319 ⊕ www.santamonica.com. **Visit California.** ☎ 916/444–4429, 800/862–2543 ⊕ www. visitcalifornia.com. **Visit West Hollywood.** ☎ 310/289–2525, 800/368–6020 ⊕ www. visitwesthollywood.com.

# INDEX

## PHOTO CREDITS

**Front cover:** stellalevi/iStockphoto [Description: Manhattan Beach pier, Los Angeles, California]. **Back cover, from left to right:** Chebyshev007 | Dreamstime.com; EHStock/iStockphoto; Shawnhemp | Dreamstime.com. **Spine:** JingleBeeZ Photo Gallery/Shutterstock. 1, LPETTET/iStockphoto. 2-3, Biansho | Dreamstime.com. 5, ames sf/Flickr. **Chapter 1: Experience Los Angeles:** 8–9, Jose Gil/iStockphoto. 16 (left), Sam Howzit/Flickr, [CC BY 2.0]. 16 (bottom right), Frek58 | Dreamstime.com. 16 (top center), Boomer/ LACVB. 16 (top right), Diana Lundin/Shutterstock. 17 (left), Lee Pettet/iStockphoto. 17 (top right), S. Greg Panosian/iStockphoto. 17 (bottom right), Famke Backx/ iStockphoto. 27, Sepavo | Dreamstime.com. 28, Heeb Christian/age fotostock. 29 (top right), Neil Emmerson/age fotostock. 29 (bottom right), stevelyan/Flickr. 30 (top), IK's World trip/Flickr. 30 (bottom), Kjetil Ree/Wikimedia Commons. 31(top left), Stepan Mazurov/Flickr. 31 (bottom left), Andaz West Hollywood. 31 (top right), mertxe iturrioz/Flickr, [CC BY-SA 2.0]. 32, Mike Simpson/Stockphoto. **Chapter 2: Downtown Los Angeles:** 33, Eddie Hernandez Photography/iStockphoto. 35, Danbreckwoldt | Dreamstime. com. 36, Meg Butler. 37, Biansho | Dreamstime.com. 39, Usataro | Dreamstime.com. 40, S. Greg Panosian/iStockphoto. 43, Meg Butler. 45, Jakob N. Layman/Grand Central Market. 47, Lilyling1982 | Dreamstime.com. **Chapter 3: Hollywood and the Studios:** 49, Sepavo | Dreamstime.com. 51, Byron W.Moore/Shutterstock. 52, David Livingston/iStockphoto. 53 (top), Clinton Steeds/Flickr. 53 (bottom), wolfsavard/Flickr. 54, SeanPavonePhoto/iStockphoto. 55, Chicco7 | Dreamstime.com. 58, Gary Bembridge/Flickr, [CC BY 2.0]. 60, Davel5957/iStockphoto. 64, Universal Studios, Hollywood. 69, David Liu/ iStockphoto. **Chapter 4: Beverly Hills and the Westside:** 71, F11photo | Dreamstime. com. 73, Lehakok | Dreamstime.com. 74, Andy Hwang/iStockphoto. 75, Nito100 | Dreamstime.com. 77, Courtesy of the Annenberg Space for Photography. 78–79, Scott Leigh/iStockphoto.81, Clucian | Dreamstime.com. 85, Zverava | Dreamstime.com. **Chapter 5: Santa Monica and the Beaches:** 87, Appalachianviews | Dreamstime.com. 89, Jose Gil/Shutterstock. 90, Nstanev | Dreamstime.com. 91, Asterixvs Dreamstime.com. 96, Naki Kouyioumtzis/age fotostock. 97 (left), Pygmy Warrior/Flickr, 97 (top right), alonozoD/Flickr. 97 (center right), Anton J. Geisser/age fotostock. 97 (bottom right), ames sf/Flickr. 100, Richard Ross with the courtesy of the J. Paul Getty Trust. 102, jonrawlinson/Flickr. **Chapter 6: Pasadena:** 105, Sydney.lorraine5 via Wikimedia Commons, [CC BY-SA 4.0]. 107, The Huntington Library, Art Collections, and Botanical Gardens. 108, maveric2003/Flickr. 111, Pasadena Convention & Visitor Bureau. 113, wikipedia.org. **Chapter 7: Nightlife:** 115, Courtesy of the Golden Gopher. 116, Hendrik Holler/age fotostock. 129 (top), Trujillo Paumie. 129 (bottom), michael balderas/iStockphoto. 130 (top left), Tamsin Slater/Flickr. 130 (top right), tannazie/Flickr. 130 (bottom center), Trujillo Paumie. 130 (bottom right), Atomazul | Dreamstime.com. 131 (bottom right), Meg Butler. 131 (bottom left), Trujillo Paumie. 131 (top left), Chez Jay. 131 (top right), bORjAmATiC/Flickr. 132 (top left), Musso & Frank Grill. 132 (bottom left), Howard Wise. 132 (top center), Never Cool in School / Leslie Kalohi/ Flickr. 132 (top right), rawkblog.blogspot.com/flickr. 132 (bottom right), arnold | inuyaki/flickr. 132 (bottom), Musso & Frank Grill. **Chapter 8: Performing Arts:** 137, WDCH, Music Center of Los Angeles County. Photo by Alex Pitt. 138, Monika Rittershaus. 141, Steve Cohn. **Chapter 9: Shopping:** 147, Blend Images / Alamy. 148, Courtesy of Vamp. **Chapter 10: Where to Eat:** 171, Sierra Prescott / Bestia. 172, wisely/Flickr. 173(top right), Gonzalo Rivero/Wikipedia.org. 173 (bottom left), tannaz/Flickr, [CC BY-SA 2.0]. 174, Andrea Alonso/Grand Central Market. **Chapter 11: Where to Stay:** 199, Andaz Hollywood. 200, Ace Hotel. **Chapter 12: Orange County and Catalina Island:** 225, Robert Holmes. 226, Marc Pagani Photography/Shutterstock. 227 (top), berned_you, Fodors.com member. 227 (bottom), Brent Reeves/Shutterstock. 228, Robert Holmes. 237, www.eric-castro.biz/Flickr. 244, Robert Holmes. 248, Scott Vickers/iStockphoto. 250, www.rwongphoto/Alamy. 253, Brett Shoal/Artistic Visuals Photography. 254, Lowe Llaguno/Shutterstock.

**About Our Writers:** All photos are courtesy of the writers except for the following: Michele Bigley, courtesy of Tony Belko; Kathy A. McDonald, courtesy of Jeff Kirshbaum.

# NOTES

# NOTES

# NOTES

# NOTES

# NOTES

# NOTES

# NOTES

# NOTES

# NOTES

# NOTES